TO

MARY CLEARY

is the honorary "chief library guide" and has
n so generously of her time as an enthusiastic
untiring supporter of the progress of the Uni-
ity Libraries, in gratitude for her profound inst, warm enthusiasm, and untiring efforts.

ISBN 0-8108-0878-1

ht © 1975 by David Perkins and Norman Tanis
Printed in the United States of America

book was first published by California State
rsity, Northridge, and is now reprinted
e Scarecrow Press, Inc., Metuchen, N.J.

NATIVE A
OF NORTH

A bibliography based on
of California State U

Com

David

Norm

The Scare

Metuchen

As the academic discipline of Native American studies is just beginning to develop it faces a problem common to other developing fields of study--a lack of bibliographic tools. The University Libraries have recognized for some time the importance of acquiring scholarly materials for the study of the Native American. Almost a decade ago we acquired a large and comprehensive collection from the family of Donald H. McGill, a professor at the University of Southern California. This collection formed a nucleus for building the comprehensive collection of Native American materials listed in this bibliography.

Native Americans of North America is the second in a series of bibliographies issued by the University Libraries. The first volume, published in 1970, is the Black Experience in the United States, compiled by Dennis C. Bakewell. Like the first, the present volume lists selected titles from the University Libraries' holdings. As such, the bibliography is intended principally for academic and public libraries serving under-graduate and advanced high school students who want to know what the best books are from among the many that have been published.

This bibliography is intended for the Native American student on this campus and at other colleges and universities throughout North America, for in a sense, this book is a search for the Native American. No book listed here contains all of the truth about its subject; indeed, scholarship seldom pretends to have grasped the whole truth. But these works, written by men who were sometimes prejudiced, sometimes enlightened, and always fascinated, represent attempts to know and understand America's native peoples.

It should be emphasized that this bibliography covers books only. Other good bibliographies exist for periodical literature and for non-book materials. Periodical literature for the past two decades is listed and abstracted in:

Smith, Dwight L.
    Indians of the United States and Canada. Santa Barbara,
    Calif., ABC Clio, 1974.

Two recent bibliographies of non-book materials are:

Minnesota Library Services Institute for Minnesota Indians
    American Indians; an annotated bibliography of selected
    library resources. 1970.

Brigham Young University, Provo, Utah. Instructional Development
Program.
    Bibliography of nonprint instructional materials on the
    American Indian. 1972.

Norman E. Tanis

Introduction

This bibliography contains a selection of books by and about the native populations of North America from the libraries of California State University, Northridge, and is divided topically. Geographic divisions within topics were made for Anthropology, Archeology, and History because these contain so many titles that alphabetical lists do not seem useful. Works on one tribe are grouped by tribal name under the heading Tribes. It seemed more useful to consolidate the material on one tribe than scatter it between several sections.

Each item within the bibliography has a unique item number. These numbers are sequential except for the addition of certain recent acquisitions which are given an extra digit; for example, 0515, 05151, 0516. The author-title index refers to these numbers. A list of numbers may be found at the end of most sections, referring to works located elsewhere that are germane to the subject of that section.

As many anthropological works are parts of series, entries in this bibliography for parts of series are indicated by a group of initials standing for the series main entry. These initials are located to the left of the call number in parenthesis. An index to the series main entry from the initialism is located just before the author-title index.

The place of publication, if not otherwise specified, is New York City. When the listed title is a reprint edition, the original date of publication in parenthesis follows the date of our copy. The book's Library of Congress classification number is at the end of each entry.

In the University Libraries, but not included in the bibliography are a number of major microform collections which contain additional research material related to Native American studies. The Human Relations Area Files (HRAF) contain many ethnographic accounts of Native American culture of importance for those seeking an anthropological perspective. The Library of American Civilization provides a well-indexed historical perspective. Microcard editions of the works represented in the American Bibliographies of Charles Evans and Joseph Sabin are available for early writings. The U. S. government documents collection is an important source of materials on Native American-governmental relations. In the field of education the Educational Research Information Center (ERIC) should be consulted; the complete texts of these reports are available.

The publication of this bibliography depended on the assistance of numerous University administrators, faculty, staff, and students. We owe special thanks to Diane Edwards who did the initial entry typing, Sue Blacker who did checking and proofing, and Julia Crippen who typed the manuscript. The book's illustrations are copies of California Indian petroglyphs; they were done by Annie Wassilak and Robert Corey.

David Perkins

CONTENTS

Maine	Pennsylvania	Georgia
New Hampshire	Delaware	Florida
Vermont	Maryland	Alabama
Massachusetts	District of Columbia	Mississippi
Rhode Island	Virginia	Louisiana
Connecticut	West Virginia	Texas
New York	North Carolina	
New Jersey	South Carolina	

Arkansas	Indiana
Tennessee	Illinois
Kentucky	Michigan
Missouri	Wisconsin
Ohio	

ANTHROPOLOGY

General

0001   AMERICAN ANTHROPOLOGIST
       Selected papers from the American anthropologist, 1888-1920.
       Evanston, Ill., Row, Peterson, 1960   E12.A75

0002   Anales de antropología. v.1-
       México, Universidad Nacional Autónoma de México, 1964-
                                                GN4.A6

0003   Assay; journal of anthropology. v. 1-
       Spring 1965- Northridge, Calif., San Fernando Valley State
       College, Anthropology Dept.   GN4.A78

0004   BANCROFT, Hubert Howe
       American antiquities, being the entire section devoted to
       the subject in the author's series on the native races.
       The Bancroft Co., 1921?   E61.B23

0005   BANDELIER, Adolph Francis Alphonse
       Pioneers in American anthropology: the Bandelier-Morgan
       letters, 1873-1883. Albuquerque, The Univ. of New Mexico Pr.,
       1940   E58.B2296

0006   BERRY, Brewton
       Almost white. Macmillan, 1963   F184.A1B43

0007   BIRKET-SMITH, Kaj
       Studies in circumpacific culture relations. København,
       Munksgaard, 1967-   AS281.D214.bd.42.nr.3

0008   BOAS, Franz
       The ethnography of Franz Boas. Chicago, Univ. of Chicago Pr.,
       1969   E77.2.B613

0009   BOAS, Franz
       Materials for the study of inheritance in man. AMS Pr., 1969
       (1928)   (CUCA)   E51.C7.v.6

0010   CALIFORNIA. STATE COLLEGE, SAN FRANCISCO. DEPT. OF ANTHROPOLOGY.
       Occasional papers in anthropology. no. 1- San Francisco, 1960-
                                                GN4.C24

0011   CARLI, Giovanni Rinaldo, conte
       Lettres américaines, dans lesquelles on examine l'origine, l'etat
       civil, politique, militaire and religieux. A Boston, et se trouve
       a Paris, chez Buisson, 1788   E61.C29

0012   COCQ, Antonius Petrus Leonardus de
       Andrew Lang. Tilburg, Zwijsen, 1968   GN21.L27C6

1

0013   Contributions to North American ethnology.
        Vol. I-VII, IX. Washington. Govt. Print. Off., 1877-93
                                                E71.C76

00131   CROSBY, Alfred W.
        The Columbian exchange; biological and cultural conse-
        quences of 1492. (Contributions in American studies,
        no. 2) Greenwood, 1972   E98.D6.C7

0014   DRIVER, Harold Edson
        Comparative studies of North American Indians. Philadelphia
        American Philosophical Society, 1957   fE77.D75

0015   DRIVER, Harold Edson
        Hoof rattles and girls' puberty rites in North and
        South America. Baltimore, Indiana Univ., 1950
                        (IUPA)   GN4.I5.mem.4-5

0016   DRIVER, Harold Edson
        Quantitative expression of cultural relationships.
        Berkeley, Univ. of California Pr., 1932
                        (UCPAE)   E51.C15.v.31.no.4

0017   DRIVER, Harold Edson
        The reliability of culture element data. Berkeley,
        Univ. of California Pr., 1938 (AR)   E51.A58.v.1.no.4

0018   DRUCKER, Philip
        The native brotherhoods: modern intertribal organizations
        of the Northwest coast. Washington, U. S. Govt. Print.
        Off., 1958   (BAEB)   E51.U55.no.168

0019   EDMONSON, Munro S.
        Status terminology and the social structure of North
        American Indians. Seattle, Univ. of Washington Pr.,
        1958   E98.S7E3

0020   Estudios de cultura náhuatl. v.1- 1959- México F1219.E8

0021   FOSTER, John Wells
        Pre-historic races of the United States of America.
        Chicago, S. C. Griggs; London, Trübner, 1878 E71.F76

0022   GIFFORD, Edward Winslow
        Tübatulabal and Kawaiisu kinship terms. Berkeley, Univ.
        of California Pr., 1917 (UCPAE)   E51.C15.v.12.no.6

00221   GLADWIN, Winifred E.
        A method for designation of cultures and their variations.
        Medallion, 1934   E78.S7.G432

0023   GRINNELL, George Bird
        When buffalo ran. New Haven, Yale Univ. Pr., 1920
                                2

0024   HALE, Horatio Emmons
        Ethnography and philology. Ridgewood, N.J., Gregg Pr., 1968
        (1846)   Q115.H16.1968

0025   HEIZER, Robert Fleming
        Languages, territories, and names of California Indian tribes.
        Berkeley, Univ. of California Pr., 1966 E78.C15H43

0026   HODGE, Frederick Webb ed.
        Handbook of American Indians north of Mexico. Washington,
        Govt. Print. Off., 1907-10 (BAEB)   E51.U55.no.30

0027   HODGE, Frederick Webb ed.
        Handbook of Indians of Canada. Kraus Reprint, 1969 (1913)
                                               E78.C2H6.1969

0028   INTERUNIVERSITY SUMMER RESEARCH SEMINAR, University of New Mexico,
        1956.
        Perspectives in American Indian culture change. Chicago,
        Univ. of Chicago Pr., 1961   E77.I55.1956

0029   JENNESS, Diamond
        The Indians of Canada. Ottawa, National Museum of Canada, 1934
                                               E78.C2J4

0030   JUDD, Neil Merton
        The Bureau of American Ethnology; a partial history. Norman,
        Univ. of Oklahoma Pr., 1967   E51.U655

0031   KLUCKHOHN, Florence (Rockwood)
        Variations in value orientations. Evanston, Ill., Row, Peterson,
        1961   E184.A1K5

0032   KROEBER, Alfred Louis
        Cultural and natural areas of native North America. Berkeley,
        Univ. of California Pr., 1939 (UCPAE) E51.C15.v.38

0033   KROEBER, Alfred Louis
        Ethnographic interpretations, 1-6. Berkeley, Univ. of California
        Pr., 1957   (UCPAE)   E51.C15.v.47.no.2

0034   KROEBER, Alfred Louis
        Ethnographic interpretations, 7-11. Berkeley, Univ. of California
        Pr., 1959   (UCPAE)   E51.C15.v.47.no.3

0035   KROEBER, Alfred Louis
        Tribes surveyed. Berkeley, Univ. of California Pr., 1939
                              (AR)   E51.A58.v.1.no.7

0036   Language, culture, and personality. Menasha, Wis., Sapir Memorial
        Publication Fund, 1941   E98.C9L25

0037   LEWIS, Oscar
        Anthropological essays. Random House, 1970 GN6.L47

3

0038   LINDQUIST, Gustavus Elmer Emanuel
          The Indian in American life. Friendship Pr., 1944
                                  E98.C9L56

0039   LINTON, Ralph ed.
          Acculturation in seven American Indian tribes.
          D. Appleton-Century Co., Inc., 1940   E98.C9L6

0040   LOEB, Edwin Meyer
          Tribal initiations and secret societies. Berkeley,
          Univ. of California Pr., 1929 (UCPAE)   E51.C15.v.25.no.3

0041   LONGACRE, William A.
          Archaeology as anthropology. Tucson, Univ. of Arizona
          Pr., 1970   E78.A7L6

0042   LOWIE, Robert Harry
          The matrilineal complex. Berkeley, Univ. of California
          Pr., 1919   (UCPAE)   E51.C15.v.16.no.2

0043   McLUHAN, T. C. comp.
          Touch the earth; a self-portrait of Indian existence.
          Outerbridge & Dienstfrey; distributed by Dutton, 1971
                                  E98.C9M24.1971

0044   MacNEISH, June Helm ed.
          Pioneers of American anthropology; the uses of biography.
          Seattle, Univ. of Washington Pr., 1966
                      (MAES)   E51.A556.v.43

0045   McNICKLE, D'Arcy
          The Indian tribes of the United States: ethnic and
          cultural survival. London, Oxford Univ. Pr., 1962
                                  E77.M176

0046   MANITOBA. UNIVERSITY. DEPT. OF UNIVERSITY EXTENSION AND
          ADULT EDUCATION.
          Resolving conflicts--a cross-cultural approach.
          Kenora, Ont. 1967   E78.C2M2

0047   MARRIOTT, Alice Lee
          Greener fields. Crowell, 1953   E98.C9M3

00471   MEAD, Margaret
          The changing culture of an Indian tribe. Capricorn
          Books, 1966   E98.S7.M33.1966

0048   MEAD, Margaret ed.
          The golden age of American anthropology. G. Braziller, 1960
                                  E77.M48

0049   Measures of men. New Orleans, Dept. of Middle American
          Research, Tulane, Univ. of Louisiana, 1936
                    (TMAI)   F1421.T95.no.7

0050   MORGAN, Lewis Henry
       The Indian journals, 1859-62. Ann Arbor, Univ. of Michigan Pr.,
       1959   E78.W5M6

00501   NUTTALL, Zelia
       The fundamental principles of Old and New world civilizations.
       Cambridge, Mass., The Museum, 1901 (PMP) E51.H337.v.2

0051   OLSON, Ronald Le Roy
       Clan and moiety in native America. Berkeley, Univ. of California
       Pr., 1933   (UCPAE)   E51.C15.v.33.no.4

0052   THE PHILADELPHIA ANTHROPOLOGICAL SOCIETY.
       Papers presented on its golden anniversary, edited by
       Jacob W. Gruber. Columbia Univ. Pr., 1967 E51.P52

0053   Phoebe Apperson Hearst memorial volume, on the twentieth
       anniversary of the organization of the Department and
       museum of anthropology of the University of California,
       September 10, 1901. Berkeley, Univ. of California Pr., 1923
                 (UCPAE)   E51.C15.v.20

0054   RESEK, Carl
       Lewis Henry Morgan. Chicago, Univ. of Chicago Pr., 1960
                            GN21.M8R4

0055   SAPIR, Edward
       Selected writings in language, culture and personality.
       Berkeley, Univ. of California Pr., 1963 (1949)
                         P27.S33.1963

0056   SMITHSONIAN INSTITUTION.
       Essays in historical anthropology of North America. City of
       Washington, The Smithsonian Institution, 1940 E61.S76

0057   Social anthropology of North American tribes.
       Chicago, The Univ. of Chicago Pr., 1937 E98.S7S6

0058   SPECK, Gordon
       Breeds and half-breeds. C. N. Potter; distributed by Crown
       Publishers, 1969   E71.S67.1969

0059   STERN, Bernhard Joseph
       Lewis Henry Morgan. Russell & Russell, 1967 (1931)
                         GN21.M8S8.1967

0060   STEWART, Omer Call
       Washo-northern Paiute peyotism, a study in acculturation.
       Berkeley and Los Angeles, Univ. of California Pr., 1944
                (UCPAE)   E51.C15.v.40.no.3

0061   SWANTON, John Reed
        Indian tribes of the lower Mississippi valley and
        adjacent coast of the gulf of Mexico. Washington,
        Govt. Print. Off., 1911 (BAEB)   E51.U55.no.43

0062   SYMINGTON, Fraser
        The Canadian Indian. Toronto, McClelland and Stewart,
        Illustrated Books Division, 1969   fE78.C2S9

0063   U. S. BUREAU OF AMERICAN ETHNOLOGY.
        Annual report. 1879/80- Washington, U. S. Govt. Print.
        1881-19   E51.U552

0064   U.S. BUREAU OF AMERICAN ETHNOLOGY.
        Bulletin. no. 1- Washington, Govt. Print. Off., 1887-
                                               E51.U55

0065   VLAHOS, Olivia
        New World beginnings: Indian cultures in the Americas.
        Fawcett, 1972 (1970)   E58.V6.1970

0066   WENNER-GREN FOUNDATION FOR ANTHROPOLOGICAL RESEARCH, NEW YORK.
        Papers on the physical anthropology of the American
        Indian. Wenner-Gren Foundation, 1951. E98.P53W4

0067   WEST, George Arbor
        Tobacco, pipes and smoking customs of the American
        Indians. Westport, Conn., Greenwood Pr., 1970
                                               E98.S7W4.1970

0068   WISSLER, Clark
        The American Indian, an introduction to the anthropology
        of the new world. Gloucester, Mass., P. Smith, 1957
        (1938)   E58.W82.1957

0069   WISSLER, Clark
        Observations on the face and teeth of the North American
        Indians. American Museum of Natural History, 1931
                        (AMNHP)   GN2.A27.v.33.pt.1

Eastern United States and Canada

0070 BLAIR, Emma Helen ed.
      The Indian tribes of the upper Mississippi valley and region
      of the Great Lakes as described by Nicolas Perrot, French
      commandant in the Northwest. Cleveland, Ohio, The Arthur H.
      Clark Co., 1911-12   E78.N8B63

0071 CLARKE, George Frederick
      Someone before us. Fredericton, N.B., Brunswick Pr., 1968
                                            E78.N9C55

0072 COTTERILL, Robert Spencer
      The southern Indians. Norman, Univ. of Oklahoma Pr., 1966 (1954)
                                            E78.S55C6

0073 HRDLIČKA, ALEŠ
      Physical anthropology of the Lenape or Delawares, and of the
      eastern Indians in general. The Museum of the American Indian,
      Heye Foundation, 1916 (BAEB)   E51.U55.no.62

0074 ILIFF, Flora (Gregg)
      People of the blue water. Harper, 1954 E78.A7I32

0075 LEWIS, Thomas McDowell Nelson
      Tribes that slumber. Knoxville, Univ. of Tennessee Pr., 1958
                                            E78.T3L42

0076 NEITZEL, Robert S.
      Archeology of the Fatherland site. American Museum of Natural
      History, 1965   (AMNHP)   GN2.A27.v.51.pt.1

0077 RITZENTHALER, Robert Eugene
      The Woodland Indians of the western Great Lakes. Garden City,
      N.Y., published for the American Museum of Natural History by
      the Natural History Pr., 1970   E78.E2R5

0078 STRONG, William Duncan
      The Indian tribes of the Chicago region. Chicago, Field
      Museum of Natural History, 1926 (CMA) GN2.F5.no.24

0079 SWANTON, John Reed
      The Indians of the southeastern United States. Washington,
      U.S. Govt. Print. Off., 1946 (BAEB)   E51.U55.no.137

0080 Symposium on Cherokee and Iroquois Culture.
      Washington, U. S. Govt. Print. Off., 1961
                                  (BAEB)   E51.U55.no.180

00801   SYMPOSIUM ON INDIANS IN THE OLD SOUTH, Athens, Ga., 1970
        <u>Red, white, and Black</u>. Athens, Southern Anthropological
        Society; distributed by the Univ. of Georgia Press, 1971
                        (SASP)   GN2.S9243.no.5

0081   TAYLOR, William Ewart
        <u>The Arnapik and Tyara sites</u>. Salt Lake City, Society for
        American Archaeology, 1968 (SAAM)   E51.S7.no.22

Western United States and Canada

0082   AGINSKY, Bernard Willard
        Central Sierra. Berkeley and Los Angeles, Univ. of California
        Pr., 1943   (AR)   E51.A58.v.8.no.4

0083   AIKENS, C. Melvin
        Fremont-Promontory-Plains relationships. Salt Lake City, Univ.
        of Utah Pr., 1966   (UUAP)   E51.U8.no.82

0084   ATKINSON, Mary Jourdan
        Indians of the Southwest. San Antonio, Naylor Co., 1958
                                             E78.S7A8.1958

0085   BAHTI, Tom
        Southwestern Indian tribes. Flagstaff, Ariz., KC Publications,
        1968   fE78.S7B184

0086   BANDELIER, Adolph Francis Alphonse
        Final report of investigations among the Indians of the
        southwestern United States. With Index. Cambridge, Mass.,
        J. Wilson and Son, 1890-92 (PAIA)   E51.A64.v.3-4

0087   BANDELIER, Adolph Francis Alphonse
        Indians of the Rio Grande valley. Albuquerque, Univ. of
        New Mexico Pr., 1937   E78.S7B3

0088   BARNETT, Homer Garner
        Oregon coast. Berkeley, Univ. of California Pr., 1937
                            (AR)   E51.A58.v.1.no.3

0089   BARRETT, Samuel
        Ancient Aztalan. Westport, Conn., Greenwood Pr., 1970
                                             E78.W8B3.1970

0090   BAUMHOFF, Martin A.
        California Athabascan groups. Berkeley, Univ. of California Pr.,
        1958   (AR)   E51.A58.v.16.no.5

0091   BERREMAN, Joel Van Meter
        Tribal distribution in Oregon. Menasha, Wis., American
        Anthropological Assoc., 1937   E78.O6B44

0092   BUSHNELL, David Ives
        Villages of the Algonquian, Siouan, and Caddoan tribes west
        of the Mississippi. Washington, Govt. Print. Off., 1922
                            (BAEB)   E51.U55.no.77

00921   BUTLER, Robert B.
        The Old Cordilleran Culture in the Pacific Northwest. Pocatello,
        Idaho, Idaho State Univ., 1961 (ISUOP) E78.I18.I4.no.5

0093   CHAPMAN, Berlin Basil
        The Otoes and Missourias. Oklahoma City, Times Journal
        Pub. Co., 1965   E99.O87C5

0094   COLLINS, Henry Bascom
        The Aleutian islands: their people and natural history.
        City of Washington, The Smithsonian Institution, 1945
                (SIWBS)   GN4.S6.no.21

0095   COLLISON, William Henry
        In the wake of the war canoe. Toronto, Musson Book Co.,
        1916?   E78.B9C7

0096   COOK, Sherburne Friend
        The aboriginal population of Alameda and Contra Costa
        Counties, California. Berkeley, Univ. of California Pr.,
        1957   (AR)   E51.A58.v.16.no.4

0097   COOK, Sherburne Friend
        The aboriginal population of the north coast of California.
        Berkeley, Univ. of California Pr., 1956
                (AR)   E51.A58.v.16.no.3

0098   COOK, Sherburne Friend
        The aboriginal population of the San Joaquin Valley,
        California. Berkeley, Univ. of California Pr., 1955
                (AR)   E51.A58.v.16.no.2

0099   DALE, Edward Everett
        The Indians of the Southwest. Norman, Pub. in cooperation
        with the Huntington Library, San Marino, Calif., by the
        Univ. of Oklahoma Pr., 1949   E78.S7D34

0100   DEBO, Angie
        The five civilized tribes of Oklahoma. Philadelphia,
        Indian Rights Assoc., 1951   E78.O45D4

0101   DENIG, Edwin Thompson
        Five Indian tribes of the upper Missouri: Sioux,
        Arickaras, Assiniboines, Crees, Crows. Norman,
        Univ. of Oklahoma Pr., 1961   E78.M82D4

0102   DORSEY, George Amos
        Indians of the Southwest. Chicago, Passenger Dept.,
        Atchison, Topeka & Santa Fe railway system, 1903
                E78.S7D7

0103   DRIVER, Harold Edson
        Girls' puberty rites in western North America.
        Berkeley and Los Angeles, Univ. of California Pr., 1941
                (AR)   E51.A58.v.6.no.2

0104   DRIVER, Harold Edson
        Northwest California. Berkeley, Univ. of California Pr.,
        1939   (AR)   E51.A58.v.1.no.6

0105   DRIVER, Harold Edson
      Southern Sierra Nevada. Berkeley, Univ. of California Pr.,
      1937   (AR)   E51.A58.v.1.no.2

0106   DRUCKER, Philip
      Cultures of the north Pacific coast. San Francisco, Chandler
      Pub. Co., 1965   E78.N78D67

0107   DRUCKER, Philip
      Indians of the Northwest coast. Pub. for the American Museum
      of Natural History by McGraw-Hill, 1955 E78.N78D7

0108   DRUCKER, Philip
      Southern California. Berkeley, Univ. of California Pr., 1937
                 (AR)   E51.A58.v.1.no.1

0109   ESSENE, Frank
      Round valley. Berkeley and Los Angeles, Univ. of California
      Pr., 1942   (AR)   E51.A58.v.8.no.1

0110   Ethnohistory in southwestern Alaska and the southern Yukon:
      method and content. Lexington, Univ. Press of Kentucky, 1970
                              E78.A3E8

0111   EWERS, John Canfield
      Indian life on the Upper Missouri. Norman, Univ. of Oklahoma
      Pr., 1968   E78.M82E94

0112   FOREMAN, Grant
      The Five civilized tribes. Norman, Univ. of Oklahoma Pr.,
      1934   E78.O45F6

01121   FOWLER, Don D.
      John Wesley Powell and the anthropology of the Canyon Country.
      Washington, U.S. Dept. of the Interior, Geological Survey;
      U. S. Govt. Print. Off., 1969   E78.C6.F6

0113   FUNDABURK, Emma Lila ed.
      Sun circles and human hands. Luverne, Ala., 1957 E78.S65F82

0114   GAYTON, Anna Hadwick
      The ghost dance of 1870 in south-central California. Berkeley,
      Univ. of California Pr., 1930 (UCPAE)   E51.C15.v.28.no.3

0115   GIFFORD, Edward Winslow
      Californian anthropometry. Berkeley, Univ. of California Pr.,
      1926   (UCPAE)   E51.C15.v.28.no.3

0116   GIFFORD, Edward Winslow
      Californian kinship terminologies. Berkeley, Univ. of Cali-
      fornia Pr., 1922   (UCPAE)   E51.C15.v.18.no.1

11

0117 GIFFORD, Edward Winslow
Clans and moieties in southern California. Berkeley,
Univ. of California Pr., 1918. (UCPAE) E51.C15.v.14.no.2

0118 GIFFORD, Edward Winslow
Dichotomous social organization in south central California. Berkeley, Univ. of California Pr., 1916
              (UCPAE)   E51.C15.v.11.no.5

0119 GLADWIN, Winifred (Jones)
The red-on-buff culture of the Gila basin. Pasadena,
Calif., Priv. print. for the Medallion, 1929
                                   E78.A7G567

0120 GODDARD, Pliny Earle
Indians of the Southwest. American Museum Pr., 1931
                                   E78.S7G53.1931

0121 GUMERMAN, George J.
Black Mesa. Prescott, Ariz., Prescott College Pr., 1970
                                   E78.A7G96

0122 HAEBERLIN, Herman Karl
The Indians of Puget Sound. Seattle, Univ. of
Washington Pr., 1952 (1930)   E78.P8H33

0123 HAGAN, William Thomas
The Sac and Fox Indians. Norman, Univ. of Oklahoma Pr.,
1958   E99.S23H33

0124 HARRINGTON, John Peabody
Central California coast. Berkeley and Los Angeles,
Univ. of California Pr., 1942 (AR) E51.A58.v.7.no.1

0125 HARVEY, Fred
American Indians. Kansas City, Mo., 1928 E78.S7H34

0126 HAWTHORN, Harry Bertram
The Indians of British Columbia. Toronto, Univ. of
Toronto Pr. and the Univ. of British Columbia, 1960 (1958)
                                   E78.B9H35.1960

0127 HEIZER, Robert Fleming
The California Indians. Berkeley, Univ. of California
Pr., 1951   E78.C15H4

0128 HONIGMANN, John Joseph
Ethnography and acculturation of the Fort Nelson
Slave. Notes on the Indians of the Great Slave lake area,
by J. Alden Mason. New Haven, Pub. for the Dept. of
Anthropology, Yale Univ., Yale Univ. Pr., 1946
              (YUPA)   GN2.Y3.no.33-34

0129   HRDLIČKA, Aleš
        The anthropology of Kodiak island. Philadelphia, The Wistar
        Institute of Anatomy and Biology, 1944   E78.A3H814

0130   HRDLIČKA, Aleš
        Contribution to the physical anthropology of California.
        Berkeley, The Univ. Pr., 1906
                            (UCPAE)   E51.C15.v.4.no.2

0131   JAMES, George Wharton
        The Indians of the Painted desert region. Boston, Little,
        Brown, and Co., 1903   E78.S7J2

0132   KELLY, Arthur Randolph
        Physical anthropology of a Mexican population in Texas.
        New Orleans, Middle American Research Institute, Tulane Univ.
        of Louisiana, 1947   (TMAI)   F1421.T95.no.13

0133   KLIMEK, Stanislaw
        The structure of California Indian culture. Berkeley, Univ.
        of California Pr., 1935 (UCPAE)   E51.C15.v.37.no.1

0134   KROEBER, Alfred Louis
        California culture provinces. Berkeley, Univ. of California
        Pr., 1920   (UCPAE)   E51.C15.v.17.no.2

0135   KROEBER, Alfred Louis
        California kinship systems. Berkeley, Univ. of California Pr.,
        1917   (UCPAE)   E51.C15.v.12.no.9

0136   KROEBER, Alfred Louis
        Elements of culture in native California. Berkeley, Univ.
        of California Pr., 1922 (UCPAE)   E51.C15.v.13.no.8

0137   KROEBER, Alfred Louis
        Handbook of the Indians in California. Washington, Govt.
        Print. Off., 1925   (BAEB)   E51.U55.no.78

0138   KROEBER, Alfred Louis
        Native culture of the Southwest. Berkeley, Univ. of
        California Pr., 1928   (UCPAE)   E51.C15.v.23.no.9

0139   KROEBER, Alfred Louis
        Types of Indian culture in California. Berkeley, The
        University Pr., 1904   (UCPAE)   E51.C15.v.2.no.3

01391   LEE, Shirley W.
        A survey of acculturation in the Intermontane Area of the
        United States. Pocatello, Idaho, Idaho St. Univ. 1967
                            (ISUOP)   E78.I18.I4.no.19

13

0140   LEWIS, Albert Buell
       Tribes of the Columbia Valley and the coast of
       Washington and Oregon. Lancaster, Pa., The New Era
       Printing Co., 1906   (AAAM)   GN2.A22.no.2

0141   LOWIE, Robert Harry
       Indians of the Plains. Pub. for the American Museum of
       Natural History by McGraw-Hill, 1954   E78.W6L68

0142   LOWIE, Robert Harry
       Notes on the social organization and customs of the
       Mandan, Hidatsa, and Crow Indians. American Museum
       of Natural History, 1917 (AMNHP)   GN2.A27.v.21.pt.1

0143   LOWIE, Robert Harry
       Plains Indian age-societies: historical and comparative
       summary. American Museum of Natural History, 1916
                 (AMNHP)   GN2.A27.v.11.pt.13

0144   LOWIE, Robert Harry
       Societies of the Crow, Hidatsa and Mandan Indians.
       American Museum of Natural History, 1913 E98.S75L6

01441   LYNCH, Thomas F.
       The Nature of the Central Andean Preceramic. Pocatello,
       Idaho, Idaho State Univ., 1967 (ISUOP) E78.I18.I4.no.21

0145   McFEAT, Tom comp.
       Indians of the North Pacific Coast. Seattle, Univ. of
       Washington Pr., 1967 (1966)   E78.N78M3

01451   MARTIN, Paul Sidney
       Table rock pueblo, Arizona. Chicago, Field Museum of
       Natural History, 1950 (FMAS)   GN2.F4.v.51.no.2

01452   MAXON, James C.
       Indians of the Lake Mead Country. Globe, Ariz., Southwest
       Park and Monument Association, 1971   E78.A7.M35

0146   MERRIAM, Clinton Hart
       Studies of California Indians. Berkeley, Univ. of
       California Pr., 1955   E78.C15M48

0147   MILLER, Joseph
       Arizona Indians. Hastings House, 1941 E78.A7M57

0148   NIBLACK, Albert Parker
       The coast Indians of southern Alaska and northern
       British Columbia. Johnson Reprint Corp., 1970 (1890)
                         E78.A3N5.1970

0149   OLIVER, Symmes Chadwick
        Ecology and cultural continuity as contributing factors
        in the social organization of the Plains Indians. Berkeley,
        Univ. of California Pr., 1962. (UCPAE) E51.C15.v.48.no.1

0150   POURADE, Richard F.
        Ancient hunters of the Far West. San Diego, Calif., Union-
        Tribune Pub. Co., 1966   E78.W5P6

0151   REAGAN, Albert B.
        Notes on the Indians of the Fort Apache region. American
        Museum of Natural History, 1930 (AMNHP) GN2.A27.v.31.pt.5

0152   REID, Hugo
        The Indians of Los Angeles County: Hugo Reid's letters of
        1852. Los Angeles, Southwest Museum, 1968
                            (LASM)   F869.L8S65.no.21

0153   ROSMAN, Abraham
        Feasting with mine enemy: rank and exchange among northwest
        coast societies. Columbia Univ. Pr., 1971 E78.N78R65

0154   SCHENCK, William Egbert
        Historic aboriginal groups of the California delta region.
        Berkeley, Univ. of California Pr., 1926 (UCPAE)
                                            E51.C15.v.23.no.2

0155   SEGER, John Homer
        Early days among the Cheyenne and Arapahoe Indians. Norman,
        Univ. of Oklahoma Pr., 1934   E99.C53S272

0156   SKINNER, Alanson Buck
        Notes on the eastern Cree and northern Saulteaux. American
        Museum of Natural History, 1911 (AMNHP) GN2.A27.v.9.pt.1

0157   SKINNER, Alanson Buck
        Political organizations, cults, and ceremonies of the Plains-
        Ojibway and Plains-Cree Indians. American Museum of Natural
        History, 1914   (AMNHP)   GN2.A27.v.11.pt.6

0158   SKINNER, Alanson Buck
        Societies of the Iowa, Kansa, and Ponca Indians. American
        Museum of Natural History, 1915 (AMNHP) GN2.A27.v.11.pt.9

01581   SLOBODIN, Richard
        Metis of the Mackenzie District. Canada, Canadian Research
        Centre for Anthropology, Saint-Paul Univ., 1966 E78.C2.S55

0159   SMITH, Mrs. Dama Margaret
        Indian tribes of the Southwest. Stanford Univ., Calif.,
        Stanford Univ. Pr., 1933   E78.S7S53

15

0160   SPIER, Leslie
        Cultural relations of the Gila river and lower Colorado
        tribes. New Haven, Pub. for the Section of Anthropology,
        Dept. of the Social Sciences, Yale Univ., by the Yale
        Univ. Pr., 1936   (YUPA)   GN2.Y3.no.3

0161   STEWART, Omer Call
        Ute-southern Paiute. Berkeley and Los Angeles, Univ. of
        California Pr., 1942   (AR)   E51.A58.v.6.no.4

0162   STRONG, William Duncan
        Aboriginal society in southern California. Berkeley,
        Univ. of California Pr., 1929 (UCPAE) E51.C15.v.26

01621   SWANSON, Earl Herbert Jr.
        The Emergence of Plateau Culture. Pocatello, Idaho,
        Idaho State Univ., 1962 (ISUOP)   E78.I18.I4.no.8

0163   UNDERHILL, Ruth Murray
        Indians of southern California. Washington, Education
        Division, U. S. Office of Indian Affairs, 1941
                                              E78.C15U35

0164   UNDERHILL, Ruth Murray
        Indians of the Pacific Northwest. Washington, U. S.
        Dept. of the Interior, Bureau of Indian Affairs, Branch
        of Education, 1960   E78.N77U47.1960

0165   U. S. DEPT. OF THE INTERIOR.
        Five civilized tribes in Oklahoma. Washington, Govt.
        Print. Off., 1913   E78.I5U516

0166   U. S. FEDERAL FIELD COMMITTEE FOR DEVELOPMENT PLANNING IN
        ALASKA.
        Alaska natives and the land. Anchorage, Alaska; For sale
        by the Supt. of Docs., U. S. Govt. Print. Off., Washington
        1968   fE78.A3U65

0167   U. S. NATIONAL PARK SERVICE.
        Indian tribes of Sequoia National Park region.
        Berkeley, 1935   E78.C15U449

0168   U. S. NATIONAL PARK SERVICE.
        Preliminary report on the ethnography of the Southwest.
        Berkeley, 1935   E78.S7U85

0169   VOEGELIN, Erminie (Wheeler)
        Northeast California. Berkeley, Univ. of California Pr.,
        1942   (AR)   E51.A58.v.7.no.2

0170   VRANGEL', Ferdinand Petrovich, Baron
       <u>Statistische und ethnographische Nachrichten über die</u>
       <u>russischen Besitzungen an der Nordwestküste von Amerika.</u>
       Osnabrück, Biblio-Verlag, 1968   DK3.B422.Folge 1, Bd.1

0171   WALKER, Edwin Francis
       <u>Indians of southern California.</u> Los Angeles, Southwest
       Museum, 1937   E78.C15W3

0172   WELSH, Herbert
       <u>Report of a visit to the Navajo, Pueblo, and Hualapais</u>
       <u>Indians of New Mexico and Arizona.</u> Philadelphia, The
       Indian Rights Assoc., 1885   E99.D1W5

0173   WHEAT, Joe Ben
       <u>Mogollon culture prior to A.D. 1000.</u> Menasha, Wis.,
       American Anthropological Assoc., 1955
                        (AAAM)   GN2.A22.no.82

0174   WISSLER, Clark
       <u>Distribution of moccasin decorations among the Plains tribes.</u>
       American Museum of Natural History, 1927
                        (AMNHP)   GN2.A27.v.29.pt.1

0175   WISSLER, Clark
       <u>North American Indians of the plains.</u> American Museum of
       Natural History, 1927   E78.W5W58

0176   WRIGHT, Muriel Hazel
       <u>A guide to the Indian tribes of Oklahoma.</u> Norman, Univ.
       of Oklahoma Pr., 1951   E78.O45W7

Mexico and Central America

0177   BEALS, Ralph Leon
        The comparative ethnology of northern Mexico before 1750.
        Berkeley, Univ. of California Pr., 1932
                            (IAM)   F1401.I22.no.2

0178   BENITZ, Fernando
        Los indios de México. México, Ediciones Era, 1968
                                            F1220.B4.1968

0179   BRAND, Donald Dilworth
        Quiroga, a Mexican municipio. Washington, U. S. Govt.
        Print. Off., 1951   (SIP)   E51.S4.no.11

01791   CASO, Alfonso
        La communidad indigena. Mexico, Secretaria de Education
        Publica, 1971   F1200.C3

0180   CONZEMIUS, Eduard
        Ethnographical survey of the Miskito and Sumu Indians
        of Honduras and Nicaragua. Washington, U.S. Govt.
        Print. Off., 1932   (BAEB)   E51.U55.no.106

0181   COOK, Sherburne Friend
        The conflict between the California Indian and white
        civilization. Berkeley and Los Angeles, Univ. of
        Calif. Pr., 1943   (IAM)   F1401.I22.no.21-24

0182   CORDRY, Donald Bush
        Mexican Indian costumes. Austin, Univ. of Texas Pr.,
        1968   fF1219.3.C75C72

0183   DAVALOS HURTADO, Eusebio
        La deformación craneana entre los Tlatelolcas. Mexico,
        Secretaria de Educacion Publica, 1951   F1219.3.C8D38

01831   DE TERRA, Helmut
        Man and mammoth in Mexico. London, Hutchinson, (1957)
                                            F1219.D4

0184   DRIVER, Harold Edson
        Ethnography and acculturation of the Chichimeca-Jonaz of
        northeast Mexico. Bloomington, Indiana Univ., 1963
                                            F1221.C53D7

0185   EDMONSON, Munro S.
        Contemporary Latin American culture. New Orleans,
        Middle American Research Institute, Tulane Univ., 1968
                            (TMAI)   F1421.T95.no.25

0186   FOSTER, George McClelland
        Empire's children; the people of Tzintzuntzan. Mexico,
        Impr. Nuevo Mundo, 1948 (SIP)   E51.S4.no.6

0187   FUENTE, Beatriz de la
        La escultura de Palenque. México, Imprento Universitaria,
        1964   F1219.1.P2F8

0188   GILLIN, John Philip
        The culture of security in San Carlos. New Orleans, Middle
        American Research Institute, Tulane Univ., 1951
                        (TMAI)   F1421.T95.no.16

0189   Handbook of Middle American Indians.
        Austin, Univ. of Texas Pr., 1964-   F1434.H3

0190   HARRIS, Marvin
        Patterns of race in the Americas. Walker, 1964 F1419.A1H3

0191   HINTON, Thomas B.
        A survey of Indian assimilation in eastern Sonora. Tucson,
        1959   F1219.1.S65H5

0192   HUMPHRIES, Frank Theodore
        The Indians of Panama. Panama, Republic of Panama, printed
        by the Panama American Publishing Co., 1944 F1565.H8

01921   KATZ, Friedrich
        The ancient American civilizations. Praeger, 1972
                                               E65.K3713.1972b

0193   LESLIE, Charles M.
        Now we are civilized. Detroit, Wayne State Univ. Pr., 1960
                                               F1221.Z3L4

0194   LOTZ, Otto
        Los habitantes primitivos de la república de Panamá. Leipzig,
        Impr. de O. Brandstetter, 1924   F1565.L97

0195   McBRYDE, Felix Webster
        Cultural and historical geography of southwest Guatemala.
        Washington, U. S. Govt. Print. Off., 1947
                        (SIP)   E51.S4.no.4

0196   MEIGS, Peveril
        The Kiliwa Indians of Lower California. Berkeley, Univ.
        of California Pr., 1939 (IAM)   F1401.I22.no.15

0197   MÖRNER, Magnus
        Race mixture in the history of Latin America. Boston, Little,
        Brown, 1967   F1419.A1M6

0198   MONTEFORTE TOLEDO, Mario
        Guatemala, monografía sociológica. México, Instituto
        de Investigaciones Sociales, Universidad Nacional
        Autónoma de México, 1965   F1463.5.M6.1965

0199   NASH, June C.
        In the eyes of the ancestors. New Haven, Yale Univ. Pr.,
        1970   F1219.3.S6N3

0200   Nativism and syncretism.
        New Orleans, Middle American Research Institute, Tulane
        Univ., 1960   (TMAI)   F1421.T95.no.19

0201   NOLASCO ARMAS, Margarita
        Notas para la antropología social del nordeste de México.
        México, Instituto Nacional de Antropología e Historia,
        1969   F1220.N653

0202   RADIN, Paul
        Mexican kinship terms. Berkeley, Univ. of California Pr.,
        1931   (UCPAE)   E51.C15.v.31.no.1

0203   REDFIELD, Robert
        The folk culture of Yucatan. Chicago, The Univ. of Chicago
        Pr., 1941   F1376.R4

0204   SAUER, Carl Ortwin
        Aztatlán: prehistoric Mexican frontier on the Pacific
        coast. Berkeley, Univ. of California Pr., 1932
                (IAM)   F1401.I22.no.1

02041   The Social anthropology of Latin America; essays in honor of
        Ralph Leon Beals. Walter Goldschmidt and Harry Hiojer,
        eds. Los Angeles, Latin American Center, Univ. of Calif.,
        1970   E65.S63

0205   SOUSTELLE, Jacques
        Daily life of the Aztecs. Stanford, Stanford Univ. Pr.,
        1970 (1961)   F1219.S723

02051   SOUSTELLE, Jacques
        The four suns; recollections and reflections of an
        ethnologist in Mexico. Grossman Publishers, 1971
                F1219.S71713.1971

0206   SOUSTELLE, Jacques
        Les Quatre soleils. Paris, Plon, 1967   F1219.S726

0207   STARR, Frederick
        In Indian Mexico. Chicago, Forbes & Co., 1908
                F1220.S78

0208   STERN, Theodore
        The rubber-ball games of the americas.   J. J. Augustin, 1950
                            (MAES)   E51.A556.v.17

0209   STRONG, William Duncan
        Archeological investigations in the Bay islands, Spanish
        Honduras. City of Washington, The Smithsonian Institution,
        1935   F1509.B3S77

0210   Summa anthropologica en homenaje a Roberto J. Weitlaner.
        México, Instituto Nacional de Antropología e Historia,
        Secretaria de Educación Pública, 1966   F1220.S8

0211   Synoptic studies of Mexican culture.
        New Orleans, Middle American Research Institute, Tulane
        Univ., 1957   (TMAI)   F1421.T95.no.17

0212   TAYLOR, Paul Schuster
        A Spanish-Mexican peasant community: Arandas in Jalisco,
        Mexico. Berkeley, Univ. of California Pr., 1933
                            (IAM)   F1401.I22.no.4

0213   TEHUACAN ARCHAEOLOGICAL BOTANICAL PROJECT.
        The prehistory of Tehuacan Valley. Austin, Pub. for the
        Robert S. Peabody Foundation, Phillips Academy, Andover,
        Mass., by the Univ. of Texas, 1967   F1219.1.T224T4

0214   TIBÓN, Gutierre
        Mujeres y diosas de México. México, Instituto Nacional
        de Antropología e Historia, 1967   F1219.3.A7T5

0215   TOZZER, Alfred Marston
        A comparative study of the Mayas and the Lacandones.   Pub.
        for the Archaeological Institute of America by the
        Macmillan Co., 1907   F1435.T75

0216   WAGLEY, Charles
        The social and religious life of a Guatemalan village.
        Menasha, Wis., American Anthropological Assoc., 1949
                            (AAAM)   GN2.A22.no.71

0217   WATERMAN, Thomas Talbot
        Bandelier's contribution to the study of ancient Mexican
        social organization. Berkeley, Univ. of California Pr.,
        1917   (UCPAE)   E51.C15.v.12.no.7

0218   WEITLANER, Roberto J.
        Los grupos indígenas del norte de Oaxaca. México, Instituto
        Nacional de Antropología e Historia, 1969 F1219.1.O11W42

0219   WEST, Robert Cooper
        <u>Cultural geography of the modern Tarascan area</u>. Washington,
        U. S. Govt. Print. Off., 1948 (SIP)   E51.S4.no.7

0220   WHETTEN, Nathan Laselle
        <u>Guatemala, the land and the people</u>. New Haven, Yale Univ.
        Pr., 1961   F1463.5.W5

0221   WILLARD, Theodore Arthur
        <u>Kukulcan, the bearded conqueror</u>. Hollywood, Calif.,
        Murray and Gee, 1941   F1435.W715

0222   ZANTWIJK, Rudolf A. M. van
        <u>Servants of the saints</u>. Assen, Van Gorcum & Comp., 1967
                                                  F1221.T3Z3.1967

General

0223   AMERICAN PHILOSOPHICAL SOCIETY, Philadelphia.
        Recent advances in American archaeology. Philadelphia,
        The American Philosophical Society, 1943
                            (PPSP)   Q11.P5.v.86.no.2

02231   ANTHROPOLOGICAL SOCIETY OF WASHINGTON, WASHINGTON, D.C.
        New interpretations of aboriginal American culture history;
        75th anniversary volume. Cooper Square, 1972 E61.A6.1972

0224   ATWATER, Caleb
        Writings. Scott and Wright, 1833   E73.A88.Spec.Coll.

02241   BALDWIN, John Denison
        Ancient America, in notes on American archaeology. Harper,
        1876   E61.B185

0225   BRENNAN, Louis A.
        No stone unturned. Random House, 1959 E61.B83

0226   BUSHNELL, Geoffrey Hext Sutherland
        The first Americans. McGraw-Hill, 1968 E61.B95.1968b

0227   CHARNAY, Désiré
        The ancient cities of the new world. Harper, 1887
                                                F1219.C49.1887

0228   CONANT, Alban Jasper
        Foot-prints of vanished races in the Mississippi Valley.
        St. Louis, C. R. Barns, 1879   E78.M75C6

0229   COOK, Sherburne Friend
        The fossilization of human bone: calcium, phosphate, and
        carbonate. Berkeley, Univ. of California Pr., 1951
                            (UCPAE)   E51.C15.v.40.no.6

0230   COOK, Sherburne Friend
        The quantitative investigation of Indian mounds. Berkeley,
        Univ. of California Pr., 1950 (UCPAE) E51.C15.v.40.no.5

0231   COOK, Sherburne Friend
        Studies on the chemical analysis of archaeological sites.
        Berkeley, Univ. of California Pr., 1965 E77.94.C6

0232   DEUEL, Leo, comp.
        Conquistadors without swords: archaeologists in the Americas.
        St. Martin's Pr., 1967   E61.D46

0233   FERDON, Edwin N.
        A trial survey of Mexican-Southwestern architectural
        parallels. Santa Fe, N.M., School of American Research,
        Museum of New Mexico, 1955   E59.A67F4

0234   FRAZER, Sir James George comp.
        Anthologia anthropolgica. The native races of America.
        London, P. Lund, Humphries & Co., Ltd., 1939
                                            E58.F75

0235   GARCÍA COOK, Angel
        Análisis tipológico de artefactos. México, Instituto
        Nacional de Antropología e Historia, 1967
                        (INAH)   F1219.M627.no.12

0236   GLADWIN, Harold Sterling
        Men out of Asia. Whittlesey House, 1947 E61.G6

0237   GUNNERSON, James H.
        Miscellaneous collected papers. Salt Lake City, Univ. of
        Utah Pr., 1962   (UUAP)   E51.U8.no.60

0238   HARDOY, Jorge Enrique
        Urban planning in pre-Columbian America. Braziller, 1968
                                            E59.C55H3

0239   HOLMES, William Henry
        Handbook of aboriginal American antiquities. Washington,
        Govt. Print. Off., 1919- (BAEB)   E51.U55.no.60

0240   HOWELLS, William White
        Craniometry and multivariate analysis. Cambridge, Mass.,
        Peabody Museum, 1966 (PMP) ·   E51.H337.v.57.no.1

0241   HRDLIČKA, Aleš
        Recent discoveries attributed to early man in America.
        Washington, Govt. Print. Off., 1918
                        (BAEB)   E51.U55.no.66

0242   HUDDLESTON, Lee Eldridge
        Origins of the American Indians. Austin, published for
        the Institute of Latin American Studies by the Univ.
        of Texas Pr., 1967   E61.H875

02421   JENNESS, Diamond ed.
        The American aborigines, their origin and antiquity; a
        collection of papers by ten authors. Russell and Russell,
        1972   E61.J53.1972

0243   JENNINGS, Jesse David
        Prehistory of North America. McGraw-Hill, 1968 E77.9.J4

                                24

0244   JOHNSON, Frederick ed.
       Radiocarbon dating; a report on the program to aid in the
       development of the method of dating. Salt Lake City, Society
       for American Archaeology, 1951 (SAAM) E51.S7.no.8

0245   JUDD, Neil Merton
       Men met along the trail. Norman, Univ. of Oklahoma Pr.,
       1968   E57.J8A3

0246   KROEBER, Alfred Louis
       Area and climax. Berkeley, Univ. of California Pr., 1936
                        (UCPAE)   E51.C15.v.37.no.3

02461 MCGIMSEY, Charles Robert
       Public Archeology. Seminar Press, 1972 E77.9.M3

0247   MACGOWEN, Kenneth
       Early man in the New World. Garden City, N.Y., Anchor Books,
       1962   E61.M143.1962

0248   MCINTIRE, William G.
       Prehistoric Indian settlements of the changing Mississippi
       River Delta. Baton Rouge, Louisiana State Univ. Pr., 1958
                                         E78.L8M3

02481 MCKERN, Sharon S.
       Exploring the unknown; mysteries in American archaeology.
       Praeger, 1972   E61.M17

0249   MACLEAN, John Patterson
       The mound builders. Cincinnati, The R. Clarke Co., 1885 (1879)
                                         E73.M17

0250   MARRIOTT, Alice Lee
       The first comers; Indians of America's dawn. David McKay,
       1968 (1960)   E98.A6M29.1968

0251   MARTIN, Paul Sidney
       Digging into history. Chicago, Natural History Museum, 1963
       (1959)   (CMA)   GN2.F5.no.38

0252   MARTIN, Paul Sidney
       Indians before Columbus. Chicago, The Univ. of Chicago Pr.,
       1947   E61.M36

02521 MEGGERS, Betty Jane
       Prehistoric America. Aldine. Atherton, 1972 E59.C95.M4

0253   MICKEY, Margaret Portia
       The Cowrie Shell Miao of Kweichow. Cambridge, Mass.,
       The Museum, 1947   (PMP)   E51.H337.v.32.no.1

0254   Middle American papers. New Orleans, Dept. of Middle
        American Research, Tulane Univ. of Louisiana, 1932
                            (TMAI)   F1421.T95.no.4

0255   MILES, Charles
        Indian and Eskimo artifacts of North America. Chicago,
        H. Regnery Co., 1963   E77.M62

0256   MOOREHEAD, Warren King
        Hematite implements of the United States, together
        with chemical analysis of various hematites. Andover,
        Mass., The Andover Pr., 1912   E51.P55

0257   MOOREHEAD, Warren King
        Prehistoric relics. Andover, Mass., The Andover Pr., 1905
                                            E56.M73

0258   MORRIS, Earl Halstead
        The Earl Morris papers. Boulder, Univ. of Colorado Pr.,
        1963-   (CUSA)   GN4.C64.no.8,10

0259   NADAILLAC, Jean Francois Albert du Pouget, marquis de
        Pre-historic America. London, J. Murray, 1885 E61.N12

0260   PANNETON, Philippe
        Un monde était leur empire. Montréal, Can., Les Éditions
        Variétés, Dussault et Péladeau, 1943   E61.P2

0261   PAYNE, Mildred Y.
        Mounds in the mist. South Brunswick, N.J., A. S. Barnes,
        1970 (1969)   E78.T3P3.1970

0262   PHILLIPS, Philip
        Archaeological survey in the Lower Mississippi Alluvial
        Valley, 1940 1947. Kraus, 1968 (1951)
                            (PMP)   E51.H337.v.25.1968

0263   PRIEST, Josiah
        American antiquities, and discoveries in the West.
        Albany, Printed by Packard, Hoffman and White, 1833
                                            E61.P925.Spec.Coll.

0264   ROBBINS, Maurice
        The Amateur archaeologist's handbook. Crowell, 1966 (1965)
                                            E77.9.R6

0265   SANDERS, William T.
        New World prehistory. Englewood Cliffs, N.J., Prentice-Hall,
        1970   E58.S25

0266   SHETRONE, Henry Clyde
       The mound-builders. Port Washington, N.Y., Kennikat Pr.,
       1964 (1930)   E73.S55.1964

0267   SILVERBERG, Robert
       Mound builders of ancient America. Greenwich, Conn.,
       New York Graphic Society, 1968   E73.S57

0268   SOCIETY FOR AMERICAN ARCHAEOLOGY.
       Seminars in archaeology: 1955. Salt Lake City, Society
       for American Archaeology, 1956 (SAAM) E51.S7.no.11

0269   STUART, George E.
       Discovering man's past in the Americas. Washington, National
       Geographic Society, 1969   E61.S9

0270   Studies in Middle America. New Orleans, Dept. of Middle
       America Research, Tulane Univ. of Louisiana, 1934
                  (TMAI)   F1421.T95.no.5a

0271   THOMAS, Cyrus
       Introduction to the study of North America archaeology.
       Cincinnati, The Robert Clarke Co., 1898 E61.T45

0272   THOMAS, Cyrus
       Work in mound exploration of the Bureau of ethnology.
       Washington, Govt. Print. Off., 1887 (BAEB) E51.U55.no.4

0273   WAUCHOPE, Robert
       Lost tribes and sunken continents. Chicago, Univ. of
       Chicago Pr., 1963 (1962)   E61.W33

0274   WAUCHOPE, Robert
       They found the buried cities. Chicago, Univ. of Chicago
       Pr., 1965   F1435.W38

0275   WENDORF, Fred
       A guide for salvage archaeology. Santa Fe, Museum of New
       Mexico Pr., 1962   E77.W42

0276   WILLEY, Gordon Randolph
       An introduction to American archaeology. Englewood Cliffs,
       N.J., Prentice-Hall, 1966-   E61.W68

0277   WILLEY, Gordon Randolph
       Method and theory in American archaeology. Chicago, Univ.
       of Chicago Pr., 1967 (1958)   E61.W7

0278   WILLIAM MARSH RICE UNIVERSITY, HOUSTON, TEX.
       Prehistoric man in the New World. Chicago, Published for
       William Marsh Rice University by the Univ. of Chicago Pr.,
       1965 (1964)   E61.W717

0279   WILMSEN, Edwin N.
        Lithnic analysis and cultural inference: a paleo-Indian case.
        Tucson, Univ. of Arizona Pr., 1970   E77.9.W54

0280   WISSLER, Clark
        Indian cavalcade. Sheridan House, 1938 E98.S7W57

0281   WORMINGTON, Hannah Marie
        Ancient man in North America. Denver, Denver Museum
        of Natural History, 1957   E61.W8.1957

Eastern United States and Canada

02811   BENSON, Elizabeth P.
        An Olmec figure at Dumbarton Oaks. Washington, Dumbarton
        Oaks, Trustees for Harvard Univ., 1971 (DO) E51.S85.no.8

02812   BINFORD, Lewis R.
        Indian site and chipped stone materials in the northern
        Lake Michigan area. Chicago, Field Museum of Natural
        History, 1963   (FMAS)   GN2.F4.v.36.no.12

0282   BLACK, Glenn Albert
        Angel Site. Indianapolis, Indiana Historical Society, 1967
                                            E78.I53B55.1967

02821   BROSE, David S.
        The Summer Island site; a study of prehistoric cultural
        ecology and social organization in the northern Lake
        Michigan area. Cleveland, Ohio, Case Western Reserve Univ.,
        1970   (CWRA)   GN2.C34.no.1

0283   BULLEN, Ripley P.
        Archaeological investigations of Green Mound, Florida.
        Orlando, Fla., Central Florida Museum, 1960
                             (ASR)   E77.8.W5.no.2

0284   BULLEN, Ripley P.
        Archaeological investigations of the Castle Windy Midden,
        Florida. Springfield, Vt., 1959 (ASR) E77.8.W5.no.1

0285   BUSHNELL, David Ives
        Indian sites below the falls of the Rappahannock, Virginia.
        City of Washington, The Smithsonian Institution, 1937
                                            E78.V7B825

0286   BUSHNELL, David Ives, Jr.
        Native cemeteries and forms of burial east of the Mississippi.
        Washington, Govt. Print. Off., 1920 (BAEB) E51.U55.no.71

0287   BUSHNELL, David Ives, Jr.
        Native villages and village sites east of the Mississippi.
        Washington, Govt. Print. Off., 1919 (BAEB) E51.U55.no.69

0288   CALDWELL, Joseph Ralston
        Trend and tradition in the prehistory of the eastern
        United States. Springfield, Published jointly by Illinois
        State Museum and American Anthropological Assoc., 1958
                             (AAAM)   GN2.A22.no.88

0289   COE, Joffre Lanning
        The formative cultures of the Carolina Piedmont.
        Philadelphia, American Philosophical Society, 1964
                        (APST)   fQ11.P6.n.s.v.54.pt.5

0290   COTTER, John L.
        Archeological excavations at Jamestown Colonial
        National Historical Park and Jamestown National
        Historic Site, Virginia. Washington, National Park
        Service, U.S. Dept. of the Interior, 1958
                        (NPSAS)   E51.U75.no.4

0291   COTTER, John L.
        Archeology of the Bynum mounds, Mississippi. Washington,
        National Park Service, U. S. Dept. of the Interior, 1951
                        (NPSAS)   E51.U75.no.1

0292   DINCAUZE, Dena Ferran
        Cremation cemeteries in eastern Massachusetts.
        Cambridge, Mass., The Museum, 1968 (PMP) E51.H337.v.59.no.1

0293   EVANS, Clifford
        A ceramic study of Virginia archeology. Washington,
        U.S. Govt. Print. Off., 1955 (BAEB)   E51.U55.no.160

0294   FITTING, James Edward
        The archaeology of Michigan. Garden City, N.Y.,
        Published for the American Museum of Natural History by
        the Natural History Pr., 1970   E78.M6F5

0295   FITTING, James Edward
        Contributions to Michigan archaeology. Ann Arbor,
        Univ. of Michigan, 1968 (UMAP)   GN2.M5.no.32

0296   FORD, James Alfred
        The Jaketown site in west-central Mississippi. American
        Museum of Natural History, 1955 (AMNHP) GN2.A27.v.45.pt.1

0297   FORD, James Alfred
        Measurements of some prehistoric design developments
        in the Southeastern States. American Museum of Natural
        History, 1952   (AMNHP)   GN2.A27.v.44.pt.3

0298   GREENGO, Robert E.
        Issaquena: an archaeological phase in the Yazoo Basin
        of the lower Mississippi Valley. Salt Lake City, Society
        for American Archaeology, 1964 (SAAM) E51.S7.no.18

0299   GRIFFIN, James Bennett ed.
        Archeology of eastern United States. Chicago, Univ. of
        Chicago Pr., 1952   fE53.G75

                                30

0300   HAAG, William George
        The archeology of coastal North Carolina. Baton Rouge,
        Louisiana State Univ. Pr., 1958   E78.N74H3.1958

0301   HANSON, Lee H.
        The Hardin Village site. Lexington, Univ. of Kentucky Pr.,
        1966   E78.K3H3

0302   HARRINGTON, Jean Carl
        Search for the Cittie of Ralegh. Washington, National
        Park Service. U.S. Dept. of the Interior, 1962
                        (NPSAS)   E51.U75.no.6

0303   HARRINGTON, Mark Raymond
        An ancient village site of the Shinnecock Indians. American
        Museum of Natural History (AMNHP)   GN2.A27.v.22.pt.5

03031   JONES, Charles Colcock
        _Antiquities of the southern Indians, particularly of the
        Georgia Tribes._ Spartanburg, S.C., Reprint Co., 1972 (1873)
                                               E78.G3.J6.1972

0304   LEWIS, Thomas McDowell Nelson
        _Hiwassee island, an archaeological account of four Tennessee
        Indian peoples._ Knoxville, The Univ. of Tennessee Pr., 1946
                                               E78.T3L4

0305   MOOREHEAD, Warren King
        The Hopewell mound group of Ohio. Chicago, Field Museum
        of Natural History, 1922 (FMAS)   GN2.F4.v.6.no.5

03051   PENDERGAST, James P.
        Cartier's Hochelaga and the Lawson site. Canada, McGill-Queen's
        Univ. Pr., 1972   E99.I69.P46

03052   PHILLIPS, Philip
        _Archaeological survey in the lower Yazoo Basin, Mississippi,
        1949-1955._ Cambridge, Mass., The Museum, 1970
                        (PMP)   E51.H337.v.60

0306   POTTER, Martha A.
        Ohio's prehistoric peoples. Columbus, Ohio Historical
        Society, 1968   E78.O3P6

0307   PRAUS, Alexis A.
        Bibliography of Michigan archaeology. Ann Arbor, Univ.
        of Michigan, 1964   (UMAP)   GN2.M5.no.22

0308   PRUFER, Olaf H.
        Blain Village and the Fort Ancient tradition in Ohio.
        Kent, Ohio, Kent State Univ. Pr., 1970 E78.O3P7

03081 QUIMBY, George Irving
       The Bayou Goula site, Iberville Parish, Louisiana.
       Chicago, Field Museum of Natural History, 1957
                      (FMAS)   GN2.F4.v.47.no.2

03082 QUIMBY, George Irving
       The Dumaw Creek site; a seventeenth century prehistoric
       Indian village and cemetery in Oceana County, Michigan.
       Chicago, Field Museum of Natural History, 1966
                      (FMAS)   GN2.F4.v.56.no.1

0309   RITCHIE, William Augustus
       The archaeology of Martha's Vineyard: a framework for
       the prehistory of southern New England. Garden City, N.Y.,
       Published for the American Museum of Natural History by
       the Natural History Pr., 1969   E78.M4R5

0310   RITCHIE, William Augustus
       The archaeology of New York State. Garden City, N.Y.,
       Pub. for the American Museum of Natural History by
       the Natural History Pr., 1965   E78.N7R476

0311   RITCHIE, William Augustus
       The pre-Iroquoian occupations of New York state.
       Rochester, N.Y., Rochester Museum of Arts and
       Sciences, 1944   E78.N7R66

0312   RITCHIE, William Augustus
       The Stony Brook site and its relation to archaic and
       transitional cultures on Long Island. Albany, Univ.
       of the State of New York, 1959   E78.N7R67

0313   RITCHIE, William Augustus
       Traces of early man in the Northeast. Albany, Univ.
       of the State of New York, 1957   E78.N7R69

0314   ROLINGSON, Martha Ann
       Late Paleo-Indian and early archaic manifestations in
       western Kentucky. Lexington, Univ. of Kentucky Pr.,
       1966   E78.K3R57

0315   ROLINGSON, Martha Ann
       Paleo-Indian culture in Kentucky. Lexington, Univ.
       of Kentucky Pr., 1964   E78.K3R6

0316   SCHWARTZ, Douglas Wright
       Conceptions of Kentucky prehistory. Lexington, Univ.
       of Kentucky Pr., 1968 (1967)   E78.K3S26

0317   SETZLER, Frank Maryl
       Peachtree mound and village site, Cherokee county, North
       Carolina. Washington, U.S. Govt. Print. Off., 1941
                                            E78.N74S5.1941

0318   SMITH, Carlyle Shreeve
        The archaeology of coastal New York. American Museum
        of Natural History, 1950 (AMNHP)   GN2.A27.v.43.pt.2

0319   SMITH, Harlan Ingersoll
        The prehistoric ethnology of a Kentucky site. American
        Museum of Natural History, 1910 (AMNHP) GN2.A27.v.6.pt.2

0320   SNOW, Charles Ernest
        Indian burials from St. Petersburg, Florida. Gainesville,
        Univ. of Florida, 1962   E98.A55S62

0321   SPECK, Frank Gouldsmith
        The celestial bear comes down to earth. Reading, Pa.,
        Reading Public Museum and Art Gallery, 1945 Q11.R4.no.7

0322   SPECK, Frank Gouldsmith
        Territorial subdivisions and boundaries of the Wampanoag,
        Massachusett, and Nauset Indians. Museum of the American
        Indian, Heye Foundation, 1928   E78.M4S7

0323   Studies in Ohio archaeology. Cleveland, Press of Western
        Reserve Univ., 1967   E78.O3S7

0324   THOMAS, Cyrus
        The circular, square, and octagonal earthworks of Ohio.
        Washington, Govt. Print. Off., 1889 (BAEB) E51.U55.no.10

0325   TORONTO. ONTARIO PROVINCIAL MUSEUM.
        Annual archaeological report. 1st-36th, 1886/87-1926/28.
        Toronto, 1888-1929?   E78.C2T6

0326   WAUCHOPE, Robert
        Archaeological survey of Northern Georgia with a test
        of some cultural hypotheses. Salt Lake City, Society for
        American Archaeology, 1966 (SAAM)   E51.S7.no.21

0327   WEBB, William Snyder
        An archeological survey of Pickwick basin in the adjacent
        portions of the states of Alabama, Mississippi and Tennessee.
        Washington, U. S. Govt. Print. Off., 1942
                        (BAEB)   E51.U55.no.129

0328   WEBB, William Snyder
        An archaeological survey of the Norris basin in eastern
        Tennessee. Washington, U. S. Govt. Print. Off., 1938
                        (BAEB)   E51.U55.no.118

0329   WEBB, William Snyder
        An archaeological survey of Wheeler basin on the Tennessee
        river in northern Alabama. Washington, U.S. Govt. Print.
        Off., 1939   (BAEB)   E51.U55.no.122

0330   WILLEY, Gordon Randolph
        Archeology of the Florida Gulf Coast. Washington,
        Smithsonian Institution, 1949   F313.W56

03301   WILLOUGHBY, Charles C.
        Indian burial places at Winthrop, Massachusetts. Cambridge,
        Mass., The Museum, 1924 (PMP)   E51.H337.v.11.no.1

Western United States and Canada

0331   Aboriginal California. Berkeley, Published for the Univ.
        of California Archaeological Research Facility by Univ.
        of California, 1963   E78.C15A5

0332   ALLISON, Vernon Charles
        The antiquity of the deposits in Jacob's cavern. American
        Museum of Natural History, 1926 (AMNHP) GN2.A27.v.19.pt.6

0333   AMSDEN, Charles Avery
        Prehistoric Southwesterners from basketmaker to pueblo.
        Los Angeles, Los Angeles Southwestern Museum, 1949
                                         E78.S7A5

0334   The archeology of pleistocene lake Mohave. Los Angeles,
        Southwest Museum, 1937 (LASM)   F869.L8S65.no.11

0335   The archaeology of two sites at Eastgate, Churchill County,
        Nevada. I. Wagon Jack Shelter, by Robert F. Heizer and
        M. A. Baumhoff. II. Eastgate Cave, by Albert B. Elsasser
        and E. R. Prince. Berkeley, Univ. of California Pr.,
        1961   (AR)   E51.A58.v.20.no.4

0336   BANDELIER, Adolph Francis Alphonse
        Hemenway southwestern archaeological expedition.
        Contributions to the history of the southwestern portion
        of the United States. Cambridge, Mass., J. Wilson and
        Son, 1890   (PAIA)   E51.A64.v.5

0337   BANDELIER, Adolph Francis Alphonse
        Historical introduction to studies among the sedentary
        Indians of New Mexico. Report on the ruins of the
        pueblo of Pecos. Boston, Cupples, Upham, 1883
                              (PAIA)   E51.A64.v.1

0338   BAUMHOFF, Martin A.
        Ecological determinants of aboriginal California populations.
        Berkeley, Univ. of California Pr., 1963
                              (UCPAE)   E51.C15.v.49.no.2

0339   BEALS, Ralph Leon
        Archaeological studies in northeast Arizona. A report on
        the archaeological work of the Rainbow Bridge-Monument Valley
        expedition. Berkeley and Los Angeles, Univ. of California
        Pr., 1945   (UCPAE)   E51.C15.v.44.no.1

0340   BIRD, Junius Bouton
        Archaeology of the Hopedale area, Labrador. American
        Museum of Natural History (AMNHP)   GN2.A27.v.39.pt.2

0341   BIRKET-SMITH, Kaj
        Ethnographical collections from the Northwest Passage.
        Copenhagen, Gyldendal, 1945 (TUEX)   G670.1921.R25.v.6.no.2

0342   BLEED, Peter
        The archaeology of Petaga Point. St. Paul, Minnesota
        Historical Society, 1969   E37.M7B55

0343   BRETERNITZ, David A.
        An appraisal of tree-ring dated pottery in the Southwest.
        Tucson, Univ. of Arizona Pr., 1966   E78.S7B7

0344   BRETERNITZ, David A.
        Archaeological excavations in Dinosaur National Monument,
        Colorado-Utah, 1964-1965. Boulder, Univ. of Colorado Pr.,
        1970   (CUSA)   GN4.C64.no.17

0345   BREW, John Otis
        Archaeology of Alkali Ridge, Southeastern Utah. Kraus
        Reprint Corp., 1968 (1946) (PMP)   E51.H337.v.21.1968

0346   BROWN, Lionel A.
        Pony Creek archeology. Lincoln, Neb., 1967 E74.I8B7

03461   BRYAN, Alan Lyle
        An Archaeological Survey of Northern Puget Sound.
        Pocatello, Idaho, Idaho State Univ., 1963
                        (ISUOP)   E78.I18.I4.no.11

03462   BRYAN, Alan Lyle
        Paleo-American Prehistory. Pocatello, Idaho, Idaho
        State Univ. 1965   (ISUOP)   E78.I18.I4.no.16

0347   BRYAN, Bruce
        Archaeological explorations on San Nicolas Island.
        Los Angeles, Southwest Museum, 1970
                        (LASM)   F869.L8S65.no.22

03471   BULLARD, William Rotch
        The Cerro Colorado site and pithouse architecture in the
        southwestern U. S. prior to A. D. 900. Cambridge, Mass.,
        The Museum, 1962   (PMP)   E51.H337.v.144.no.2

0348   BUSHNELL, David Ives
        Burials of the Algonquian, Siouan and Caddoan tribes
        west of the Mississippi. Washington, Govt. Print. Off.,
        1927   (BAEB)   E51.U55.no.83

349   BUTLER, B. Robert
        A guide to understanding Idaho archaeology. Pocatello,
        Idaho State Univ. Museum, 1968   E78.I18B86.1968

0350   CALDWELL, Warren Wendell
            The Black Partizan site. Lincoln, Neb., River Basin
            Surveys, 1966   E78.S63C3

0351   CALDWELL, Warren Wendell
            Hells Canyon archeology. Lincoln, Neb., 1967 E78.N77C29

0352   CALIFORNIA. UNIVERSITY. UNIVERSITY AT LOS ANGELES.
            ARCHAEOLOGICAL SURVEY.
            Report. 1958/59- Los Angeles, Dept. of Anthropology and
            Sociology. Univ. of California   F863.C26

0353   CAMPBELL, Elizabeth Warder (Crozer)
            An archeological survey of the Twenty Nine Palms region.
            Los Angeles, Southwest Museum, 1931 (LASM) F869.L8S65.no.7

0354   CAMPBELL, Elizabeth Warder (Crozer)
            The Pinto basin site. Los Angeles, Southwest Museum, 1935
                        (LASM)   F869.L8S65.no.9

03541   CAPES, Katherine H.
            Contributions to the Prehistory of Vancouver Island.
            Pocatello, Idaho, Idaho State Univ. 1964
                        (ISUOP)   E78.I18.I4.no.15

0355   CARLETON, James Henry
            Diary of an excursion to the ruins of Abó, Quarra, and
            Gran Quivira in New Mexico in 1853. Santa Fe, Stagecoach
            Pr., 1965   E78.S7C3.1965

0356   Chapters in the prehistory of eastern Arizona. Chicago,
            Field Museum of Natural History, 1962-
                        (FMAS)   GN2.F4.v.53,55,57

0357   COLLINS, Henry Bascom
            Archeology of St. Lawrence island, Alaska. City of
            Washington, The Smithsonian Institution, 1937 F912.S2C6

0358   COLTON, Harold Sellers
            Black sand. Albuquerque, Univ. of New Mexico Pr., 1960
                                                 E78.A7C73

0359   COLTON, Harold Sellers
            A survey of prehistoric sites in the region of Flagstaff,
            Arizona. Washington, U. S. Govt. Print. Off., 1932
                        (BAEB)   E51.U55.no.104

0360   COLTON, Mary Russell Ferrell
            The little-known small house ruins in the Coconino Forest.
            Lancaster, Pa., Pub. for the American Anthropological Assoc.,
            1918   (AAAM)   GN2.A22.no.24

03601   CONFERENCE OF WESTERN ARCHAEOLOGISTS ON PROBLEMS OF POINT
         TYPOLOGY.
         The First Conference of Western Archaeologists on Problems
         of Point Typology. Pocatello, Idaho, Idaho State Univ.,
         1962   (ISUOP)   E78.I18.I4.no.10

0361   Contributions to California archaeology.
         no. 1- June 1956- Los Angeles, Archaeological Research
         Associates   E78.C15C685

0362   COOK, Sherburne Friend
         Expeditions to the interior of California, Central Valley,
         1820-1840. Berkeley, Univ. of California Pr., 1962
                              (AR)   E51.A58.v.20.no.5

0363   COOK, Sherburne Friend
         The physical analysis of nine Indian mounds of the lower
         Sacramento Valley. Berkeley, Univ. of California Pr.,
         1951   (UCPAE)   E51.C15.v.40.no.7

03631   CORLISS, David W.
         Neck width of Projectile points; an index of culture
         continuity and change. Pocatello, Idaho, Idaho State
         Univ., 1972   (ISUOP)   E78.I18.I4.no.29

0364   COSGROVE, Cornelius Burton
         Caves of the upper Gila and Hueco areas, in New Mexico
         and Texas. Krause Reprint Corp., 1968 (1947)
                              (PMP)   E51.H337.v.24.no.2.1⟨

03641   COSGROVE, Harriet (Silliman)
         ...The Swarts ruin: a typical Mimbres site in southwestern
         New Mexico: report of the Mimbres valley expedition,
         seasons of 1924-1927. Cambridge, Mass., The Museum, 1967
                              (PMP)   E51.H337.v.15.no.1.1⟨

0365   CRAMPTON, Charles Gregory
         The San Juan Canyon historical sites. Salt Lake City,
         Univ. of Utah Pr., 1964 (UUAP)   E51.U8.no.70

0366   CRESSMAN, Luther Sheeleigh
         The sandal and the cave. Portland, Or., Beaver Books,
         1962   E78.06C72

0367   CUMMINGS, Byron
         Kinishba. Tucson, Ariz., Hohokam Museums Association
         and the Univ. of Arizona, 1940   E78.A7C9

0368   CURTIS, Freddie
         Arroyo Sequit. Archaeological Survey Association of
         Southern California, 1959   E78.C15C87

                                38

03681   DAIFUKU, Hiroshi
         Jeddito 264; a report on the excavation of a Basket Maker
         III-Pueblo I site in northeastern Arizona. Cambridge, Mass.,
         The Museum, 1961   (PMP)   E51.H337.v.33.no.1

0369   DANSON, Edward Bridge
         An archaeological survey of west central New Mexico and
         east central Arizona. Cambridge, Mass., The Museum, 1957
                                 (PMP)   E51.H337.v.44.no.1

0370   DAUGHERTY, Richard D.
         Early man in the Columbia intermontane province. Salt Lake
         City, Univ. of Utah Pr., 1956 (UUAP)   E51.U8.no.24

0371   DEAN, Jeffrey S.
         Chronological analysis of Tsegi phase sites in northeastern
         Arizona. Tucson, Univ. of Arizona Pr., 1969 QK477.A74.no.3

0372   DeLAGUNA, Frederica
         Archeology of the Yakutat Bay area, Alaska. Washington,
         U.S. Govt. Print. Off., 1964   E78.A3D4

0373   DiPESO, Charles Corradino
         The Reeve ruin of southeastern Arizona. Dragoon, Ariz.,
         Amerind Foundation, 1958   E78.A7D48

0374   ELSASSER, Albert B.
         The archaeology of Bowers Cave, Los Angeles County,
         California. Berkeley, Univ. of California Archaeological
         Research Facility, Dept. of Anthropology, 1963
                                                 F863.C255.no.59

0375   ERDMAN, James A.
         Environment of Mesa Verde, Colorado. Washington, U.S.
         National Park Service, 1969 (NPSAS)   E51.U75.no.7-B

0376   FEWKES, Jesse Walter
         Antiquities of the Mesa Verde National Park, Cliff Palace.
         Washington, Govt. Print. Off., 1911 (BAEB) E51.U55.no.51

0377   FEWKES, Jesse Walter
         Antiquities of the Mesa Verde National Park, Sprucetree
         house. Washington, Govt. Print. Off., 1909
                                 (BAEB)   E51.U55.no.41

0378   FEWKES, Jesse Walter
         Excavations at Casa Grande, Arizona, in 1906-07. Washington,
         Smithsonian Institution, 1907   E78.A7F4

0379   FEWKES, Jesse Walter
        <u>Preliminary report on a visit to the Navaho national</u>
        <u>monument, Arizona.</u> Washington, Govt. Print. Off.,
        1911   (BAEB)   /51.U55.no.50

0380   FISCHER-MØLLER, Knud
        <u>Skeletal remains of the central Eskimos.</u> Copenhagen,
        Gyldendal, 1937   (TUEX)   G670.1921.R25.v.3.no.1

0381   FORD, James Alfred
        <u>Greenhouse: a Troyville-Coles Creek period site in</u>
        <u>Avoyelles Parish, Louisiana.</u> American Museum of Natural
        History, 1951   (AMNHP)   GN2.A27.v.44.pt.1

0382   FORD, James Alfred
        <u>Poverty Point, a late archaic site in Louisiana.</u> American
        Museum of Natural History, 1956 (AMNHP) GN2.A27.v.46.pt.1

0383   FOWKE, Gerard
        <u>Archeological investigations: I. Cave explorations</u>
        <u>in the Ozark region of central Missouri. II. Cave ex-</u>
        <u>plorations in other states. III. Explorations along</u>
        <u>the Missouri river bluffs in Kansas and Nebraska. IV.</u>
        <u>Aboriginal house mounds. V. Archeological work in</u>
        <u>Hawaii</u>. Washington, Govt. Print. Off., 1922
                   (BAEB)   E51.U55.no.76

0384   GAGLIANO, Sherwood M.
        <u>Occupation sequences at Avery Island.</u> Baton Rouge,
        Louisiana State Univ. Pr., 1967   E78.L8G3

0385   GEROW, Bert A.
        <u>An analysis of the University Village complex.</u> Stanford?,
        Calif., 1968   E78.C15G34

0386   GIDDINGS, James Louis
        <u>The archaeology of Cape Denbigh</u>. Providence, Brown Univ.
        Pr., 1964   E78.A3G5

0387   GIFFORD, Edward Winslow
        <u>Archaeology of the southern San Joaquin valley,</u>
        <u>California</u>. Berkeley, Univ. of California Pr., 1926
                 (UCPAE)   E51.C15.v.23.no.1

0388   GIFFORD, Edward Winslow
        <u>Californian bone artifacts.</u> Berkeley and Los Angeles,
        Univ. of California Pr., 1940 (AR)   E51.A58.v.3.no.2

0389   GIFFORD, Edward Winslow
        <u>Composition of California shellmounds.</u> Berkeley, Univ.
        of California Pr., 1916 (UCPAE)   E51.C15.v.12.no.1

0390   GLADWIN, Harold Sterling
        Excavations at Snaketown: material culture. Tucson,
        Reprinted for the Arizona State Museum by the Univ. of
        Arizona Pr., 1965   E78.A7G546

0391   GREENWOOD, Roberta S.
        The Browne site. Salt Lake City, Society for American
        Archaeology, 1969   (SAAM)   E51.S7.no.23

03911   GRUHN, Ruth
        The Archaeology of Wilson Butte Cave South-Central Idaho.
        Pocatello, Idaho, Idaho State Univ., 1961
                  (ISUOP)   E78.I18.I4.no.6

03912   GUERNSEY, Samuel James
        ...Basket-maker caves of northeastern Arizona: report
        on the explorations, 1916-17. Cambridge, Mass., The Museum,
        1921   (PMP)   E51.H337.v.8.no.2

0392   GUERNSEY, Samuel James
        Explorations in northeastern Arizona; report on the
        archaeological fieldwork of 1920-1923. Cambridge, Mass.,
        The Museum, 1931   (PMP)   E51.H337.v.12.no.1

0393   HARRINGTON, Mark Raymond
        An ancient site at Borax Lake, California. Los Angeles,
        Southwest Museum, 1948 (LASM)   F869.L8S65.no.16

0394   HARRINGTON, Mark Raymond
        Gypsum cave, Nevada. Los Angeles, Southwest Museum, 1933
                  (LASM)   F869.L8S65.no.8

0395   HARRINGTON, Mark Raymond
        A Pinto site at Little Lake, California. Los Angeles,
        Southwest Museum, 1957 (LASM)   F869.L8S65.no.17

0396   HARRINGTON, Mark Raymond
        Tule Springs, Nevada. Los Angeles, Southwest Museum, 1961
                  (LASM)   F869.L8S65.no.18

0397   HAURY, Emil Walter
        Recently dated Pueblo ruins in Arizona. City of Washington,
        The Smithsonian Institution, 1931   E78.A7H3

0398   HAURY, Emil Walter
        The stratigraphy and archaeology of Ventana Cove, Arizona.
        Tucson, Univ. of Arizona Pr., 1950   F813.V4H3

0399   HAYES, Alden C.
        The archeological survey of Wetherill Mesa, Mesa Verde
        National Park, Colorado. Washington, National Park Service,
        U.S. Dept. of the Interior; for sale by the Superintendent
        of Documents, U.S. Govt. Print. Off., 1964
                  (NPSAS)   E51.U75.no.7-A

0400   HEIZER, Robert Fleming
        Archaeology and the prehistoric Great Basin lacustrine
        subsistence regime as seen from Lovelock Case, Nevada.
        Berkeley, Univ. of California Archaeological Research
        Facility, 1970   (UCAC)   E51.C2.no.10

0401   HEIZER, Robert Fleming
        The archaeology of central California: a comparative
        analysis of human bone from nine sites. Berkeley, Univ.
        of California Pr., 1949 (AR)   E51.A58.v.12.no.2

0402   HEIZER, Robert Fleming
        The archaeology of Humboldt Cave, Churchill County,
        Nevada. Berkeley, Univ. of California Pr., 1956
                        (UCPAE)   E51.C15.v.47.no.1

0403   HEIZER, Robert Fleming
        Archaeology of the Uyak site, Kodiak Island, Alaska.
        Berkeley, Univ. of California Pr., 1956
                        (AR)   E51.A58.v.17.no.1

0404   HENSHAW, Henry Wetherbee
        Perforated stones from California. Washington, Govt.
        Print. Off., 1887   (BAEB)   E51.U55.no.2

0405   HESTER, James J.
        Studies at Navajo period sites in the Navajo Reservior
        District. Santa Fe, Museum of New Mexico Pr., 1963
                        (MNMP)   E78.N65S3.no.9

0406   HEWETT, Edgar Lee
        Ancient life in the American Southwest. Biblo and
        Tannen, 1968 (1930)   E78.S7H5.1968

0407   HEWETT, Edgar Lee
        Antiquities of the Jemez Plateau, New Mexico.
        Washington, Govt. Print. Off., 1906 (BAEB) E51.U55.no.32

0408   HILL, James N.
        Broken K pueblo. Tucson, Univ. of Arizona Pr., 1970
                        E99.P9H5

0409   HOEBEL, Edward Adamson
        The archaeology of Bone Cave, Miller County, Missouri.
        American Museum of Natural History, 1946
                        (AMNHP)   GN2.A27.v.40.pt.2

0410   HOFFMAN, John Jacob
        The La Roche sites. Lincoln, Neb., 1968 E78.S63H59

0411   HOFFMAN, John Jacob
       Molstad Village. Lincoln, Neb., 1967   E78.S63H6

0412   HOUGH, Walter
       Antiquities of the upper Gila and Salt river valleys
       in Arizona and New Mexico. Washington, Govt. Print.
       Off., 1907   (BAEB)   E51.U55.no.35

0413   HOUGH, Walter
       Archaeological field work in northeastern Arizona. The
       Museum-Gates expedition of 1901. Washington, Govt. Print.
       Off., 1903   E78.A7H8

0414   HOWE, Carrol B.
       Ancient tribes of the Klamath country. Portland, Or.,
       Binfords & Mort, 1968   E78.06H6

0415   HUNT, Alice
       Archeology of the Death Valley salt pan. Johnson Reprint,
       1971 (1960)   (UUAP)   E51.U8.no.47.1971

0416   JEANÇON, Jean Allard
       Excavations in the Chama valley, New Mexico. Washington,
       Govt. Print. Off., 1923 (BAEB)   E51.U55.no.81

0417   JENKS, Albert Ernest
       Minnesota's Browns valley man and associated burial
       artifacts. Menasha, Wis., American Anthropological Assoc.,
       1937   (AAAM)   GN2.A22.no.49

0418   JENNINGS, Jesse David
       Danger Cave. Salt Lake City, Univ. of Utah Pr., 1957
                           (SAAM)   E51.S7.no.14

0419   JOHNSON, Keith L.
       Site LAn-2; a late manifestation of the Topanga complex
       in southern California prehistory. Berkeley, Univ. of
       California Pr., 1966   (AR)   E51.A58.v.23

0420   JOHNSON, LeRoy
       Toward a statistical overview of the archaic cultures of
       central and southwestern Texas. Austin, Texas Memorial
       Museum, 1967   GN37.A8T4.no.12

0421   JOHNSTON, Richard B.
       The Hitchell site. Lincoln, Neb., 1967 E78.S63J63

0422   JONES, Philip Mills
       Archaeological investigations on Santa Rosa Island in
       1901. Berkeley, Univ. of California Pr., 1956
                           (AR)   E51.A58.v.17.no.2

43

0423   JUDD, Neil Merton
        Archeological observations north of the Rio Colorado.
        Washington, Govt. Print. Off., 1926 (BAEB) E51.U55.no.82

0424   JUDD, Neil Merton
        The excavation and repair of Betatakin. Washington, 1930
                                                 F817.N32J8

0425   KIDDER, Alfred Vincent
        Archeological explorations in northeastern Arizona.
        Washington, Govt. Print. Off., 1919 (BAEB) E51.U55.no.65

0426   KIDDER, Alfred Vincent
        The artifacts of Pecos. New Haven, Pub. for Phillips
        Academy by the Yale Univ. Pr.; London, H. Milford, Oxford
        Univ. Pr., 1932   E78.N65K37

0427   KIDDER, Alfred Vincent
        An introduction to the study of Southwestern archaeology,
        with a preliminary account of the excavations at Pecos.
        New Haven, Yale Univ. Pr., 1962   E78.S7K5.1962

0428   KOWTA, Makoto
        The Sayles complex. Berkeley, Univ. of California Pr.,
        1969   E78.C15K67

0429   LAMBERT, Marjorie F.
        Paa-ko, archaeological chronicle of an Indian village
        in north central New Mexico. Santa Fe, School of
        American Research, 1954   E78.N65L35

0430   LANNING, Edward P.
        Archaeology of the Rose Spring site, INY-372. Berkeley,
        Univ. of California Pr., 1963 (UCPAE)   E51.C15.v.49.no.3

0431   LAWRENCE, Barbara
        Mammals found at the Awatovi site. Kraus, 1968 (1951)
                            (PMP)   E51.H337.v.35.no.3.196

0432   LEHMER, Donald Jayne
        Arikara archeology: the Bad River phase. Lincoln,
        Neb., 1968   E78.S63L4

0433   LEHMER, Donald Jayne
        The Fire Heart Creek site. Lincoln, Neb., 1966 E78.N75L4

0434   LEHMER, Donald Jayne
        Introduction to Middle Missouri archaeology. Washington,
        National Park Service, U.S. Govt. Print. Off., 1971
                                                 E78.M82L45

0435   LEIGHTON, Alexander Hamilton
        Gregorio, the hand-trembler. Cambridge, Mass., The Museum,
        1949   (PMP)   E51.H337.v.40.no.1

0436   LIPE, William D.
        1958 excavations, Glen Canyon area. Salt Lake City, Univ.
        of Utah Pr., 1960   (UUAP)   E51.U8.no.44

0437   LISTER, Florence (Cline)
        Earl Morris and southwestern archaeology. Albuquerque,
        Univ. of New Mexico Pr., 1968   E99.P9L5

0438   LISTER, Robert Hill
        The Coombs site. Salt Lake City, Univ. of Utah Pr., 1959-
                        (UUAP)   E51.U8.no.41

0439   LISTER, Robert Hill
        Excavations at Hells Midden, Dinosaur National Monument.
        Boulder, Univ. of Colorado Pr., 1951 (CUSA) GN4.C64.no.3

0440   LOCKETT, H. Claiborne
        Woodchuck Cave. Flagstaff, Northern Arizona Society
        of Science and Art, 1953 (MNAB)   F806.M95.no.26

0441   LOS ANGELES. SOUTHWEST MUSEUM.
        Archeological explorations in southern Nevada. Los Angeles,
        Southwest Museum, 1930 (LASM)   F869.L8S65.no.4

0442   LOUD, Llewellyn Lemont
        Lovelock Cave. Berkeley, Univ. of California Pr., 1929
                        (UCPAE)   E51.C15.v.25.no.1

0443   LOUD, Llewellyn Lemont
        The Stege mounds at Richmond, California. Berkeley,
        Univ. of California Pr., 1924 (UCPAE) E51.C15.v.17.no.6

0444   McGREGOR, John Charles
        The Cohonina culture of northwestern Arizona. Urbana,
        Univ. of Illinois Pr., 1951   E78.A7M15

0445   McGREGOR, John Charles
        Southwestern archaeology. Urbana, Univ. of Illinois Pr.,
        1965   E78.S7M15.1965

04451   MARTIN, Paul Sidney
        The archaeology of Arizona; a study of the southwest
        region. American Museum of Natural History, Natural
        History Press, Doubleday, 1973   E78.A7.M298

04452   MARTIN, Paul Sidney
         Late Mogollon communities; four sites of the Tularqwa
         phase, western New Mexico. Chicago, Field Museum of
         Natural History, 1957 (FMAS)   GN2.F4.v.49.no.1

0446   MATHIASSEN, Therkel
         Archaeological collections from the Western Eskimos.
         Copenhagen, Gyldendal, 1930 (TUEX) G670.1921.R25.v.10.no.1

0447   MATHIASSEN, Therkel
         Archaeology of the Central Eskimos. Copenhagen, Gyldendal,
         1927   (TUEX)   G670.1921.R25.v.4.pt.1,2

0448   MATHIASSEN, Therkel
         Eskimo relics from Washington land and Hall land. København.
         B. Lunos, 1928   G670.1920-23.J8.Nr.3

0449   MATHIASSEN, Therkel
         Material culture of the Igluik Eskimos. Copenhagen,
         Gyldendal, 1928   (TUEX)   G670.1921.R25.v.6.no.1

0450   MERA, Harry Percival
         Reconnaissance and excavation in southeastern New Mexico.
         Menasha, Wis., American Anthropological Assoc., 1938
                                 (AAAM)   GN2.A22.no.51

04501   MILLER, Ronald
         The Archaeological Framework of the Southwest Missouri
         Ozarks. Hollister, Mo., World Archaeological Society,
         1971   E78.M8.M47

0451   MORRIS, Earl Halstead
         An aboriginal salt mine at Camp Verde, Arizona. The
         American Museum of Natural History, 1928
                                 (AMNHP)   GN2.A27.v.30.pt.3

0452   MORSS, Noel
         The ancient culture of the Fremont river in Utah. Cambridge.
         Mass., The Museum, 1931 (PMP)   E51.H337.v.12.no.3

0453   MORSS, Noel
         Archaeological explorations on the middle Chinlee, 1925.
         Menasha, Wis., Pub. for the American Anthropological
         Assoc., 1927   (AAAM)   GN2.A22.v.34

0454   NELSON, Nels Christian
         The Ellis Landing shellmound. Berkeley, The University
         Pr., 1910   (UCPAE)   E51.C15.v.7.no.5

0455   NELSON, Nels Christian
         Shellmounds of the San Francisco Bay region. Berkeley,
         The University Pr., 1909 (UCPAE)   E51.C15.v.7.no.4

04551   NESBITT, Paul Edward
       Stylistic locales and ethnographic groups: petroglyphs
       of the Lower Snake River. Pocatello, Idaho, Idaho State
       Univ., 1968   (ISUOP)   E78.I18.I4.no.23

0456   NEWELL, H. Perry
       The George C. Davis site, Cherokee County, Texas. Menasha,
       Wis., Pub. jointly by the Society for American Archaeology
       and the Univ. of Texas, 1949 (SAAM)   E51.S7.no.5

04561   NEWMAN, Thomas M.
       Cascadia Cave. Pocatello, Idaho, Idaho State Univ., 1966
               (ISUOP)   E78.I18.I4.no.18

0457   NOMLAND, Gladys Ayer
       Bear River ethnography. Berkeley, Univ. of California Pr.,
       1938   (AR)   E51.A58.v.2.no.2

0458   OETTEKING, Bruno
       The skeleton from mesa house. Los Angeles, Southwest
       Museum, 1930   (LASM)   F869.L8S65.no.5

0459   OLSON, Ronald Le Roy
       Chumash prehistory. Berkeley, Univ. of California Pr., 1930
               (UCPAE)   E51.C15.v.28.no.1

0460   ORR, Phil C.
       Prehistory of Santa Rosa Island. Santa Barbara, Calif.,
       Santa Barbara Museum of Natural History, 1968 E78.C1507

04601   OSBORNE, Douglas
       Archaeological Tests in the Lower Grand Coulee, Washington.
       Pocatello, Idaho, Idaho State Univ., 1967
               (ISUOP)   E78.I18.I4.no.20

0461   OSBORNE, Douglas comp.
       Contributions of the Wetherill Mesa archeological project.
       Salt Lake City, Society for American Archaeology, 1965
               (SAAM)   E51.S7.no.19

0462   OSWALT, Wendell H.
       The ethnoarcheology of Crow Village, Alaska. Washington,
       U. S. Govt. Print. Off., 1967 (BAEB) E51.U55.no.199

0463   PECK, Stuart L.
       An archaeological report on the excavation of a prehistoric
       site at Zuma Creek, Los Angeles County, California.
       Archaeological Survey Association of Southern California, 1955
                          E78.C15P35

0464   PECK, Stuart L.
        Some pottery from the Sand Hills, Imperial County, California.
        Los Angeles, Southwest Museum, 1953   E78.C15P36

0465   PETTITT, George Albert
        The Quileute of La Push, 1775-1945. Berkeley, Univ. of
        California Pr., 1950   (AR)   E51.A58.v.14.no.1

0466   PHENICE, Terrell W.
        An analysis of the human skeletal material from burial
        mounds in north central Kansas. Lawrence, Kan., 1969
                                                E78.K16P5

04661   POWERS, William Roger
        Archaeological Excavations in Willow Creek Canyon South-
        eastern Idaho 1966. Pocatello, Idaho, Idaho State Univ.,
        1969   (ISUOP)   E78.I18.I4.no.25

0467   PRUDDEN, Theophil Mitchell
        A further study of prehistoric small house ruins in the
        San Juan watershed. Lancaster, Pa., Pub. for the American
        Anthropological Assoc., 1918 (AAAM)   GN2.A22.no.21

0468   RAINEY, Froelich Gladstone
        Archaeology in central Alaska. American Museum of Natural
        History, 1939   (AMNHP)   GN2.A27.v.36.pt.4

0469   RAINEY, Froelich Gladstone
        Eskimo prehistory: the Okvik site on the Punuk Islands.
        American Museum of Natural History, 1941
                                (AMNHP)   GN2.A27.v.37.pt.4

0470   RAY, Verne Frederick
        Plateau. Berkeley, Univ. of California Pr., 1942
                                (AR)   E51.A58.v.8.no.2

0471   Reconstructing prehistoric Pueblo societies. Albuquerque,
        Univ. of New Mexico Pr., 1970   E99.P9R25

0472   ROBERTS, Frank Harold Hanna
        Archeological remains in the White-water district, eastern
        Arizona. Washington, U.S. Govt. Print. Off., 1939-40
                                (BAEB)   E51.U55.no.121,126

0473   ROBERTS, Frank Harold Hanna
        Early pueblo ruins in the Piedra district, southwestern
        Colorado. Washington, U. S. Govt. Print. Off., 1930
                                (BAEB)   E51.U55.no.96

0474   ROBERTS, Frank Harold Hanna
        The ruins at Kiatuthlanna, eastern Arizona. Washington,
        U. S. Govt. Print. Off., 1931   E78.A7R64

0475   ROBERTS, Frank Harold Hanna
        Shabik'eschee village a late Basket maker site in the
        Chaco Canyon, New Mexico. Washington, U. S. Govt. Print.
        Off., 1929   (BAEB)   E51.U55.no.92

0476   ROGERS, David Banks
        Prehistoric man of the Santa Barbara coast. Santa Barbara,
        Santa Barbara Museum of Natural History, 1929   F868.S23R72

0477   ROHN, Arthur H.
        Mug House, Mesa Verde National Park--Colorado. Washington,
        U. S. National Park Service, 1971 (NPSAS) E51.U75.no.7-D

0478   ROWE, Chandler W.
        The effigy mound culture of Wisconsin. Westport, Conn.,
        Greenwood Pr., 1970   E78.W8R68.1970

0479   SACRAMENTO ANTHROPOLOGICAL SOCIETY.
        Paper. no. 1- Sacramento, 1964-   E51.S2

0480   SCHENCK, William Egbert
        Archaeology of the northern San Joaquin valley. Berkeley,
        Univ. of California Pr., 1929 (UCPAE) E51.C15.v.25.no.4

0481   SCHENCK, William Egbert
        The Emeryville shellmound final report. Berkeley,
        Univ. of California Pr., 1926 (UCPAE)   E51.C15.v.23.no.3

0482   SCHMIDT, Erich Friedrich
        Time-relations of prehistoric pottery types in southern
        Arizona. American Museum of Natural History, 1928
                            (AMNHP)   GN2.A27.v.30.pt.5

0483   SCHROEDER, Albert H.
        The archeological excavations at Willow Beach, Arizona, 1950.
        Salt Lake City, Univ. of Utah Pr., 1961
                            (UUAP)   E51.U8.no.50

0484   SCHROEDER, Albert H.
        Archeology of Zion Park. Salt Lake City, Univ. of Utah Pr.,
        1955   (UUAP)   E51.U8.no.22

04841   SCHWARZE, David Martin
        Geology of the lava hot springs area, Idaho. Pocatello,
        Idaho, Idaho State Univ., 1960 (ISUOP) E78.I18.I4.no.4

0485   SEAMAN, Norma Gilm
        Indian relics of the Pacific Northwest. Portland, Or.,
        Binfords and Mort, 1967   E78.N77S4.1967

0486   SINCLAIR, William John
        The exploration of the Potter creek cave. Berkeley, The
        Univ. Pr., 1904   (UCPAE)   E51.C15.v.2.no.1

0487   SINCLAIR, William John
        Recent investigations bearing on the question of the
        occurrence of neocene man in the auriferous gravels of the
        Sierra Nevada. Berkeley, The University Pr., 1908
                         (UCPAE)   E51.C15.v.7.no.2

0488   SMITH, Carlyle Shreeve
        The Two Teeth Site. Lincoln, Neb., River Basin Surveys,
        Museum of Natural History, Smithsonian Institution, 1968
                               E78.S63S57

0489   SMITH, Harlan Ingersoll
        The archaeology of the Yakima valley. American Museum of
        Natural History, 1910 (AMNHP)   GN2.A27.v.6.pt.1

0490   SMITH, Marian Wesley
        Archaeology of the Columbia-Fraser region. Cattle Point,
        a stratified site in the southern northwest coast region
        by Arden R. King. Menasha, Wis., Society for American
        Archaeology, 1950   (SAAM)   E51.S7.no.6-7

0491   SMITH, Watson
        Painted ceramics of the western mound at Awatovi. Cambridge,
        Mass., The Museum, 1971 (PMP)   E51.H337.v.38

0492   SOUTHWESTERN ANTHROPOLOGICAL RESEARCH GROUP.
        The distribution of prehistoric population aggregates.
        Prescott, Ariz., Prescott College Pr., 1971 E78.S7S58

0493   SPAULDING, Albert Clanton
        Archaeological investigations on Agattu, Aleutian Islands.
        Ann Arbor, Univ. of Michigan, 1962 (UMAP) GN2.M5.no.18

0494   SPIER, Leslie
        An outline for a chronology of Zuñi ruins. American
        Museum of Natural History, 1917 (AMNHP) GN2.A27.v.18.pt.3

0495   STEEN, Charlie R.
        Excavations at Tse-Ta'a, Canyon de Chelly National
        Monument, Arizona. Washington, Supt. of Docs., U.S.
        Govt. Print. Off., 1966 (NPSAS)   E51.U75.no.9

0496   STEWARD, Julian Haynes
        Ancient caves of the Great Salt lake region. Washington,
        U.S. Govt. Print. Off., 1937 (BAEB)   E51.U55.no.116

0497   STRONG, Emory M.
        Stone age in the Great Basin. Portland, Or., Binfords
        and Mort, 1969   E78.G67S7

0498   STRONG, William Duncan
             Archaeology of the Dalles-Deschutes region. Berkeley,
             Univ. of California Pr., 1930   (UCPAE) E51.C15.v.29.no.1

0499   SWANNACK, Jervis D.
             Big Juniper House, Mesa Verde National Park--Colorado.
             Washington, U. S. National Park Service, 1969 [i.e. 1970]
                                 (NPSAS)   E51.U75.no.7-C

04991   SWANSON, Earl Herbert
             Birch Creek Papers No. 1, an Archaeological Reconnaissance
             in the Birch Creek Valley of Eastern Idaho. Idaho, Idaho State
             Univ., 1964   (ISUOP)   E78.I18.I4.no.13,14,17,27

04992   SWANSON, Earl Herbert   Jr.
             Reconnaissance and the Archaeological Survey System of the
             University Museum. Pocatello, Idaho, Idaho State Univ. 1963
                                 (ISUOP)   E78.I18.I4.no.12

04993   SWANSON, Earl Herbert   Jr.
             Utazytekan Prehistory. Pocatello, Idaho, Idaho State Univ.,
             1968   (ISUOP)   E78.I18.I4.no.22

0500   SYMPOSIUM ON PLEISTOCENE AND RECENT ENVIRONMENTS OF THE CENTRAL
             PLAINS, UNIVERSITY OF KANSAS, 1968.
             Pleistocene and Recent environments of the Central Great
             Plains. Lawrence, Univ. Pr. of Kansas, 1970 QE741.S95.1968

0501   TREGANZA, Adan Eduardo
             An archaeological survey of the Yuki area. Berkeley, Univ.
             of California Pr., 1950   (AR)   E51.A58.v.12,no.3

0502   TREGANZA, Adan Eduardo
             The Topanga culture; final report on excavations, 1948.
             Berkeley, Univ. of California Pr., 1958
                                 (AR)   E51.A58.v.20.no.2

0503   TREGANZA, Adan Eduardo
             The Topanga culture; first season's excavation of the Tank
             Site, 1947. Berkeley, Univ. of California Pr., 1950
                                 (AR)   E51.A58.v.12.no.4

0504   UHLE, Max
             The Emeryville shellmound. Berkeley, The University Pr.,
             1907   (UCPAE)   E51.C15.v.7.no.1

0505   U. S. COMMITTEE ON ENVIRONMENTAL STUDIES FOR PROJECT CHARIOT.
             Environment of the Cape Thompson region, Alaska. Oak Ridge,
             Tenn., United States Atomic Energy Commission, Div. of
             Technical Information, 1966   QH105.A4A57

0506   U. S. NATIONAL PARK SERVICE.
        Material culture of the Pima, Papago, and western Apache.
        Berkeley, Calif., National Park Service, 1934   E99.P6U5

0507   VIVIAN, R. Gordon
        Gran Quivira. Washington, National Park Service, U. S.
        Dept. of the Interior, 1964 (NPSAS)   E51.U75.no.8

0508   VIVIAN, R. Gordon
        The Hubbard Site and other tri-wall structures in New
        Mexico and Colorado. Washington, National Park Service,
        U. S. Dept. of the Interior, 1959 (NPSAS) E51.U75.no.5

0509   VIVIAN, R. Gordon
        The Three-C site. Albuquerque, Univ. of New Mexico Pr.,
        1965   (NMPA)   GN2.N4.no.13

0510   WALKER, Winslow Metcalf
        The Troyville mounds, Catahoula parish, La. Washington,
        U. S. Govt. Print. Off., 1936 (BAEB) E51.U55.no.113

05101   WARREN, Claude N.
        The view from Wenas: a study in plateau prehistory.
        Pocatello, Idaho, Idaho State Univ., 1968
                          (ISUOP)   E78.I18.I4.no.24

05102   WASLEY, William Warwick
        The Archaeological Survey of the Arizona State Museum.
        Tucson, Arizona State Museum, Univ. of Arizona, 1964
                                         E77.9.W36.1964

0511   WASLEY, William Warwick
        Salvage archaeology in Painted Rocks Reservoir, western
        Arizona. Tucson, Univ. of Arizona Pr., 1965 E78.A7W3

0512   WEBB, Clarence H.
        The Belcher Mound. Salt Lake City, Society for American
        Archaeology, 1959   (SAAM)   E51.S7.no.16

0513   WEDEL, Waldo Rudolph
        Archaeological investigations at Buena Vista lake, Kern
        county, California. Washington, U. S. Govt. Print Off.,
        1941   (BAEB)   E51.U55.no.130

0514   WEDEL, Waldo Rudolph
        An introduction to Kansas archeology. Washington, U. S.
        Govt. Print. Off., 1959 (BAEB)   E51.U55.no.174

0515   WEDEL, Waldo Rudolph
        Prehistoric man on the Great Plains. Norman, Univ. of
        Oklahoma Pr., 1961   E78.W5W4

0516   WEDEL, Waldo Rudolph
        Prehistory and the Missouri Valley development program.
        Washington, Smithsonian Institution, 1948   E78.M82W42

0517   WENDORF, Fred
        Pipeline archaeology. Santa Fe, Pub. jointly by the
        Laboratory of Anthropology and the Museum of Northern
        Arizona, Flagstaff, 1956   E78.S7W45

0518   WEYER, Edward Moffat
        An Aleutian burial. American Museum of Natural History,
        1929   (AMNHP)   GN2.A27.v.31.pt.3

0519   WEYER, Edward Moffat
        Archaeological material from the village site at Hot Springs,
        Port Möller, Alaska. American Museum of Natural History, 1930
                            (AMNHP)   GN2.A27.v.31.pt.4

0520   WILFORD, Lloyd Alden
        Burial mounds of central Minnesota. St. Paul, Minnesota
        Historical Society, 1969   E78.M7W54

0521   WILL, George Francis
        Archaeology of the Missouri valley. American Museum of
        Natural History, 1924 (AMNHP)   GN2.A27.v.22.pt.6

0522   WILSON, Gilbert Livingstone
        The Hidatsa earthlodge. American Museum of Natural History,
        1934   (AMNHP)   GN2.A27.v.33.pt.5

05221   WOOD, W. Raymond
        Biesterfeldt: a post-contact coalescent site on the north-
        eastern plains. Washington, Smithsonian Institution Pr., 1971
                            (SCA)   fGN1.S54.no.15

0523   WOODBURY, Angus Munn
        Notes on the human ecology of Glen Canyon. Salt Lake City,
        Univ. of Utah Pr., 1965   (UUAP)   E51.U8.no.74

0524   WOODBURY, Richard Benjamin
        Prehistoric agriculture at Point of Pines, Arizona.
        Salt Lake City, Univ. of Utah Pr., 1961 (SAAM) E51.S7.no.17

0525   WORMINGTON, Hannah Marie
        Prehistoric Indians of the southwest. Denver, Colorado
        Museum of Natural History, 1947   E78.S8W67

0526   ANGULO V., Jorge
    Un tlamanalli encontrado en Tlatelolco. México, Instituto
    Nacional de Antropología e Historia, 1966   F1219.1.M5A7

05261   BECQUELIN, Pierre
    Archeologia de la region de Nebaj (Guatemala). France,
    Paris, Institute d'ethnologie, 1969   F1465.1.N4.B4

0527   BENNETT, Wendell Clark
    Excavations at Tiahuanaco. American Museum of Natural
    History, 1934   (AMNHP)   GN2.A27.v.34.pt.3

0528   BOWDITCH, Charles Pickering ed.
    Mexican and Central American antiquities, calendar systems,
    and history. Washington, Govt. Print. Off., 1904
                      F1219.B78

0529   BRAINERD, George Walton
    The archaeological ceramics of Yucatan. Berkeley, Univ.
    of California Pr., 1958 (AR)   E51.A58.v.19

0530   BRUNHOUSE, Robert Levere
    Sylvanus G. Morley and the world of the ancient Mayas.
    Norman, Univ. of Oklahoma Pr., 1971   F1435.M76B7

0531   CASO, Alfonso
    Los calendarios prehispánicos. México, 1967 F1219.3.C2C35

0532   CASO, Alfonso
    El tesoro de Monte Alban. México, Instituto Nacional de
    Antropología e Historia, 1969   fF1219.1.011C34

0533   The Chronicles of Michoacán. Norman, Univ. of Oklahoma Pr.,
    1970   F1219.1.M55R43

0534   COE, Michael D.
    An early stone pectoral from southeastern Mexico.
    Washington, Dumbarton Oaks Trustees for Harvard University,
    1966   (SCAA)   E51.S85.no.1

0535   COOK, Sherburne Friend
    Erosion morphology and occupation history in western Mexico.
    Berkeley, Univ. of California Pr., 1963
                 (AR)   E51.A58.v.17.no.3

0536   DAHLGREN DE JORDÁN, Barbro
        La mixteca, su cultura e historia prehispánicas. Mexico,
        Universidad Nacional Autónoma de México, 1966 F1221.M7D3.1966

0537   DRUCKER, Philip
        Ceramic sequences at Tres Zapotes, Veracruz, Mexico.
        Washington, U. S. Govt. Print. Off., 1943
                              (BAEB)   E51.U55.no.140

0538   DRUCKER, Philip
        Ceramic stratigraphy at Cerro de las Mesas, Veracruz,
        Mexico. Washington, U. S. Govt. Print. Off., 1943
                              (BAEB)   E51.U55.no.141

0539   DRUCKER, Philip
        Excavations at La Venta, Tabasco, 1955. Washington,
        U. S. Govt. Print. Off., 1959 (BAEB) E51.U55.no.170

0540   DUMBARTON OAKS CONFERENCE ON THE OLMEC, 1967.
        Dumbarton Oaks Conference on the Olmec. Washington,
        Dumbarton Oaks Research Library and Collection, Trustees
        for Harvard Univ., 1968   F1219.D9.1967

0541   EKHOLM, Gordon Frederick
        Excavations at Guasave, Sinaloa, Mexico. American Museum
        of Natural History, 1942 (AMNHP)   GN2.A27.v.38.pt.2

0542   EKHOLM, Gordon Frederick
        Excavations at Tampico and Panuco in the Huasteca, Mexico.
        American Museum of Natural History, 1944
                              (AMNHP)   GN2.A27.v.38.pt.5

05421   EKHOLM, Susanna M.
        Mound 30a and the Early Preclassic Ceramic Sequence of
        Izapa, Chiapas, Mexico. New World Archaeological Foundation,
        1969   (NWAF)   E51.N38.no.25

0543   FIELD, Frederick Vanderbilt
        Thoughts on the meaning and use of pre-Hispanic Mexican
        sellos. Washington, Dumbarton Oaks, Trustees for Harvard
        University, 1967   (SCAA)   E51.S85.no.3

0544   FRANCO C., José Luis
        Objetos de hueso de la época precolombina. México, Museo
        Nacional de Antropología Instituto Nacional de Antropología
        e Historia, 1968   F1219.3.B6F7

0545   GARCÍA COOK, Angel
        Chimalhuacán: un artefacto asociado a megafauna. México,
        Instituto Nacional de Antropología e Historia, 1968 F1219.G2

0546   GIFFORD, Edward Winslow
        Surface archaeology of Ixtlan del Rio, Nayarit. Berkeley,
        Univ. of California Pr., 1950   (UCPAE)   E51.C15.v.43.no.2

0547   GRAHAM, Ian
        Archaeological explorations in El Paten, Guatemala.   New
        Orleans, Dept. of Middle American Research, Tulane Univ.,
        1967   (TMAI)   F1421.T95.no.33

0548   HELFRITZ, Hans
        Mexican cities of the gods.   Praeger, 1970   F1219.3.A7H413

0549   HEYERDAHL, Thor
        Archaeological evidence of pre-Spanish visits to the
        Galápagos Islands.   Salt Lake City, Society for American
        Archaeology, 1956   (SAAM)   E51.S7.no.12

0550   HUMBOLDT, Alexander, freiherr von,
        Sites des Cordillères et monuments des peuples indigènes
        de l'Amerique.   Paris, Legrand, Pomey et Crouzet, 1868?
                                              F1219.H92.1868

05501   JOYCE, Thomas Athol
        Central American and West Indian archaeology; being an
        introduction to the archaeology of the states of Nicaragua,
        Costa Rica, Panama, and the West Indies.   Blom, 1971
                                              F1434.J89.1971b

0551   JOYCE, Thomas Athol
        Mexican archaeology.   London, P. L. Warner, 1920
                                              F1219.J89.1920

0552   KELLY, Isabel Truesdell
        The archaeology of the Autlán-Tuxcacuesco area of Jalisco.
        Berkeley, Univ. of California Pr., 1945-49
                          (IAM)   F1401.I22.no.26-27

0553   KELLY, Isabel Truesdell
        Excavations at Apatzingan, Michoacan.   Johnson Reprint,
        1963 (1947)   F1219.1.M55K.1963

0554   KROEBER, Alfred Louis
        Archaic culture horizons in the valley of Mexico.
        Berkeley, Univ. of California Pr., 1925
                          (UCPAE)   E51.C15.v.17.no.7

0555   LADD, John
        Archeological investigations in the Parita and Santa Maria
        zones of Panama.   Washington, U. S. Govt. Print. Off.,
        1964   F1565.L3

05551   LEE, Thomas A. Jr.
        The Artifacts of Chiapa de Corzo, Chiapas, Mexico. New
        World Archaeological Foundation, 1969 (NWAF) E5.N38.no.26

05552   LINNE, Sigvald
        ...Mexican highland cultures; archaeological researches
        at Teotihuacan, Calpulalpan and Chalchicomula in 1934/35.
        Stockholm, 1942   fF1219.L6

0556   LISTER, Robert Hill
        Archaeological excavations in the northern Sierra Madre
        Occidental, Chihuahua, and Sonora, Mexico. Boulder, Univ.
        of Colorado Pr., 1958 (CUSA)   GN4.C64.no.7

0557   LISTER, Robert Hill
        The present status of the archaeology of western Mexico:
        a distributional study. Boulder, Univ. of Colorado Pr.,
        1955   (CUSA)   GN4.C64.no.5

0558   LORENZO, José Luis
        La etapa lítica en México. México, Instituto Nacional de
        Antropología e Historia, 1967   F1219.L866

0559   LORENZO, José Luis
        Las zonas arqueológicas de los volcanes Iztaccíhuatl y
        Popocatépetl. México, Instituto Nacional de Antropología
        e Historia, 1957   F1219.L67

0560   LOTHROP, Samuel Kirkland
        Metals from the Cenote of Sacrifice, Chichen Itza, Yucatan.
        Cambridge, Mass., The Museum, 1952 (PMP) fE51.H336.v.10.no.2

0561   McCOWN, Theodore Doney
        Pre-Incaic Huamachuco: survey and excavations in the region
        of Huamachuco and Cajabamba. Berkeley and Los Angeles, Univ.
        of California Pr., 1945 (UCPAE)   E51.C15.v.39.no.4

0562   MacNEISH, Richard S.
        An early archaeological site near Panúco, Vera Cruz.
        Philadelphia, American Philosophical Society, 1954
                  (APST)   fQ11.P6.n.s.v.44.pt.5

0563   MacNEISH, Richard S.
        Preliminary archaeological investigations in the Sierra
        de Tamaulipas, Mexico. Philadelphia, American Philosophical
        Society, 1958   (APST)   fQ11.P6.n.s.v.48.pt.6

0564   MALER, Teobert
        Explorations in the department of Peten, Guatemala and
        adjacent region: Motul de San José; Peten-Itza. Cambridge,
        Mass., The Museum, 1910 (PMM)   FE51.H336.v.4.no.3

0565   MALER, Teobert
       Explorations in the department of Peten, Guatemala and
       adjacent region: Topoxté; Yaxhá; Benque Viejo; Naranjo.
       Cambridge, Mass., The Museum, 1908   (PMM)   fE51.H336.v.4

0566   MALER, Teobert
       Explorations in the department of Peten, Guatemala,
       Tikal. Cambridge, Mass., The Museum, 1911
                              (PMM)   fE51.H336.v.5.no.1

0567   MALER, Teobert
       Explorations of the upper Usumatsintla and adjacent region;
       Altar de sacrificos; Seibal; Itsimte-Sacluk; Cankuen.
       Cambridge, Mass., The Museum, 1908   (PMM)   fE51.H336.n.4.no.1

0568   MASSEY, William C.
       A burial case in Baja California, the Palmer collection,
       1887. Berkeley, Univ. of California Pr., 1961
                              (AR)   E51.A58.v.16.no.8

0569   MERWIN, Raymond Edwin
       The ruins of Holmul, Guatemala. Cambridge, Mass., The
       Museum, 1932   (PMM)   fE51.H336.v.3.no.2

0570   MESSMACHER, Miguel
       Colima. México, Instituto Nacional de Antropología
       e Historia de la Secretaría de Educación Pública, 1966
                              F1219.1.C75M4

0571   MEXICO. DEPARTAMENTO DE MONUMENTOS PREHISPÁNICOS.
       Atlas arqueológico de la República Mexicana. México,
       Instituto Nacional de Antropología e Historia, 1959-
                              ref.F1219.M622

0572   MEXICO. INSTITUTO NACIONAL DE ANTROPOLOGÍA E HISTORIA.
       Copilco-Cuicuilco; guía oficial. México, 1966 F1219.M625.196

0573   MEXICO. INSTITUTO NACIONAL DE ANTROPOLOGÍA E HISTORIA.
       Guía oficial de El Tajín. México, 1966 F1219.1.T2M4

0574   MEXICO. INSTITUTO NACIONAL DE ANTROPOLOGÍA E HISTORIA.
       Guía oficial de Tula. México, 1966   F1219.1T8M4.1966

0575   MEXICO. INSTITUTO NACIONAL DE ANTROPOLOGÍA E HISTORIA.
       Monte Albán [y] Mitla, guía oficial. México, D. F., 1957
                              F1219.1.M65M49

0576   MEXICO. INSTITUTO NACIONAL DE ANTROPOLOGÍA E HISTORIA.
       Palenque: official guide. Mexico, 1955 F1219.1.P3M4

0577   MEXICO. INSTITUTO NACIONAL DE ANTROPOLOGÍA E HISTORIA.
        Tula; official guide. Mexico, 1957   F1219.1.T8M7

0578   MILLON, René Francis
        The Pyramid of the Sun at Teotihuacán, 1959 investigations.
        Philadelphia, American Philosophical Society, 1965
                            (APST)   fQ11.P6.n.s.v.55.pt.6

0579   MIRAMBELL SILVA, Lorena E.
        Técnicas lapidarias prehispánicas. México, Instituto
        National de Antropologia e Historia, 1968
                            (INAH)   F1219.M627.no.14

0580   MORRIS, Earl Halstead
        Notes on excavations in the Aztec ruin. American Museum
        of Natural History, 1928 (AMNHP)   GN2.A27.v.26.pt.5

0581   NOGUERA, Eduardo
        La cerámica arqueológica de Mesoamérica. México, Universidad
        Nacional Autónoma de México, 1965   F1219.3.P8N62

0582   Oaxaca archives. Stanford, Stanford Univ. Pr., 1968 F1219.1.O1103

0583   PADDOCK, John ed.
        Ancient Oaxaca. Stanford, Stanford Univ. Pr., 1966
                                             F1219.1.O11P25

0584   Papers on Mesoamerican archaeology. Berkeley, Univ. of California
        Pr., 1968   (UCAC)   E51.C2.no.5

0585   PARSONS, Elsie Worthington (Clews)
        Mitla, town of the souls. Chicago, The Univ. of Chicago Pr.,
        1936   F1391.M6P3

0586   PIÑA CHÁN, Roman
        Archeological research in the lower Grijalva River region,
        Tabasco and Chiapa. Provo, Utah, Brigham Young Univ.,
        1967   E51.N38.no.22

0587   PIÑA CHAN, Román
        Una visión del México prehispánico. México, Instituto de
        Investigaciones Históricas, Universidad Nacional Autónoma
        de México, 1967   F1219.P665

0588   POPL VUH
        Popol vuh. Norman, Univ. of Oklahoma Pr., 1950 F1465.P8385.1950

0589   PORTER, Muriel Noé
        Excavations at Chupícurao, Guanajuato, Mexico. Philadelphia,
        American Philosophical Society, 1956   F1219.1.C54P6

0590   RITTLINGER, Herbert
        Jungle quest. London, Odhams Pr., 1961 F1221.L2R53

0591   RIVET, Paul
        Mayas cities. London, Elek Books; Putnam, 1960
                                  F1435.R573

0592   ROYS, Lawrence
        Preliminary report on the ruins of Aké, Yucatan.
        Salt Lake City, Society for American Archaeology, 1966
                   (SAAM)   E51.S7.no.20

0593   ROYS, Ralph Loveland
        The ethno-botany of the Maya. New Orleans, Dept. of
        Middle American Research, Tulane Univ., 1931
                   (TMAI)   F1421.T95.no.2

0594   RUPPERT, Karl
        Chichen Itza. Washington, Carnegie Institution of Wash-
        ington, 1952   F1219.1.C455R8

0595   SÁENZ, César A.
        Nuevas exploraciones y hallazgos en Xochicalco, 1965-1966.
        México, Instituto Nacional de Antropología e Historia, 1967
                                  F1219.1.M64S29

0596   SANSORES, Manuel Cirerol
        "_Chi Cheen Itsa_." Yucatan, Mex., 1956 F1376.S35

0597   SÉJOURNÉ, Laurette
        Arqueología del Valle de México. México, Instituto
        Nacional de Antropología e Historia, 1970- F1219.1.M53S4

0598   SÉJOURNÉ, Laurette
        Un palacio en la Ciudad de los Dioses, Teotihuacán.
        México, Instituto Nacional de Antropología e Historia,
        1959   fF1219.1.T27S418

0599   SMITH, Robert Eliot
        Ceramic sequence at Uaxactun, Guatemala. New Orleans,
        Middle American Research Institute, Tulane Univ., 1955
                   (TMAI)   F1421.T95.no.20

0600   SMITHSONIAN INSTITUTION-HARVARD UNIVERSITY ARCHEOLOGICAL
        EXPEDITION TO NORTHWESTERN HONDURAS, 1936.
        Preliminary report on the Smithsonian Institution-Harvard
        University archeological expedition to northwestern Honduras,
        _1936_. City of Washington, The Smithsonian Institution, 1938
                                F1505.S65
0601   _Sources of stones used in prehistoric Mesoamerican sites_.
        Berkeley, Univ. of California, Dept. of Anthropology, 1965
                   (UCAC)   E51.C2.no.1

0602   STARR, Frederick
       The little pottery objects of Lake Chapala, Mexico.
       Chicago, Univ. of Chicago Pr., 1897   F1219.S78

0603   STARR, Frederick
       The Mapa de Cuauhtlantzinco or Códice Campos. Chicago,
       Univ. of Chicago Pr., 1898   F1219.S8

0604   STARR, Frederick
       Notes on Mexican archaeology. Chicago, Univ. of Chicago
       Pr., 1894   F1219.S82

0605   STIRLING, Matthew Williams
       Stone monuments of southern Mexico. Washington, U. S.
       Govt. Print. Off., 1943 (BAEB)   E51.U55.no.138

0606   SUTTON, Ann
       Among the Maya ruins. Chicago, Rand McNally, 1968 (1967)
                                               F1435.S86S9

0607   TEHUACAN ARCHAEOLOGICAL-BOTANICAL PROJECT.
       Report. 1st-3d. 1961-64. Andover, Mass., Robert S.
       Peabody Foundation for Archaeology.   F1219.T38

0608   TERRA, Hellmut de
       Tepexpan man. Johnson Reprint, 196- (1949) F1219.T37.1960z

0609   THOMPSON, Edward Herbert
       Archaeological researches in Yucatan. Cambridge, Mass.,
       The Museum, 1904   (PMM)   fE51.H336.v.3.no.1

0610   TOLSTOY, Paul
       Surface survey of the northern Valley of Mexico: the classic
       and post-classic periods. Philadelphia, American Philo-
       sophical Society, 1958 (APST)   fQ11.P6.n.s.v.48.pt.5

0611   TOZZER, Alfred Marston
       Excavation of a site at Santiago Ahuitzotla, D. F. Mexico.
       Washington, U. S. Govt. Print. Off., 1921
                               (BAEB)   E51.U55.no.74

0612   TOZZER, Alfred Marston
       A preliminary study of the prehistoric ruins of Nakum,
       Guatemala. Cambridge, Mass., The Museum, 1913
                               (PMM)   fE51.H336.v.5.no.3

0613   TOZZER, Alfred Marston
       A preliminary study of the prehistoric ruins of Tikal,
       Guatemala. Cambridge, Mass., The Museum, 1911
                               (PMM)   fE51.H336.v.5.no.2

                               61

0614   Tulane university expedition to middle America. 1st, 1925.
        New Orleans, Tulane Univ. of Louisiana, 1926-27
                            (TMAI)   F1421.T95.no.1

0615   VAILLANT, George Clapp
        Excavations at Ticoman. American Museum of Natural
        History, 1931   (AMNHP)   GN2.A27.v.32.pt.2

0616   VAILLANT, George Clapp
        Excavations at Zacatenco. American Museum of Natural
        History 1930.   (AMNHP)   GN2.A27.v.32.pt.1

0617   VAILLANT, Suzannah (Beck)
        Excavations at Gualupita. American Museum of Natural
        History, 1934   (AMNHP)   GN2.A27.v.35.pt.1

0618   VAN DE VELDE, Paul
        The black pottery of Coyotepec, Oaxaca, Mexico. Los
        Angeles, Southwest Museum, 1939 (LASM) F869.L8S65.no.13

0619   VON HAGEN, Victor Wolfgang
        Maya explorer, John Lloyd Stephens and the lost cities of
        central America and Yucatán. Norman, Univ. of Oklahoma
        Pr., 1948   F1435.S84V65

0620   WALLRATH, Matthew
        Excavations in the Tehuantecpec region, Mexico. Philadelphia,
        American Philosophical Society, 1967 (APST) fQ11.P6.n.s.v.57.pt

0621   WATERMAN, Thomas Talbot
        The delineation of the day-signs in the Aztec manuscripts.
        Berkeley, Univ. of California Pr., 1961
                            (UCPAE)   E51.C15.v.11.no.6

0622   WAUCHOPE, Robert
        Excavations at Zacualpa, Guatemala. New Orleans, 1948
                            (TMAI)   F1421.T95.no.14

0623   WEIANT, Clarence Wolsey
        An introduction to the ceramics of Tres Zapotes, Veracruz,
        Mexico. Washington, D. C., 1943 (BAEB) E51.U55.no.139

0624   WILLIAMS GARCÍA, Jorge
        Protección juridica de los bienes arqueológicos e historicos.
        Xalapa, Ver., Universidad Veracruzana, 1967
                            (UVIA)   F1219.1.V47J3.no.3

0625   WORMINGTON, Hannah Marie
        Origins, indigenous period. Mexico, Pan American Institute
        of Geography and History, 1953 (PAIP) F1401.P153.no.153

0626   YOUNG, Philip D.
        <u>Ngawbe; tradition and change among the Western Guaymí</u>
        <u>of Panama</u>.   Urbana, Univ. Of Illinois Pr., 1971
                                        F1565.2.G8Y6

0627   ADAIR, John
      The Navajo and Pueblo silversmiths. Norman, Univ. of
      Oklahoma Pr., 1944   E98.A7A17

0628   ADAMS, Richard E. W.
      The ceramics of Alter de Sacrificios. Cambridge, Mass.,
      The Museum, 1971   (PMP)   E51.H337.v.63.no.1

0629   ALBERS, Anni
      Pre-Columbian Mexican miniatures. Praeger, 1970
                                  fF1219.3.A7A38.1970

0630   ALCINA FRANCH, José
      Las "pintaderas" mejicanas y sus relaciones. Madrid,
      Consejo Superior de Investigaciones Científicas, Instituto
      "Gonzalo Fernández de Oviedo," 1958   F1219.3.A7A4

0631   ALSBERG, John L.
      Ancient sculpture from western Mexico. Berkeley, Nicole
      Gallery, 1968   fF1219.3.A7A45

06311   American Indian art; form and tradition. Dutton, 1972   E98.A7.A44

0632   AMON CARTER MUSEUM OF WESTERN ART, FORT WORTH, TEX.
      Quiet Triumph. Fort Worth, Amon Carter Museum of Western
      Art with the cooperation of the School of American Research,
      Santa Fe, 1966   E78.S7A48

0633   ANTON, Ferdinand
      Ancient Mexican art. Putnam, 1969   fF1219.3.A7A513.1969

0634   ANTON, Ferdinand
      Pre-Columbian art and later Indian tribal arts. H. N. Abrams,
      1968   E59.A7A5

06341   APPLETON, LeRoy H.
      American Indian design and decoration. Dover, 1971
                              E59.A7.A6.1971

0635   APPLETON, Le Roy H.
      Indian art of the Americas. Scribner, 1950   fE59.A7A66

0636   BARBEAU, Charles Marius
      Totem poles. Ottawa, R. Duhamel, Queen's Printer, 1964
                              E98.T65B37.1964

0637   BARCLAY, Isabel
      Art of the Canadian Indians and Eskimos. Ottawa, National
      Ballery of Canada, in collaboration with the National Museum
      of Man, 1969   E98.A7B3

0638   BERNAL, Ignacio
        Ancient Mexico in colour. McGraw-Hill, 1968
                                 fF1219.3.A7B38.1968b

0639   BERNAL, Ignacio
        Cien obras maestras del Museo Nacional de Antropología.
        México, J. Bolea; Distribución: Avandaro, 1969
                               fF 1219.3.A7B39

0640 BLISS, Robert Woods
        Pre-Columbian art. Phaidon Publishers, distributed by
        Garden City Books, 1957   fE59.A7B55

0641   BOOS, Frank H.
        The ceramic sculptures of ancient Oaxaca. South Brunswick,
        N.J., A. S. Barnes, 1966   fF1219.1.O11B65.1966

0642   BRENNER, Anita
        Idols behind altars. Biblo and Tannen, 1967 (1929)
                         N6550.B7.1967

0643   BRENNER, Anita
        The influence of technique on the decorative style in
        the domestic pottery of Culhuacan. AMS Pr., 1969 (1931)
                  (CUCA)   E51.C7.v.13

0644   BRODY, J. J.
        Indian painters and white patrons. Albuquerque, Univ.
        of New Mexico Pr., 1971   E98.A7B7.1971

0645   BROOKLYN INSTITUTE OF ARTS AND SCIENCES. MUSEUM.
        Art of the eastern Plains Indians. Brooklyn, N.Y.,
        Brooklyn Museum, 1964   E78.G73B69

0646   BUSHNELL, David Ives
        Drawings by George Gibbs in the far Northwest, 1849-1851.
        City of Washington, The Smithsonian Institution, 1938
                        E78.N77B8

0647   BUSHNELL, Geoffrey Hext Sutherland
        Ancient American pottery. London, Faber and Faber, 1955
                        E59.P8B8.1955

0648   BUSHNELL, Geoffrey Hext Sutherland
        Ancient arts of the Americas. F. A. Praeger, 1965
                        E59.A7B97

0649   CAIN, Harvey Thomas
        Petroglyphs of central Washington. Seattle, Univ. of
        Washington Pr., 1950   E98.P6C3

0650   CHICAGO. ART INSTITUTE.
        Animal sculpture in pre-Columbian art. Chicago, 1957 E59.A7C4

0651   COE, Michael D.
        The jaguar's children: pre-classic central Mexico.
        Museum of Primitive Art; distributed by the New York
        Graphic Society, Greenwich, Conn., 1965 F1219.3.A7C56

0652   CONNER, Stuart W.
        Rock art of the Montana High Plains. Santa Barbara?, 1971
                                        E78.M9C6

0653   COVARRUBIAS, Miguel
        The eagle, the jaguar, and the serpent. Knopf, 1954 E98.A7C68

0654   COVARRUBIAS, Miguel
        Indian art of Mexico and Central America. Knopf, 1966
                                        F1219.3.A7C58

06541   DARBOIS, Dominique
        Indian and Eskimo art of Canada. Ryerson, 1971 E78.C2.D1313

0655   DEWDNEY, Selwyn H.
        Indian rock paintings of the Great Lakes. Toronto,
        Pub. for the Quetico Foundation by Univ. of Toronto Pr.,
        1962   E98.P6D4

0656   DISSELHOFF, Hans Dietrich
        The art of ancient America. Crown Publishers, 1964 (1960)
                                        E59.A7D513

0657   DOCKSTADER, Frederick J.
        Indian art in America. Greenwich, Conn., New York Graphic
        Society, 1962   E98.A7D57.1962

0658   DOCKSTADER, Frederick J.
        Indian art in Middle America. Greenwich, Conn., New York
        Graphic Society, 1964   F1219.3.A7D6

0659   DOUGLAS, Frederic Huntington
        Indian art of the United States. Pub. for the Museum of
        Modern Art by Arno Pr., 1969 (1941)   E98.A7D6.1969

0660   DUFF, Wilson
        Arts of the raven: masterworks by the northwest coast
        Indian. Vancouver, 1967   E78.N78D8

0661   DUNN, Dorothy
        American Indian painting of the Southwest and Plains areas.
        Albuquerque, Univ. of New Mexico, 1968 E98.A7D8

                            67

0662   EARL H. MORRIS MEMORIAL POTTERY COLLECTION.
             The Earl H. Morris Memorial Pottery Collection. Boulder,
             Univ. of Colorado Pr., 1969 (CUSA)   GN4.C64.no.16

0663   EASBY, Elizabeth Kennedy
             Before Cortés, sculpture of Middle America. Metropolitan
             Museum of Art; distributed by New York Graphic Society,
             1970   E59.A7E17

06631   1877: Plains Indian sketch books of Zo-Tom and Howling Wolf.
             Flagstaff, Arizona, Northland Pr., 1969 E98.A7.E4

0664   EMMERICH, André
             Art before Columbus. Simon and Schuster, 1963 F1219.3.A7E48

0665   EMMERICH, André
             Sweat of the sun and tears of the moon: gold and silver
             in pre-Columbian art. Seattle, Univ. of Washington Pr., 1965
                                E59.A7E6

0666   ENCISO, Jorge
             Design motifs of ancient Mexico. Dover Publications, 1953
                         F1219.3.A7E53

0667   Essays in pre-Columbian art and archaeology, by Samuel K. Lothrop
             and others. Cambridge, Harvard Univ. Pr., 1961 E59.A7E8

0668   EWERS, John Canfield
             Plains Indian painting. Stanford Univ., Calif., Stanford
             Univ. Pr.; London, H. Milford, Oxford Univ. Pr., 1939
                            E98.A7E93

0669   EXPOSITION OF INDIAN TRIBAL ARTS, INC.
             Introduction to American Indian art. The Exposition of
             Indian Tribal Arts, Inc., 1931   E98.A7E95

0670   FEDER, Norman
             American Indian art. Harry N. Abrams, Inc., 1971 E98.A7F38

0671   FEDER, Norman
             North American Indian painting. Museum of Primitive Art;
             distributed by the New York Graphic Society, Greenwich,
             Conn., 1967   E98.A7F4

0672   FEDER, Norman
             Two hundred years of North American Indian art. Praeger,
             1971   E98.A7F43.1972

0673   FOLSOM, Franklin
             America's ancient treasures. Rand McNally, 1971 ref.E56.F64

06731   FOWLER, Don D.
      In a sacred manner we live; photographs of the North
      American Indian by Edward S. Curtis. Barre, Mass.,
      Barre Publishers, 1972   E77.5F6

0674   GARFIELD, Viola Edmundson
      The wolf and the raven. Seattle, Univ. of Washington
      Pr., 1948   E98.T65G32

0675   GARZA TARAZONA, Silvia
      Yugos, hachas, y palmas. Mexico, Museo Nacional de Antropologia,
      1968   GN37.M383.no.9

0676   GAY, Carlo T. E.
      Mezcala stone sculpture. Greenwich, Conn., Distributed by
      the New York Graphic Society, 1967   F1219.1.G93G3

06761   GAY, Carlo T. E.
      Xochipala: the beginning of Olmec art. Princeton, N.J.,
      Distributed by Princeton Univ., 1972   F1219.1.G93.G32

06762   GENDROP, Paul
      Arte prehispanico en Mesoamericano. Mexico, Editorial
      Trillas, 1970   F1219.3.A7.G4

0677   GRANT, Campbell
      Rock art of the American Indian. Crowell, 1967 E98.P6G7

06771   GREENE, Merle
      Maya sculpture from the southern lowlands, highlands and
      pacific piedmont. Lederer, Street, and Zeus, 1972
                                   F1435.3.A7.G693

0678   GRIDLEY, Marion Eleanor comp.
      America's Indian statues. Chicago, The Amerindian, 1966
                                   NB205.G7

0679   GUNTHER, Erna
      Art in the life of the Northwest Coast Indians. Portland,
      Or., Portland Art Museum, 1966   E78.N78G8

0680   HALPIN, Marjorie
      Catlin's Indian gallery: the George Catlin paintings in
      the United States National Museum. Washington City, The
      Smithsonian Institution, 1965   ND237.C35H32

0681   HARCOURT, Raoul d'
      Arts de l'Amérique. Paris, Éditions du Chêne, 1948 E59.A7H28

0682   HARNER, Michael J.
      Art of the Northwest Coast. Berkeley, Univ. of California, 1965
                                   E78.N78H3

06821   HARVEY, Byron
        Ritual in Pueblo art; Hopi life in Hopi painting.
        Museum of the American Indian, Heye Foundation, 1970
                        (HFM)   E51.N42.v.24

06822   HEIKAMP, Detlef
        Mexico and the Medici.   Edam, 1972   F1219.3.A7.H37

0683   HODGE, Gene Meany
        The kachinas are coming. Flagstaff, Ariz., Northland Pr.,
        1967 (1963)   fE99.P9H66.1967

0684   HOLM, Oscar William
        Northwest coast Indian art.   Seattle, Univ. of Washington
        Pr., 1965   E78.N78H6

0685   HOLMES, William Henry
        Ancient pottery of the Mississippi valley. Washington,
        Smithsonian Institution, Bureau of Ethnology, 1886
                                                E98.P8H5.1886

0686   HOLMES, William Henry
        Art in shell of the ancient Americans. Washington,
        Smithsonian Institution, Bureau of Ethnology, 1883
                                                E98.A7H6

06861   HORAN, James David
        The McKenney-Hall Portrait Gallery of American Indians.
        Crown, 1972   fE89.H67.1972

0687   HOOVER, Francis Louis
        Molas from the San Blas Islands.   1969? F1565.8.A7H6

0688   HOTZ, Gottfried
        Indian skin paintings from the American Southwest. Norman,
        Univ. of Oklahoma Pr., 1970   E98.A7H7213
0689   INVERARITY, Robert Bruce
        Art of the Northwest Coast Indians.   Berkeley, Univ. of
        California Pr., 1950   E98.A7I5

0690   JACKSON, A. T.
        Picture-writing of Texas Indians.   Austin, Tex., The
        University, 1938   E98.P6J23

0691   JAMES, George Wharton
        Poetry and symbolism of Indian basketry.   Point Loma,
        Calif., Printed at the Aryan Theosophical Pr., 1913
                                                E98.B3J3

0692   JOYCE, Thomas Athol
        Maya and Mexican art.   London, "The Studio," Ltd., 1927
                                                F1435.J84

06921   KAMPEN, Michael Edwin
        The sculptures of El Tajin, Veracruz, Mexico. Florida,
        Univ. of Florida Pr., 1972   F1219.1.T2.K35

0693   KANE, Paul
        Paul Kane's frontier. Austin, Published for the Amon Carter
        Museum, Fort Worth, and the National Gallery of Canada by
        the Univ. of Texas Pr., 1971   fND249.K3H3

0694   KEITHAHN, Edward Linnaeus
        Monuments in cedar. Seattle, Superior Pub. Co., 1963
                                                E98.T65K4.1963

0695   KELEMEN, Pál
        Medieval American art. Dover Publications, 1969 E59.A7K4.1969

0696   KELLY, Isabel Truesdell
        The carver's art of the Indians of northwestern California.
        Berkeley, Univ. of California Pr., 1930
                            (UCPAE)   E51.C15.v.24.no.7

0697   KIRKLAND, Forrest
        The rock art of Texas Indians. Austin, Univ. of Texas Pr.,
        1967   fE78.T4K5

0698   KROEBER, Alfred Louis
        Basket designs of the Indians of northwestern California.
        Univ. of California Pr., 1905 (UCPAE) E51.C15.v.2.no.4

0699   KROEBER, Alfred Louis
        Basketry designs of the mission Indians. American Museum
        Pr., 1926   E98.B3K932.1926

0700   KUBLER, George
        The art and architecture of ancient America. Baltimore,
        Penguin Books, 1962   E59.A7K8

0701   KUBLER, George
        The iconography of the art of Teotihuacán. Washington,
        Dumbarton Oaks Trustees for Harvard University, 1967
                            (SCAA)   E51.S85.no.4

0702   LA JOLLA, CALIF. ART CENTER.
        Indian art of the Northwest coast. La Jolla, Calif., 1962
                                                E98.A7L3

0703   LEFF, Jay C.
        Ancient art of Latin America from the collection of Jay
        C. Leff. Brooklyn Museum, 1966   E59.A7L37

0704   LEHMANN, Henri
        Pre-Columbian ceramics. London, Elek Books, 1962
                                      E59.P8L43.1962

0705   LINNÉ, Sigvald
        Treasures of Mexican art. Stockholm, Nordisk Rotogravyr, 1956
                                      F1219.3.A7L513

0706   LOS ANGELES CO., CALIF. MUSEUM OF ART, LOS ANGELES.
        Sculpture of ancient west Mexico, Nayarit, Jalsico,
        Colima. Los Angeles, 1970   F1219.3.A7L6

0707   LOS ANGELES COUNTY MUSEUM, LOS ANGELES.
        Gold before Columbus. Los Angeles, 1964 E59.A7L6

0708   LOTHROP, Samuel Kirkland
        Treasures of ancient America: the arts of the pre-Columbian
        civilizations from Mexico to Peru. Skira; book trade
        distribution in the United States by the World Pub. Co.,
        Cleveland, 1964   fE65.L6

0709   McCRACKEN, Harold
        George Catlin and the old frontier. Dial Pr., 1959
                                      fND237.C35M3.1959

0710   MASON, Bernard Sterling
        The book of Indian-crafts and costumes. Ronald Pr. Co.,
        1946   E98.C8M3.1946a

0711   MASON, Otis Tufton
        Aboriginal American basketry. Washington, 1904
                                      GN431.M38

0712   MATTHEWS, Washington
        The Catlin collection of Indian paintings. Washington,
        Govt. Print. Off., 1892   E77.M33

07121   MEADE, Edward F.
        Indian rock drawings of the Pacific Northwest. Sidney,
        B.C., Gray's Pub., 1971   E78.N78.M4

0713   MEIGHAN, Clement Woodward
        Indian art and history. Los Angeles, Dawson's Book Shop,
        1969   F1219.3.A7M42.Spec.Coll.

07131   MERA, Harry Percival
        Pueblo designs; 176 illustrations of the "rain bird".
        Dover, 1970   E99.P9.M4.1970

4   MERA, Harry Percival
       Pueblo Indian embroidery. Santa Fe, the Univ. of New
       Mexico Pr., 1943   fE98.E5M4

5   MEXICO (CITY) MUSEO NACIONAL DE ANTROPOLOGIA.
       Arte preclasico. México, 1968   F1219.3.P8M4

6   MILES, Charles
       American Indian and Eskimo basketry, a key to identification.
       San Francisco, P. Bovis, 1969   E98.B3M5

61   MILLER, Marjorie
       Indian arts and crafts; a complete "how to" guide to
       Southwestern Indian handicrafts. Los Angeles, Nash Pub.,
       1972   E98.A7.M5

7   MONTANA. HISTORICAL SOCIETY.
       An art perspective of the historic Pacific Northwest.
       Butte, Mont., Ashton's, 1963   N6528.M6

8   MONTI, Franco
       Precolumbian terracottas. Hamlyn, 1969 E59.A7M633

9   MOOREHEAD, Warren King
       Stone ornaments used by Indians in the United States and
       Canada. Andover, Mass., Andover Pr., 1917 E98.A7M83

20   The Natalie Wood collection of pre-Columbian ceramics from
       Chupícuaro, Guanajuato, México, at UCLA. Los Angeles,
       Museum and Laboratories of Ethnic Arts and Technology,
       Univ. of California, 1969   F1219.1.C54N3

201 NAVAJO SCHOOL OF INDIAN BASKETRY, LOS ANGELES.
       Indian basket weaving. Dover, 1971   F98.B3.N3.1971

21   NEW YORK (CITY). MUSEUM OF MODERN ART.
       American sources of modern art, May 10 to June 30, 1933,
       the Museum of Modern Art. . .New York. Reprint ed.
       Published for the Museum of Modern Art by Arno Pr., 1969
       (1933)   E59.A7N4.1969

22   NEW YORK. MUSEUM OF MODERN ART.
       Twenty centuries of Mexican art. The Museum of Modern
       Art, in collaboration with the Mexican Government, 1940.
                       N6550.N4

23   NEW YORK. MUSEUM OF PRIMITIVE ART.
       Precolumbian art in New York. Distributed by New York
       Graphic Society, Greenwich, Conn., 1969 fE98.A7N4

24   NEW YORK. MUSEUM OF PRIMITIVE ART.
       Stone sculpture from Mexico. 1959   F1219.3.A7N4

0725   OGLESBY, Catharine
        Modern primitive arts of Mexico, Guatemala, and the Southwest.
        Freeport, N.Y., Books for Libraries Pr., 1969 E98.A705.1969

0726   PETERSEN, Karen Daniels
        Plains Indian art from Fort Marion. Norman, Univ. of
        Oklahoma Pr., 1971   E78.G73P4

0727   PHILADELPHIA MUSEUM OF ART.
        The Louise and Walter Arensberg Collection. Philadelphia,
        1954   N685.A6

0728   PORTLAND, OR. ART MUSEUM.
        Native arts of the Pacific Northwest. Stanford, Stanford
        Univ. Pr., 1949   E98.A7P6

0729   PRINCETON UNIVERSITY. ART MUSEUM.
        Art of the Northwest coast. Princeton, N.J., Princeton
        Print. Co., 1969   E78.N78P7

07291   PRUCHA, Francis Paul
        Indian peace medals in American History. Madison, State
        Historical Society of Wisconsin, 1971   E98.M35.P7

0730   ROBERTSON, Donald
        Pre-Columbian architecture. G. Braziller, 1963 E59.A7R6

0731   ROBINSON, Alambert E.
        The basket weavers of Arizona. Albuquerque, Univ. of
        New Mexico Pr., 1954   E98.B3R62

0732   ROEHM, Marjorie (Catlin) ed.
        The letters of George Catlin and his family. Berkeley,
        Univ. of California Pr., 1966   ND237.C35R6

07321   ROSENTHAL, Joe
        Indians; a sketching odyssey. Clarke, Irwin, 1971
                         F E78.C2.R68

0733   SANFORD, Trent Elwood
        The story of architecture in Mexico. W. W. Norton & Co.,
        Inc., 1947   NA750.S3

0734   SCHAAFSMA, Polly
        The Rock Art of Utah. Cambridge, Mass., The Museum,
        1971   (PMP)   E51.H337.v.65

0735   SCHUSTER, Alfred B.
        The art of two worlds. Praeger, 1959 N6501.5.S34

0736   SEATTLE. CENTURY 21 EXPOSITION, 1962.
        Northwest coast Indian art. Seattle?, 1962? E78.N78S4

0737   SETON, Julia (Moss)
        American Indian arts, a way of life. Ronald Press Co.,
        1962   E98.A7S4

0738   SIDES, Dorothy (Smith)
        Decorative art of the southwestern Indians. Dover
        Publications, 1961   E98.A7S53.1961

0739   SIEBERT, Erna
        Indianerkunst der amerikanischen Nordwestküste. Hanau,
        Germany, W. Dausien, 1967   fE78.N78S5

0740   SIEBERT, Erna
        North American Indian art: masks, amulets, wood carvings
        and ceremonial dress from the North-West coast. London,
        Hamlyn, 1967   fE78.N78S513

0741   SMITH, Robert Eliot
        The pottery of Mayapan. Cambridge, Mass., The Museum, 1971
                  (PMP)   E51.H337.v.66

07411   SMITH, Watson
        Kiva mural decorations at Awatovi an Kawalka-a: with a
        survey of other wall paintings in the pueblo southwest.
        Cambridge, Mass., The Museum, 1952 (PMP) E51.H337.v.37

07412   SNODGRASS, Jeanne O.
        American Indian painters; a biographical directory.
        Museum of the American Indian Heye Foundation, 1968
                  (HFM)   Ref.E51.N42.v.21.pt.1

0742   SOUSTELLE, Jacques
        L'Art du Mexique ancien. Paris, Arthaud, 1966 F1219.3.A7S6

0743   SOUSTELLE, Jacques
        Arts of ancient Mexico. Viking Pr., 1967 F1219.3.A7S613.1967a

0744   STEWARD, Julian Haynes
        Petroglyphs of California and adjoining states. Berkeley,
        Univ. of California Pr., 1929 (UCPAE) E51.C15.v.24.no.2

0745   STUMP, Sarain
        There is my people sleeping. Sidney, B. C. Gray's Pub.,
        1970   E98.A7S85

0746   TANNER, Clara Lee
        Southwest Indian craft arts. Tucson, Univ. of Arizona Pr.,
        1968   fE78.S7T3

0747   TANNER, Clara Lee
           Southwest Indian painting. Tucson, Univ. of Arizona Pr.,
           1957   fE98.A7T35

07471   THOMAS GILCREASE INSTITUTE OF AMERICAN HISTORY AND ART,
           Tulsa, Okla., Library.
           The Gilcrease-Hargrett catalogue of imprints. Norman Univ.
           of Oklahoma Pr., 1972   Z1209.s.U5.T48

07472   THOMSON, Charlotte
           Ancient art of the Americas from New England collections;
           exhibition and catalogue. Boston, Mass., Museum of Fine
           Arts, 1971   E59.A7.T5

0748   TOLEDO MUSEUM OF ART.
           The art of the North American Indian of the United
           States. Toledo, Ohio, 1946   E98.A7T6

0749   TOSCANO, Salvador
           Arte precolombino de México y de la América central.
           México, Instituto de Investigaciones Estéticas, Universidad
           Nacional Autónoma de México, 1944   fF1219.3.A7T6

0750   VAILLANT, George Clapp
           Indian arts in North America. Harper and Brothers, 1939
                                       E98.A7V25

0751   VANCOUVER, B. C. ART GALLERY.
           People of the Potlach. Vancouver, 1956 E98.A7V3

0752   VIENNA. MUSEUM FÜR VÖLKERKUNDE.
           Die mexikanischen Sammlungen. Wien, 1965 F1219.3.A7V5

0753   VON WINNING, Hasso
           Pre-Columbian art of Mexico and Central America.
           Abrams, 1968   fF1219.3.A7V6

0754   WARDWELL, Allen
           The gold of ancient America. Greenwich, Conn.,
           Distributed by New York Graphic Society, 1968 E59.A7W3

07541   WASHINGTON (STATE). UNIVERSITY. MUSEUM.
           Crooked beak of heaven; masks and other ceremonial art
           of the Northwest coast, by Bill Holm. Seattle, Univ.
           of Washington Pr., 1972   E78.N78.W3

0755   WESTHEIM, Paul
           L'art du Mexique précolombien. Paris, Payout, 196-
                             F1219.3.A7W4

0756   WESTHEIM, Paul
        The art of ancient Mexico. Garden City, N.Y., Anchor Books,
        1965   F1219.3.A7W413

0757   WESTHEIM, Paul
        The sculpture of ancient Mexico. Doubleday, 1963
                                                     F1219.3.A7W43

0758   WHATCOM MUSEUM OF HISTORY AND ART.
        Arts of a vanished era. Bellingham, Wash., 1968   E78.N78W48

0759   WHERRY, Joe H.
        The totem pole Indians. W. Funk, 1964   E78.N78W5

0760   WICKE, Charles R.
        Olmec: an early art style of Pre-columbian Mexico. Tucson,
        Univ. of Arizona Pr., 1971   F1219.W53

0761   WINGERT, Paul Stover
        American Indian sculpture. J. J. Augustin, 1949   E98.A7W5

0762   WINTER, George
        The journals and Indian paintings of George Winter,
        1837-1839. Indianapolis, Indiana Historical Society, 1948
                                                     ND237.W77A25

0763   WUTHENAU, Alexander von
        The art of terracotta pottery in pre-Columbian Central
        and South America. Crown Publishers, 1970 (1969)   E59.A7W813

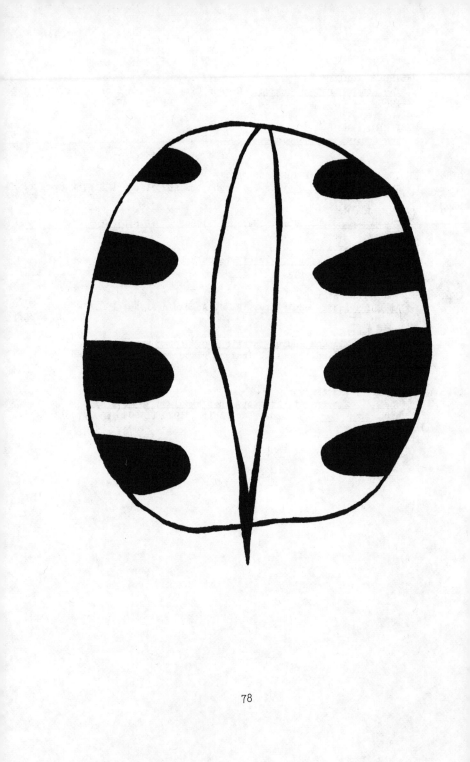

07631   Abstracts in anthropology.
        v. 1- Feb. 1970- Westport, Conn., Greenwood Periodicals
                        ref GN1.A15

0764   Abstracts of New World archaeology.
        v. 1- 1959- Salt Lake City, University of Utah Pr.
                        ref. E51.S73

0765   AZCUÉ Y MANCERA, Luis
        Códices indígenas. México, Editorial Orion, 1966 Z1426.A9

0766   BERNAL, Ignacio
        Bibliografía de arqueología y etnografía: Mesoamérica y Norte
        de México, 1514-1960. México, Instituto Nacional de Antro-
        pología e Historia, 1962   f.ref.Z1209.B45

0767   CALIFORNIA. HUMBOLDT STATE COLLEGE, ARCATA. LIBRARY.
        Indians of North America: guide to resources in Humboldt
        State College Library. Arcata, Calif., 1970 ref.Z1209.C35

0768   CALIFORNIA. STATE COLLEGE, SACRAMENTO. LIBRARY.
        Native Americans; a bibliography for young people.
        Sacramento, 1970   ref.Z1209.C38

07681   CORRELL, J. Lee
        Navajo bibliography with subject index. Window Rock,
        Ariz., Research Section, Navajo Parks and Recreation,
        Navajo Tribe, 1969   ref Z1210.N3.C6

0769   DE PUY, Henry Farr
        A bibliography of the English colonial treaties with the
        American Indians. AMS Pr., 1971 (1917) Z1209.2.U5D44.1971

0770   DOCKSTADER, Frederick J.
        The American Indian in graduate studies. Museum of the
        American Indian, Heye Foundation, 1957 ref.Z1209.D6.1957

0771   FENTON, William Nelson
        American Indian and white relations to 1830. Chapel Hill,
        Pub. for the Institute of Early American History and Culture,
        Williamsburg, Va., by the Univ. of North Carolina Pr., 1957
                        Z1209.F38

0772   FIELD, Thomas Warren
        Catalogue of the library belonging to Mr. Thomas W. Field.
        C. C. Shelley, 1875   ref.Z1209.F456

0773 FIELD, Thomas Warren
An essay towards an Indian bibliography. Scribner,
Armstrong and Co., 1873   ref.Z1209.F45

0774 FOREMAN, Carolyn (Thomas)
Oklahoma imprints, 1835-1907. Norman, Univ. of Oklahoma
Pr., 1936   Z1325.F71

0775 HARDING, Anne Dinsdale comp.
Bibliography of articles and papers on North American
Indian art. Washington, Dept. of the Interior, Indian
Arts and Crafts Board, 1938   ref.Z1209.H26

0776 HARGRETT, Lester
A bibliography of the constitutions and laws of the
American Indians. Cambridge, Mass., Harvard Univ. Pr.,
1947   ref.Z1209.H28

0777 HARVARD UNIVERSITY. PEABODY MUSEUM OF ARCHAEOLOGY AND
ETHNOLOGY. LIBRARY.
Catalogue: authors. Boston, G. K. Hall, 1963
                                    f.ref.Z5119.H35

0778 HARVARD UNIVERSITY. PEABODY MUSEUM OF ARCHAEOLOGY AND
ETHNOLOGY. LIBRARY.
Catalogue: subjects. Boston, G. K. Hall, 1963
                                    f.ref.Z5119.H36

0779 HAYWOOD, Charles
A bibliography of North American folklore and folksong.
Dover Publications, 1961   ref.Z5984.U5H32

0780 HEIZER, Robert Fleming
A bibliography of California archaeology. Berkeley,
Univ. of California, Dept. of Anthropology, 1970
                    (UCAC)   E51.C2.no.6

0781 HELLMUTH, Nicolas M.
A bibliography of the 16th-20th century Maya of the
southern lowlands. Greeley, Museum of Anthropology,
Univ. of Northern Colorado, 1970   F1346.025.no.2

0782 Index to literature on the American Indian: 1970.
American Indian Historical Society, 1972 ref.Z1209.I5

0783 JILLSON, Willard Rouse
A selected bibliography on the American Indian. Frankfort,
Ky., Roberts Print. Co., 1964   Z1209.J5

0784 JONES, Julie
Bibliography for Olmec sculpture. Library, Museum of
Primitive Art, 1963   Z1210.04J6
                      80

0785 KLUCKHOHN, Clyde
A bibliography of the Navaho Indians. J. J. Augustin, 1940
ref.Z1210.N3K7

0786 LINES, Jorge A.
Anthropological bibliography of aboriginal Costa Rica.
San José, Tropical Science Center, 1967 ref.Z1208.C6L5

0787 LINES, Jorge A.
Anthropological bibliography of aboriginal Guatemala, British
Honduras. San José, Costa Rica, Tropical Science Center, 1967
ref.Z1208.G8L5

0788 LINES, Jorge A.
Anthropological bibliography of aboriginal El Salvador.
San José, Costa Rica, Tropical Science Center, 1965
ref.Z1208.S2L5.1965

0789 LINES, Jorge A.
Anthropological bibliography of aboriginal Honduras.
San José, Costa Rica, Tropical Science Center, 1966
ref.Z1208.H6L5

0790 MARTÍNEZ, Héctor
Bibliografía indígena andina peruana, 1900-1968. Lima,
Ministerio de Trabajo y Communidades, Instituto Indigenista
Peruano, 1968- ref.Z1209.M3

0791 MINNESOTA HISTORICAL SOCIETY.
Chippewa and Dakota Indians. St. Paul, 1969 ref.Z1210.C5M5

0792 MURDOCK, George Peter
Ethnographic bibliography of North America. New Haven,
Human Relations Area Files, 1960 ref.Z1209.M8.1960

0793 NEWBERRY LIBRARY, CHICAGO. EDWARD E. AYER COLLECTION.
Dictionary catalog of the Edward E. Ayer Collection of
Americana and American Indians in the Newberry Library.
Boston, G. K. Hall, 1961 f.ref.Z1209.N4

0794 NEWBERRY LIBRARY, CHICAGO. EDWARD E. AYER COLLECTION.
Narratives of captivity among the Indians of North America.
Chicago, The Newberry Library, 1912 ref.Z1209.N53

0795 PILLING, James Constantine
Bibliography of the Algonquin languages. Washington, Govt.
Print. Off., 1891 (BAEB) E51.U55.no.13

0796 PILLING, James Constantine
Bibliography of the Athapascan languages. Washington, Govt.
Print. Off., 1892 (BAEB) E51.U55.no.14

0797   PILLING, James Constantine
Bibliography of the Chinookan languages (including the
Chinook jargon). Washington, Govt. Print. Off., 1893
                 (BAEB)   E51.U55.no.15

0798   PILLING, James Constantine
Bibliography of the Muskhogean languages. Washington,
Govt. Print. Off., 1889 (BAEB)   E51.U55.no.9

0799   PILLING, James Constantine
Bibliography of the Siouan languages. Washington, Govt.
Print. Off., 1887   (BAEB)   E51.U55.no.5

0800   PILLING, James Constantine
Bibliography of the Wakashan languages. Washington,
Govt. Print. Off., 1894 (BAEB)   E51.U55.no.19

0801   PILLING, James Constantine
Proof-sheets of a bibliography of the languages of the
North American Indians. Brooklyn, N.Y., Central Book
Co., 196-? (1885)   ref.Z7118.P64.1885a

0802   RADER, Jesse Lee
South of forty. Norman, Univ. of Oklahoma Pr., 1947
                        ref.Z1251.S83R33

0803   RIDDELL, Francis A.
A bibliography of the Indians of central California.
Sacramento, State of California, Resources Agency,
Dept. of Parks and Recreation, Div. of Beaches and
Parks, 1962   ref.Z1209.R47

0804   RIDDELL, Francis A.
A bibliography of the Indians of northeastern California.
Sacramento, State of California, Resources Agency, Dept.
of Parks and Recreation, Div. of Beaches and Parks, 1962
                    ref.Z1209.R49

0805   RIDDELL, Francis A.
A bibliography of the Indians of northwestern California.
Sacramento, Resources Agency, Dept. of Parks and Re-
creation, Div. of Beaches and Parks, 1962 ref.Z1209.R5

0806   RIDDELL, Francis A.
A bibliography of the Indians of southern California.
Sacramento, State of California, Resources Agency, Dept.
of Parks and Recreation, Div. of Beaches and Parks, 1962
                    ref.Z1209.R515

0807   ROUSE, Irving
        An anthropological bibliography of the eastern seaboard.
        New Haven, The Federation, 1947 (i.e. 1948)
                        (ESAF)   E51.E212.no.1

0808   SAUNDERS, Lyle
        A guide to materials bearing on cultural relations in New
        Mexico. Albuquerque, The Univ. of New Mexico Pr., 1944
                           ref.Z1315.S35

0809   SAVILLE, Marshall Howard
        Bibliographic notes on Palenque, Chiapas. Museum of the
        American Indian, Heye Foundation, 1928
                      (HFM)   E51.N45.v.6.no.5

0810   SAVILLE, Marshall Howard
        Bibliographic notes on Xochicalco, Mexico. Museum of the
        American Indian, Heye Foundation, 1928
                      (HFM)   E51.N45.v.6.no.6

0811   SHOOK, Edwin M.
        Anthropological bibliography of aboriginal Panama.
        San José, Costa Rica, Tropical Science Center, 1965
                           ref.Z1209.S52.1965

0812   SPRAGUE, Roderick
        A preliminary bibliography of Washington archaeology.
        Pullman, Wash., Washington State Univ., Laboratory of
        Anthropology, 1967   ref.Z5114.S68

0813   SUMMER INSTITUTE OF LINGUISTICS.
        Twenty-fifth anniversary bibliography of the Summer
        Institute of Linguistics. Glendale, Calif., 1960 ref.Z7120.S8

0814   U. S. BUREAU OF AMERICAN ETHNOLOGY. BULLETIN. (INDEXES)
        Index to Bulletins 1-100 of the Bureau of American Ethnology.
        Washington, U. S. Govt. Print. Off., 1963 ref.Z1209.U49

0815   U. S. DEPT. OF THE INTERIOR. LIBRARY.
        Biographical and historical index of American Indians and
        persons involved in Indian affairs. Boston, G. K. Hall,
        1966   f.ref.E77.U52

0816   WARDWELL, Allen
        Annotated bibliography of Northwest Coast Indian art.
        Library, Museum of Primitive Art, 1970 Z1209.W34

0817   ANDERSON, Rufus
        Memoir of Catharine Brown, a Christian Indian of the Cherokee
        nation. Boston, S. T. Armstrong, 1825 E90.B87A4.Spec.Coll.

0818   BLACK ELK, Oglala Indians
        Black Elk speaks. W. Morrow & Co., 1932 E90.B82B7

0819   BLOWSNAKE, Sam
        Crashing Thunder; the autobiography of an American Indian.
        D. Appleton and Co., 1926   E90.C9B55

08191   BOULANGER, Tom
        An Indian remembers, my life as a trapper in Northern
        Manitoba. Winnipeg, Peguis Publishers, 1971 E78.M25.B6

0820   BRININSTOOL, Earl Alonzo
        Dull Knife (a Cheyenne Napoleon). Hollywood, Calif.,
        Priv. pub. by E. A. Brininstool, 1935 E90.D8B7

0821   BRITT, Albert
        Great Indian chiefs. Freeport, N.Y., Books for Libraries
        Pr., 1969   E89.B75.1969

0822   CUERO, Delfina
        The autobiography of Delfina Cuero, a Diegueno Indian.
        Los Angeles, Dawson's Book Shop, 1968 E90.C945A3.Spec.Coll.

0823   CUMMINGS, Byron
        Indians I have known. Tucson, Arizona Silhouettes, 1952
                                         E89.C85

0824   EASTMAN, Charles Alexander
        From the deep woods to civilization. Boston, Little, Brown,
        and Co., 1923   E90.E14E14.1923

0825   EASTMAN, Charles Alexander
        Indian boyhood. Boston, Little, Brown, 1923 (1902) E98.C5E2

0826   EASTMAN, Charles Alexander
        Indian heroes and great chieftains. Boston, Little, Brown,
        and Co., 1918   E89.E13

0827   FAULK, Odie B.
        The Geronimo campaign. Oxford Univ. Pr., 1969 E90.G4F3

0828   FOREMAN, Grant
        Sequoyah. Norman, Univ. of Oklahoma Pr., 1970 (1938) E90.S47F6

0829   GOODRICH, Samuel Griswold
        Lives of celebrated American Indians. Boston, Bradbury,
        Soden & Co., 1843   E58.G654

0830   GRIDLEY, Marion Eleanor ed.
        Indians of today. Chicago, Millar Pub. Co., 1947 (i.e. 1948)
                                 E89.G75.1947

0831   HEBARD, Grace Raymond
        Washakie. Cleveland, The Arthur H. Clark Co., 1930
                         E90.W31H4

0832   HOWARD, Helen Addison
        War chief Joseph. Caldwell, Id., The Caxton Printers, Ltd.,
        1952 (1941)   E90.J8H68

08321   HOWARD, Oliver Otis
        Nez Perce Joseph; an account of his ancestors, his lands,
        his confederates, his enemies, his murders, his war, his
        pursuit and capture. Da Capo, 1972   E83.877.J83.1972

0833   HUGHES, Thomas
        Indian chiefs of southern Minnesota. Minneapolis, Ross
        and Haines, 1969   E89.H93.1969

0834   JACKSON, Clyde L.
        Quanah Parker, last chief of the Comanches. Exposition Pr.,
        1963   E90.P19J3

0835   JOHNSTON, Charles Haven Ladd
        Famous Indian chiefs. Boston, The Page Co., 1921
                    E89.J72

0836   JOSEPHY, Alvin M.
        The patriot chiefs. Viking Pr., 1965 (1961) E89.J78

08361   KINO, Eusebio Francisco
        Kino's biography of Francisco Javier Saeta. Rome,
        Jesuit Historical Institute; St. Louis, Mo., St. Louis
        Univ., 1971   E.99.P6.S35.1971

0837   KROEBER, Theodora
        Almost ancestors. San Francisco, Sierra Club, 1968
                    E89.K7

0838   KROEBER, Theodora
        Ishi in two worlds. Berkeley, Univ. of California Pr.,
        1961   E90.I8K7

0839   LEFT HANDED, Navaho Indian
        Son of Old Man Hat. Lincoln, Univ. of Nebraska Pr., 1967 (1938)
                                            E90.L4L5.1967

0840   LINDERMAN, Frank Bird
        American; the life story of a great Indian, Plenty-coups,
        chief of the Crows. The John Day Co., 1930 E90.P56L7

0841   MACEWAN, John Walter Grant
        Tatanga Mani: Walking Buffalo of the Stonies. Edmonton,
        Alta., M. G. Hurtig, 1969   E90.W27M3

0842   McNICOL, Donald Monroe
        The Amerindians, from Acuera to Sitting Bull, from Donnacona
        to Big Bear. Frederick A. Stokes Co., 1937 E77.M177

0843   McSPADDEN, Joseph Walker
        Indian heroes. Crowell, 1950   E77.M32.1950

0844   MARQUIS, Thomas Bailey
        A warrior who fought Custer. Minneapolis, The Midwest Co.,
        1931   E90.W8M35

0845   MITCHELL, Emerson Blackhorse
        Miracle hill; the story of a Navaho boy. Norman, Univ.
        of Oklahoma Pr., 1967   E90.M5A3

0846   MOUNTAIN WOLF WOMAN
        Mountain Wolf Woman, sister of Crashing Thunder. Ann
        Arbor, Univ. of Michigan Pr., 1961   E90.M6A3

0847   NOWELL, Charles James
        Smoke from their fires; the life of a Kwakiutl chief.
        Hamden, Conn., Archon Books, 1968 (1941) E90.K85N6.1968

0848   O'MEARA, Walter
        Daughters of the country. Harcourt, Brace & World, 1968
                                                E98.W8O4

0849   PEIRCE, Ebenezer Weaver
        Indian history, biography and genealogy. North Abington,
        Mass., Z.G. Mitchell, 1878   E90.M4P3

08491   PORTER, C. Fayne
        Our Indian heritage; profiles of 12 great leaders. Philadelphia,
        Chilton, 1967, 1964   E89.P6

0850   POZAS ARCINIEGA, Ricardo
        Juan Pérez Jolote. Mexico, Fondo de Cultura Económica, 1965
                                                F1221.T9P69.1965

87

0851   POZAS ARCINIEGA, Ricardo
        Juan the Chamula. Berkeley, Univ. of California Pr.,
        1962   F1221.T9P693

0852   QUOYAWAYMA, Polingaysi
        No turning back. Albuquerque, Univ. of New Mexico Pr.,
        1964   E90.Q6A3

0853   RED FOX, Chief
        The memoirs of Chief Red Fox. McGraw-Hill, 1971
                                          E90.R4A3

0854   RICH, John M.
        Chief Seattle's unanswered challenge. Fairfield, Wash.,
        Ye Galleon Pr., 1970 (1947)   E90.S4R5.1970

0855   SABIN, Edwin Legrand
        Boys' book of Indian warriors and heroic Indian women.
        Philadelphia. G. W. Jacobs & Co., 1918 E89.S12

0856   SANDOZ, Mari
        Crazy Horse, the strange man of the Oglalas. Hastings
        House, 1965 (1942)   E90.C94S3.1965

0857   SCOTT, Lalla
        Karnee; a Paiute narrative. Reno, Univ. of Nevada Pr.,
        1966   E90.L88S3

0858   SEKAQUAPTEWA, Helen
        Me and mine. Tucson, Univ. of Arizona Pr., 1969
                                          E90.S45A3

0859   STANDING BEAR, Luther, Dakota chief
        My Indian boyhood. Houghton Mifflin Co., 1931 E90.S8S8

0860   SUN BEAR (Chippewa Indian)
        Buffalo hearts. Healdsburg, Calif., Naturegraph, 1970
                                          E98.C9S87

0861   SWEEZY, Carl
        The Arapaho way. C. N. Potter, 1966   E90.S85A3

0862   TAYLOR, Rose (Schuster)
        The last survivor. San Francisco, Johnck & Seeger, 1932
                                          E90.L37T3

0863   THATCHER, Benjamin Bussey
        Indian biography. A. L. Fowle, 1900   E89.T36.1900

0864   THORNTON, Mildred Valley (Stinson)
        Indian lives and legends. Vancouver, Mitchell Pr., 1966
                                          E78.B9T5

0865   TWO LEGGINGS
            Two Leggings; the making of a Crow warrior. Crowell, 1967
                                                E90.T9A3

0866   VOIGHT, Virginia Frances
            Mohegan chief, the story of Harold Tantaquidgeon. Funk &
            Wagnalls Co., Inc., 1965   E90.T16V6

0867   WHITE HORSE EAGLE, Osage chief
            We Indians, the passing of a great race. London,
            T. Butterworth, 1931   E90.W5W52

0868   WHITEWOLF, Jim
            Jim Whitewolf: the life of a Kiowa Indian. Dover
            Publications, 1969   E90.W55A3

0869   WOOD, Norman Barton
            Lives of famous Indian chiefs. Chicago, L. W. Walter,
            1906   E89.W87.1906

0870   WOODWARD, Grace Steele
            Pocahontas. Norman, Univ. of Oklahoma Pr., 1969   E90.P6W6

0871   ZITKALA-SA
            American Indian stories. Washington, Hayworth Publishing
            House, 1921   E90.Z82

0872   ACOSTA, José de
        Historia natural y moral de las Indias.
        México, Fondo de Cultura Económica, 1962   E141.A286

0873   ANDERSON, John Richard Lane
        Vinland voyage. Funk & Wagnalls, 1967   E105.A5.1967b

0874   ANGHIERA, Pietro Martire d'
        The decades of the Newe Worlde or West India. Ann Arbor,
        Mich., University Microfilms, 1966   E141.A58.1555a

0875   ARBER, Edward
        The first three English books on America. Westminster,
        A.Constable and Co., 1895   E141.A66

0876   BATAILLON, Marcel
        Las Casas et la défense des indiens. Paris, Julliard, 1971
                                                E125.C4B28

0877   BLEGEN, Theodore Christian
        The Kensington rune stone. St. Paul, Minnesota Historical
        Society, 1968   E105.B65

0878   BREBNER, John Bartlet
        The explorers of North America, 1492-1806. Cleveland, Ohio,
        World Publishing, 1966   E101.B83.1966

0879   BRINE, Lindesay
        Travels amongst American Indians, their ancient earth-works
        and temples. London, S. Low, Marston & Co., Ltd., 1894
                                                E58.B84

0880   BUNNELL, Lafayette Houghton
        Discovery of the Yosemite. Los Angeles, G. W. Gerlicher, 1911
                                                F868.Y6B9.1911

0881   CÁRDENAS, Juan de
        Problemas y secretos maravillosos de las Indias. Madrid,
        Ediciones Cultura Hispánica, 1945   E141.C19

0882   CARTIER, Jacques
        Navigations to Newe Fraunce. Ann Arbor, Mich., University
        Microfilms, 1966   E133.C3C443.1580a

0883   CASSOU, Jean
        La dé-ouverte du Nouveau monde, vue d'ensemble. Paris,
        A. Michel, 1966   E101.C35

0884   CATLIN, George
        Episodes from Life among the Indians, and Last rambles.
        Norman, Univ. of Oklahoma Pr., 1959   E58.C3535

0885   CATLIN, George
        Last rambles amongst the Indians of the Rocky mountains and
        the Andes. London, S. Low and Marston, 1868   E58.C352.1868

0886   CATLIN, George
        Letters and notes on the manners, customs, and condition
        of the North American Indians, written during eight years'
        travel amongst the wildest tribes of Indians in North
        America in 1832, 33, 34, 35, 36, 37, 38, and 39. Minneapolis,
        Ross & Haines, 1965   E77.C38.1965

0887   CHATEUABRIAND, François Auguste René, vicomte de
        Travels in America. Lexington, Univ. of Kentucky Pr.,
        1969   E164.C4983

0888   CHEYNEY, Edward Potts
        European background of American history, 1300-1600.
        F. Ungar Pub. Co., 1966   E101.C53.1966

0889   CULBERTSON, Thaddeus Ainsworth
        Journal of an expedition to the Mauvaises Terres and the
        Upper Missouri in 1850. Washington, U.S. Govt. Print. Off.,
        1952   (BAEB)   E51.U55.no.147

0890   DEACON, Richard
        Madoc and the discovery of America. G. Braziller, 1967
        (1966)   E109.W4D18.1967b

0891   DIAZ-ALEJO, R. ed.
        América y el viejo mundo. Buenos Aires, J. Gil, 1942
                                                E101.D5

08911   ENTERLINE, James Robert
        Viking America; the Norse crossings and their legacy.
        Doubleday, 1972   E105.E58

0892   FISCHER, Joseph
        The discoveries of the Norsemen in America. B. Franklin,
        1970 (1903)   E105.F53.1970

0893   FISKE, John
        The discovery of America. Houghton, Mifflin and Co., 1920
                                                E101.F58

0894   Flateyjarbók.
        London, New York, etc., Norroena Society, 1906 fE105.F59

08941   FONTAINE, John
       The journal of John Fontaine; an Irish Huguenot son in Spain
       and Virginia, 1710-1719. Williamsburg, Va., Colonial
       Williamsburg Foundation; distributed by the Univ. Pr.
       of Virginia, 1972   F229.F6615

0895   GATHORNE-HARDY, Geoffrey Malcolm
       The Norse discoverers of America. Oxford, Clarendon P.,
       1970   E105.G26.1970

0896   GORDON, Cyrus Herzl
       Before Columbus. Crown, 1971   E103.G65.1971

08961   GRAY, Edward Francis
       Leif Eriksson, discoverer of America, A.D. 1003.
       Kraus, 1972   E105.E68.1972

0897   HALL, Charles Francis
       Life with the Esquimaux. Rutland, Vt., C. E. Tuttle Co.,
       1970   G665.1860.H182.1970

0898   HALL, Charles Francis
       Narrative of the second Arctic expedition made by
       Charles F. Hall. Washington, Govt. Print. Off., 1879
                       G665.1862.H2

0899   HANKE, Lewis
       Bartolomé de las Casas. The Hague, M. Nijhoff, 1951
                       E125.C4H32

0900   HARRISSEE, Henry
       The diplomatic history of America. London. B. F. Stevens,
       1897   E110.H32

0901   HARRISSEE, Henry
       The discovery of North America. Amsterdam, N. Israel,
       1961   E101.H32.1961

0902   HELPS, Sir Arthur
       The life of Las Casas. Philadelphia, Lippincott, 1868
                       E125.C4H4.1868

0903   HERRERA Y TORDESILLAS, Antonio de
       The general history of the vast continent and islands
       of America. London, Printed by J. Batley, 1725-26
                       E141.H59.Spec.Coll.

0904   HIGGINSON, Thomas Wentworth
       Young folks' book of American explorers. Longmans, Green
       and Co., 1895   E101.H634

0905   HODGSON, Adam
        Remarks during a journey through North America in the
        years 1819, 1820, and 1821. Westport, Conn., Negro
        Universities Pr., 1970   E165.H69.1970

0906   HOLAND, Hjalmar Rued
        America, 1355-1364. Duell, Sloan and Pearce, 1946
                                              E105.H68

0907   HOLAND, Hjalmar Rued
        Explorations in America before Columbus. Twayne
        Publishers, 1956   E105.H69

0908   HOLAND, Hjalmar Rued
        Westward from Vinland. Duell, Sloan & Pearce, 1940
                                              E105.H73

09081   HOVGAARD, William
        The voyages of the Norsemen to America. (The American-
        Scandinavian Foundation, 1914) Kraus, 1971 E105.H89.1971

0909   HOWITT, Emanuel
        Selections from letters written during a tour through the
        United States. Nottingham, Printed and sold by J. Dunn,
        1820   E165.H86.Spec.Coll.

0910   JOHNSTON, Charles Haven Ladd
        Famous discoverers and explorers of America. Freeport,
        N.Y., Books for Libraries Pr., 1971 (1917)E101.J73.1971

0911   LAMB, Harold
        New found world. Doubleday, 1955   E101.L2

0912   LANDSVERK, Ole Godfred
        Ancient Norse messages on American stones. Glendale, Calif.,
        Norseman Pr., 1969   E105.L23

0913   LEACOCK, Stephen Butler
        The dawn of Canadian history. Toronto, Glasgow, Brook &
        Co., 1922   E101.L43

0914   LEHNER, Ernst
        How they saw the new world. Tudor Pub. Co., 1966 E101.L45

0915   LEVILLIER, Roberto
        América la bien llamada. Buenos Aires, Editorial G. Kraft,
        1948   fE101.L49

0916   LORANT, Stefan
        The new world. Duell, Sloan & Pearce, 1946 fE141.L88

0917   LOWERY, Woodbury
        The Spanish settlements within the present limits of the
        United States, 1513-1561. Russell & Russell, 1959
                                                E123.L68.1959

0918   MALAURIE, Jean
        The last kings of Thule. Crowell, 1956 G750.M34

0919   Man across the sea. Austin, Univ. of Texas Pr., 1971 E103.M34

0920   MEARES, John
        Voyages made in the years 1788 and 1789 from China to the
        North-West coast of America. Amsterdam, N. Israel;
        New York, Da Capo Pr., 1967 (1790)   F851.5.M47.1790a

0921   MERTZ, Henriette
        Pale ink. Chicago, 1953   E109.C5M4

0922   MONGÉ, Alf
        Norse medieval cryptography in runic carvings. Glendale,
        Calif., Norseman Pr., 1967   E105.M78

0923   MORISON, Samuel Eliot
        The European discovery of America. Oxford Univ. Pr., 1971
                                                E101.M85

0924   MORISON, Samuel Eliot
        Portuguese voyages to America in the fifteenth century.
        Cambridge, Harvard Univ. Pr., 1940   E109.P8M67

0925   MOWAT, Farley
        Westviking. Boston, Little, Brown, 1965 E105.M89

0926   NEWTON, Arthur Percival ed.
        The great age of discovery. London, Univ. of London Pr., Ltd,
        1932   E101.N48

0927   The Norse discovery of America. London, New York, etc.,
        Norroena Society, 1907 (1905)   E105.N86.1907

0928   The Northmen, Columbus and Cabot, 985-1503: The voyages of
        the Northmen. C. Scribner's Sons, 1906 E101.N87

0929   NUÑEZ CABEZA DE VACA, Alvar
        The journey of Alvar Nuñez Cabeza de Vaca. Chicago,
        Rio Grande Pr., 1964   E125.N9N96

0930   O'GORMAN, Edmundo
        The invention of America. Bloomington, Indiana Univ. Pr.,
        1961   E110.O42

0931   OLESON, Tryggvi J.
        Early voyages and northern approaches, 1000-1632.
        Toronto, McClelland and Stewart; New York, Oxford Univ.
        Pr., 1964 (1963)   E105.048

0932   OVIEDO Y VALDÉS, Gonzalo Fernández de
        Sumario de la natural historia de las Indias. México,
        Fondo de Cultura Económica, 1950   E141.0972

0933   PARRY, Sir William Edward
        Journal of a second voyage for the discovery of a
        northwest passage from the Atlantic to the Pacific.
        Greenwood Pr., 1969 (1824)   G650.1821.P223

0934   POHL, Frederick Julius
        Atlantic crossings before Columbus. Norton, 1961
                                            E103.P6

0935   POHL, Frederick Julius
        The Viking explorers. T. Y. Crowell Co., 1966 E105.P65

09351   POHL, Frederick Julius
        The Viking settlements of North America. Potter, 1972
                                            E105.P66.1972

0936   The Quest for America. Praeger Pub., 1971 E101.Q4

0937   QUINN, David Beers comp.
        North American discovery, circa 1000-1612. Columbia,
        Univ. of South Carolina Pr., 1971   E101.Q5.1971b

09371   RANDOLPH, J. Ralph
        British travelers among the southern Indians, 1660-1763.
        Oklahoma, Univ. of Oklahoma Pr., 1973   E78.S65.R3

0938   RASMUSSEN, Knud Johan Victor
        Across Arctic America. G. P. Putnam's Sons, 1927
                                            G670.1921.R35

0939   RASMUSSEN, Knus Johan Victor
        Fra Grønland til Stillehavet, rejser og mennesker.
        København, Gyldendal, Nordisk Forlag, 1925-1926
                                            G650.1921.R3

0940   REMAN, Edward
        The Norse discoveries and explorations in America.
        Berkeley, Univ. of California Pr., 1949 E105.R4

0941   REEVES, Arthur Middleton ed. and tr.
        The finding of Wineland the good. Burt Franklin, 1967
        (1895)   E105.R38.1967

0942   SANSON, Nicolas
        America, 1667. Cleveland, Bloch, 1959-   E143.S243

0943   SCHRAG, Peter
        The European mind and the discovery of a new world.
        Boston, Heath, 1965   E101.S29

0944   *Spanish explorers in the southern United States, 1528-1543*.
        C. Scribner's Sons, 1925 (1907)   E123.S75

0945   STEFANSSON, Vilhjalmur
        The friendly Arctic. Greenwood Pr., 1969 (1943)
                                            G670.1908.A522

0946   STEVENS, Henry
        *Historical and geographical notes on the earliest discoveries
        in America, 1453-1530*. B. Franklin, 1970 E101.S84.1970

0947   THÓRDARSON, Matthias
        The Vinland voyages. American Geographical Society, 1930
                                            E105.T36

0948   TORNØE, Johannes Kristoffer
        Columbus in the Arctic? Oslo, 1965   E105.T69

0949   TORNØE, Johannes Kristoffer
        Early American history. Oslo, Universitets Forlaget; New York,
        Humanities Pr., 1965   E105.T7.1965

0950   VÁZQUEZ DE ESPINOSA, Antonio
        Compendio y descripción de las Indias Occidentales.
        Washington, Smithsonian Institution, 1948 E143.V32

0951   VÁZQUEZ DE ESPINOSA, Antonio
        Description of the Indies, c. 1620. Washington, Smithsonian
        Institution Pr., 1968   E143.V33.1968

0952   VIERECK, Phillip   ed.
        The new land. John Day Co., 1967   E141.V5

09521   VIGNAUD, Henry
        Toscanelli and Columbus. Books for Libraries Pr., 1971
                                            E110.V69.1971

0953   WAHLGREN, Erik
        The Kensington stone. Madison, Univ. of Wisconsin Pr., 1958
                                            E105.W33

0954   WEAVER, John Carrier
        Beyond the "Western Sea". Tucson, Univ. of Arizona Pr., 1965
                                            E103.W4

97

0955   WEIR, Ruth Cromer
            Leif Ericson, explorer. Abingdon-Cokesbury Pr., 1951
                                        E105.W4

0956   WEISE, Arthur James
            The discoveries of America in the year 1525. Putnam, 1884
                                        E101.W42

0957   WELZL, Jan
            Thirty years in the golden north. The Macmillan Co., 1932
                                        G825.W4.1932a

0958   WRIGHT, Louis Booker   comp.
            West and by north. Delacorte Pr., 1971   E101.W9

0959   BENNETT, Edna Mae
        Turquoise and the Indian. Denver, Sage Books, 1966   E78.S7B4

0960   CASTELLÓ YTURBIDE, Teresa
        El traje indígena en México. México, Instituto Nacional
        de Antropología e Historia, 1965-66   fF1219.3.C75C3.Spec.Coll.

0961   FOSTER, George McClelland
        A primitive Mexican economy. J. J. Augustin, 1942
                            (MAES)   E51.A556.v.5

0962   GREGG, Josiah
        Commerce of the prairies. Norman, Univ. of Oklahoma Pr., 1954
                                            F800.G83.1954

0963   LINDEBORG, Karl Hartvig
        Economic analysis of minimum-size farms for various levels
        of income on the Fort Hall Indian Reservation. Moscow,
        Univ. of Idaho, Bureau of Business and Economic Research,
        1961   HC107.I2I17.no.4

0964   McNITT, Frank
        The Indian Traders. Norman, Univ. of Oklahoma Pr., 1962
                                            E98.C7M25

0965   PEAKE, Ora Brooks
        A history of the United States Indian factory system, 1795-1822.
        Denver, Sage Books, 1954   E98.C7P4

0966   QUIMBY, George Irving
        Indian culture and European trade goods. Madison, Univ. of
        Wisconsin Pr., 1966   E78.G7Q49

0967   SAUM, Lewis O.
        The fur trader and the Indian. Seattle, Univ. of Washington Pr.,
        1965   E77.S28

0968   SNODGRASS, Marjorie P.
        Economic development of American Indians and Eskimos,
        1930 through 1967: a bibliography. Washington, U.S. Bureau
        of Indian Affairs; for sale by the Supt. of Docs., U. S.
        Govt. Print. Off., 1968 (i.e. 1969)   ref.Z1209.S56

0969   _Studies in Middle American economics_. New Orleans, Middle
        American Research Institute, Tulane Univ., 1968
                            (TMAI)   F1421.T95.no.29

0970   TAX, Sol
        <u>Penny capitalism: A Guatemalan Indian economy</u>. Washington,
        U. S. Govt. Print. Off., 1953 (SIP)   E51.S4.no.16

0971   TAXAY, Don
        <u>Money of the American Indians and other primitive currencies
        of the Americas</u>.   Nummus Pr., 1970   E59.M7T3

0972   TERRELL, John Upton
        <u>Traders of the Western morning</u>.   Los Angeles, Southwest
        Museum, 1967   E98.C7T4

0973   ALL-INDIAN STATEWIDE CONFERENCE ON CALIFORNIA INDIAN EDUCATION.
1st, NORTH FORK, CALIF.
California Indian education: report of the First All-Indian
Statewide Conference on California Indian Education. Modesto,
Calif., Ad Hoc Committee on California Indian Education, 1967
                         E97.A4.1967

0974   ANDERSON, Kenneth Eugene
The educational achievement of Indian children. Lawrence?,
Kansas., Bureau of Indian Affairs, Dept. of the Interior, 1953
                         E97.A5

09741   AURBACH, Herbert A.
The status of American Indian education. Univ. Park, Pennsylvania
State Univ., 1970   E97.A9

0975   BEATTY, Willard Walcott
Education for action. Chilocco, Okl., Printing Dept.,
Chilocco Agricultural School, 1944   E97.B34

0976   BERGMAN, Robert
Problems of cross-cultural educational research and evaluation:
The Rough Rock Demonstration School. Minneapolis, Univ. of
Minnesota, 1969   E97.B36

0977   BERRY, Brewton
The education of American Indians. Washington, U. S. Dept. of
Health, Education and Welfare, Office of Education, Bureau of
Research, 1968   E97.B37

0978   BRYDE, John F.
The Indian student. Vermillion, S. D., Dakota Pr., 1970
(1966)   E97.B75.1970

0979   BRYDE, John F.
Indian students and guidance. Boston, Houghton Mifflin Co.,
1971   E98.P95B68

0980   CHAPMAN, William McKissack
Remember the wind. Philadelphia, Lippincott, 1965 E97.6.S15C5

0981   EASTMAN, Elaine (Goodale)
Pratt, the red man's Moses. Norman, Univ. of Oklahoma Pr.,
1935   E97.P915

09811   Education of American Indians.
         Distributed by the Office of Community Programs, Center for
         Urban and Regional Affairs, Minn., Univ. of Minnesota, (1970)
         (National study of American Indians, ed., v.2)   E97.E4

09812   FUCHS, Estelle
         To live on this earth; American Indian education.   Doubleday,
         1972   E97.F8

0982   GARRARD, James Lathrop
         A survey of the education of the Indians of Mexico as a
         factor in their incorporation into modern Mexican society.
         Ann Arbor, University Microfilms, 1970   LC2631.G3.1970

09821   HALL, Geraldine
         Kee's home; a beginning Navajo/English reader.   Flagstaff,
         Northland Pr., 1972   PM2007.H25.1972

09822   HAVIGHURST, Robert J.
         The education of Indian children and youth; summary report
         and recommendations.   Distributed by the Office of Community
         Programs, Minn., Univ. of Minnesota, 1970, (National study
         of American Indians, ed., v.5)   E97.H3

0983   HENRY, Jeannette
         Textbooks and the American Indian.   San Francisco, Indian
         Historian Pr., 1970   E76.6.H44

09831   JONES, Louis Thomas
         Amerindian education.   San Antonio, Texas, Naylor Co., 1972
                                                   E97.J65

0984   KELLY, William H.
         A study of southern Arizona schoolage Indian children,
         1966-67.   Tucson, Bureau of Ethnic Research, Dept. of
         Anthropology, Univ. of Arizona, 1967   E78.A7K35

0985   KING, Alfred Richard
         The school at Mopass.   Holt, Rinehart and Winston, 1967
                                                   E78.Y8K5

0986   McCALLUM, James Dow ed.
         The letters of Eleazar Wheelock's Indians.   Hanover, N.H.,
         Dartmouth College Publications, 1932   E97.6.M5M2

0987   MALONEY, Gertrude Coyte
         A study of the Pueblo Indians developed in grade III,
         the University elementary school, the University of California
         at Los Angeles.   Sacramento, Printed in California State
         Print. Off., G. H. Moore, State Printer, 1938
                                     refL124.B62.v.7.no.10.1938

0988   NATIONAL RESEARCH CONFERENCE ON AMERICAN INDIAN EDUCATION,
        PENNSYLVANIA STATE UNIVERSITY, 1967.
        Proceedings. Kalamazoo, Mich., Society for the Study of
        Social Problems, cover 1967   E97.N29.1967

0989   NEW, Lloyd H.
        Institute of American Indian Arts; cultural difference as
        the basis for creative education. Washington, U.S. Indian
        Arts and Crafts Board; for sale by the Supt. of Docs.,
        U.S. Govt. Print. Off., 1968 (NAA)   E98.A7N36.no.1

0990   OFFICER, James E.
        Indians in school. Tucson, Bureau of Ethnic Research,
        Univ. of Arizona, 1956   E97.5.O34

09901   OHANNESSIAN, Sirarpi
        The study of the problems of teaching English to American
        Indians; report and recommendation, July 1967. Washington,
        Center for Applied Linguistics, 1968 (?) E97.O5

0991   ORATA, Pedro Tamesis
        Fundamental education in an Amerindian community. Washington?,
        U. S. Dept. of the Interior, Bureau of Indian Affairs, 1953
                                                E97.O7

0992   PAYNE, Lois Estelle
        A brief history of the education of the Indians of Oregon
        and Washington. Stanford, Calif., 1935 E97.P3

0993   PETERSON, Shailer Alvarey
        How well are Indian children educated? Washington, U. S.
        Indian Service, 1948   E97.P45

0994   POTTS, Alfred M. ed.
        Developing curriculum for Indian children. Alamosa, Colo.,
        Center for Cultural Studies, Adams State College, 1964 E97.P56

0995   POWERS, Joseph F.
        Brotherhood through education. Fayette, Upper Iowa Univ.,
        1965   E97.P6

0996   PRATT, Richard Henry
        Battlefield and classroom. New Haven, Yale Univ. Pr., 1964
                                                E97.6.C2P89.1964

0997   PRESTON, Caroline Eldredge
        Psychological testing with northwest coast Alaskan Eskimos.
        Provincetown, Mass., 1964   LB1101.G4.v.69.p.323-419

0998   SMITH, Anne Marie
        Indian education in New Mexico. Albuquerque, Division of
        Government Research, Institute for Social Research and
        Development, Univ. of New Mexico, 1968 E97.S6

09981   Teachers and curriculum for American Indian youth.
        Distributed by the Office of Community Programs, Center
        for Urban and Regional Affairs, Minn., University of
        Minnesota (1970) (National study of American Indians ed.,
        v.3)   E97.T4

0999   U. S. SUPERINTENDENT OF INDIAN SCHOOLS.
        Course of study for the Indian schools of the United
        States, industrial and literary. Washington, Govt. Print.
        Off., 1901   E97.U59

1000   WALL, Claude Leon
        History of Indian education in Nevada, 1861-1951. Reno,
        Univ. of Nevada Pr., 1952   E97.W3

1001   WOODS, Richard G.
        Education-related preferences and characteristics of
        college-aspiring urban Indian teenagers: a preliminary
        report. Minneapolis, Training Center for Community
        Programs, Univ. of Minnesota, 1969 E78.M7W6

1002   YOUNG, Robert Fitzgibbon ed.
        Comenius in England. Arno, 1971 (1932) LB475.C6Y63.1971

1003   ZURCHER, Louis A.
        The leader and the lost. Worcester, Mass., 1967
                       LB1101.G4.v.76.p.23-93

1004   ABEL, Annie Heloise
        The American Indian as slaveholder and seccessionist.
        Cleveland, The Arthur H. Clark Co., 1915   E540.I3A19

1005   ABEL, Annie Heloise
        The American Indian under reconstruction. Cleveland,
        The Arthur H. Clark Co., 1925   E540.I3A22

1006   ADAIR, James
        Adair's History of the American Indians. Argonaut Pr.,
        1966   E77.A22.1966

10061   ADLER, Bill, comp.
        The American Indian; the first victim. Morrow, 1972
                                                 E77.2.A3

1007   AMERICAN HERITAGE
        Book of Indians. American Heritage Heritage Pub. Co.;
        book trade distribution by Simon & Schuster, 1961   E58.A53

1008   American Indians: facts and future.
        Arno Pr., 1970   E98.E2A45

1009   ANDRIST, Ralph K.
        The long death. Macmillan, 1964   E78.W5A593

1010   Anecdotes of the American Indians, Illustrating their
        eccentricities of character. A. V. Blake, 1844   E77.A59

1011   ARMILLAS, Pedro
        Programma de historia de la América indígena. Washington,
        Unión Panamericana, 1961   E16.A72.1961

10111   Assorted research papers. Distributed by the Office of Community
        Programs, Center for Urban and Regional Affairs, Minn., Univ.
        of Minnesota, 1970 (National study of American Indians, ed.,
        v.1)   E97.A8

1012   BAHR, Howard M. comp.
        Native Americans today: sociological perspectives. Harper &
        Row, 1972   E98.S67B3

1013   BAITY, Elizabeth (Chesley)
        Americans before Columbus. Viking Pr., 1961   E58.B18.1961

1014   BALDWIN, Gordon Cortis
        Games of the American Indian. Norton, 1969   E98.G2B3.1969b

1015   BALDWIN, Gordon Cortis
        Race against time. Putnam, 1966   E77.9.B3

1016   BALLESTEROS GAIBROIS, Manuel
        Indigenismo americano. Madrid, Ediciones Cultura
        Hispánica, 1961   E59.G6B3

1017   BARBÉ-MARBOIS, François, marquis de
        Our revolutionary forefathers. Duffield & Co., 1929
                                        E163.B23

1018   BEACH, William Wallace ed.
        The Indian miscellany. Albany, J. Munsell, 1877
                                        E77.B36

1019   BELOUS, Russell E.
        Will Soule. Los Angeles, Ward Ritchie Pr., 1969
                                        fE77.5.B4

1020   BENEDICT, Burton
        Indians in a plural society. London, H. M. Stationery
        Off., 1961   JV33.G7A48.no.34

1021   BENNDORF, Helga
        Indianer Nordamerikas 1760-1860. Aus der Sammlung Speyer.
        (Ausstellung. Katalog.) Offenbach a.M., Deutsches Ledermuseum,
        Deutsches Schuhmuseum, 1968   E56.B4

1022   BRANDON, William
        The American heritage Book of Indians. Dell Pub. Co.,
        1964 (1961)   E58.B813

1023   BRENNAN, Lois A.
        American dawn. Macmillan, 1970   E57.B7

1024   BRINTON, Daniel Garrison
        The American race. Johnson Reprint, 1970 (1891)
                                        E58.B86.1970

1025   BRINTON, Daniel Garrison
        Essays of an Americanist. I. Ethnologic and archaeologic.
        II. Mythology and folk lore. III. Graphic systems and
        literature. IV. Linguistic. Philadelphia, D. McKay,
        1890?   E54.B85

1026   BRONSON, Ruth Muskrat
        Indians are people, too. Friendship Pr., 1944 E77.B86

1027   BROWN, Frederick Martin
        America's yesterday. Philadelphia, Lippincott, 1937
                                        E58.B875

1028   BURBANK, Elbridge Ayer
        Burbank among the Indians. Caldwell, Id., The Caxton
        Printers, Ltd., 1944   E78.W5B8

1029   CADILLAC, Antoine de la Mothe
        The western country in the 17th century. Chicago, Lakeside
        Pr., 1947   E78.N76C3

1030   CARR, Emily
        Klee Wyck. Farrar & Rinehart, Inc., 1942 E78.B9C37.1942

1031   CASAS, Bartolomé de las
        Apologética historia sumaria. México, 1967 E85.C3.1967

1032   CATLIN, George
        Adventures of the Ojibbeway and Ioway Indians in England,
        France, and Belgium. London, The author, 1852 E77.C414

1033   CATLIN, George
        The boy's Catlin. My life among the Indians. C. Scribner's
        Sons, 1909   E77.C395

1034   CATLIN, George
        Catlin's notes of eight years' travels and residence in
        Europe, with his North American Indian collection. London,
        The author, 1848   E77.C412

1035   CATLIN, George
        Die Indianer und die während eines achtjährigen Aufenthalts
        unter den wildesten ihrer Stämme erlebten Abenteuer und Schicksale
        von G. Catlin. Berlin-Friedenau, Verlag Continent, 1924
                                                E77.C398.1924

1036   CATLIN, George
        North American Indians. Edinburgh, J. Grant, 1926 E77.C3973

1037   CATTERMOLE, E. G.
        Famous frontiersmen, pioneers and scouts. Chicago, M. A. Donohue,
        1890?   E85.C37.1890

1038   COLLIER, John
        The Indians of the Americas. W. W. Norton, 1947   E58.C6

1039   COMAS, Juan
        Los Congresos Internacionales de Americanistas. Mexico,
        Instituto Indigenista Interamericano, 1954   E51.I73

1040   COMAS, Juan
        Una década de Congresos Internacionales de Americanistas,
        1952-1962. México, Universidad Nacional Autónoma de México,
        1964   E51.I7292.1964

1041   CONVOCATION OF AMERICAN INDIAN SCHOLARS, 1st, PRINCETON
        UNIVERSITY, 1970.
        Indian voices. San Francisco, Indian Historian Pr.,
        1970   E77.2.C6.1970

1042   CURTIS, Edward S.
        Indian days of the long ago. Yonkers-on-Hudson, N.Y.,
        World Book Co., 1914   E78.W5C9

1043   CURTIS, Edward S.
        The North American Indian. Johnson Reprint, 1970 (1907-30)
                                                      E77.C97.1970

10431   DAHLBERG, Edward comp.
        The gold of Ophir; travels, myths, and legends in the
        new world. Dutton, 1972   E77.2D3.1972

1044   DANIELS, Walter Machray ed.
        American Indians. Wilson, 1957   E77.D3

1045   DEBO, Angie
        A history of the Indians of the United States. Norman,
        Univ. of Oklahoma Pr., 1970   E77.D34

1046   DELLENBAUGH, Frederick Samuel
        The North-Americans of yesterday. G. Putnam's Sons, 1901
                                                      E77.D35

1047   DELORIA, Ella Cara
        Speaking of Indians. Friendship Pr., 1944 E77.D355

1048   DELORIA, Vine
        We talk, you listen: new tribes, new turf. Macmillan,
        1970   E184.A1D33

1049   DENNIS, Henry C.
        The American Indian, 1492-1970. Dobbs Ferry, N.Y.,
        Oceana, 1971   E77.D393

1050   DENVER. PUBLIC LIBRARY.
        David F. Barry: catalog of photographs. Denver, 1960
                                                      ref.E77.D4

1051   DENVER CONFERENCE WITH THE INDIAN ELDERS, 1968.
        Can the redman help the white man? G. Church, 1970
                                                      E76.D45.1968

1052   DE VOTO, Bernard Augustine
        The course of empire. Boston, Houghton Mifflin, 1952
                                                      E179.5.D4

1053   DODGE, Richard Irving
        Our wild Indians: thirty-three years' personal experience
        among the Red Men of the great West. Hartford, Conn.,
        A. D. Worthington, 1890   E78.W5D6.1890

1054   DOUGLAS-LITHGOW, Robert Alexander
        Dictionary of American-Indian place and proper names in
        New England. Salem, Mass., Salem Pr.: The Salem Pr. Co.,
        1909   ref.F2.D72

1055   DRAKE, Samuel Gardner
        Biography and history of the Indians of North America,
        from its discovery. Boston, B.B. Mussey & Co., 1851 E77.D71

1056   DRAKE, Samuel Gardner
        Indian captivities. Auburn, Derby and Miller, 1851 (1839)
                                                   E85.D772.Spec.Coll.

1057   DRIVER, Harold Edson ed.
        The Americas on the eve of discovery. Englewood Cliffs, N.J.,
        Prentice-Hall, 1964   E58.D67

1058   DRIVER, Harold Edson
        Indians of North America. Chicago, Univ. of Chicago Pr., 1961
                                                   E58.D68

1059   EASTBURN, Robert
        The dangers and sufferings of Robert Eastburn, and his
        deliverance from Indian captivity. Cleveland, The Burrows
        Brothers Co., 1904   E87. 12

1060   EASTMAN, Edwin
        Seven and nine years among the Comanches and Apaches;
        an autobiography. Toyahvale, Tex., Frontier Book, 1964 (1879)
                                                   E87.E13.1879a

1061   ECKERT, Allan W.
        Wilderness empire. Boston, Little, Brown, 1969 E195.E25

1062   EGGAN, Frederick Russell
        The American Indian. Chicago, Aldine Pub. Co., 1966 E98.S7E4

1063   EMBREE, Edwin Rogers
        Indians of the Americas; historical pageant. Boston,
        Houghton Mifflin Co., 1939   E58.E63

1064   ERASMUS, Charles J.
        Man takes control. Minneapolis, Univ. of Minnesota Pr.,
        1961   F1219.1.S65E7

1065   FARB, Peter
       Man's rise to civilization as shown by the Indians of
       North America from primeval times to the coming of the
       industrial state. Dutton, 1968   E77.F36

1066   FARRAND, Livingston
       Basis of American history, 1500-1900. Harper & Brothers,
       1904   E77.F3

1067   FASSINI, Lillian Davids
       Indians of America. Racine, Wis., Whitman Publishing Co.,
       1935   E77.F38.Spec.Coll.

1068   FINLEY, James Bradley
       Life among the Indians. Cincinnati, Curts & Jennings,
       185-   E77.F5.1850z

1069   FOHLEN, Claude
       L'agonie des Peaux-Rouges. Paris, Resma, 1970 E77.F63

1070   FORBES, Jack D. ed.
       The Indian in America's past. Englewood Cliffs, N.J.,
       Prentice-Hall, 1964   E77.F68

1071   FORBES, Jack D.
       Native Americans of California and Nevada. Healdsburg,
       Calif., Naturegraph Publishers, 1969   E78.C15F6

1072   FOREMAN, Grant
       Indian removal. Norman, Univ. of Oklahoma Pr., 1953
                             E78.I5F67.1953

1073   FROST, John
       Pioneer mothers of the West. Boston, Lee and Shepard, 1859
                          CT3260.F7

1074   FROST, John
       Thrilling adventures among the Indians. Philadelphia,
       J. W. Bradley, 1849   E85.F93.Spec.Coll.

1075   FYNN, Arthur John
       The American Indian as a product of environment. Boston,
       Little, Brown, and Co., 1907   E99.P9F9

1076   GAMIO, Manuel
       Consideraciones sobre el problema indígena. México,
       Instituto Indigenista Interamericano, 1966 E58.G3.1966

1077   GARLAND, Hamlin
       The book of the American Indian. Harper & Brothers,
       1923   fE77.G23.Spec.Coll.

1078   GLASER, Lynn comp.
        Engraved America. Philadelphia, Ancient Orb Pr.; dist. by
        R. V. Boswell, Beverly Hills, Calif., 1970   fE178.5.G55.Spec.Coll.

1079   GOODRICH, Samuel Griswold
        History of the Indians, of North and South America. Boston,
        Bradbury, Soden, 1844   E58.G65

1080   GOODRICH, Samuel Griswold
        The manners, customs, and antiquities of the Indians of
        North and South America. Boston, Bradbury, Soden and Co., 1844
                                              E58.G657

1081   GRAVES, Charles Sumner
        Before the white man came. Yreka, California., The Siskiyou
        1934   E78.C15G62

1082   GRINNELL, George Bird
        The North American Indians of to-day. London, C.A. Pearson,
        1900   fE77.G85.1900

1083   GRINNELL, George Bird
        The story of the Indian. D. Appleton and Co., 1895 E78.W5G8

1084   GRISHAM, Noel
        A serpent for a dove. Austin, Tex., Jenkins Pub., 1971   E77.G88

1085   GWALTNEY, John L.
        The thrice shy. Columbia Univ. Pr., 1970 F1221.C56G9

1086   HAGAN, William Thomas
        The Indian in American history. Macmillan, 1963   E77.H14

1087   HARKINS, Arthur M.
        Attitudes and characteristics of selected Wisconsin Indians.
        Minneapolis, Univ. of Minnesota, Training Center for Community
        Programs, 1969   E78.M7H28

1088   HASTINGS, Mrs. Susannah (Willard) Johnson
        A narrative of the captivity of Mrs. Johnson. Springfield,
        Mass., H.R. Huntting Co., 1907   E87.H36

1089   HAVIGHURST, Robert James
        American Indian and white children; a sociopsychological
        investigation. Chicago, Univ. of Chicago Pr., 1955 E98.C5H38

1090   HEATH, Monroe
        Our American Indians at a glance. Menlo Park, Calif.,
        Pacific Coast Pub., 1961   E77.H4

1091   HIBBEN, Frank Cummings
        The lost Americans. Crowell, 1961 (1946) E58.H5

1092   HILL, J. L.
        The passing of the Indian and buffalo. Long Beach,
        Calif., G. W. Moyle, 1917?   E77.H58

1093   HONORÉ, Pierre
        In quest of the White God. London, Hutchinson, 1963
                                        E65.H683.1963

1094   HUGHES, John Taylor
        Doniphan's Expedition. Chicago, Rio Grande Pr., 1962
                                        E405.2.H94

1095   HUGHES, John Taylor
        Doniphan's expedition and the conquest of New Mexico
        and California. Topeka, Kan., The author, 1907 E405.2.H9

1096   HULBERT, Winifred
        Indian Americans. Friendship Pr., 1932 E77.H92

1097   HUMFREVILLE, James Lee
        Twenty years among our hostile Indians. Hunter & Co.,
        1903   E78.W5H92.1903

1098   HUNTER, John Dunn
        Memoirs of a captivity among the Indians of North
        America. London, Printed for Longman, Hurst, Rees, Orme,
        and Brown, 1824   E87.H94.1824.Spec.Coll.

1099   HUNTINGTON, Ellsworth
        The red man's continent. New Haven, Yale Univ. Pr.,
        1921   E173.C555.v.1

1100   HYDE, George E.
        Indians of the High Plains: from the prehistoric period
        to the coming of Europeans. Norman, Univ. of Oklahoma Pr.,
        1959   E78.W5H97

1101   HYDE, George E.
        Indians of the woodlands: from prehistoric times to
        1725. Norman, Univ. of Oklahoma Pr., 1962 E77.H98

1102   INTERNATIONAL CONGRESS OF AMERICANISTS. 29th, NEW YORK, 1949.
        Selected papers. Chicago, Univ. of Chicago Pr., 1951-52
                                        E65.I57

1103   JOHNSTON, Bernice Eastman
        Speaking of Indians, with an accent on the Southwest.
        Tucson, Univ. of Arizona Pr., 1970   E78.S7J66

1104   JONES, Daniel Webster
          Forty years among the Indians. Salt Lake City, Utah,
          Juvenile Instructor Office, 1890   E85.J76

1105   JONES, Louis Thomas
          Indians at work and play. San Antonio, Naylor, 1971 E98.G2J6

1106   JOSEPHY, Alvin M.
          The Indian heritage of America. Knopf, 1968   E58.J6

1107   KAPLAN, Bert
          A study of Rorschach responses in four cultures. Cambridge,
          Mass., The Museum, 1954 (PMP)   E51.H337.v.42.no.2

1108   KELEMEN, Pál
          Battlefield of the gods. London, G. Allen & Unwin, Ltd.,
          1937   F1219.K58

1109   KENNER, Charles L.
          A history of New Mexican-Plains Indian relations. Norman,
          Univ. of Oklahoma Pr., 1969   E78.N65K33

1110   KING, James T.
          War Eagle. Lincoln, Univ. of Nebraska Pr., 1963 E181.C315K5

1111   KIRK, Ruth
          The oldest man in America. Harcourt, Brace, Jovanovich,
          1970   E78.W3K5

1112   LA FARGE, Oliver ed.
          The changing Indian. Norman, Univ. of Oklahoma Pr., 1942
                                              E77.L24

1113   LA FARGE, Oliver
          A pictorial history of the American Indian. Crown Publishers,
          1956   fE77.L245

1114   LAFITAU, Joseph François
          Moeurs des sauvages ameriquains, comparées aux moeurs des
          premiers temps. Paris, Saugrain l'aîné (etc.), 1724 E58.L16

1115   LAUBER, Almon Wheeler
          Indian slavery in colonial times within the present limits
          of the United States. Columbia Univ., 1913 H31.C64.no.134

1116   LEUPP, Francis Ellington
          The Indian and his problem. C. Scribner's Sons, 1910 E77.L65

1117   LEUPP, Francis Ellington
          In Red man's land. Fleming H. Revell Co., 1914 E77.L64

1118   LEVINE, Stuart   comp.
            The American Indian today. Deland, Fla., Everett Edwards,
            1968   E77.2.L4

1119   LINDQUIST, Gustavus Elmer Emanuel
            The red man in the United States. George H. Doran Co.,
            1923   E77.L74

1120   LOCKE, Raymond Friday   comp.
            The American Indian. Los Angeles, Mankind Pub., 1970
                                                      E77.2.L6

1121   LONG, John
            John Long's voyages and travels in the years 1768-1788.
            Chicago, R. R. Donnelley & Sons Co., 1922   E77.L843

11211   Look to the mountain top. Gousha, 1972   E77.2L65

1122   McCREIGHT, Major Israel
            Firewater and forked tongues.   Pasadena, Calif., Trail's
            End Pub. Co., 1947   E77.M113

1123   MACFARLAN, Allan A.
            Book of American Indian games. Association Pr., 1958
                                                      E98.G2M25

1124   MACGREGOR, Frances M. (Cooke)
            Twentieth century Indians. G. P. Putnam's Sons, 1941
                                                      E77.M114

1125   McINTOSH, John
            The origin of the North American Indians. Cornish,
            Lamport & Co., 1853   E77.M127

1126   McKENNEY, Thomas Loraine
            The Indian tribes of North America, with biographical
            sketches and anecdotes of the principal chiefs. Edinburgh,
            J. Grant. 1933-34   E77.M135

1127   McKENNEY, Thomas Loraine
            Memoirs, official and personal. Paine and Burgess, 1846
                                                      E77.M14

1128   McLAUGHLIN, James
            My friend the Indian. Boston, Houghton Mifflin, 1910
                                                      E77.M162

1129   MACLEAN, John
            The Indians, their manners and customs. Toronto, W. Briggs,
            1889   E78.C2M16

1130   MAC-LEAN y ESTENÓS, Roberto
        Indios de América. México, Instituto de Investigaciones
        Sociales, Universidad Nacional Autónoma de México, 1962
                                    E58.M16

1131   MACLEOD, William Christie
        The American Indian frontier. A. A. Knopf, 1928 E58.M17

1132   McNICKLE, D'Arcy
        They came here first. Philadelphia, J. B. Lippincott Co.,
        1949   E58.M18

1133   MAREK, Kurt W.
        The first America. Harcourt Brace Jovanovich, 1971 E77.9.M3713

1134   MARRIOTT, Alice Lee
        American epic. Putnam, 1969   E77.M28

1135   MAYER, Brantz
        Observations on Mexican history and archaeology. Washington,
        Smithsonian Institution, 1856   Q11.S68.v.9.no.4

1136   MEANS, Philip Ainsworth
        History of the Spanish conquest of Yucatan and of the
        Itzas. Cambridge, Mass., The Museum, 1917
                            (PMP)   E51.H337.v.7

1137   MELLING, John
        Right to a future. Toronto, Published jointly by the
        Anglican Church of Canada and the United Church of Canada,
        1967   E78.C2M4

1138   MESSITER, Charles Alston
        Sport and adventures among the North American Indians.
        Abercrombie & Fitch, 1966   E88.M4.1966

1139   MEXICO. INSTITUTO NACIONAL DE ANTROPOLOGÍA E HISTORIA.
        Anales. t. 1- 1939/40- México, Secretaría de Educacion
        Pública   F1219.M6245

1140   MINER, William Harvey
        The American Indians, north of Mexico. Cambridge, Mass.,
        The University Pr., 1917   E77.M66

1141   MOGRIDGE, George
        The book of the Indians of North America. D. Appleton, 1844
                                    E77.M695

11411   MOGUIN, Wayne comp.
        Great documents in American Indian history. Praeger, 1973
                                    E77.2M66

115

1142   NAGLER, Mark
        Indians in the city. Ottawa, Canadian Research Centre
        for Anthropology, Saint Paul Univ., 1970   E78.05N3

1143   NATIONAL GEOGRAPHIC SOCIETY, Washington, D. C.
        National Geographic on Indians of the Americas.
        Washington, 1963 (1955)   E58.N3.1963

1144   NICOLAU d'OLWER, Luis ed.
        Cronistas de las culturas precolombinas. México, Fondo
        de Cultura Económica, 1963   E58.N5

1145   North American Indians in historical perspective.
        Random, 1971   E77.N63

1146   OGDEN, Peter Skene
        Traits of American Indian life & character, by a fur
        trader. San Francisco, Grabhorn Pr., 1933   E78.W3032

1147   O'MEARA, Walter
        The last portage. Boston, Houghton Mifflin, 1962
                                                   E87.T16056

1148   OSWALT, Wendell H.
        This land was theirs. Wiley, 1966   E77.08

1149   OWEN, Roger C. comp.
        The North American Indians. Macmillan, 1967 E77.2.093

1150   PALMER, Rose Amelia
        The North American Indians. Smithsonian Institution
        Series, Inc., 1929   E77.P17

1151   PARSONS, Elsie Worthington (Clews) ed.
        American Indian life, by several of its students.
        B. W. Huebsch, Inc., 1922   E58.P26

11511   PERROT, Nicolas
        Memoire sur les moeurs, costumes et relligion des
        sauvages de l'amerique septentrionale. Johnson Rep.,
        1968   E77.P45.1968

1152   PRITTS, Joseph
        Incidents of border life. Lancaster, Pa., G. Hills,
        1841   E85.P95.Spec.Coll.

1153   QUINN, Charles Russell
        Edward H. Davis and the Indians of the southwest United
        States and northwest Mexico. Downey, Calif., E. Quinn,
        1965   E88.D3Q5

1154   RADIN, Paul
            The story of the American Indian. Boni & Liveright, 1927
                                                    E58.R13.1927

1155   RAPHAEL, Ralph B.
            The book of American Indians. Greenwich, Conn., Fawcett
            Pub., 1953   E77.R18

1156   RAY, Verne Frederick
            Primitive pragmatists. Seattle, Univ. of Washington Pr.,
            1963   E99.M7R3

1157   Reference encyclopedia of the American Indian.
            B. Klein, 1967   ref.E76.2.R4

1158   RISTER, Carl Coke
            Border captives. Norman, Univ. of Oklahoma Pr., 1940
                                                    E85.R58

1159   RIVER BASIN SURVEYS.
            Papers. no. 1- Washington, U. S. Govt. Print. Off.,
            1953-   E51.U55

1160   ROGERS, Robert
            A concise account of North America. Johnson Rep., 1966
            (1765)   E162.R69.1966

1161   ROSENBLAT, Angel
            La población indígena y el mestizaje en América. Buenos
            Aires, Nova, 1954   E59.S7R6.1954

1162   SALOMON, Julian Harris
            The book of Indian crafts & Indian lore. Harper & Brothers,
            1928   E77.S2

1163   Schlesier, Karl H.
            The Indians of the United States. Wichita, Kan., Wichita
            State Univ., 1969   AS36.W62.no.81

1164   SCHOOLCRAFT, Henry Rowe
            The American Indians. Buffalo, G. H. Derby, 1851 E77.S3

1165   SCHOOLCRAFT, Henry Rowe
            Historical and statistical information respecting the
            history, condition and prospects of the Indian tribes of
            the United States. Paladin Pr., reprinted 1969 (1851-57)
                                                    fE77.S383

1166   SCHOOLCRAFT, Henry Rowe
            Information respecting the history, condition and prospects
            of the Indian tribes of the United States. Philadelphia,
            Lippincott, Grambo, 1851-57   fE77.S382.Spec.Coll.

1167   SCHOOLCRAFT, Henry Rowe
        The literary voyager. East Lansing, Michigan State
        Univ. Pr., 1962   E77.S405

1168   SCHOOLCRAFT, Henry Rowe
        Personal memoirs of a residence of thirty years with
        the Indian tribes on the American frontiers. Philadelphia,
        Lippincott, Grambo and Co., 1851   E77.S43.Spec.Coll.

1169   SCHRIEKE, Bertram Johannes Otto
        Alien Americans. The Viking Pr., 1936 E184.A1S36

1170   SELLARDS, Elias Howard
        Early man in America. Austin, Univ. of Texas Pr., 1952
                                                 E58.S44

1171   SETON, Ernest Thompson
        The book of woodcraft and Indian lore. Garden City,
        Doubleday, Page, 1912   SK601.S52

1172   SEYMOUR, Flora Warren (Smith)
        Lords of the valley. London, New York, Longmans, Green
        and Co., 1930   E195.J682

1173   SEYMOUR, Flora Warren (Smith)
        The story of the red man. Longmans, Green and Co.,
        1929   E77.S526

1174   SEYMOUR, Mrs. Flora Warren (Smith)
        We called them Indians. D. Appleton-Century Co., Inc.,
        1940   E77.S53

11741   SHEEHAN, Bernard W.
        Seeds of extinction; Jeffersonian philanthropy and the
        American Indian. North Carolina, Institute of Early
        American History and Culture, University of North
        Carolina Press, 1973   E93.S54

1175   SHORT, John Thomas
        The North Americans of antiquity. Harper & Brothers,
        1881   E58.S55.1881

1176   SMITH, De Cost
        Indian experiences. Caldwell, Id., The Caxton Printers,
        Ltd., 1943   E78.W5S66

1177   SMITH, Marian Wesley
        Indians of the urban Northwest. AMS Pr., 1969 (1949)
                        (CUCA)   E51.C7.v.36.1969

118

1178   SPENCER, Oliver M.
       The Indian captivity of O.M. Spencer. Chicago,
       R. R. Donnelley & Sons Co., 1917   E87.S746

1179   SPENCER, Robert F.
       The native Americans. Harper & Row, 1965 E77.S747

1180   SPICER, Edward Holland
       Cycles of conquest. Tucson, Univ. of Arizona Pr., 1962
                             E78.S7S6

1181   SPICER, Edward Holland
       A short history of the Indians of the United States.
       Van Nostrand Reinhold Co., 1969   E77.S754

1182   SPOONER, Walter Whipple
       The back-woodsmen. Cincinnati, W. E. Dibble & Co., 1883
                           E85.S76

1183   STARR, Frederick
       American Indians. Boston, D. C. Heath & Co., 1898 E77.S79

1184   STEELE, Zadock
       The Indian captive. Springfield, Mass., The H. R. Huntting Co.,
       1908   E87.S82

1185   STEINER, Stanley
       The new Indians. Harper & Row, 1967   E77.S83

11851   STORM, Hyemeyohsts
       Seven arrows. Harper, 1972   E98.S7.W56

1186   STOUTENBURGH, John Leeds
       Dictionary of the American Indian. Philosophical Library,
       1960   ref.E77.S84

1187   STOW, Edith
       Boys' games among the North American Indians. Dutton, 1924
                           E98.G2S8

1188   STRATTON, Royal B.
       Captivity of the Oatman girls. Literature House 1970 (1859)
                           E87.O13

1189   SWANTON, John Reed
       The Indian tribes of North America. Washington, U.S. Govt.
       Print. Off., 1952   (BAEB)   E51.U55.no.145

1190   TERRELL, John Upton
       American Indian almanac. World Pub. Co., 1971 E77.T34.1971

1191   THOMAS, Cyrus
        The Indians of North America in historic times. Philadelphia,
        Printed for subscribers only by G. Barrie & Sons, 1903
                                        E178.H7.v.2.

1192   TIBBLES, Thomas Henry
        Buckskin and blanket days. Doubleday, 1957 E78.W5T52

1193   TROTTER, George A.
        From feather, blanket, and tepee. Vantage Pr., 1955
                                        E78.W6T7

1194   UNDERHILL, Ruth Murray
        Red Man's America. Chicago, Univ. of Chicago Pr., 1953
                                        E77.U456

1195   VAN EVERY, Dale
        Ark of empire. Morrow, 1963   E310.V3

1196   VAN EVERY, Dale
        Forth to the wilderness. New American Library, 1962
        (1961)   E195.V3.1962

1197   VERRILL, Alpheus Hyatt
        The American Indian, North, South and Central America.
        D. Appleton and Co., 1930 (1927)   E58.V53

1198   VERRILL, Alpheus Hyatt
        Old civilizations of the new world. Tudor Publishing Co.,
        1938   E58.V55.1938

1199   VERRILL, Alpheus Hyatt
        Our Indians. G. P. Putnam's Sons, 1935 E77.V47

11991   VOGEL, Virgil J. comp.
        This country was ours; a documentary history of the
        American Indian. Harper, 1972   E77.2V63.1972

1200   WADDELL, Jack O. comp.
        The American Indian in urban society. Boston, Little,
        Brown, 1971   E98.S67W3

1201   WALKER, Deward E. comp.
        The emergent native Americans. Boston, Little, Brown,
        1972   E77.2.W3

1202   WALTERS, Madge Hardin (Smith)
        Early days and Indian ways. Los Angeles, Westernlore Pr.,
        1956   E78.W5W3

1203   WALTON, William
        The captivity and sufferings of Benjamin Gilbert and his
        family, 1780-83. Cleveland, Burrows Bros. Co., 1904   E87.G45

1204   WARDEN, David Baillie
        A statistical, political, and historical account of the
        United States of North America. Edinburgh, Printed for
        A. Constable, 1819   E165.W25

1205   WARING, Antonio J.
        The Waring papers. Cambridge, Mass., The Museum, 1968
                                                E78.S65W3

1206   WASHBURN, Wilcomb E. ed
        The Indian and the white man. Anchor Books, 1964   E77.W3

1207   WAX, Murray Lionel
        Indian Americans. Englewood Cliffs, N.J., Prentice-Hall,
        1971   E77.W4

1208   WHIPPLE, Henry Benjamin
        Lights and shadows of a long episcopate. Macmillan, 1899
                                                E78.M7W5

1209   WILLIAMS, John
        The redeemed captive returning to Zion. Kraus Reprint, 1969
                                                E87.W734.1969

1210   WILSON, Edmund
        Red, black, blond, and olive. Oxford Univ. Pr., 1956   G469.W55

1211   WISE, Jennings Cropper
        The red man in the new world drama. Macmillan, 1971
                                                E77.W796.1971

1212   WISSLER, Clark
        Adventurers in the wilderness. New Haven, Yale Univ. Pr.,
                                                E178.5.P22.v.1.

1213   WISSLER, Clark
        Indians of the United States. Doubleday, 1966 E77.W799.1966

1214   WISSLER, Clark
        The relation of nature to man in aboriginal America.
        Oxford Univ. Pr., 1926   E77.W82

1215   ASCHMANN, Homer
        The central desert of Baja California: demography and
        ecology. Berkeley, Univ. of California Pr., 1959
                            (IAM)   F1401.I22.no.42

1216   BARRETT, Samuel Alfred
        The ethno-geography of the Pomo and neighboring Indians.
        Berkeley, Univ. of California Pr., 1908
                            (UCPAE)   E51.C15.v.6.no.1

1217   BERREMAN, Joel Van Meter
        Tribal distribution in Oregon. Menasha, Wis., American
        Anthropological Assoc., 1937 (AAAM) GN2.A22.no.47

1218   BORAH, Woodrow Wilson
        The aboriginal population of central Mexico on the eve of
        the Spanish conquest. Berkeley, Univ. of California Pr.,
        1963   (IAM)   F1401.I22.no.45

1219   BORAH, Woodrow Wilson
        The population of central Mexico in 1548. Berkeley, Univ.
        of California Pr., 1960 (IAM)   F1401.I22.no.43

1220   CANADIAN ARCTIC EXPEDITION, 1913-1918.
        Report. Ottawa, King's Printer, 1919-46 G670.1913.C3

1221   Cartas, informes, diarios y derroteros.
        Culicán, Mex., 1927   F1231.C32.Spec.Coll.

1222   COOK, Sherburne Friend
        The historical demography and ecology of the Teotlalpan.
        Berkeley, Univ. of California Pr., 1949
                            (IAM)   F1401.I22.no.33

1223   COOK, Sherburne Friend
        The Indian population of central Mexico, 1531-1610.
        Berkeley, Univ. of California Pr., 1960
                            (IAM)   F1401.I22.no.44

1224   COOK, Sherburne Friend
        The population of the Mixteco Alta, 1520-1960. Berkeley,
        Univ. of California Pr., 1968 (IAM) F1401.I22.no.50

1225   COOK, Sherburne Friend
        Population trends among the California mission Indians.
        Berkeley and Los Angeles, Univ. of California Pr., 1940
                            (IAM)   F1401.I22.no.17

1226   HEWETT, Edgar Lee
        The physiography of the Rio Grande valley, New Mexico,
        in relation to Pueblo culture. Washington, Govt. Print.
        Off., 1913   (BAEB)   E51.U55.no.54

1227   KNOWLTON, Clark S. ed.
        Indian and Spanish American adjustments to arid and
        semiarid environments. Lubbock, Texas, Texas Technological
        College, 1964   HD209.K5

1228   KROEBER, Alfred Louis
        California place names of Indian origin. Berkeley,
        Univ. of California Pr., 1916 (UCPAE) E51.C15.v.12.no.2

12281   NEOG, Prafulla
        Chicago Indians; the effects of urban migration.
        Indiana, St. Augustine's Ctr. Am., 1970 E78.I3.N46

1229   OSGOOD, Cornelius
        The distribution of the northern Athapaskan Indians.
        New Haven, Pub. for the Section of Anthropology,
        Dept. of the Social Sciences, Yale Univ., by the Yale
        Univ. Pr.; London, H. Milford, Oxford Univ. Pr., 1936
                    (YUPA)   GN2.Y3.no.7

1230   RYDJORD, John
        Indian place-names: their origin, evolution, and meanings.
        Norman, Univ. of Oklahoma Pr., 1968   E98.N2R9

1231   SAUER, Carl Ortwin
        Aboriginal population of northwestern Mexico. Berkeley,
        Univ. of California Pr., 1935 (IAM) F401.I22.no.10

1232   SAUER, Carl Ortwin
        The distribution of aboriginal tribes and languages in
        northwestern Mexico. Berkeley, Univ. of California Pr.,
        1934   (IAM)   F1401.I22.no.5

1233   U. S. BUREAU OF THE CENSUS.
        Indian population in the United States and Alaska. 1910.
        Washington, U. S. Govt. Print. Off., 1915 f.ref.E77.U5

1234   WATERMAN, Thomas Talbot
        The Kepel fish dam. Berkeley, Univ. of California Pr.,
        1938   (UCPAE)   E51.C15.v.35.no.6

12341   WEIL, Thomas E.
        Area handbook for Panama. Washington, D. C., U. S.
        Govt. Print. Off., 1972   F1563.W36

1235   WILSON, Herbert Earl
        The lore and the lure of Sequoia. Los Angeles, Wolfer
        Printing Co., 1928   QK495.S5W5

1236   WISSLER, Clark
        Changes in population profiles among the northern plains
        Indians. American Museum of Natural History, 1936
                        (AMNHP)   GN2.A27.v.36.pt.1

1237   WISSLER, Clark
        Population changes among the northern Plains Indians.
        New Haven, Pub. for the Section of Anthropology, Dept.
        of the Social Sciences, Yale Univ., by the Yale Univ.
        Pr.; London, H. Milford, Oxford Univ. Pr., 1936
                        (YUPA)   GN2.Y3.no.1

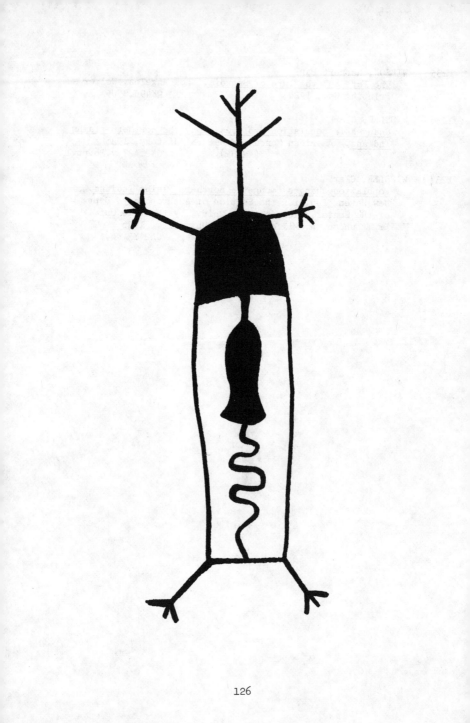

1238   ARNY, William Frederick Milton
        Indian agent in New Mexico. Santa Fe, N.M., Stagecoach Pr.,
        1967   E78.N65A84

1239   ATKIN, Edmond
        The Appalachian Indian frontier. Lincoln, Univ. of
        Nebraska Pr., 1967   E91.A8.1967

1240   ATKIN, Edmond
        Indians of the Southern Colonial frontier. Columbia,
        Univ. of South Carolina Pr., 1954   E91.A8.1954

1241   Attitudes of the colonial powers toward the American Indians.
        Salt Lake City, Univ. of Utah Pr., 1969   E59.G6A87

1242   BASAURI, Carlos
        La población indígena de México. México, Secretaría
        de Educación Pública. 1940   F1220.B27

1243   BROOKINGS INSTITUTION, WASHINGTON, D.C. INSTITUTE FOR GOVERNMENT
        RESEARCH.
        The problem of Indian administration. Baltimore, Md.,
        The Johns Hopkins Pr., 1928   E93.B873

1244   BROWNE, John Ross
        The California Indians, a clever satire on the government's
        dealings with its Indian wards. Indian Board of Co-operation,
        1919?   E78.C15B68

1245   BURNETTE, Robert
        The tortured Americans. Englewood Cliffs, N.J., Prentice-Hall,
        1971   E93.B973

1246   CAHN, Edgar S.
        Our brother's keeper: the Indian in white America.
        Washington, New Community Pr.; distributed by the World
        Pub. Co., New York, 1969   E98.E2C3

1247   CALIFORNIA. ATTORNEY GENERAL'S OFFICE.
        History and proposed settlement: claims of California Indians.
        Sacramento, State Print. Off., 1944   E78.C15C3

1248   CALIFORNIA. STATE ADVISORY COMMISSION ON INDIAN AFFAIRS.
        Final report to the Governor and the Legislature. Sacramento,
        1969   E78.C15A47

1249   CALIFORNIA. STATE ADVISORY COMMISSION ON INDIAN AFFAIRS.
        Progress report to the Governor and the Legislature
        on Indians in rural and reservation areas. Sacramento,
        1966   E98.E2C33

1250   CARDINAL, Harold
        The unjust society: the tragedy of Canada's Indians.
        Edmonton, Alberta, M. G. Hurtig, 1969   E92.C35

1251   Chronicles of American Indian protest. Fawcett, 1971
                                          E77.2.C5

1252   COHEN, Felix S.
        Handbook of Federal Indian law. Albuquerque, Univ. of
        New Mexico Pr., 1971 (1942)   fKF8205.A33.1971

1253   COHEN, Felix S.
        The legal conscience. New Haven, Yale Univ. Pr., 1960
                                          KB199.J9C6

1254   COMMISSION ON THE RIGHTS, LIBERTIES, AND RESPONSIBILITIES
        OF THE AMERICAN INDIAN.
        The Indian, America's unfinished business. Norman,
        Univ. of Oklahoma Pr., 1966   E93.C72

1255   DELORIA, Vine comp.
        Of utmost good faith. San Francisco, Straight Arrow
        Books, 1971   E93.D38

1256   DIXON, Joseph Kossuth
        The vanishing race, the last great Indian council.
        Doubleday, Page & Co., 1914 (1913)   E77.D6

1257   ELLIS, Richard N.
        General Pope and U. S. Indian policy. Albuquerque,
        Univ. of New Mexico Pr., 1970   E93.E45

12571   ELLIS, Richard N.
        The western American Indian: case studies in tribal
        history. Lincoln, Univ. of Nebraska Pr., 1972   E93.E46

1258   FANSHEL, David
        Far from the reservation. Metuchen, N. J., Scarecrow,
        1972   HV875.F15

1259   FEY, Harold Edward
        Indians and other Americans; two ways of life meet.
        Harper, 1959   E93.F37

1260   FOREMAN, Grant
        Advancing the frontier, 1830-1860. Norman, The Univ. of
        Oklahoma Pr., 1933   E93.F64

1261   FOREMAN, Grant
        The last trek of the Indians. Chicago, Univ. of Chicago Pr.,
        1946   E93.F67

1262   FRITZ, Henry Eugene
        The movement for Indian assimilation, 1860-1890. Philadelphia,
        Univ. of Pennsylvania Pr., 1963   E93.F96

1263   GESSNER, Robert
        Massacre; a survey of today's American Indian. J. Cape
        and H. Smith, 1931   E93.G39

1264   GOODNER, James
        Indian Americans in Dallas: migrations, missions, and styles
        of adaptation. Minneapolis, Training Center for Community
        Programs, Univ. of Minnesota, 1969   E78.T4G6

1265   HAGAN, William Thomas
        American Indians. Chicago, Univ. of Chicago Pr., 1961 E93.H2

1266   HAGAN, William Thomas
        Indian police and judges. New Haven, Yale Univ. Pr., 1966
                KB79.I6H3

1267   HANKS, Jane (Richardson)
        Law and status among the Kiowa Indians. J. J. Augustin, 1940
               (MAES)   E51.A556.v.1

1268   HARKINS, Arthur M.
        Attitudes of Minneapolis agency personnel toward urban
        Indians. Minneapolis, Training Center for Community
        Programs, Univ. of Minnesota, 1968   E78.M7H285

1269   HARMON, George Dewey
        Sixty years of Indian affairs, political, economic, and
        diplomatic, 1789-1850. Kraus Reprint, 1969 (1941) E93.H274.1969

1270   HERTZBERG, Hazel W.
        The search for an American Indian identity. Syracuse, N.Y.,
        Syracuse Univ. Pr., 1971   E91.H47

1271   HOOPES, Alban W.
        Indian affairs and their administration. Philadelphia,
        Univ. of Pennsylvania Pr.; London, H. Milford, Oxford
        Univ. Pr., 1932   E93.H76

1272   HORSMAN, Reginald
        Expansion and American Indian policy, 1783-1812. East
        Lansing, Michigan State Univ. Pr., 1967   E93.H79

1273   HORSMAN, Reginald
        Matthew Elliott, British Indian agent.   Detroit,
        Wayne State Univ. Pr., 1964   E92.E45H6

1274   HUMPHREY, Seth King
        The Indian dispossessed. Boston, Little, Brown, and Co.,
        1906   E93.H928

1275   INDIAN RIGHTS ASSOCIATION.
        Annual report of the Board of directors. 1st-52d, 1883-1934.
        Philadelphia, Office of the Indian Rights Association,
        1884-1934.   E93.I39

1276   JACKSON, Helen Maria (Fiske) Hunt
        A century of dishonor. Boston, Little, Brown, 1905
                                                   E93.J13.1905

1277   JACOBS, Wilbur R.
        Diplomacy and Indian gifts. Stanford, Stanford Univ. Pr.,
        1950   E195.J2

12771   JACOBS, Wilbur R.
        Dispossessing the American Indian; Indians and whites
        on the colonial frontier. Scribner, 1972 E91.J3.1972

1278   JOHNSON, Kenneth M.
        K-344. Los Angeles, Dawson's Book Shop, 1966
                                                   KF8208.J6.Spec.Coll.

1279   JONES, Douglas C.
        The Treaty of Medicine Lodge. Norman, Univ. of Oklahoma
        Pr., 1966   E78.G73J6

1280   JOSEPHY, Alvin M. comp.
        Red power: the American Indians' fight for freedom.
        American Heritage Pr., 1971   E93.J67

1281   KELLY, Roger E.
        American Indians in small cities: a survey of urban
        acculturation in two northern Arizona communities.
        Flagstaff, Dept. of Rehabilitation, Northern Arizona
        University, 1966   E78.A7K33

12811   KICKINGBIRD, Kirke
        One hundred million acres. Macmillan, 1973 E98.L3.K52

130

1282   KNEALE, Albert H.
           Indian agent. Caldwell, Id., Caxton Printers, 1950 E93.K6

1283   LA FARGE, Oliver
           As long as the grass shall grow. Alliance Book Corp.,
           Longmans, Green & Co., 1940   E93.L17

1284   LAKE MOHONK CONFERENCE ON THE INDIAN.
           Report. 1st-35th; 1883-1929. Mohonk Lake, N.Y., etc.,
           1883-1930   E93.L19

1285   LEAGUE OF WOMEN VOTERS OF MINNEAPOLIS.
           Indians in Minneapolis. Minneapolis, 1968   E78.M7L4

1286   LEVITAN, Sar A.
           Big brother's Indian programs with reservations. McGraw-Hill,
           1971   E93.L66

1287   LLAGUNA, José A.
           La personalidad jurídica del indio y el III Concilio
           Provincial Mexicano, 1585. Mexico, Editorial Porrua,
           1963   F1219.3.L4L5

1288   McGILLYCUDDY, Julia E. (Blanchard)
           McGillycuddy, agent. Stanford Univ., Calif., Stanford
           Univ. Pr.; London , H. Milford, Oxford Univ. Pr., 1941
                                                       E78.S63M15

1289   MANYPENNY, George Washington
           Our Indian wards. Cincinnati, R. Clark & Co., 1880 E93.M29

1290   MARDOCK, Robert Winston
           The reformers and the American Indian. Columbia, Univ. of
           Missouri Pr., 1971   E93.M37

1291   MEYER, William
           Native Americans: the new Indian resistance. International
           Publishers, 1971   E93.M58

1292   MOHR, Walter Harrison
           Federal Indian relations, 1774-1788. AMS Pr., 1971
                                                       E93.M74.1971

1293   MOOREHEAD, Warren King
           The American Indian in the United States, period 1850-1914.
           Freeport, N.Y., Books for Libraries Pr., 1969 E93.M8.1969

12931   MORRIS, Alexander
           The treaties of Canada with the Indians of Manitoba. (Coles
           Canadian Collection) Canada, Coles Pubs., 1971 (1880)
                                                       E92.M87.1880a

131

1294   MORSE, Jedidiah
        A report to the Secretary of War of the United States on
        Indian affairs. A. M. Kelley, 1970 (1822) E77.M88.1970

12941   NAACP LEGAL DEFENSE AND EDUCATIONAL FUND .
        An even chance. NAACP, 1971   E97.3.N2

1295   NAMMACK, Georgiana C.
        Fraud, politics, and the dispossession of the Indians.
        Norman, Univ. of Oklahoma Pr., 1969   E93.N22

1296   NEW MEXICO. EMPLOYMENT SECURITY COMMISSION.
        Minority groups in New Mexico. New Mexico, 1969
                                                F805.M5A3

1297   PEARCE, Roy Harvey
        The savages of America. Baltimore, Johns Hopkins Pr.,
        1953   E93.P4

1298   PEITHMANN, Irvin M.
        Broken peace pipes. Springfield, Ill., Thomas, 1964
                                                E77.P4

1299   PIERRE, George
        American Indian crisis. San Antonio, Naylor Co., 1971
                                                P91.P53

1300   POWERS, Mabel
        The Indian as peacemaker. Fleming H. Revell Co., 1932
                                                E95.P88

1301   PRIEST, Loring Benson
        Uncle Sam's stepchildren. Octagon Books, 1969 (1942)
                                                E93.P95.1969

1302   PRUCHA, Francis Paul
        American Indian policy in the formative years: the Indian
        trade and intercourse acts, 1780-1834. Cambridge, Mass.,
        Harvard Univ. Pr., 1962   E93.P965

1303   PRUCHA, Francis Paul comp.
        The Indian in American history. Holt, Rinehart & Winston,
        1971   E93.P966

1304   PRUCHA, Francis Paul
        Lewis Cass and American Indian policy. Detroit, Pub.
        for the Detroit Historical Society by Wayne State Univ.
        Pr., 1967   E93.C34P7

1305   ROBERTSON, Heather
        Reservations are for Indians. Toronto, J. Lewis & Samuel,
        1970   E78.C2R62

1306   SCHMECKEBIER, Laurence Frederick
          The Office of Indian affairs. Baltimore, Md.,
          The Johns Hopkins Pr., 1927   E93.S34

13061   SCHULTZ, George A.
          An Indian Canaan: Isaac McCoy and the vision of an Indian
          state. Norman, Univ. of Oklahoma Pr., 1972 E93.M122.S3

13062   SHUMIATCHER, Morris Cyril
          Welfare: hidden backlash. Toronto, McClelland and Stewart,
          1971   E78.C2.S47

1307   SCHUSKY, Ernest Lester
          The right to be Indian. Board of National Missions of the
          United Presbyterian Church in cooperation with the Institute
          of Indian Studies, State Univ. of South Dakota, 1965 E93.S36

1308   SEYMOUR, Flora Warren (Smith)
          Indian agents of the old frontier. D. Appleton-Century Co.,
          Inc., 1941   E93.S48

1309   SIMPSON, Lesley Byrd
          Studies in the administration of the Indians in New Spain.
          Berkeley, Univ. of California Pr., 1934
                    (IAM)   F1401.I22.no.16

1310   SMITH, Archilla
          Indian justice. Oklahoma City, Okla., Harlow Pub. Co.,
          1934   K643.H6S57

1311   SORKIN, Alan L.
          American Indians and Federal aid. Washington, Brookings
          Institution, 1971   E93.S66

1312   SOUTH CAROLINA (COLONY).
          Documents relating to Indian affairs. Columbia, South Carolina,
          Archives Dept., 1958-70.   E78.S6S6

1313   Speeches on the passage of the bill for the removal of the
          Indians, delivered in the Congress of the United States,
          April and May, 1830. Boston, Perkins and Marvin, 1830 E93.S64

1314   STEWART, Julian Haynes
          Basin-plateau aboriginal sociopolitical groups. Washington,
          U.S. Govt. Print. Off., 1938 (BAEB)   E51.U55.no.120

1315   TATUM, Lawrie
          Our red brothers and the peace policy of President Ulysses S.
          Grant. Lincoln, Univ. of Nebraska Pr., 1970 E93.T22.1970

13151   TAYLOR, Theodore W.
        The States and their Indian Citizens. U. S. Bureau of
        Indian Affairs, 1972   E93.T27

1316   THOMSON, Charles
        An enquiry into the causes of the alienation of the
        Delaware and Shawanese Indians from the British interest.
        St. Clair Shores, Mich., Scholarly Pr., 1970 E78.P4T4.1970

1317   Uncommon controversy; fishing rights of the Muckleshoot,
        Puyallup, and Nisqually Indians. Seattle, Univ. of
        Washington Pr., 1970   E78.W3U25.1970

1318   U. S. BOARD OF INDIAN COMMISSIONERS.
        Annual report of the Board of Indian commissioners to
        the secretary of the interior. 1st-63rd; 1869-1931/32.
        Washington, U. S. Govt. Print. Off., 1870-1932 E93.U58

1319   U. S. BOARD OF INDIAN COMMISSIONERS.
        Report upon the conditions and needs of the Indians of
        the northwest coast. Washington, D.C., 1915 E78.N77U5

1320   U. S. BUREAU OF INDIAN AFFAIRS.
        The official correspondence of James S. Calhoun while
        Indian agent at Santa Fe and superintendent of Indian
        affairs in New Mexico. Washington, U. S. Govt. Print.
        Off., 1915   E78.N65U58

1321   U. S. COMMISSION ON ORGANIZATION OF THE EXECUTIVE BRANCH
        OF THE GOVERNMENT.
        Social security and education, Indian affairs. Washington,
        U. S. Govt. Print. Off., 1949   JK643.C47A55.no.15

1322   U. S. COMMISSION TO THE FIVE CIVILIZED TRIBES.
        Laws, decisions, and regulations affecting the work of
        the commissioner to the five civilized tribes, 1893 to
        1906. Washington, U. S. Govt. Print. Off., 1906 E78.I5U47

1323   U. S. CONGRESS. HOUSE. COMMITTEE ON INDIAN AFFAIRS.
        California Indians jurisdictional act. Washington,
        U. S. Govt. Print. Off., 1937   E78.C15U37

1324   U. S. CONGRESS. HOUSE. COMMITTEE ON INDIAN AFFAIRS.
        Indian conditions and affairs. Washington, U. S. Govt.
        Print. Off., 1935   E93.U6622

1325   U. S. CONGRESS. HOUSE. COMMITTEE ON INDIAN AFFAIRS.
        Indians of the United States. Washington, U. S. Govt.
        Print. Off., 1919   E93.U6623

1326   U. S. CONGRESS. SENATE. COMMITTEE ON INDIAN AFFAIRS.
Survey of conditions of the Indians in the United States.
Washington, U. S. Govt. Print. Off., 1929-   E93.U6773.1929

1327   U. S. CONGRESS. SENATE. COMMITTEE ON THE JUDICIARY.
Juvenile delinquency (Indians). Washington, U. S. Govt.
Print. Off., 1955   E98.C87U5.1955

1328   U. S. CONGRESS. SENATE. SELECT COMMITTEE ON AFFAIRS IN
INDIAN TERRITORY.
Report of the Select committee to investigate matters
connected with affairs in the Indian territory with
Hearings, November 11, 1906-January 9, 1907. Washington,
U. S. Govt. Print. Off., 1907   E78.I5U38

1329   U. S. DIVISION OF INDIAN HEALTH. PROGRAM ANALYSIS AND SPECIAL
STUDIES BRANCH.
Indians on Federal reservations in the United States:
a digest. Washington, 1958-63   E93.U6914

1330   WALKER, Francis Amasa
The Indian question. Boston, J. R. Osgood and Co., 1874
                           E93.W17

1331   WASHBURN, Wilcomb E.
Red man's land/white man's law. Scribner, 1971 KF8205.W38

1332   WHITE, Eugene E.
Experiences of a special Indian agent. Norman, Univ. of
Oklahoma Pr., 1965   E93.W58.1965

1333   WISCONSIN. STATE HISTORICAL SOCIETY.
The Indian in modern America. Madison, 1956 E91.W58

1334   WISSLER, Clark
Red man reservations. Collier Books, 1971 E98.S7W57.1971

13341 WUTTUNEE, William I
Ruffled feathers; Indians in Canadian society. Canada,
Bell Books, 1971   E92.W87

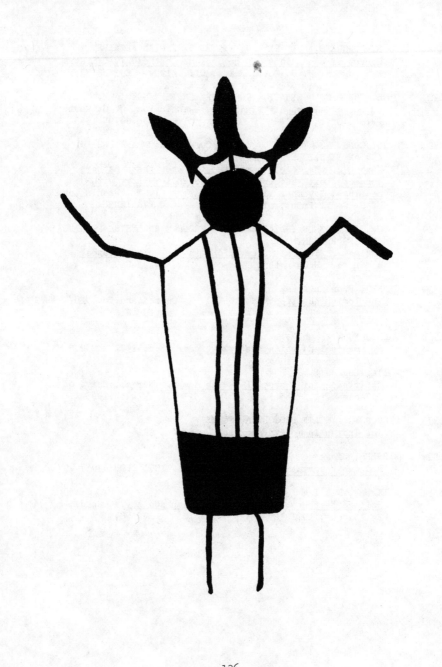

136

1335   ALDEN, John Richard
        John Stuart and the Southern colonial frontier. Gordian Pr.,
        1966 (1944)   F212.S7A6.1966

1336   BAKER-CROTHERS, Hayes
        Virginia and the French and Indian war. Chicago, The Univ.
        of Chicago Pr., 1928   F229.B33

1337   BARCIA CARBALLIDO Y ZÚÑIGA, Andrés González de
        Barcia's chronological history of the continent of Florida.
        Westport, Conn., Greenwood Pr., 1970 (1951) fF314.B243.1970

1338   BARTRAM, John
        Travels in Pensilvania and Canada. Ann Arbor, University
        Microfilms, 1966   F122.B133.1966

1339   BARTRAM, William
        Travels. New Haven, Yale Univ. Pr., 1958 F213.B2893

1340   BARTRAM, William
        The travels of William Bartram. Macy-Masius, 1928 F213.B288

1341   BERLANDIER, Luis
        The Indians of Texas in 1830. Washington, Smithsonian
        Institution Pr., 1969   E78.T4B413.1969

1342   BEVERLEY, Robert
        The history and present state of Virginia. Chapel Hill,
        Pub. for the Institute of Early American History and Culture
        at Williamsburg, Virginia, by the Univ. of North Carolina Pr.,
        1947   F229.B593

1343   BOLTON, Herbert Eugene ed.
        Athanase de Mezieres and the Louisiana-Texas frontier,
        1768-1780. Cleveland, The Arthur H. Clark Co., 1914 F373.B69

13431   BOLTON, Reginald Pelham
        Indian life of long ago in the city of New York.
        I. J. Friedman, 1971   E78.N7.B67.1971

1344   BONNELL, George William
        Topographical description of Texas. Waco, Tex., Texian Pr.,
        1964   F390.B71.1840a

1345   BOSSU, Jean Bernard
        Travels in the interior of North America, 1751-1762. Norman,
        Univ. of Oklahoma Pr., 1962   F372.B737

1346   BRICKELL, John
        The natural history of North Carolina. Murfreesboro, N.C.,
        Johnson Pub. Co., 1968 (1737)   F257.B843.1968

1347   BRINTON, Daniel Garrison
        The Floridian peninsula. Paladin Pr., 1969   F314.B85.1969

1348   CARTER, Robert Goldthwaite
        On the border with Mackenzie. Antiquarian Pr., 1961
                                               F391.C337.1961

1349   CARUSO, John Anthony
        The Mississippi Valley frontier. Indianapolis,
        Bobbs-Merrill, 1966   F352.C35

1350   CLARK, Joshua Victor Hopkins
        Indian camp-fires. Derby & Jackson, 1860 (1854)
                                               F127.06C4.1860

1351   COLDEN, Cadwallader
        The history of the five Indian nations depending on
        the Province of New-York in America. Ithaca, N.Y.,
        Great Seal Books, 1958   E99.I7C64.1958

1352   CORKRAN, David H.
        The Carolina Indian frontier. Columbia, S. C., Pub. for
        the South Carolina Tricentennial Commission by the Univ.
        of South Carolina Pr., 1970   F272.C8

1353   CRANE, Verner Winslow
        The southern frontier, 1670-1732. Ann Arbor, Univ. of
        Michigan Pr., 1956 (1929)   F272.C73

1354   CRAVEN, Wesley Frank
        White, red, and black: the seventeenth century Virginian.
        Charlottesville, Univ. Pr. of Virginia, 1971   F229.C897

1355   CRÈVECOEUR, Michel Guillaume St. Jean de
        Eighteenth-century travels in Pennsylvania and New York.
        Lexington, Univ. of Kentucky Pr., 1961   F153.C923

1356   DE FOREST, John William
        History of the Indians of Connecticut from the earliest
        known period to 1850. Hartford, W. J. Hamersley, 1853
                                               E78.C7D4

1357   DENTON, Daniel
        A brief description of New-York. Ann Arbor, Mich.,
        University Microfilms, 1966   F122.D37.1670a

1358   DE VORSEY, Louis
       The Indian boundary in the southern colonies, 1763-1775.
       Chapel Hill, Univ. of North Carolina Pr., 1966   F212.D4

1359   DICKINSON, Jonathan
       Jonathan Dickinson's journal. New Haven, Printed for the
       Yale Univ. Pr.; London, for sale by H. Milford at the
       Oxford Univ. Pr., 1945   F314.D52

1360   DONCK, Adriaen van der
       A description of the New Netherlands. Syracuse, N. Y.,
       Syracuse Univ. Pr., 1968   F122.1.D6613.1968

1361   DOUGLAS, Claude Leroy
       The gentlemen in the white hats. Dallas, Tex.,
       South-west Pr., 1934   F391.D73

1362   FEATHERSTONHAUGH, George William
       A canoe voyage up the Minnay Sotor. St. Paul, Minnesota
       Historical Society, 1970   F353.F28.1970

1363   FLETCHER, John Gould
       John Smith--Also Pocahontas. Brentano's, 1928 F229.S7174

1364   FORSYTH, George Alexander
       The story of the soldier. D. Appleton and Co., 1900 F181.F73

1365   GRANT, Anne (MacVicar)
       Memoirs of an American lady. Research Rep., 1970 (1808)
                                           F122.G7.1970

1366   GREGG, Alexander
       History of the old Cheraws. Spartanburg, S. C., Reprint Co.,
       1965 (1867)   F266.S53.no.9

1367   HANNA, Charles Augustus
       The wilderness trail. G. P. Putnam's Sons, 1911 F152.H24

1368   HARE, Lloyd Custer Mayhew
       Thomas Mayhew, patriarch to the Indians (1593-1682).
       D. Appleton and Co., 1932   F67.M526

1369   HARRIOT, Thomas
       A brief and true report of the new found land of Virginia.
       History Book Club, 1951   F229.H27

1370   HECKEWELDER, John Gottlieb Ernestus
       History, manners and customs of the Indian nations who
       once inhabited Pennsylvania and the neighboring states.
       Philadelphia, Historical Society of Pennsylvania, 1881
                                           E78.P4H4.1876

1371   HENNEPIN, Louis
        A description of Louisiana. Ann Arbor, University Microfilms,
        1966   F352.H56.1966

1372   HENNEPIN, Louis
        Father Louis Hennepin's Description of Louisiana.
        Minneapolis, Pub. for the Minnesota Society of the Colonial
        Dames of America, Univ. of Minnesota Pr., 1938 F352.H564

1373   HENNEPIN, Louis
        A new discovery of a vast country in America. Chicago,
        A. C. McClurg & Co., 1903   F352.H76

13731   Indian Tribes of Texas. Texas, Texian Pr., 1971 E78.T4.I46

13732   JOHNSON, Robert
        Nova Britannia. Da Capo, 1969 (1609) F229.J67.1609a

1374   JONES, Hugh
        The present state of Virginia. Chapel Hill, Pub. for
        Virginia Historical Society by Univ. of North Carolina
        Pr., 1956   F229.J78.1956

1375   KETCHUM, William
        An authentic and comprehensive history of Buffalo.
        St. Clair Shores, Mich., Scholarly Pr., 1970 F129.B8K42

1376   KOONTZ, Louis Knott
        The Virginia frontier, 1754-1763. Baltimore, Johns Hopkins Pr.,
        1925   F229.K82

1377   LANNING, John Tate
        The Spanish missions of Georgia. Chapel Hill, Univ. of
        North Carolina Pr., 1935   F289.L35

1378   LAWSON, John
        A new voyage to Carolina. Chapel Hill, Univ. of North
        Carolina Pr., 1967   F257.L40.1967

1379   LEDERER, John
        The discoveries of John Lederer. Charlottesville,
        Univ. of Virginia Pr., 1958   F229.L46.1958

1380   LEE, Enoch Lawrence
        Indian ways in North Carolina, 1663-1763. Raleigh, N. C.,
        Carolina Charter Tercentenary Commission, 1963 F257.L5

1381   MacMINN, Edwin
        On the frontier with Colonel Antes. Camden, N.J.,
        S. Chew & Sons, Printers, 1900   F149.M16

13811   MAILS, Thomas E.
              The mystic warriors of the plains.   Doubleday, 1972
                                                    fE78.G73.M34

1382   MONTAULT de MONBERAUT, Henri
              Mémoire justificatif. University, Univ. of Alabama Pr., 1965
                                                    E78.F6M63

1383   MORFI, Juan Agustín
              History of Texas, 1673-1779. Albuquerque, The Quivira
              Society, 1935   F389.M72.Spec.Coll.

1384   NEW YORK (COLONY).
              An abridgment of the Indian affairs contained in four volumes,
              transacted in the colony of New York, from the year 1678 to
              the year 1751, by Peter Wraxall. B. Blom, 1968 (1915)
                                                    E78.N7N6.1968

1385   NEW YORK (STATE) LEGISLATURE. ASSEMBLY. SPECIAL COMMITTEE TO
         INVESTIGATE THE INDIAN PROBLEM.
              Report of Special committee to investigate the Indian problem
              of the state of New York, appointed by the Assembly of 1888.
              Albany, The Troy Press Co., Printers, 1889   E78.N7N77

1386   NEWCOMB, William Wilmon
              The Indians of Texas, from prehistoric to modern times.
              Austin, Univ. of Texas Pr., 1961   E78.T4N4

13861   ORCUTT, Samuel
              The Indians of the Housatonic and Naugatuck Valleys.
              J. E. Edwards, 1972   E78.C7.06.1972

1387   OXENDINE, Clifton
              A social and economic history of the Indians of Robeson
              County, North Carolina. Nashville, George Peabody College
              for Teachers, Library Photoduplication Service, 1970 (1934)
                                                    E78.N7409.1970

1388   PERKINS, James Handasyd
              Annals of the West. Cincinnati, J. R. Albach, 1847 (1846)
                                                    F351.P44.Spec.Coll.

1389   PIKE, James
              Scout and ranger. Princeton, Princeton Univ. Pr., 1932
                                                    F391.P63

13891   PRATSON, Frederick John
              Land of the four directions. Viking Pr., 1970 E78.M2.P7

1390   READING, Robert S.
              Arrows over Texas. San Antonio, Naylor Co., 1967
                                                    E78.T4R4.1967

1391   ROMANS, Bernard
        A concise natural history of East and West Florida.
        Gainesville, Univ. of Florida Pr., 1962 F314.R75.1775a

1392   RUTTENBER, Edward Manning
        History of the Indian tribes of Hudson's River.
        Albany, N.Y., J. Munsell, 1872   E78.N7R9

1393   SKINNER, Alanson Buck
        The Indians of Manhattan Island and vicinity. American
        Museum of Natural History, 1921?   E78.N7S6.1921

1394   SMITH, John
        The generall historie of Virginia, New-England, and the
        Summer Isles. London, Produced for the World Pub. Co.,
        Cleveland, by G. Rainbird Ltd., 1966 fF229.S612.Spec.Coll.

1395   TRELEASE, Allen W.
        Indian affairs in colonial New York: the seventeenth
        century. Ithaca, N.Y., Cornell Univ. Pr., 1960 E78.N7T7

1396   TROBRIAND, Philippe Régis Denis de Keredern, comte de
        Military life in Dakota. St. Paul, Alvord Memorial
        Commission, 1951   F351.M685.v.2

1397   URLSPERGER, Samuel comp.
        Detailed reports on the Salzburger emigrants who
        settled in America. Athens, Univ. of Georgia Pr.,
        1968-   F295.S1U813

1398   VAUGHAN, Alden T.
        New England frontier. Boston, Little, Brown, 1965 F7.V3

1399   VOLWILER, Albert Tangeman
        George Croghan and the westward movement, 1741-1782.
        Cleveland, Ohio, The Arthur H. Clark Co., 1926
                                                F152.V943.1926

1400   WALLACE, Ernest
        Ranald S. Mackenzie on the Texas frontier. Lubbock, Tex.,
        West Texas Museum Assoc., 1964   F391.M167W3

1401   WALLACE, Paul A. W.
        Conrad Weiser, 1696-1760. Philadelphia, Univ. of
        Pennsylvania Pr.; London, H. Milford, Oxford Univ. Pr.,
        1945   F152.W45W34

1402   WHITE, Henry
        The early history of New England. Johnson Reprint, 1970
        (1841)   F7.W586.1970

1403   WHITE, Henry
        Indian battles. D. W. Evans & Co., 1859 F7.W59

1404   WILLIAMS, John Lee
        The Territory of Florida. Gainesville, Univ. of Florida Pr.,
        1962   F311.W65.1837a

Northwest Territory, Lower Mississippi Valley

1405   BARTLETT, William W.
        History, tradition and adventure in the Chippewa valley.
        Chippewa Falls, Wis., The Chippewa Printery, 1929
                                            F587.C5B2

1406   BRICE, Wallace A.
        History of Fort Wayne. Fort Wayne, Ind., D. W. Jones & Son,
        Printers, 1868   F534.F7B8

1407   BROWN, William Horace
        The glory seekers. Chicago, A. C. McClurg & Co., 1906
                                            F396.B87

1408   BUTTERFIELD, Consul Willshire
        History of the Girty's. Cincinnati, R. Clarke & Co.,
        1890   F517.G52

1409   CHICAGO & NORTHWESTERN RAILWAY COMPANY.
        The Indian, the Northwest, 1600-1900. Chicago,
        Chicago & North-western railway, 1901   E78.N8C5

14091   COLTON, Calvin
        Tour of the American lakes, and among the Indians of the
        North-West Territory, in 1830: disclosing the character
        and prospects of the Indian race. Kennikat, 1972
                                            E77.C72.1972

1410   CROCKETT, David
        The adventures of Davy Crockett. Scribner, 1955
                                            F436.C76.1955

1411   CROCKETT, David
        Life of David Crockett. Philadelphia, J. E. Potter and
        Co., 1865   F436.C936

1412   CROGHAN, George
        George Croghan's journal of his trip to Detroit in 1767.
        Ann Arbor, Mich., University Microfilms, 1967 (1939)
                                            F483.C76

1413   DOWNES, Randolph Chandler
        Council fires on the upper Ohio. Pittsburgh, Univ. of
        Pittsburgh Pr., 1940   F517.D69

1414   ECKERT, Allan W.
        The frontiersmen. Boston, Little, Brown, 1967
                                            F517.K362

1415 FERNOW, Berthold
      The Ohio Valley in colonial days. B. Franklin, 1971
                                          F517.F47.1971

1416 FILSON, John
      The discovery, settlement, and present State of Kentucke.
      Corinth Books, 1962   F454.F485

1417 FOREMAN, Grant
      Indians & pioneers. New Haven, Yale Univ. Pr.; London,
      H. Milford, Oxford Univ. Pr., 1930   F396.F71

1418 HULBERT, Archer Butler
      Military roads of the Mississippi basin. Cleveland, Ohio,
      The A. H. Clark Co., 1904   HE355.H9.v.8

1419 KINIETZ, William Vernon
      The Indians of the western Great Lakes, 1615-1760.
      Ann Arbor, Univ. of Michigan Pr., 1940 E78.N76K5

1420 KRAUSKOPF, Frances ed. and tr.
      Ouiatanon documents. Indianapolis, Indiana Historical
      Society, 1955   F521.I41.v.18.no.2

1421 McCLUNG, John Alexander
      Sketches of western adventure. Arno, 1969 F517.M1322

1422 McKNIGHT, Charles
      Our western border. Johnson Repr., 1970 (1876) F517.M15.1970

1423 PEITHMANN, Irvin M.
      Indians of southern Illinois. Springfield, Ill., C. C. Thomas,
      1964   E78.I3P42.1964

1424 QUIMBY, George Irving
      Indian life in the Upper Great Lakes, 11,000 B.C. to A.D. 1800.
      Chicago, Univ. of Chicago Pr., 1960   E78.G7Q5

1425 SMITH, William Henry
      The St. Clair papers. Cincinnati, R. Clark & Co., 1882
                                      F483.S15

1426 SOSIN, Jack M.
      Whitehall and the wilderness. Lincoln, Univ. of Nebraska Pr.,
      1961   F483.S6

1427 TEMPLE, Wayne Calhoun
      Indian villages of the Illinois country. Springfield, Ill.,
      State of Illinois, 1958   E78.I3T4

1428   TRENT, William
      Journal of Captain William Trent from Logstown to Pickawillany, A. D. 1752. Arno, 1971 (1871)   F517.T79.1971

1429   TURNER, Frederick Jackson
      The character and influence of the Indian trade in Wisconsin. B. Franklin, 1970   E78.W8T9.1970

1430   VAN EVERY, Dale
      Men of the western waters.   Boston, Houghton Mifflin, 1956   F517.V3

1431   ARMSTRONG, Moses Kimball
        The early empire builders of the great West. St. Paul, Minn.,
        E. W. Porter, 1901   F655.A73

14311   BAILEY, Minnie Thomas
        Reconstruction in Indian territory; a story of avarice,
        discrimination, and opportunism. (Kennikat Press national
        university publications. Series in American studies)
        Kennikat, 1972   E78.I5.B34

1432   BARNARD, Evan G.
        A rider of the Cherokee strip. Boston, New York, Houghton
        Mifflin Co., 1936   F596.B25

1433   BEADLE, John Hanson
        Western wilds. Cincinnati, Chicago, Jones Brothers & Co.,
        1878   F594.B37

1434   BECKWOURTH, James P.
        The life and adventures of James P. Beckwourth. Harper &
        Brothers, 1856   F592.B39.Spec.Coll.

1435   BONSAL, Stephen
        Edward Fitzgerald Beale. G. P. Putnam's Sons, 1912 F593.B36

1436   BRONSON, Edgar Beecher
        Reminiscences of a ranchman. G. H. Doran, 1910 F594.B82

1437   BROWN, Mark Herbert
        The frontier years. Bramhall House, 1955 F595.H87B7.1955

1438   CAMPION, J. S.
        On the frontier. London, Chapman & Hall, 1878 F594.C195

1439   CARVER, Jonathan
        Three years travels throughout the interior parts of North
        America. Printed by John Russell, for David West No. 56,
        Cornhill, Boston, 1797   F597.C382.Spec.Coll.

1440   COLLINS, Hubert Edwin
        Warpath & cattle trail. Morrow, 1933   F596.C72.1933

1441   CONOVER, George W.
        Sixty years in southwest Oklahoma. Anadarko, Okl.,
        N. T. Plummer, 1927   F697.C75

1442   CRAWFORD, Samuel Johnson
        Kansas in the sixties. Chicago, A. C. McClurg & Co.,
        1911   F686.C89

1443   CUSTER, Elizabeth (Bacon)
        Following the guidon. Harper & Brothers, 1890 F594.C88

1444   CUSTER, George Armstrong
        My life on the plains. Sheldon and Co., 1874 F594.C97

1445   CUSTER, George Armstrong
        Wild life on the plains and horrors of Indian warfare.
        St. Louis, Royal Publishing Co., 1891 F594.C981

1446   DEBO, Angie
        And still the waters run. Gordian Pr., 1966 E78.I5D4.1966

1447   DELANO, Alonzo
        Life on the plains and among the diggings. Miller, Orton &
        Co., 1857   F593.D34

1448   DODGE, Richard Irving
        The hunting grounds of the great West. London,
        Chatto & Windus, 1878   F594.D64.1878

1449   DODGE, Richard Irving
        The Plains of the great West and their inhabitants. Archer
        House, 1959   F594.D63.1959

1450   DOMENECH, Emmanuel Henri Dieudonné
        Seven years' residence in the great deserts of North
        America. London, Longman, Green, Longman, and Roberts,
        1860   F593.D653.Spec.Coll.

1451   DOWNEY, Fairfax Davis
        Indian-fighting army. C. Scribner's Sons, 1941 F594.D65

1452   DRANNAN, William F.
        Thirty-one years on the plains and in the mountains.
        Chicago, T. W. Jackson, 1900   F593.D76.1900

1453   ELLSWORTH, Henry Leavitt
        Washington Irving on the prairie. American Book Co.,
        1937   F697.E58

1454   FARNHAM, Thomas Jefferson
        Travels in the great western prairies, the Anahuac and
        Rocky mountains, and in the Oregon territory.
        Poughkeepsie, N.Y., Killey and Lossing, Printers, 1841
                                                F592.F225.Spec.Coll.

1455   GRINNELL, George Bird
       Beyond the old frontier. C. Scribner's Sons, 1913 F591.G84

1456   HAFEN, Le Roy Reuben ed.
       Relations with the Indians of the Plains, 1857-1861.
       Glendale, Calif., A. H. Clark Co., 1959 F591.F35.v.9

1457   HAMILTON, William Thomas
       My sixty years on the plains. Columbus, Ohio,
       Reprinted by Long's College Book Co., 1951 (1905) F591.H37

1458   HANSON, Joseph Mills
       The conquest of the Missouri. Murray Hill Books, Inc.,
       1946   F597.H35

1459   HARKINS, Arthur M.
       The social programs and political styles of Minneapolis
       Indians: an interim report. Minneapolis, Univ. of Minnesota,
       Training Center for Community Programs, 1969 E78.M7H3

1460   HEBARD, Grace Raymond
       The Bozeman trail. Glendale, Calif., Arthur H. Clark Co.,
       1960 (1922)   F591.H4.1960

1461   HITCHCOCK, Ethan Allen
       A traveler in Indian territory. Cedar Rapids, Ia.,
       Torch Pr., 1930   F697.H67

1462   HOPEWELL, Menra
       Legends of the Missouri and Mississippi. London, New York,
       E. F. Beadle, 1864?   F598.H79

1463   HORN, Tom
       Life of Tom Horn. Norman, Univ. of Oklahoma Pr., 1964
                                           F595.H797.1964

1464   INMAN, Henry
       The Great Salt Lake trail. Minneapolis, Ross & Haines, 1966
                                           F591.I575.1966

1465   IRVING, Washington
       A tour on the prairies. Norman, Univ. of Oklahoma Pr.,
       1956   F697.I78.1956

1466   JAMES, Marquis
       The Cherokee strip. Viking Pr., 1945 E175.5.J3A3

1467   JONES, Robert Huhn
       The Civil War in the Northwest. Norman, Univ. of Oklahoma Pr.
       1960   F597.J62

1468   KEATING, William Hypolitus
        Narrative of an expedition to the source of St. Peter's
        River, Lake Winnepeek, Lake of the Woods, &c., &c.
        Philadelphia, H. C. Carey & I. Lea, 1824 F597.L845.Spec.Coll.

1469   KELSEY, D. M.
        History of our wild West and stories of pioneer life from
        experiences of Buffalo Bill, Wild Bill, Kit Carson, David
        Crockett, Sam Houston, Generals Crook, Miles and Custer,
        Geronimo, Sitting Bull, great Indian chiefs, and other
        famous frontiersmen and Indian fighters. Willey Book Co.,
        1928   F591.K4

1470   LAMAR, Howard Roberts
        Dakota Territory, 1861-1889. New Haven, Yale Univ. Pr.,
        1958 (1956)   F655.L25

1471   LANG, John D.
        Report of a visit to some of the tribes of Indians, located
        west of the Mississippi river. Press of M. Day & Co., 1843
                          E77.L26.Spec.Coll.

1472   LARPENTEUR, Charles
        Forty years a fur trader on the upper Missouri. F. P. Harper,
        1898   F598.L33

1473   LIBBY, Orin Grant ed.
        The Arikara narrative of the campaign against the hostile
        Dakotas, June, 1876. Bismarck, N. D., 1920 F631.N86.v.6

1474   McFARLING, Lloyd ed.
        Exploring the northern plains, 1804-1876. Caldwell, Idaho,
        Caxton Printers, 1955   F591.M14

1475   MARCY, Randolph Barnes
        Thirty years of Army life on the border. Philadelphia,
        Lippincott, 1963 (1962)   F593.M33.1963

1476   MELINE, James Florant
        Two thousand miles on horseback. Catholic Publication
        Society, 1872   F594.M49

1477   MOORE, John M.
        The West. Wichita Falls, Tex., Wichita Printing Co.,
        1935   F596.M67

1478   NELSON, Bruce Opie
        Land of the Dacotahs. Lincoln, Univ. of Nebraska Pr.,
        1964 (1946)   F598.N42.1964

1479   NELSON, John Young
        Fifty years on the trail. Norman, Univ. of Oklahoma Pr.,
        1963   F591.N42.1963

1480   NEWSON, Thomas McLean
        Thrilling scenes among the Indians. Chicago, Donohue &
        Henneberry, 1890   E78.N8N5.1890

1481   NICOLLET, Joseph Nicolas
        The journals of Joseph N. Nicollet. St. Paul, Minnesota
        Historical Society, 1970   F606.N468

1482   NYE, Wilbur Sturtevant
        Carbine & lance. Norman, Univ. of Oklahoma Pr., 1969
                                          F694.N95.1969

1483   PARKMAN, Francis
        The Oregon Trail. Madison, Univ. of Wisconsin Pr., 1969
                                          F592.P284.1969

1484   PETERS, De Witt Clinton
        Kit Carson's life and adventures. Hartford, Conn., Dustin,
        Gilman & Co.; Cincinnati, Queen City Publishing Co., 1874
                                          F592.C398

1485   POURTALÈS, Albert, Graf von
        On the western tour with Washington Irving. Norman,
        Univ. of Oklahoma Pr., 1968   F697.P613

1486   PRESCOTT, Philander
        The recollections of Philander Prescott. Lincoln,
        Univ. of Nebraska Pr., 1966   F606.P74.1966

1487   PRETTYMAN, William S.
        Indian Territory. Norman, Univ. of Oklahoma Pr., 1957
                                          F697.P74

1488   REMINGTON, Frederic
        Pony tracks. Harper & Brothers, 1895   F595.R38

1489   RICKEY, Don
        Forty miles a day on beans and hay. Norman, Univ. of
        Oklahoma Pr., 1963   F594.R53

1490   ROGERS, Fred Blackburn
        Soldiers of the overland. San Francisco, Grabhorn Pr.,
        1938   F594.R65.Spec.Coll.

1491   SCHOOLCRAFT, Henry Rowe
        Expedition to Lake Itasca. East Lansing, Michigan State
        Univ. Pr., 1958   F597.S36.1958

1492   SIMONIN, Louis Laurent
        The Rocky Mountain West in 1867. Lincoln, Univ. of
        Nebraska Pr., 1966   F594.S613

1493   SMET, Pierre Jean de
        Life, letters and travels of Father Pierre-Jean de Smet,
        S. J., 1801-1873. F. P. Harper, 1905 (1904) F591.S63

1494   SMET, Pierre Jean de
        Western missions and missionaries. P. J. Kenedy, 1859
                                              F593.S634

1495   STREETER, Daniel Willard
        An Arctic rodeo. G. P. Putnam's Sons, 1929 F608.S7

1496   TALLENT, Annie D.
        The Black Hills. St. Louis, Nixon-Jones Printing Co.,
        1899   F657.B6T2

1497   TAUNTON, Francis B.
        Sidelights of the Sioux wars. London, English Westerners'
        Society, 1967   F591.E49.no.2

1498   TOWNSHEND, Richard Baxter
        Last memories of a tenderfoot. London, J. Lane, 1926
                                              F595.T75

1499   TROBRIAND, Phillippe Régis Denis de Keredern, comte de
        Army life in Dakota. Chicago, The Lakeside Pr.,
        R. R. Donnelley & Sons Co., 1941   F655.T842

1500   U. S. NATIONAL PARK SERVICE.
        Soldier and brave. Harper & Row, 1963 F591.U59

1501   U. S. WAR DEPT.
        Reports of explorations and surveys. Washington,
        B. Tucker, Printer, 1855-61   fF593.U58

1502   WELLMAN, Paul Iselin
        The Indian wars of the West. Doubleday, 1954 (1947)
                                              F591.W4.1954

1503   WERNER, Herman
        On the western frontier with the United States Cavalry
        fifty years ago. n.p., 1934   F595.W4

1504   WHEELER, Homer Webster
        Buffalo days. Indianapolis, Bobbs-Merrill Co., 1925
                                              F594.W56

1505   WHEELER, Homer Webster
        The frontier trail. Los Angeles, Times-Mirror Pr., 1923
                                              F594.W57

1506   ABERT, James William
        Western America in 1846-1847. San Francisco, J. Howell, 1966
                                      fF800.A6.1966

1507   BAILEY, Lynn Robison
        Bosque Redondo. Pasadena, Calif., Socio-Technical Books,
        1970   F804.S8B3

1508   BAILEY, Lynn Robison
        Indian slave trade in the Southwest. Los Angeles,
        Westernlore Pr., 1966   E78.S7B19

1509   BANDELIER, Adolph Francis Alphonse
        The Southwestern journals of Adolph F. Bandelier, 1880-1882.
        Albuquerque, Univ. of New Mexico Pr., 1966 E78.S7B32

1510   BARNES, William Croft
        Apaches & longhorns. Los Angeles, The Ward Ritchie Pr., 1941
                                      F811.B27

1511   BELL, William Abraham
        New tracks in North America. Albuquerque, N. M., Horn and
        Wallace, 1965   F786.B43.1965

1512   BENAVIDES, Alonso de
        Fray Alonso de Benavides' revised Memorial of 1634.
        Albuquerque, Univ. of New Mexico Pr., 1945 F799.B44

1513   BENAVIDES, Alonso de
        The memorial of Fray Alonso de Benavides, 1630. Albuquerque,
        Horn and Wallace, 1965   F799.B43.1965

1514   BENAVIDES, Alonso de
        Memorial of 1630. Washington, Academy of American Franciscan
        History, 1954   F799.B46

1515   BORG, Carl Oscar
        The great Southwest. Santa Ana, Calif., The Fine Arts Pr., 1936
                                      F786.B75

1516   BROWNE, John Ross
        Adventures in the Apache country. Harper & Brothers, 1869
                                      F786.B87

1517   BRUGGE, David M.
        Navajos in the Catholic Church records of New Mexico, 1694-1875.
        Window Rock, Ariz., Research Section, Parks and Recreation Dept.,
        The Navajo Tribe, 1968   E78.N65B7

1518   CARR, Harry
        The West is still wild. Boston and New York, Houghton
        Mifflin Co., 1932   F786.C28

1519   CHAPIN, Frederick Hastings
        The land of the cliff-dwellers. Boston, Appalachian
        Mountain Club, 1892   F786.C46

1520   COLTON, Harold Sellers
        Days on the Painted desert and in the San Francisco
        mountains. Flagstaff, Ariz., 1927   F817.P2C6

1521   COZZENS, Samuel Woodworth
        The marvelous country. Amherst, N. S., Rogers & Black,
        1874   F801.C88.1874

1522   DAVID, Robert Beebe
        Finn Burnett, frontiersman. Glendale, Calif.,
        Arthur H. Clark Co., 1937   F761.B87

1523   DOBIE, James Frank
        Apache gold & Yaqui silver. Boston, Little, Brown and
        Co., 1947   F786.D62.1947

1524   DOBIE, James Frank   ed.
        Southwestern lore. Hatboro, Pa., Folklore Associates,
        1965 (1931)   F786.D645.1965

1525   FERGUSSON, Erna
        New Mexico, a pageant of three peoples. Knopf, 1964
                                             F796.F35.1964

1526   FERGUSSON, Harvey
        Rio Grande. Knopf, 1933   F796.F38

1527   FORBES, Jack D.
        Apache, Navaho, and Spaniard. Norman, Univ. of Oklahoma
        Pr., 1960   E78.S7F6

1528   FORREST, Earle Robert
        Missions and pueblos of the old Southwest. Cleveland,
        Arthur H. Clark Co., 1929   F786.F67

1529   GARCIA, Andrew
        Tough trip through paradise, 1878-1879. Boston,
        Houghton Mifflin, 1967   F731.G3

1530   GILLMOR, Frances
        Traders to the Navajos. Boston, Houghton Mifflin, 1934
                                             F786.G46

1531   GLADWIN, Harold Sterling
            A history of the ancient Southwest. Portland, Me.,
            Bond Wheelwright Co., 1957   E78.S7G52

1532   GOTTFREDSON, Peter ed.
            History of Indian depredations in Utah. Salt Lake City,
            Press of Skelton Pub. Co., 1919   E78.U55G68

1533   GRANT, Blanche Chloe
            When old trails were new. The Press of the Pioneers, Inc.,
            1934   F804.T2G74

1534   HACKETT, Charles Wilson ed.
            Revolt of the Pueblo Indians of New Mexico and Otermín's
            attempted reconquest, 1680-1682. Albuquerque, The Univ.
            of New Mexico Pr., 1970 (1942)   F799.H1249.1970

1535   HAFEN, Le Roy Reuben
            Fort Laramie and the pageant of the West, 1834-1890.
            Glendale, Calif. Arthur H. Clark Co., 1938 F761.H24

1536   HEWETT, Edgar Lee
            Landmarks of New Mexico. Albuquerque, Univ. of New Mexico Pr.
            and School of American Research, 1947 F801.H58.1947

1537   HODGE, Frederick Webb
            History of Hawikuh, New Mexico. Los Angeles, Southwest
            Museum, 1937   F799.H67

1538   HORGAN, Paul
            The heroic triad. Holt, Rinehart and Winston, 1970 F790.A1H6

1539   JAMES, George Wharton
            A little journey to some strange places and peoples in our
            southwestern land. Chicago, A. Flanagan Co., 1911 F786.J27

1540   JONES, Oakah L.
            Pueblo warriors & Spanish conquest. Norman, Univ. of Oklahoma
            Pr., 1966   F799.J76

1541   KINO, Eusebio Francisco
            Historical memoir of Pimería Alta. Berkeley, Univ. of
            California Pr., 1948 (1919)   F799.K55.1919

1542   KLUCKHOHN, Clyde
            To the foot of the rainbow. London, Everleigh Nash & Grayson,
            1928   F786.K66

1543   LAUT, Agnes Christina
            Through our unknown Southwest. McBride, Nast & Co., 1913
                                               F786.L38

1544   LUMMIS, Charles Fletcher
        <u>The land of poco tiempo</u>. Albuquerque, Univ. of New
        Mexico Pr., 1966   F801.L96.1966

1545   LYMAN, Albert R.
        <u>Indians and outlaws</u>. Salt Lake City, Bookcraft, 1962
                                                F832.S4L9

15451   MARRIOTT, Alice Lee
        <u>These are the people</u>. Santa Fe, N. M., Laboratory of
        Anthropology, 1951   E78.S7.M3

1546   MEADERS, Margaret
        <u>The Indian situation in New Mexico</u>. Albuquerque,
        Bureau of Business Research, Univ. of New Mexico, 1963
                                                E78.N65M4

1547   MEGINNESS, John Franklin
        <u>Biography of Frances Slocum, the lost sister of Wyoming</u>.
        Williamsport, Pa., Heller Bros. Printing House, 1891
                                                E87.S63

1548   MILLER, Joseph
        <u>Monument Valley and the Navajo country, Arizona [and]
        Utah</u>. Hastings House, 1951   F817.M6M5

1549   MUNK, Joseph Amasa
        <u>Southwest sketches</u>. Putnam, 1920   F786.M95

1550   NADEAU, Remi A.
        <u>Fort Laramie and the Sioux Indians</u>. Englewood Cliffs,
        N. J., Prentice-Hall, 1967   F769.F6N3

1551   PÉREZ DE LUXÁN, Diego
        <u>Expedition into New Mexico made by Antonio de Espejo,
        1582-1583</u>. Los Angeles, The Quivira Society, 1929
                                                F799.P43.Spec.Coll.

1552   POINT, Nicolas
        <u>Wilderness kingdom, Indian life in the Rocky Mountains:
        1840-1847: the journals & paintings of Nicolas Point</u>.
        Holt, Rinehart and Winston, 1967   fE78.N77P6

1553   PRIESTLEY, John Boynton
        <u>Journey down a rainbow</u>. Harper, 1955   F786.P95.1955a

1554   PRUDDEN, Theophil Mitchell
        <u>On the great American plateau</u>. G. P. Putnam's Sons, 1906
                                                F786.P97

156

1555   RISTER, Carl Coke
       The southwestern frontier--1865-1881. Cleveland,
       Arthur H. Clark Co., 1928   F786.R6

1556   ROBINSON, William Henry
       Under turquoise skies. Macmillan, 1928 F786.R73

1557   ROSS, Adeline Rebecca
       Indian life in Wyoming. 1911   E78.W9R6

1558   SEDGWICK, Mary Katrine (Rice)
       Acoma, the sky city. Cambridge, Harvard Univ. Pr., 1927
                           F798.S43.1927

1559   SIGÜENZA Y GÓNGORA, Carlos de
       The Mercurio volante of Don Carlos de Sigüenza y Góngora.
       Los Angeles, The Quivira Society, 1932 F799.S58.Spec.Coll.

1560   SMET, Pierre Jean de
       Origin, progress, and prospects of the Catholic Mission to
       the Rocky Mountains. Fairfield, Wash., Ye Galleon Pr., 1967
                           F737.B6S5

1561   SMITH, Dama Margaret
       I married a ranger. Stanford, Calif., Stanford Univ. Pr.;
       London, H. Milford, Oxford Univ. Pr., 1930 F788.S615

1562   Southwest Indian country: Arizona, New Mexico, Southern Utah,
       and Colorado.
       Menlo Park, Calif., Lane Books, 1970   E78.S7S57

1563   SPRING, John A.
       John Spring's Arizona. Tucson, Univ. of Arizona Pr., 1966
                         F811.S77

1564   THOMAS, Alfred Barnaby ed. and tr.
       Forgotten frontiers. Norman, Univ. of Oklahoma Pr., 1932
                         F799.T48

1565   THOMAS, Alfred Barnaby
       The Plains Indians and New Mexico, 1751-1778. Albuquerque,
       Univ. of New Mexico Pr., 1940   F799.T49

1566   THRAPP, Dan L.
       Al Sieber, chief of scouts. Norman, Univ. of Oklahoma Pr.,
       1964   F811.S5T5

1567   TOPPING, E. S.
       The chronicles of the Yellowstone. St. Paul, Pioneer Press Co.,
       1888   F722.T6

1568   TREGO, Frank H.
        Boulevarded old trails in the great Southwest. Greenberg,
        1929   F786.T78

1569   U. S. ARMY. CORPS OF TOPOGRAPHICAL ENGINEERS.
        Report of an expedition down the Zuni and Colorado Rivers.
        Washington, B. Tucker, Senate Print., 1854
                                          F788.U57.1854.Spec.Coll.

1570   VARGAS ZAPATA Y LUXÁN PONZE DE LEÓN, Diego de
        First expedition of Vargas into New Mexico, 1692.
        Albuquerque, N. M., University of New Mexico Pr., 1940
                                          F799.V282

1571   WALGAMOTT, Charles Shirley
        Six decades back. Caldwell, Id., Caxton Printers, Ltd.,
        1936   F746.W29

1572   WALLACE, Susan Arnold (Elston)
        The land of the Pueblos. Troy, N.Y., Nims & Knight, 1889
        (1888)   F801.W18.1889

1573   WATERS, William Elkanah
        Life among the Mormons. Moorhead, Simpson & Bond, 1868
                                          F826.W33

1574   WELLS, Edmund W.
        Argonaut tales, stories of the gold seekers and the
        Indian scouts of early Arizona. F. H. Hitchcock, 1927
                                          F811.W45

1575   WETHERILL, Hilda (Faunce)
        Desert wife. Boston, Little, Brown, 1934 F811.W48

1576   WHIPPLE, Amiel Weeks
        The Whipple report. Los Angeles, Westernlore Pr., 1961
                                          F786.W575

1577   WRIGHT, William
        Washoe rambles. Los Angeles, Westernlore Pr., 1963
                                          F841.W76.1963

1578   ANDERSON, Hobson Dewey
        Alaska natives. Stanford, Calif., Stanford University Pr.,
        1935   F909.A54

1579   ARMSTRONG, A. N.
        Oregon. Fairfield, Wash., Ye Galleon Pr., 1969 F880.A73.1969

1580   BANCROFT, Hubert Howe
        The works of Hubert Howe Bancroft. San Francisco,
        A. L. Bancroft & Co., 1882-90   F851.B215

1581   BEECHEY, Frederick William
        An account of a visit to California, 1826-'27. San Francisco,
        Printed at the Grabhorn Pr. for the Book Club of California,
        1941   fF864.B4.1941.Spec.Coll.

1582   BOSCANA, Gerónimo
        Chinigchinich. Santa Ana, Calif., Fine Arts Pr., 1933
                          fF869.S34B7.Spec.Coll.

1583   BUTLER, Evelyn I.
        Alaska, the land and the people. Viking Pr., 1957 F904.B88

1584   CARRIGHAR, Sally
        Moonlight at midday. Knopf, 1969 (1958) F909.C3

1585   CHALFANT, Willie Arthur
        The story of Inyo. Los Angeles, Citizens Print Shop, Inc.,
        1933   F868.I6C4.1933

1586   COX, Ross
        The Columbia River. Norman, Univ. of Oklahoma Pr., 1957
                          F880.C69.1957

1587   CRAWFORD, Medorem
        Journal of Medorem Crawford. Fairfield, Wash., Ye Galleon Pr.,
        1967   F871.S72.1967

1588   CULLETON, James
        Indians and pioneers of old Monterey. Fresno, Academy of
        California Church History, 1950   F869.M7C8

1589   DE LAGUNA, Frederica
        Chugach prehistory. Seattle, Univ. of Washington Pr., 1967
        (1956)   F906.D36.1967

1590 DRURY, Clifford Merrill
      Elkanah and Mary Walker. Caldwell, Id., The Caxton
      Printers, Ltd., 1940   F880.W24

1591 DRURY, Clifford Merrill
      Henry Harmon Spalding. Caldwell, Id., The Caxton
      Printers, Ltd., 1936   F880.S69

1592 DRYDEN, Cecil
      Up the Columbia for furs. Caldwell, Id., The Caxton
      Printers, Ltd., 1950 (1949)   F880.D78

1593 _Early California travel series_. 1-50.
      Los Angeles, G. Dawson, 1951-61. F856.E174.Spec.Coll.

1594 EELLS, Myron
      History of Indian missions on the Pacific coast.
      Oregon, Washington and Idaho. Philadelphia, Union Pr.,
      1882   E78.N8E2

1595 FAGES, Pedro
      The Colorado river campaign, 1781-1782. Berkeley,
      Calif., Univ. of California Pr., 1913   F851.A15.v.3.no.2

1596 FAGES, Pedro
      _A historical, political, and natural description of
      California._ Berkeley, Univ. of California Pr., 1937
                                      F864.F165

1597 FARNHAM, Thomas Jefferson
      Life, adventures and travels in California. Nafis &
      Cornish, 1850 (1848)   F864.F23.1850.Spec.Coll.

1598 FORBES, Alexander
      _California: a history of Upper and Lower California
      from their first discovery to the present time_.
      London, Smith, Elder and Co., 1839   F864.F6.Spec.Coll.

1599 FRIENDS, SOCIETY OF. AMERICAN FRIENDS SERVICE COMMITTEE.
      Indians of California, past and present. San Francisco,
      1960   E78.C15F7.1960

1600 HEIZER, Robert Fleming
      Francis Drake and the California Indians, 1579.
      Berkeley and Los Angeles, Univ. of California Pr., 1947
                  (UCPAE)   E51.C15.v.42.no.3

1601 HILL, Joseph John
      The history of Warner's ranch and its environs.
      Los Angeles, Priv. Print., 1927   F867.H64

1602   JAMES, George Wharton
       The lake of the sky. Pasadena, Calif., The Radiant Life Pr.,
       1921   F868.T2J3.1921

1603   JAMES, George Wharton
       Through Ramona's country. Boston, Little, Brown and Co.,
       1909 (1908)   F867.J35

1604   LARKIN, Thomas Oliver
       The affair at Monterey, October 20 & 21, 1842. Los Angeles,
       Zamorano Club, 1964   F864.L288.Spec.Coll.

1605   LEE, Bourke
       Death valley. Macmillan, 1930   F868.D2L34

16051   LEVI-STRAUSS, Claude
       L'Homme nu. Paris, Plon, 1971   E78.N77.L4

1606   LONGINOS MARTÍNEZ, José
       Journal. San Francisco, J. Howell Books, 1961 F864.L87.1961

1607   MARSHALL, Robert
       Arctic village. H. Smith and R. Haas, 1933 F909.M37

1608   Memorias para la historia natural de California. 1-
       México, Vargas Bea, 1945-   F864.M4

1609   A Mission record of the California Indians, from a manuscript
       in the Bancroft library. Berkeley, Univ. of California Pr.,
       1908   (UCPAE)   E51.C15.v.8.no.1

1610   PARKER, Samuel
       Journal of an exploring tour beyond the Rocky Mountains
       under the direction of the A. B. C. F. M. Minneapolis,
       Ross & Haines, 1967 (1838)   F880.P22.1967

16101   REID, William
       Out of the silence. Outerbridge and Dienstfrey, 1971
                         E78.N78.R4

1611   REVERE, Joseph Warren
       Naval duty in California. Oakland, Calif., Biobooks, 1947
                     F865.R4.1947.Spec.Coll.

1612   ROBINSON, Alfred
       Life in California. Da Capo Pr., 1969 F864.R65.1969

1613   ROGERS, George William
       Alaska in transition. Baltimore, Published for Resources
       for the Future by Johns Hopkins Pr., 1960 HC107.A45R6

1614   ROSS, Alexander
        Adventures of the first settlers on the Oregon or Columbia
        river. Chicago, R. R. Donnelley & Sons Co., 1923 F880.R812

1615   ROSS, Alexander
        The fur hunters of the far West. Chicago, R. R. Donnelley
        & Sons Co., 1924   F880.R84

1616   SAN MARTÍN, José
        Memoria y proposiciones del señor don José San Martín.
        México, Vargas Rea, 1943   F864.S2

1617   SANTA MARIA, Vicente
        The first Spanish entry into San Francisco Bay, 1775.
        San Francisco, J. Howell, 1971   fF868.S156S2

1618   SCHWATKA, Frederick
        Report of a military reconnaissance in Alaska. Washington,
        D. C., U. S. Govt. Print. Off., 1885   F908.S35

1619   SECURITY TRUST & SAVINGS BANK, LOS ANGELES.
        El pueblo, Los Angeles before the railroads. Los Angeles,
        Equitable Branch of the Security Trust & Savings Bank,
        1928   F869.L8S44

1620   STUART, Robert
        The discovery of the Oregon trail. C. Scribner's Sons,
        1935   F880.S925

1621   TARAVAL, Sigismundo
        The Indian uprising in Lower California, 1734-1737.
        Los Angeles, The Quivira Society, 1931 F864.T252.Spec.Coll.

1622   TAYLOR, Katherine Ames
        Lights and shadows of Yosemite. San Francisco, H. S.
        Crocker Co., Inc. 1926   F868.Y6T2

1623   THOMPSON, William
        Reminiscences of a pioneer. San Francisco, 1912 F881.T46

16231   U. S. DEPT. OF THE INTERIOR
        Rolls of certain Indian tribes in Oregon and Washington.
        (Incl. U. S. 59th Cong., 2nd sess. House Document no. 133
        Date in book: 1969) Ye Galleon, 1970   E78.O6.U5.1969

1624   VENEGAS, Miguel
        A natural and civil history of California. London,
        J. Rivington and J. Fletcher, 1759   F864.V4.Spec.Coll.

1625   WALKER, Ernest Pillsbury
        <u>Alaska: America's continental frontier outpost</u>.
        City of Washington, The Smithsonian Institution, 1943
                            (SIWBS)   GN4.S6.no.13

1626   WEBB, Edith (Buckland)
        <u>Indian life at the old missions</u>. Los Angeles,
        W. F. Lewis, 1952   F864.W4

1627   WINTHROP, Theodore
        <u>The canoe and the saddle</u>. Tacoma, J. H. Williams, 1913 (1863)
                                            F891.W82

1628   WORK, John
        <u>The Snake Country expedition of 1830-1831</u>. Norman,
        Univ. of Oklahoma Pr., 1971   F880.W9

1629   BAILEY, Alfred Goldsworthy
        The conflict of European and Eastern Algonkian cultures
        1504-1700. Toronto, Univ. of Toronto Pr., 1969
                                        F1021.B25.1969

1630   BARBEAU, Charles Marius
        Indian days in the Canadian Rockies. Toronto,
        Macmillan Co. of Canada Ltd., 1923   E78.C2B23

1631   CANADA. DEPT. OF MARINE AND FISHERIES.
        Report on the Dominion government expedition to
        Hudson Bay and the Arctic islands on board the D. G. S.
        Neptune, 1903-1904. Ottawa, Government Printing Bureau,
        1906   F1060.9.C221

1632   CARTIER, Jacques
        The voyages of Jacques Cartier. Ottawa, F. A. Acland,
        Printer, 1924   F1001.C128.no.11

1633   CHAMPLAIN, Samuel de
        Voyages of Samuel de Champlain, 1604-1618. Barnes &
        Noble, 1952   F1030.1.C494.1952

1634   CHARLEVOIX, Pierre Francois Xavier
        Journal of a voyage to North America. Ann Arbor, Mich.,
        University Microfilms, 1966   F1030.C503

1635   DENYS, Nicolas
        Description & natural history of the coasts of North
        America (Acadia). Greenwood Pr., 1968 F1038.D43.1968

1636   DOBBS, Arthur
        An account of the countries adjoinint to Hudson's Bay
        in the North-west part of America. Wakefield, Eng.,
        S. R. Publishers; Johnson Reprint, 1967 (1744)
                                        F1060.7.D63.1967

1637   DOUVILLE, Raymond
        La Vie quotidienne des Indiens au Canada à l'époque
        de la colonisation française. Paris, Hachette, 1967
                                        E78.C2D6

1638   FARAUD, Henri, bp of Anemour
        Dix-huit ans chez les sauvages. Wakefield, Yorkshire,
        Eng., S. R. Publishers, 1965 (1866) F1060.8.F21.1866a

1639   GREENBIE, Sydney
        Frontiers and the fur trade. John Day Co., 1929 F1030.G78

1640   HAYES, John F.
        Wilderness mission. Toronto, Ryerson Pr., 1969 F1030.7.H38

1641   HEARNE, Samuel
        Coppermine journey. Boston, Little, Brown, 1958 F1060.7.H445

1642   HEARNE, Samuel
        A journey from Prince of Wale's Fort in Hudson's Bay to the
        Northern Ocean. Greenwood Pr., 1968   F1060.7.H42.1968

1643   HENRY, Alexander
        New light on the early history of the greater Northwest.
        Minneapolis, Ross & Haines, 1965   F1060.7.H52.1965

1644   HENRY, Alexander
        Travels and adventures in Canada. Ann Arbor, Mich.,
        University Microfilms, 1966   F1013.H52.1809a

1645   HOWARD, Joseph Kinsey
        Strange empire. Morrow, 1952   F1060.9.H68

1646   ISELY, Bliss
        Blazing the way west. C. Scribner's Sons, 1939 F1030.I76

1647   JESUITS. LETTERS FROM MISSIONS (NORTH AMERICA).
        Black gowns and redskins. London, New York, Longmans,
        Green, 1956   F1030.7.C965.1956

1648   JESUITS. LETTERS FROM MISSIONS (NORTH AMERICA).
        The Indians of North America. Harcourt, Brace & Co., 1927
                                               F1030.7.C964

1649   KANE, Paul
        Wanderings of an artist among the Indians of North America
        from Canada to Vancouver's island and Oregon. Toronto,
        The Radisson Society of Canada, Ltd., 1925 F1060.8.K163

1650   KENNEDY, John Hopkins
        Jesuit and savage in new France. Hamden, Conn., Archon
        Books, 1971 (1950)   F1030.7.K44.1971

1651   KENTON, Edna
        With hearts courageous. Liveright Pub. Corp., 1948
                                               F1030.7.K46.1948

1652   LAHONTAN, Louis Armand de Lom d'Arce, baron de
        Dialogues curieux entre l'auteur et un sauvage de bon sens
        qui a voyagé. Baltimore, The Johns Hopkins Pr.; Paris,
        A. Margraff, 1931   F1030.L145
                                165

1653   LAHONTAN, Louis Armand de Lom d'Arce, baron de
        New voyages to North-America. Chicago, A. C. McClurg,
        1905   F1030.L184

1654   LE CLERCQ, Chrétien
        New relations of Gaspesia. Greenwood Pr., 1968
                              F1054.G2L5.1968

1655   LESCARBOT, Marc
        History of New France. Greenwood Pr., 1968
                              F1030.L6553.1968

1656   LESCARBOT, Marc
        Nova Francia, a description of Acadia, 1606. Harper &
        Brothers, 1928   F1030.L656

1657   MACKENZIE, Sir Alexander
        Alexander Mackenzie's voyage to the Pacific ocean in
        1793. Chicago, The Lakeside Pr., R. R. Donnelley &
        Sons Co., 1931   F1060.7.M178

1658   MACKENZIE, Sir Alexander
        Exploring the Northwest Territory. Norman, Univ. of
        Oklahoma Pr., 1966   F1060.7.M1773

1659   MACKENZIE, Sir Alexander
        The journals and letters of Sir Alexander Mackenzie.
        Cambridge, Eng., Published for the Hakluyt Society at
        the University Pr., 1970   F1060.7.M13

1660   RADISSON, Pierre Esprit
        Voyages of Peter Esprit Radisson. P. Smith, 1943
        (i.e. 1853)   F1060.9.R16

1661   RALPH, Julian
        On Canada's frontier. Harper & Brothers, 1892
                              F1060.9.R16

1662   ROSS, Eric
        Beyond the river and the bay. Toronto, University of
        Toronto Pr., 1970   F1060.7.R84

1663   ROUSTANG, François ed.
        An autobiography of martyrdom. St. Louis, Herder,
        1964   F1030.7.R873

1664   SAGARD-Théodat, Gabriel
        The long journey to the country of the Hurons.
        Greenwood Pr., 1968   F1030.S135.1939a

1665   SAUNDERS, Audrey
        Algonquin story. Toronto, Ontario Dept. of Lands and
        Forests, 1963   F1059.A4S3.1963

1666   TACHÉ, Alexandre Antonin
        <u>Vingt années de missions dans le nordouest de l'Amérique</u>.
        East Ardsley, Yorks., S. R. Publishers; New York, Johnson
        Reprint Corp.; La Haye, Mouton & Co., 1969 (1866)
                              F1060.T118.1969

1667   TALBOT, Francis Xavier
        <u>Saint among the Hurons</u>. Garden City, N.Y., Doubleday, 1956
        (1949)   F1030.8.B8T28.1956

1668   WORK, John
        <u>The journal of John Work</u>. Cleveland, Arthur H. Clark Co.,
        1923   F1060.W92

1669   YOUNG, Egerton Ryerson
        <u>By canoe and dog-train among the Cree and Salteaux Indians</u>.
        Hunt and Eaton, 1890   F1060.9.Y72

Mexico

1670   ANGULA V., Jorge
        Un posible códice de El Mirador, Chiapas. México,
        Departamento de Prehistoria, Instituto Nacional de
        Antropología e Historia, 1970   F1219.A6

1671   AUGUR, Helen
        Zapotec. Garden City, N.Y., Doubleday, 1954
                                                F1321.A8.1954

1672   BAEGERT, Jakob
        Noticias de la península americana de California.
        México, Antigua Librería Robredo de J. Porrúa e Hijos,
        1942   F1246.B15

1673   BAEGERT, Jakob
        Observations in Lower California. Berkeley, Univ. of
        California Pr., 1952   F1246.B143

1674   BANDELIER, Adolph Francis Alphonse
        A scientist on the trail. Berkeley, Calif., Quivira
        Society, 1949   F1215.B22.1967

1675   BERLIN, Heinrich
        Fragmentos desconocidos del Codice de Yanhuitlán.
        México, J. Porrua, 1947   F1391.Y3B4

1676   BERNAL, Ignacio
        Mexico before Cortez. Garden City, N.Y., Doubleday,
        1963   F1219.1.M53B43

1677   BERNAL, Ignacio
        3000 years of art and life in Mexico. H. N. Abrams,
        1968   F1219.B5313

1678   BOTURINI BENADUCCI, Lorenzo
        Tezcoco en los últimos tiempos de sus antiguos reyes.
        México, 1970   F1219.1.T4B7.1970

1679   BRADEN, Charles Samuel
        Religious aspects of the conquest of Mexico. AMS,
        1966   F1230.B79.1966

16791   BRUNDAGE, Burr Cartwright
        A rain of darts; the Mexica Aztecs. Austin, Univ. of
        Texas Pr., 1972   F1219.B89

1680 BYAM DAVIES, Claude Nigel
Los señoríos independientes del Imperio Azteca. México,
Instituto Nacional de Antropología e Historia, 1968   F1219.B99

1681 CAMPBELL, Camilla
Star mountain. McGraw-Hill, 1968   F1210.C3.1968

1682 CANALS FRAU, Salvador
Las civilizaciones prehispánicas de América. Buenos Aires,
Editorial Sudamericana, 1959   E65.C35.1959

1683 CANSECO VINCOURT, Jorge
La guerra sagrada. México, Instituto Nacional de Antropología
e Historia, 1966   F1219.C285

1684 CHÁVEZ, Ezequiel Adeodato
Apuntes sobre la colonia. México, Jus, 1958 F1201.F5.no.52-54

1685 CLAVIJERO, Francisco Javier
Historia antigua de México. México, Editorial Porrúa,
1958-59.   F1219.C6293.1958

1686 CLAVIJERO, Francisco Javier
The history of Mexico. London, G. G. J. and J. Robinson, 1787
F1219.C62.Spec.Coll.

1687 CODEX AUBIN
Historia de la nación mexicana. Madrid, J. Porrúa Turanzas,
1963   F1219.C6368

1688 CODEX LAUD.
Códice Laud. Mexico, Instituto Nacional de Antropología de
Historia, 1961   (INAH)   F1219.M627.no.5

1689 CODEX OSUNA
Codice Osuna. México, Ediciones del Instituto Indigenista
Interamericano, 1947   F1231.0852

1690 COE, Michael D.
Mexico. Praeger, 1962   F1219.C757

1691 Corpus antiquitatum Americanesium:
México. México, Instituto Nacional de Antropología e
Historia, 1964-   F1221.Z3C6.Spec.Coll.

1692 COVARRUBIAS, Miguel
Mexico south, the isthmus of Tehuantepec. Knopf, 1954 (1946)
F1359.C6.1954

1693 DIVEN, Thomas J.
Aztecs and Mayas. v. 1- Chicago, The Antiquarian Co., 1909-
F1219.D61

169

16931   GANN, Thomas William Francis
        Ancient cities and modern tribes: exploration and
        adventure in Maya lands. C. Scribner's Sons, 1926
                                        F1435.G17

1694   GARCÍA CUBAS, Antonio
        The republic of Mexico in 1876. Mexico, "La Enseñanza"
        Print. Office, 1876   F1208.G26

1695   GARCÍA GRANADOS, Rafael
        Diccionario biográfico de historia antigua de Méjico.
        Méjico, Instituto de Historia, 1952-53 (i.e. 1955)
                                        F1219.G27

16951   GAY, Carlo T. E.
        Chalcacingo. Portland, Or., International Scholarly Book
        Services, 1972   fF1219.1.C38.G3.1972

1696   GIBSON, Charles
        Tlaxcala in the sixteenth century. New Haven, Yale
        Univ. Pr., 1952   F1366.G4

1697   GILLMOR, Frances
        The King danced in the marketplace. Tucson, Univ. of
        Arizona Pr., 1964   F1219.G47.1964

1698   GOTARI, Eli de
        La ciencia en la historia de México. México, Buenos
        Aires, Fondo de Cultura Económica, 1963 F1219.e.S35G6

1699   GRANBERG, Wilbur J.
        People of the maguey. Praeger, 1970   F1221.O86G7

1700   GRIFFEN, William B.
        Culture change and shifting populations in central
        northern Mexico. Tucson, Univ. of Arizona Pr., 1969
                                        F1261.G7

1701   GRIFFITH, James S.
        Legacy of conquest. Colorado Springs, Taylor Museum of
        the Colorado Springs Fine Arts Center, 1967 F1219.3.A7G68

1702   GURRÍA LACROIX, Jorge
        Códice Entrada de los españoles en Tlaxcala. México,
        Universidad Nacional Autónoma de México, 1966 F1219.G95

1703   HEDRICK, Basil Calvin
        The north Mexican frontier. Carbondale, Southern Illinois
        Univ. Pr., 1971   F1219.H45

1704   HEWETT, Edgar Lee
        Ancient life in Mexico and Central America. Tudor, 1943
        (1936)   F1219.H48

1705   Historia tolteca-chichimeca. México, Antigua Libería Robredo,
        1947   F1219.H676

1706   HUERTA PRECIADO, María Teresa
        Rebeliones indígenas en el noreste de México en la época
        colonial. México, Instituto Nacional de Antropologia e
        Historia, 1966   F1231.H8.1966

1707   Indian Mexico: past and present. Los Angeles, Latin American
        Center, Univ. of California, 1967   F1219.I44

1708   IXTLILXOCHITL, Fernando de Alva
        Ally of Cortés. El Paso, Texas, Western Pr., 1969 F1230.1973

1709   JIMÉNEZ, Luz
        De Porfirio Díaz a Zapata. México, UNAM, Instituto de
        Investigaciones Históricas, 1968   F1391.M55J5.1968

1710   KEEN, Benjamin
        The Aztec image in Western thought. New Brunswick, N.J.
        Rutgers Univ. Pr., 1971   F1219.K43

1711   Los Lacandones. México, Instituto Nacional de Antropología
        e Historia, 1967-   F1221.L2L3

1712   LANDA, Diego de
        Landa's Relacion de las cosas de Yucatan, a translation.
        Cambridge, Mass., The Museum, 1941
                            (PMP)   E51.H337.v.18

1713   LANDA, Diego de
        Relación de las cosas de Yucatán. México, Editorial
        Porrúa, 1959   F1376.L246.1959

1714   LAWRENCE, David Herbert
        Mornings in Mexico. Knopf, 1934 (1927) F1215.L4

1715   LEANDER, Birgitta
        Códice de Otlazpan (acompañado de un facsimile del códice)
        XIII. Mexico, Instituto de Antropología e Historia, 1967
                                                    fF1219.1.O8L4

1716   LEÓN PORTILLA, Miguel ed.
        The broken spears. Boston, Beacon Pr., 1962 F1230.L383

1717   LEÓN PORTILLA, Miguel
        Imagen del México antiguo. Buenos Aires, Editorial
        Universitaria de Buenos Aires, 1963   F1219.L5555

1718   LEÓN PORTILLA, Miguel comp.
        Testimonios sudcalifornianos. México, UNAM. 1970
                                                    F1391.L32L4

1719   LUMHOLTZ, Karl Sofus
        Unknown Mexico. C. Scribner's Sons, 1902 F1215.L93

1720   MATA TORRES, Ramón
        Los huicholes. Guadalajara, México, Casa de la Cultura
        Jalisciense, 1970   F1296.M3

1721   MÉNDEZ PLANCARTE, Gabriel ed.
        Humanistas del siglo XVIII. México, Universidad Nacional
        Autónoma de México, 1962   F1210.M46.1962

17211   MITCHELL, James Leslie
        The conquest of the Maya. Dutton, 1935 F1435.M68.1935

1722   MORENO TOSCANO, Alejandra
        Fray Juan de Torquemada y su Monarquía indiana.
        Xalapa, Universidad Veracruzana, 1963   F1219.T68M6

1723   MOTOLINIA, Toribio
        Historia de los indios de la Nueva España. México,
        D. F., Chávez Hayhoe, 1941   F1219.M92.1941

1724   MOTOLINIA, Toribio
        History of the Indians of New Spain. Washington,
        Academy of American Franciscan History, 1951 F1219.M9223

1725   NORMAN, Benjamin Moore
        Rambles in Yucatan. J. & H. G. Langley, 1843 F1376.N84

1726   OCAMPO, Javier
        Las ideas de un día. México, Colegio de México, 1969
                                                    F1232.025

1727   OCH, Joseph
        Missionary in Sonora. San Francisco, California Historical
        Society, 1965   F1346.03

1728   ODENA, Lina
        Totonacos y Huastecos. México, INAH, 1968 F1220.T603

1729   OLSON, Charles
        Mayan letters. London, Cape, 1968   F1376.04

1730   OROZCO Y BERRA, Manuel
        Historia antigua y de la conquista de México. México,
        Editorial Porrúa, 1960   F1219.O75.1960

1731   ORTEGA, José de
        Historia del Nayarit. México, Tipografía de E. Abadiano,
        1887   F1231.O77

1732   PEISSEL, Michel
        The lost world of Quintana Roo. Dutton, 1963 F1333.P4

1733   PETERSON, Frederick A.
        Ancient Mexico. Putnam, 1959   F1219.P42

1734   PIÑA CHAN, Román
        Las culturas preclásicas de la cuenca de México.
        México, Fondo de Cultura Económica, 1955 F1219.P42

1735   POWELL, Philip Wayne
        Soldiers, Indians & silver. Berkeley, Univ. of California
        Pr., 1952   F1231.P68

1736   RADIN, Paul
        The sources and authenticity of the history of the
        ancient Mexicans. Berkeley, Univ. of California Pr.,
        1920   (UCPAE)   E51.C15.v.17.no.1

1737   REED, Alma M.
        The ancient past of Mexico. Crown Publishers, 1966 F1219.R3

1738   REED, Nelson
        The Caste War of Yucatan. Stanford, Calif., Stanford
        Univ. Pr., 1964   F1376.R43

1739   ROBERTSON, Thomas A.
        A southwestern Utopia. Los Angeles, W. Ritchie Pr.,
        1964   HX656.T62R6.1964

1740   ROSENBLAT, Angel
        La población de América en 1492. México, Colegio de
        México, 1967   F1219.3.S7R6

17401   ROYS, Ralph Loveland
        The Indian background of colonial Yucatan. Norman, Univ.
        of Oklahoma Pr., 1972   F1219.1.Y8.R6.1972

1741   SAHAGÚN, Bernardino de
        General history of the things of New Spain. Santa Fe, N.M.
        School of American Research, 1950—   F1219.S1319

1742　　SAHAGÚN, Bernardino de
　　　　　Historia general de las cosas de Nueva España. México,
　　　　　Porrúa, 1956　　　　　　　　　　　　F1219.S331

17421　SAHAGUN, Bernardino de
　　　　　A history of ancient Mexico. Blaine Ethridge, 1971
　　　　　(1932)　　　　　　　　　　　　　F1219.S132

1743　　SALVATIERRA, Juan María de
　　　　　Selected letters about Lower California. Los Angeles,
　　　　　Dawson's Book Shop, 1971　　　F1246.S1713.Spec.Coll.

1744　　SANDERS, William T.
　　　　　Mesoamerica. Random House, 1968　　　F1219.S18.1968

1745　　SAUER, Carl Ortwin
　　　　　Colima of New Spain in the sixteenth century. Berkeley,
　　　　　Univ. of California Pr., 1948　(IAM)　F1401.I22.no.29

1746　　SCHOLES, France Vinton　ed.
　　　　　Don Diego Quijada, alcalde mayor de Yucatán, 1561-1565.
　　　　　México, Antigua Librería Robredo, de J. Porrúa e Hijos,
　　　　　1938　　　　　　　　　　　　　　F1376.Q67

1747　　SCHOLES, France Vinton
　　　　　The Maya Chontal Indians of Acalan-Tixchel. Norman,
　　　　　Univ. of Oklahoma Pr., 1968　　　　F1376.S486.1968

1748　　SCHOLES, Walter Vinton
　　　　　The Diego Ramirez visita. Columbia, Univ. of Missouri,
　　　　　1946　　　　　　　　　　　　　　F1231.S35

1749　　SCHWATKA, Frederick
　　　　　In the land of cave and cliff dwellers. Cassell Pub.
　　　　　Co., 1893　　　　　　　　　　　　F1261.S39

1750　　SÉJOURNÉ, Laurette
　　　　　La pensée des anciens Mexicains. Paris, F. Maspero,
　　　　　1966　　　　　　　　　　　　　　F1219.S45

17501　SHEARER, Tony
　　　　　Lord of the Dawn: Quetzalcoatl, the plumed serpent of
　　　　　Mexico. Healdsburg, Calif., Naturegraph Pub., 1971
　　　　　　　　　　　　　　　　　　　　F1219.S47

1751　　SOUSTELLE, Jacques
　　　　　Mexico. London, Varrie & Rockliff the Cresset P.,
　　　　　1969　　　　　　　　　　　　　F1219.S7253.1969

1752　　SOUSTELLE, Jacques
　　　　　Mexique, terre indienne. Paris, B. Grasset, 1936
　　　　　　　　　　　　　　　　　　　　F1215.S698

1753   SOUSTELLE, Jacques
        La Vie quotidienne des Azteques à la veille de la conquête
        espagnole. Paris, Hachette, 1955   F1219.S72

17531   SOUSTELLE, Jacques
        Les Azteques. Paris, Presses Universitaires de France,
        1970   F1219.S714

1754   SPINDEN, Herbert Joseph
        Ancient civilizations of Mexico and Central America.
        American Museum Pr., 1922   F1219.S766

1755   STEININGER, George Russell
        Three dollars a year. Detroit, B. Ethridge Books, 1971
        (1935)   F1221.Z3S7.1971

1756   TAVERA ALFARO, Xavier comp.
        Dos etapas de la independencia. Morelia, Departamento
        de Difusión Cultural e Intercambio Universitario, 1966
                                            F1232.T2

1757   THOMPSON, John Eric Signey
        Mexico before Cortez. C. Scribner's Sons, 1940 (1933)
                                            F1219.T46

1758   TORQUEMADA, Juan de
        Monarquía indiana. México, Universidad Nacional Autónoma
        de México, 1964   F1219.T68.1964

17581   VIGIL, Jose Maria
        Nezahualcoyotl. Mexico, Govierno Del Estado de Mexico, 1972
                                            F1219.N48.1972

1759   VIVÓ, Jorge Abilio
        Razas y lenguas indígenas de México. México, D. F.,
        "Industrial Gráfica, S. A.", 1941 (PAIP) F1401.P153.no.52

1760   VON HAGEN, Victor Wolfgang
        The ancient sun kingdoms of the Americas: Aztec, Maya,
        Inca. Cleveland, World Pub. Co., 1961 E65.V6

1761   WEBER, David J. comp.
        The extranjeros. Santa Fe, Stagecoach Pr., 1967 F1392.A5W43

1762   WOLF, Eric Robert
        Sons of the shaking earth. Chicago, Univ. of Chicago Pr.,
        1959   F1210.W6

1763   ZUÑIGA, Ignacio
        Rápida ojeada al Estado de Sonora. México, Vargas Rea,
        1948   F1346.Z8.1948

1764   ZURITA, Alonso de
           <u>Life and labor in ancient Mexico</u>. New Brunswick, N.J.,
           Rutgers Univ. Pr., 1963   F1219.Z943

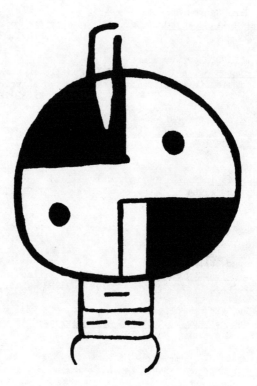

Central America

1765   ARMELLADA, Cesáreo de
        La causa indigena americana en las Cortes de Cádiz.
        Madrid, Ediciones Cultura Hispanica, 1959 F1412.A7

1766   BIESANZ, John Berry
        The people of Panama. Columbia Univ. Pr., 1964 (1955)
                                                F1563.8.B5

1767   BUNZEL, Ruth Leah
        Chichicastenango, a Guatemalan village. Seattle, Univ.
        of Washington Pr., 1959   F1476.V5B8

1768   CARBIA, Rómulo D.
        Historia de la leyenda Negra Hispano-Americana. Madrid,
        Consejo de la Hispanidad, 1944   F1410.C265

1769   CARRO, Venancio Diego
        España en America. Madrid, Librería Ope, 1963 F1410.C265

1770   CASAS, Bartolomé de las
        Bartolomé de las Casas. Knopf, 1971   F1411.C4273.1971

1771   CASAS, Bartolomé de las
        Doctrina. México, Universidad Nacional Autónoma, 1951
                                          F1411.C319.1951

1772   CASAS, Bartolomé de las
        Historia de las Indias. México, Fondo de Cultural Económica,
        1951   F1411.C4674.1951

1773   CASAS, Bartolomé de las
        The tears of the Indians. Stanford, Calif., Academic Reprints,
        1953? (1656)   F1411.C424.1656a

1774   COE, William R.
        Tikal. Philadelphia, Univ. Museum, Univ. of Pennsylvania,
        1967   F1465.1.T5C6

1775   FERGUSSON, Erna
        Guatemala. Knopf, 1942   F1464.F47

1776   HANKE, Lewis
        Aristotle and the American Indians. Chicago, H. Regnery Co.,
        1959   F1411.H33

1777   HANKE, Lewis
        The first social experiments in America. Gloucester, Mass.
        P. Smith, 1964 (1935)   F1411.H35.1964

1778   HANKE, Lewis
       The Spanish struggle for justice in the conquest of
       America. Philadelphia, Univ. of Pennsylvania Pr., 1949
                      F1411.H37

1779   HELMS, Mary W.
       Asang. Gainesville, Univ. of Florida Pr., 1971 F1529.M9H4

1780   HELPS, Sir Arthur
       The Spanish conquest in America. AMS, 1966   F1411.H482

1781   IVANOFF, Pierre
       Mayan enigma. Delacorte Pr., 1971   F1435.1.P47I8513

1782   KELSEY, Vera
       Four keys to Guatemala. Funk & Wagnalls, 1952
                      F1463.K45.1952

1783   KONETZKE, Richard ed.
       Colección de documentos para la historia de la formación
       social de Hispanoamérica, 1493-1810. Madrid, Consejo
       Superior de Investigaciones Científicas, 1953- F1410.K6

1784   LA FARGE, Oliver
       Santa Eulalia. Chicago, Univ. of Chicago Pr., 1947
                      F1465.3.R4L3

17841   MELENDEZ CHAVERRI, Carlos
       La Ilustracion en el antiguo reino de Guatemala.
       Costa Rica, San Jose, Editorial Universitaria Centroamericana,
       1970   F1463.5.M4

1785   MILES, Suzanne W.
       The sixteenth-century Pokom-Maya. Philadelphia, American
       Philosophical Society, 1957   F1465.2.P6M5

1786   MITCHELL-HEDGES, Frederick Albert
       Land of wonder and fear. Century Co., 1931 F1432.M67

1787   OAKES, Maud van Cortlandt
       The two crosses of Todos Santos. Pantheon Books, 1951
                      F1465.2.M303

1788   O'NEALE, Lila Morris
       Textiles of highland Guatemala. Johnson Reprint, 1966(1945)
                      F1465.3.T4057.1945a

1789   PAN AMERICAN INSTITUTE OF GEOGRAPHY AND HISTORY. COMMISSION
       ON HISTORY.
       El mestizaje en la historia de Ibero-América. Mexico, D.F.,
       1962   F1419.A1P2

1790   PIÑA, CHÁN, Román
        Jaina, la casa en el agua. México, Instituto Nacional de
        Antropología e Historia, 1968   F1435.1.J3P5

1791   PUXLEY, W. Lavallin
        The magic land of the Maya. London, G. Allen & Unwin Ltd.,
        1928   F1432.P97

1792   SIGÜENZA Y GÓNGORA, Carlos de
        Obras históricas. México, Editorial Porrúa, 1960
                                               F1412.S5.1960

1793   STEPHENS, John Lloyd
        Incidents of travel in Central America, Chiapas, and
        Yucatan. Harper & Brothers, 1841-43   F1432.S83

1794   TAX, Sol
        Heritage of conquest. Cooper Square Pub., 1968 (1952)
                                               F1434.T3.1968

1795   THOMPSON, Edward Herbert
        People of the serpent. Boston and New York, Houghton
        Mifflin Co., 1932   F1435.T483

1796   Tratado de Indias de Monseñor [de] Chiapa y el Doctor Sepúlveda.
        Caracas, Academia Nacional de la Historia, 1962   F1411.C47

1797   ZAVALA, Silvio Arturo
        Contribución a la historia de las instituciones coloniales
        en Guatemala. Guatemala, Universidad de San Carlos de
        Guatemala, 1967   F1465.Z39.1967

1798   ZAVALA, Silvio Arturo
        New viewpoints on the Spanish colonization of America.
        Russell & Russell, 1968 (1943)   F1411.Z373.1968

1799   ABEL, Annie Heloise
       The American Indian as participant in the civil war.
       Johnson Reprint Corp., 1970 (1919)   E540.I3A2.1970

1800   BATES, Charles Francis
       Custer's Indian battles. Bronxville, N.Y., 1936 fE467.1.C99B3

1801   BEAL, Merrill D.
       "I will fight no more forever." Seattle, Univ. of Washington
       Pr., 1963   E83.877.B4

1802   BEARD, Reed
       The battle of Tippecanoe. Chicago, Donohue & Henneberry,
       Printers, 1889   E83.81.B35

1803   BEMROSE, John
       Reminiscences of the Second Seminole War. Gainesville,
       Univ. of Florida Pr., 1966   E83.835.B4

1804   BIGELOW, John
       On the bloody trail of Geronimo. Los Angeles,
       Westernlore Pr., 1968   E83.88.B5.1968

1805   BIRD, Harrison
       War for the west, 1790-1813. Oxford Univ. Pr., 1971 E55.1.B5

1806   BISHOP, Mrs. Harriet E.
       Dakota war whoop: or, Indian massacres and war in Minnesota,
       of 1862-3. Minneapolis, Ross & Haines, 1970 E83.86.B622.1970

1807   BLACK HAWK, Sauk Chief
       Black Hawk (Ma-ka-tai-me-she-kia-kiak). Urbana, Univ. of
       Illinois Pr., 1955   E83.83.B635

1808   BLEDSOE, Anthony Jennings
       Indian wars of the Northwest, a California sketch. Oakland,
       Biobooks, 1956   E83.84.B64.1956

1809   BOURKE, John Gregory
       An Apache campaign in the Sierra Madre. Scribner, 1958
                                               E83.88.B76.1958

1810   BOURKE, John Gregory
       On the border with Crook. Columbus, Ohio, Long's College
       Book Co., 1950   E83.866.B77.1950

18101   BOURKE, John Gregory
        With General Crook in the Indian Wars. Palo Alto,
        Osborne, 1968   E83.866.B79

1811   BOYLE, William Henry
        Personal observations on the conduct of the Modoc War.
        Los Angeles, Dawson's Book Shop, 1959 E83.87.B6.Spec.Coll.

18111   BRADLEY, Arthur Granville
        The fight with France for North America. Arno, 1971
                                               E199.B8.1971

1812   BRADY, Cyrus Townsend
        Indian fights and fighters. Lincoln, Univ. of Nebraska Pr.,
        1971   E83.866.B82.1971

1813   BRAM, Joseph
        An analysis of Inca militarism. J. J. Augustin, 1941
                        (MAES)   E51.A556.v.4

1814   BRANDES, Raymond
        Troopers West: military and Indian affairs on the
        American frontier. San Diego, Calif., Frontier Heritage
        Pr., 1970   E83.866.B83

1815   BRILL, Charles J.
        Conquest of the southern plains. Oklahoma City, Golden
        Saga Publishers, 1938   E83.869.B75

1816   BRININSTOOL, Earl Alonzo
        Fighting Red Cloud's warriors. Columbus, Ohio,
        The Hunter-trader-trapper Co., 1926   E83.866.B85

1817   BRININSTOOL, Earl Alonzo
        Troopers with Custer. Harrisburgh, Pa., Stackpole Co.,
        1952   E83.876.B85.1952

1818   BROWN, Dee Alexander
        Bury my heart at Wounded Knee. Holt, Rinehart & Winston,
        1971 (1970)   E81.B75.1971

1819   BROWN, Dee Alexander
        Fort Phil Kearny, an American saga. Putnam, 1962
                                               E83.866.B87

1820   BROWN, Dee Alexander
        The Galvanized Yankees. Urbana, Univ. of Illinois Pr.,
        1963   E83.863.B7

18201   BROWN, Dee Alexander
        Showdown at Little Big Horn. Berkeley Pub., 1971
                                               E83.876.B87.1971

1821   BROWN Mark Herbert
        The flight of the Nez Perce. Putnam, 1967   E83.877.B7

1822   BUCK, Daniel
        Indian outbreaks. Minneapolis, Ross & Haines, 1965
                                             E83.86.B93.1965

1823   BUNN, Matthew
        A journal of the adventures of Matthew Bunn. Chicago, 1962
                                             E83.79.B94.1796a

1824   BURNS, Robert Ignatius
        The Jesuits and the Indian wars of the Northwest. New Haven,
        Yale Univ. Pr., 1966   E83.84.B9

1825   BYRNE, Patrick Edward
        Soldiers of the plains. Minton, Balch & Co., 1926   E83.866.B98

1826   CARRINGTON, Frances (Courtney)
        My army life and the Fort Phil. Kearney massacre.
        Philadelphia & London, J. B. Lippincott Co., 1911 (1910)
                                             E83.866.C31

1827   CHALMERS, Harvey
        The last stand of the Nez Perce. Twayne Publishers, 1962
                                             E83.877.C5

1828   COHEN, Myer M.
        Notices of Florida and the campaigns. Gainesville,
        Univ. of Florida Pr., 1964   E83.835.C67.1836a

1829   COLE, Cyrenus
        I am a man. Iowa City, Ia., The State Historical Society
        of Iowa, 1938   E83.83.B638

1830   COLTON, Ray Charles
        The Civil War in the western territories: Arizona, Colorado,
        New Mexico, and Utah. Norman, Univ. of Oklahoma Pr., 1959
                                             E470.9.C7

1831   CROOK, George
        General George Crook, his autobiography. Norman, Univ. of
        Oklahoma Pr., 1946   E83.866.C93

18311   CROOK, George
        Resume of operations against Apache Indians, 1882-1886.
        United Kingdom, Johnson-Taunton Military, 1971 E83.88.C7.1971

1832   CRUSE, Thomas
        Apache days and after. Caldwell, Id., The Caxton Printers,
        Ltd., 1941   E83.866.C95

1833   DARLINTON, Mary Carson (O'Hara) comp.
        History of Col. Henry Bouquet and the western frontiers
        of Pennsylvania, 1747-1764. Arno, 1971 (1920) E83.76.B75.1971

18331   DILLON, Richard H.
        Burnt-out fires. Prentice, 1973   E83.87.D5.1973

1834   DOWNEY, Fairfax Davis
        The Buffalo Soldiers in the Indian Wars. McGraw-Hill, 1969
                                               UA30.D6

1835   DRAKE, Benjamin
        The great Indian chief of the West: or, Life and
        adventures of Black Hawk. Cincinnati, H. M. Rulison,
        1857 (1848)   E83.83.B656

1836   DUNN, Jacob Piatt
        Massacres of the mountains. Harper & Brothers, 1886 E81.D92

1837   ECCLESTON, Robert
        The Mariposa Indian War, 1850-1851. Salt Lake City,
        Univ. of Utah Pr., 1957   E83.85.E3

1838   ECKERT, Allan W.
        The conquerors. Boston, Little, Brown, 1970 E83.76.E27

1839   EMMITT, Robert
        The last war trail. Norman, Univ. of Oklahoma Pr., 1954
                                               E83.879.E55

1840   FINERTY, John Frederick
        War-path and bivouac. Chicago, Donohue & Henneberry,
        1890   E83.866.F5

18401   FLINT, Timothy
        Indian wars of the West. (First American frontier)
        Arno, 1971   E81.F62.1971

18402   FORBES, John
        Writings of General John Forbes relating to his service
        in North America. Arno, 1971   E199.F694.1971

1841   FRINK, Maurice
        Fort Defiance & the Navajos. Boulder, Colo., Pruett Pr.,
        1968   E83.859.F7

1842   FROST, John
        Indian wars of the United States. Auburn, Derby and Miller,
        1852   E81.F943

1843   FROST, John
        <u>Indian wars of the United States, from the discovery to</u>
        <u>the present time</u>. Philadelphia, J. B. Smith & Co., 1857 (1850)
                                        E81.F95.Spec.Coll.

1844   GIDDINGS, Joshua Reed
        <u>The exiles of Florida</u>. Arno, 1969   E83.817.G45.1969

1845   GRAHAM, William Alexander
        <u>The Custer myth</u>. Harrisburg, Pa., Stackpole Co., 1953
                                        E83.876.G7

1846   GRINNELL, George Bird
        <u>Two great scouts and their Pawnee battalion</u>. Cleveland,
        Arthur H. Clark Co., 1928   E83.866.N86

1847   HALBERT, Henry Sale
        <u>The Creek War of 1813 and 1814</u>. University, Univ. of
        Alabama Pr., 1969

1848   HARRIS, William
        <u>A Rhode Islander reports on King Philip's War</u>. Providence,
        Rhode Island Historical Society, 1963   E83.57.H3.1963

1849   HEARD, Isaac V. D.
        <u>History of the Sioux war and massacres of 1862 and 1863</u>.
        Harper & Brothers, 1863   E83.86.H43

18491   HIBBERT, Christopher
        <u>Wolfe at Quebec</u>. Cleveland, World Pub. Co., 1959   E199.H54

1850   HOIG, Stan
        <u>The Sand Creek Massacre</u>. Norman, Univ. of Oklahoma Pr.,
        1961   E83.863.H68

1851   HOYT, Epaphras
        <u>Antiquarian researches</u>. Greenfield, Mass., Printed by
        A. Phelps, 1824   E82.H86.Spec.Coll.

1852   HUBBARD, William
        <u>A narrative of the Indian wars in New-England</u>. Brattleborough:
        Pub. by William Fessenden, 1814   E82.H872.1814

1853   KEIM, De Benneville Randolph
        <u>Sheridan's troopers on the borders: a winter campaign</u>
        <u>on the plains</u>. Freeport, N.Y., Books for Libraries Pr.,
        1970   E83.866.K27.1970

1854   KELLY, Lawrence C.
        <u>Navajo roundup</u>. Boulder, Colo., Pruett Pub. Co., 1970
                                        E83.859.K44

1855   KEYES, Erasmus Darwin
        Fifty years' observations of men and events, civil and
        military. C. Scribner's Sons, 1884   E181.K48

1856   KING, Charles
        Campaigning with Crook. Norman, Univ. of Oklahoma Pr.,
        1964   E83.866.K553

1857   King Philip's War narratives. Ann Arbor, Mich., University
        Microfilms, 1966   E83.67.K5

1858   KNIGHT, Oliver
        Following the Indian wars. Norman, Univ. of Oklahoma Pr.,
        1960   E83.866.K58

1859   KUHLMAN, Charles
        Legend into history: the Custer mystery. Harrisburg, Pa.,
        Stackpole Co., 1952   E83.876.K87.1952

1860   LAUMER, Frank
        Massacre! Gainesville, Univ. of Florida Pr., 1968
                                                E83.835.L37

1861   LEACH, Douglas Edward
        Flintlock and tomahawk. Macmillan, 1958 E83.67.L42

1862   LECKIE, William H.
        The military conquest of the southern plains. Norman,
        Univ. of Oklahoma Pr., 1963   E83.866.L4

1863   LEE, L. P.
        History of the Spirit lake massacre. Fairfield, Wash.,
        Ye Galleon Pr., 1967   E83.857.L46.1967

1864   LINCOLN, Charles Henry
        Narratives of the Indian wars, 1675-1699. Barnes & Noble,
        1952   E82.L73.1952

18641   LOUDON, Archibald comp.
        A selection of some of the most interesting narratives
        of outrages committed by the Indians in their wars with
        the white people. (First American Frontier) Arno, 1971
                                                E85.L88.1971

1865   LUMMIS, Charles Fletcher
        General Crook and the Apache wars. Flagstaff, Ariz.,
        Northland Pr., 1966   E83.866.C942

1866   MAHON, John K.
        History of the Second Seminole War, 1835-1842. Gainesville,
        Univ. of Florida Pr., 1967   E83.835.M3

186

1867   MANRING, Benjamin Franklin
        The conquest of the Coeur d'Alenes, Spokanes and Palouses.
        Spokane, Wash., Printed by Inland Printing Co., 1912
                                            E83.84.M28

1868   MANTE, Thomas
        The history of the late war in North-America. Research
        Reprints, 1970 (1772)   E199.M29.1970

1869   MARQUIS, Thomas Guthrie
        The war chief of the Ottawas. Toronto, Glasgow, Brook
        & Co., 1922   E83.76.M35

18691   MARSHALL, J. T.
        The Miles expedition of 1874-1875: an eyewitness account
        of the Red River war. Austin, Texas, Encino Pr., 1971
                                            E83.875.M3

18692   MARSHALL, Samuel Lyman Atwood
        Crimsoned prairie; the wars between the United States and
        the Plains Indians during the winning of the West. Scribner,
        1972   E83.866.M36

1870   MATHER, Increase
        Early history of New England. Boston, The Editor, 1864
                                            E82.M42

1871   MAURY, Dabney Herndon
        Recollections of a Virginian in the Mexican, Indian, and
        civil wars. C. Scribner's Sons, 1897   E415.9.M3M3

1872   MILES, Nelson Appleton
        Personal recollections and observations of General
        Nelson A. Miles. Chicago, New York, Werner Co., 1896
                                            E83.866.M65

1873   MILES, Nelson Appleton
        Serving the Republic. Harper & Brothers, 1911 E83.866.M65

1874   MURRAY, Keith A.
        The Modocs and their war. Norman, Univ. of Oklahoma Pr.,
        1959   E83.87.M87

1875   NICHOLS, Roger L.
        General Henry Atkinson. Norman, Univ. of Oklahoma Pr.,
        1965   E340.A85N5

1876   NICOLAY, John George
        Lincoln's secretary goes West. La Crosse, Wis., Sumac Pr.,
        1965   E83.86.N5

1877   NORTHROP, Henry Davenport
         Indian horrors. Detroit, Ellsworth & Brey, 1891? E81.N87

1878   NYE, Elwood L.
         Marching with Custer. Glendale, Calif., A. H. Clark,
         1964   fE83.876.N9

1879   NYE, Wilbur Sturtevant
         Plains Indian raiders. Norman, Univ. of Oklahoma Pr.,
         1968   E83.866.N9

1880   OEHLER, Charles M.
         The great Sioux uprising. Oxford Univ. Pr., 1959 E83.86.033

1881   OSTRANDER, Alson Bowles
         An army boy of the sixties. Yonkers-on-Hudson, N.Y.,
         World Book Co., 1924   E83.866.085

1882   PARKMAN, Francis
         History of the conspiracy of Pontiac, and the war of the
         North American tribes against the English colonies after
         the conquest of Canada. A. L. Burt, pref. 1851 E83.76.P37

1883   PECKHAM, Howard Henry
         Pontiac and the Indian uprising. Russell & Russell, 1970
                                               E83.76.P4.1970

1884   PENHALLOW, Samuel
         The history of the wars of New-England with the Eastern
         Indians. Kraus Reprint, 1969 (1859) E197.P39.1969

1885   QUAIFE, Milo Milton ed.
         The siege of Detroit in 1763: the Journal of Pontiac's
         Conspiracy, and John Rutherfurd's Narrative of a captivity.
         Chicago, R. R. Donnelley, 1958   E83.76.Q3

1886   REMINGTON, Frederic
         Remington's frontier sketches. Chicago. New York, etc.,
         Werner Co., 1898   E83.866.R38.Spec.Coll

1887   RIDDLE, Jeff C. Davis
         The Indian history of the Modoc war, and the causes that
         led to it. San Francisco, Printed by Marnell & Co., 1914
                                               E83.87.R54

1888   RISTER, Carl Coke
         Border command. Norman, Univ. of Oklahoma Pr., 1944
                                               E467.1.S54R5

1889   RUSSELL, Don
            Custer's last. Fort Worth, Tex., Amon Carter Museum of
            Western Art, 1968   E83.876.R8

1890   RUSSELL, Donald Bert
            One hundred and three fights and scrimmages. Washington, D.C.,
            United States Cavalry Assoc., 1936   E83.866.B47

1891   SANDOZ, Mari
            The Battle of the Little Bighorn. Philadelphia, Lippincott,
            1966   E83.876.S2

1892   SCANLAN, Charles Martin
            Indian massacre and captivity of Hall girls. Milwaukee, Wisc.,
            Reic Pub. Co., 1915   E83.83.S28

1893   SCHMITT, Martin Ferdinand
            Fighting Indians of the West. Bonanza Books, 1948
                                                     fE83.866.S3.1948b

1894   SECOY, Frank Raymond
            Changing military patterns on the Great Plains (17th century
            through early 19th century). Locust Valley, N. Y.,
            J. J. Augustin, 1953   (MAES)   E51.A556.v.21

1895   SPRAGUE, John Titcomb
            The origin, progress, and conclusion of the Florida War.
            Gainesville, Univ. of Florida Pr., 1964 E83.835.S77.1848a

1896   SPRING, Agnes (Wright)
            Caspar Collins. Columbia Univ. Pr., 1927 E83.86.C71

18961   SPRINGER, Charles H.
            Soldiering in Sioux country: 1865. San Diego, Frontier
            Heritage Pr., 1971   E83.86.S63

1897   STEVENS, Hazard
            The life of Isaac Ingalls Stevens. Boston and New York,
            Houghton, Mifflin and Co., 1900   F880.S845

1898   STEWART, Edgar Irving
            Custer's luck. Norman, Univ. of Oklahoma Pr., 1964 (1955)
                                                     E83.866.S85

1899   TEBBEL, John William
            The compact history of the Indian Wars. Hawthorn Books, 1966
                                                     E81.T42

1900   TERRELL, John Upton
            Faint the trumpet sounds. D. McKay Co., 1966 E83.876.T4

1901   THOMSON, John Lewis
        History of the war of the United States with Great
        Britain in 1812. Philadelphia, Lippincott, 1887
                                        E354.T5.1887

1902   THRAPP, Dan L.
        General Crook and the Sierra Madre adventure. Norman,
        Univ. of Oklahoma Pr., 1971   E83.866.C94T45

1903   THWAITES, Reuben Gold
        Documentary history of Dunmore's war, 1774. Madison,
        Wisconsin Historical Society, 1905   E83.77.T54

1904   TOLMAN, Newton F.
        The search for General Miles. Putnam, 1968 E83.866.M66T6

1905   TRUMBULL, Henry
        History of the discovery of America. Boston, G. Clark,
        1833 (1819)   E81.T92

1906   TUTTLE, Charles Richard
        History of the border wars of two centuries. Chicago,
        C. A. Wall & Co., 1874   E81.T96

1907   U. S. WAR DEPT.
        Letter from the secretary of war, transmitting documents
        in relation to hostilities of Creek Indians. Washington,
        Blair & Rives, Printers, 1836   E83.836.U5

1908   VAN EVERY, Dale
        A company of heroes. Morrow, 1962   E263.N84V3

1909   VAUGHN, Jesse Wendell
        The Battle of Platte Bridge. Norman, Univ. of Oklahoma Pr.,
        1963   E83.86.V3

1910   VAUGHN, Jesse Wendell
        Indian fights. Norman, Univ. of Oklahoma Pr., 1966
                                           E83.866.V29

1911   VAUGHN, Jesse Wendell
        With Crook at the Rosebud. Harrisburg, Pa., Stackpole Co.,
        1956   E83.876.V3

1912   WARE, Eugene Fitch
        The Indian War of 1864. Topeka, Kan., 1911   E83.863.W26

1913   WELLMAN, Paul Iselin
        Death in the desert. Macmillan, 1935   E81.W46

1914   WELLMAN, Paul Iselin
           Death on the prairie. London, W. Faulsham & Co., 1956
                                        E83.866.W35.1956

1915   THE WESTERNERS. POTOMAC CORRAL.
           Great western Indian fights. Lincoln, Univ. of Nebraska Pr.,
           1966? (1960)   E81.W49.1966

1916   WILSON, Frazer Ells
           The peace of Mad Anthony. Greenville, O., C. R. Kemble,
           printer, 1909   E83.794.W75

1917   WITHERS, Alexander Scott
           Chronicles of border warfare. Parsons, W. Va., McClain
           Printing, 1970   E81.W82.1970

1918   WOOD, Leonard
           Chasing Geronimo. Albuquerque, Univ. of New Mexico Pr., 1970
                                        E83.88.W6

1919   YAGER, Willard E.
           The Onéota. Oneonta, N. Y., Oneonta Herald Print, 1912
           (1913)   E81.Y13

192

1920   AMERICAN HERITAGE.
        Discoverers of the New World. American Heritage Pub. Co.;
        distribution by Golden Pr., 1960   jE101.A49

1921   BALCH, Glenn
        Little Hawk and the free horses. Crowell, 1957 jPZ7.B18Li

1922   BAUER, Helen
        California Indian days. Garden City, N. Y., Doubleday, 1963
                                                    jE78.C15B3

1923   BECK, Ruth Everett
        The little buffalo robe. H. Holt and Co., 1914 jPZ7.B3808L

1924   BERGER, Josef
        Discoverers of the New World. American Heritage Pub. Co.;
        book trade and institutional distribution by Harper & Row,
        1960   jE101.B53

1925   BERKE, Ernest
        The North American Indians. Garden City, N. Y., Doubleday,
        1963   jE77.B48

1926   BLEEKER, Sonia
        The Apache Indians. Morrow, 1951   jE99.A6B6

1927   BLEEKER, Sonia
        The Cherokee. Morrow, 1952   jE99.C5B54

1928   BLEEKER, Sonia
        The Chippewa Indians. Morrow, 1968   jE99.C6B64

1929   BLEEKER, Sonia
        Horsemen of the western plateaus. Morrow, 1967 (1957)
                                               jE99.N5B5

1930   BLEEKER, Sonia
        Indians of the longhouse. Morrow, 1950 jE99.I7B63.1950

1931   BLEEKER, Sonia
        The Mission Indians of California. Morrow, 1956 jE78.C15B55

1932   BLEEKER, Sonia
        The Pueblo Indians. Morrow, 1967   jE99.P9B5

1933   BLEEKER, Sonia
        The sea hunters, Indians of the Northwest Coast. Morrow, 1969
                                               jE78.N77B53

1934   BLEEKER, Sonia
        The Seminole Indians. Morrow, 1966   jE99.S28B55.1966

1935   BRINDZE, Ruth
        The story of the totem pole. Vanguard Pr., 1951 jE98.T65B7

1936   BUFF, Mary (Marsh)
        Dancing Cloud, the Navajo Boy. Viking Pr., 1957 jPZ7.B89Dan5

1937   BUFF, Mary (Marsh)
        Kemi, an Indian boy before the white man came. Los Angeles,
        Ward Ritchie Pr., 1966   jPZ7.B89Ke

1938   BULLA, Clyde Robert
        Eagle Feather. Crowell, 1953   jPZ7.B912Eag

1939   CLARK, Ann (Nolan)
        The desert people. Viking Pr., 1967 (1962) jE99.P25C57

1940   CLARK, Ann (Nolan)
        In my mother's house. The Viking Pr., 1941 jPZ9.C374In

1941   CLARK, Ann (Nolan)
        The little Indian basket maker. Los Angeles, Melmont
        Publishers, 1957   jE98.B3C53

1942   CLARK, Ann (Nolan)
        The little Indian pottery maker. Los Angeles, Melmont
        Publishers, 1955   jPZ10.C56

1943   COBLENTZ, Catherine (Cate)
        Sequoya. David McKay, 1962 (1946)   jE99.C5C67.1946b

19431   CREIGHTON, Luella Sanders Bruce
        Tecumseh: the story of the Shawnee chief. St. Martin's Pr.,
        1965   jE99.S35.C7

1944   DARBOIS, Dominique
        Achouna, boy of the Arctic. Chicago, Follett Pub. Co.,
        1962   jPZ9.D165Ac

1945   DINES, Glen
        Dog soldiers. Macmillan, 1961   jE99.C53D5

1946   DOBRIN, Norma Zane
        Delawares. Chicago, Melmont Publishers, 1963 jE99.D2D6

1947   DORIAN, Edith M.
        Hokahey! McGraw-Hill, 1957   jE77.D68

1948   EDWARDS, Charles Lincoln
        Jose, a story of the Desert Cahuilla. Los Angeles,
        Hesperian Pr., 1930   194   jE99.S39E3

1949   ELTING, Mary
        The first book of Eskimos. F. Watts, 1952   jE99.E7E4

1950   ELTING, Mary
        The first book of Indians. F. Watts, 1950   jE77.E5

1951   ESTEP, Irene
        Iroquois. Chicago, Melmont Publishers, 1961 jE99.I7E8

1952   FABER, Doris
        The life of Pocahontas. Englewood Cliffs, N. J., Prentice-Hall,
        1966 (1963)   jE90.P6F3

1953   FENTON, Carroll Lane
        Cliff dwellers of Walnut Canyon. J. Day Co., 1960   jE78.A7F38

1954   FISHER, Anne (Benson)
        Stories California Indians told. Berkeley, Calif.,
        Parnassus Pr., 1957   jE98.F6F5

1955   FISHER, Olive Margaret comp.
        Totem, tipi, and tumpline. Toronto, 1957 (1955) jE78.C2F5

1956   FLEISCHMANN, Glen
        The Cherokee Removal, 1838. Watts, 1971 JE99.C5F68

1957   GARST, Doris Shannon
        Crazy Horse. Boston, Houghton Mifflin, 1950 jE90.C94G3

1958   GARST, Doris Shannon
        Sitting Bull, champion of his people. J. Messner, 1965 (1946)
                                      jE99.D1S605

1959   GILLHAM, Charles Edward
        Beyond the Clapping mountains. Macmillan, 1968 (1943)
                                      jE99.E7G44

1960   GLUBOK, Shirley
        The art of the Eskimo. Harper & Row, 1964 jE99.E7G6

1961   GRAFF, Stewart
        Squanto: Indian adventurer. Champaign, Ill., Garrard Pub. Co.,
        1965   jE90.S77G7

1962   GRANT, Bruce
        American Indians, yesterday and today. Dutton, 1960
                                      jE77.G78.1960

1963   GRESHAM, Elizabeth
        The world of the Aztecs. Walker, 1961 jF1219.G75

1964   GRIDLEY, Marion Eleanor
        Indians of yesterday. Chicago, New York, M. A. Donohue & Co.,
        1940   jE77.G83.Spec.Coll.

1965   HARRIS, Christie
        Once upon a totem. Antheneum, 1966 (1963) jE98.F6H29

1966   HEIDERSTADT, Dorothy
        Indian friends and foes. D. McKay Co., 1967 (1958) jE89.H4

1967   HEIDERSTADT, Dorothy
        More Indian friends and foes. D. McKay Co., 1963 jE89.H42

1968   HOFSINDE, Robert
        The Indian and his horse. Morrow, 1960 jE98.H55H6

1969   HOFSINDE, Robert
        Indian games and crafts. Morrow, 1957 (i.e. 1968) jE98.G2H6

1970   HOFSINDE, Robert
        Indian music makers. Morrow, 1967   jML3557.H7

1971   HOFSINDE, Robert
        Indian picture writing. Morrow, 1959   jE98.P6H6

1972   HOFSINDE, Robert
        Indian sign language. Morrow, 1956   jE98.S5H6

1973   HOFSINDE, Robert
        Indians at home. Morrow, 1964   jE98.D9H6

1974   HOOKE, Hilda Mary
        Thunder in the mountains, legends of Canada. Toronto,
        New York, Oxford Univ. Pr., 1947   jE98.F6H6.1947

1975   HUNT, Walter Bernard
        The golden book of Indian crafts and lore. Golden Pr.,
        1954   jE98.C8H83

1976   ISRAEL, Marion Louise
        Cherokees. Chicago, Melmont Publishers, 1961 jE99.C5I8

1977   JAMES, Harry Clebourne
        A day in Oraibi. Los Angeles, Melmont Publishers, 1959
                            jE99.H7J23

1978   JANVIER, Thomas Allibone
        In the Aztec treasure house. Walker, 1961 jPZ7.J2815In

1979   JOHNSON, Dorothy M.
        Warrior for a lost nation. Philadelphia, Westminster Pr.,
        1969   jE99.D1J56

1980   KIDD, Kenneth E.
        Canadians of long ago. Toronto, Longmans, Green, 1951
                                        jE78.C2K5

1981   KIRK, Ruth
        David, young chief of the Quileutes. Harcourt, Brace & World,
        1967   jE99.Q5K5

1982   KROEBER, Theodora
        Ishi, last of his tribe. Berkeley, Calif., Parnassus Pr.,
        1964   jE90.I8K72

1983   LA FARGE, Oliver
        The American Indian. Golden Pr., 1960 jE77.L246.1960

1984   LAMKIN, Nina B.
        Around America with the Indian. S. French, 1933- jE98.D8L3

1985   MACMILLAN, Cyrus
        Glooskap's country. Toronto, New York, Oxford Univ. Pr.,
        1957   jE98.F6M18

1986   McNEER, May Yonge
        The American Indian story. Ariel Books, 1963 jE77.M175

1987   MARRIOTT, Alice Lee
        Indians of the Four Corners. Crowell, 1952 jE99.P9M34

1988   MARRIOTT, Alice Lee
        Indians on horseback. Crowell, 1948 jE78.W5M3

1989   MARTIN, Frances Gardiner (McEntee)
        Nine tales of Raven. Harper, 1951 jE98.F6M26

1990   MAXWELL, Moreau S.
        Eskimo family. Chicago, Encyclopaedia Britannica Pr.;
        distributed in association with Meredith Pr., Des Moines,
        1962   jE99.E7M46

1991   MEADOWCROFT, Enid (La Monte)
        Crazy Horse, Sioux warrior. Champaign, Ill., Garrard Pub. Co.,
        1965   jE90.C94M4

1992   MOON, Grace (Purdie)
        Chi-Weé. Garden City, N. Y., Doubleday, Page & Co., 1925
                                        jPZ8.1.M779Chi

1993   MORRIS, Loverne
        The American Indian as farmer. Chicago, Melmont Publishers,
        1963   jE98.A3M6

1994   MYRON, Robert
      Shadow of the hawk. Putnam, 1964   jE74.03M9

1995   PINE, Tillie S.
      The Indians knew. Whittlesey House, 1957 jE77.P6

1996   RACHLIS, Eugene
      Indians of the plains. American Heritage Pub. Co.;
      Book Trade Dist. by Meredith Pr., 1960 jE78.W5R3

1997   RAMBEAU, John
      Chumash boy. San Francisco, Field Educational Publications,
      1968   jE99.C815R3

1998   ROLAND, Albert
      Great Indian chiefs. Crowell-Collier Pr., 1966 jE89.R6

1999   RUSSELL, Don
      Sioux buffalo hunters. Chicago, Encyclopaedia Britannica Pr.;
      distributed in association with Meredith Pr., Des Moines, 1962
                               jE99.D1R8

2000   RUSSELL, Solveig Paulson
      Navaho land, yesterday and today. Chicago, Melmont Publishers,
      1961   jE99.N3R8

2001   SCHEELE, William E.
      The earliest Americans. Cleveland, World Pub. Co., 1963
                             jE61.S3

2002   SCHOOLCRAFT, Henry Rowe comp.
      The fire plume. Dial Pr., 1969   jPZ8.1.S354Fi

2003   SEXTON, Bernard
      Gray Wolf stories. Macmillan, 1921   jPZ8.1.S459Gr.1921

2004   SHIPPEN, Katherine Binney
      Leif Eriksson, first voyager to America. Harper, 1951
                             jE105.S57

2005   SHOWERS, Paul
      Indian festivals. Crowell, 1969   jE98.R3S45

2006   STEELE, William O.
      Westward adventure. Harcourt, Brace & World, 1962
                           jF209.3.S8

20061 Tales of Eskimo Alaska.
      Anchorage, Alaska Methodist Univ. Pr., 1971 jE99.E7.T14

20062 TRAVELLER BIRD
      The path to Snowbird Mountain; Cherokee legends. Farrar,
      Strauss and Giroux, 1972   jE99.C5.T7

2007   TRAVEN, B.
         The creation of the sun and moon. Hill and Wang, 1968
                                                jPZ8.1.T68Cr

2008   TUNIS, Edwin
         Indians. Cleveland, World Pub. Co., 1959 jE77.T93

2009   UNDERHILL, Ruth Murray
         People of the Crimson Evening. Riverside, U. S. Indian
         Service 1951   jPZ7.U417Pe

20091   WALTRIP, Lela
         Indian women; thirteen who played a part in the history of
         America from earliest days to now. D. McKay Co., 1964
                                                jE98.W8.W3

2010   WASHBURNE, Heluiz (Chandler)
         Children of the blizzard. J. Day Co., 1952 jE99.E7W38

2011   WYATT, Edgar
         Geronimo, the last Apache war chief. Whittlesey House, 1952
                                                jE99.A6W9

2012   ARROYO DE LA CUESTA, Felipe de
Grammar of the Mutsun language spoken at the Mission of
San Juan Bautista, Alta California. AMS, 1970 (1861)
PM1977.A8.1970

2013   ARROYO DE LA CUESTA, Felipe de
A vocabulary or phrase book of the Mutsun language of
Alta California. AMS, 1970 (1862)   PM1978.A8.1970

2014   BERLIN, Overton Brent
Tzeltal numeral classifiers. The Hague, Mouton, 1968
PM4461.B45

2015   BILLS, Garland D.
An introduction to spoken Bolivian Quechua. Austin,
Publ. for the Institute of Latin American Studies by the
Univ. of Texas Pr., 1969   PM6303.B5

2016   BLOOMFIELD, Leonard
The Menomini language. New Haven, Yale Univ. Pr., 1962
PM1761.B55

2017   BOAS, Franz
Handbook of American Indian languages. Washington, U. S.
Govt. Print. Off., 1911- (BAEB)   E51.U55.no.40

2018   BOAS, Franz
Kathlamet texts. Washington, U. S. Govt. Print. Off.,
1901   (BAEB)   E51.U55.no.26

2019   BOGORAZ, Vladimïr Germanovich
Koryak texts. Leyden, E. J. Brill, Ltd.; G. E. Stechert & Co.,
Agents, 1917   PM75.6.B6

2020   BRADLEY, Cornelius Beach
On plotting the inflections of the voice. Berkeley,
Univ. of California Pr., 1916 (UCPAE) E51.C15.v.12.no.5

2021   BRIGHT, William ed.
Studies in California linguistics. Berkeley, Univ. of
California Pr., 1964   (CUPL)   P25.C25.v.34

20211   BROUSSARD, James Francis
Louisiana Creole dialect. Kennikat, 1972 PM7854.L6.B7.1972

2022   CHILAM BALAM BOOKS. CHUMAYEL BOOK.
The Book of Chilam Balam of Chumayel. Norman, Univ. of Oklahoma
Pr., 1967   fF1435.C53.1967

2023   CODY, Iron Eyes
        Indian talk. Healdsburg, Calif., Naturegraph Publishers,
        1970   E98.S5C63

2024   COMAS, Juan
        Características físicas de la familia lingüística maya.
        México, Universidad Nacional Autónoma de México, 1966
                                   F1435.C73

20241   Comparative studies in Amerindian languages. Esther Matteson
        ed. The Hague, Mouton, 1972   PM108.C6

2025   CONKLIN, Harold C.
        Hanunóo-English vocabulary. Berkeley, Univ. of California
        Pr., 1953   (CUPL)   P25.C25.v.9

2026   CRAWFORD, John Chapman
        Tototepec Mixe phonotagmemics. Norman, Summer Institute
        of Linguistics of the Univ. of Oklahoma, 1963 (1960)
                             PM4011.C7.1963

2027   CUOQ, Jean André
        Etudes philologiques sur quelques langues sauvages de
        L'Amérique. Johnson Repr., 1966 (1866) PM206.C8.1966

2028   DÁVALOS, Juan Benjamin
        Gramática elemental de la lengua quechua. Lima, Imp.
        "Ariel," 1938?   PM6303.D3

2029   DIXON, Roland Burrage
        Linguistic families of California. Berkeley, Univ. of
        California Pr., 1919   (UCPAE)   E51.C15.v.16.no.3

2030   DORSEY, James Owen
        Omaha and Ponka letters. Washington, U. S. Govt. Print.
        Off., 1891   (BAEB)   E51.U55.no.11

2031   ELIOT, John
        The Indian primer. Edinburgh, A. Elliot, 1877 (1669)
                            PM1739.E6.1669a

2032   EMENEAU, Murray Barnson
        Kota texts. Berkeley, Univ. of California Pr., 1944-46
                (CUPL)   P25.C25.v.2,no.1-2

2033   EMENEAU, Murray Barnson
        Kota texts. Berkeley, Univ. of California Pr., 1944-46
                (CUPL)   P25.C25.v.3.no.1-2

2034   ESCOBAR, Alberto
        Cuatro fonologías quechuas. Lima, Universidad Nacional
        Mayor de San Marcos, 1967   PM6309.E8

2035   FRACHTENBERG, Leo Joachim
        Lower Umpqua texts, and Notes on the Kusan dialects.
        AMS, 1969 (1914)   (CUCA)   E51.C7.v.4.1969

2036   FUCHS, Anna
        Morphologie des Verbs im Cahuilla. The Hague, Mouton, 1970
                                                PM731.F8

2037   GARIBAY KINTANA, Angel María
        Llave del náhuatl. México, Imprenta Mayli, s. a., 1940
                                                PM4063.G37

2038   GATSCHET, Albert Samuel
        A dictionary of the Atakapa language accompanied by text
        material. Washington, U. S. Govt. Print. Off., 1932
                        (BAEB)   E51.U55.no.108

2039   GIBBS, George
        Alphabetical vocabularies of the Clallam and Lummi.
        AMS, 1970 (1863)   PM895.G5.1970

2040   GIBBS, George
        Alphabetical vocabulary of the Chinook language. AMS, 1970
        (1863)   PM843.G5.1970

2041   GIBBS, George
        A dictionary of the Chinook Jargon. AMS, 1970 (1863)
                                                PM848.G4.1970

2042   GILBERTI, Maturino
        Diccionario de la lengua tarasca o de Michoacán. Guadalajara,
        México, 1962   ref.PM4298.G6.1962

2043   GODDARD, Pliny Earle
        Texts and analysis of Cold lake dialect, Chipewyan. American
        Museum of Natural History, 1912 (AMNHP) GN2.A27.v.10.pt.1-2

2044   GONZÁLEZ HOLGUIN, Diego
        Vocabulario de la lengua general de todo el Perú llamada
        lengua qquichua o del Inca. Lima, Impr. Santa María, 1952
                                                ref.PM6306.G6.1952

2045   GOOSSEN, Irvy W.
        Navajo made easier. Flagstaff, Ariz., Northland Pr., 1967
                                            PM2007.G7

20451   Grammatical sketch of the Heve language. Buckingham Smith,
        trans. AMS, 1970 (1861)   PM1171.G8.1970

2046   GREGORES, Emma
        A description of colloquial Guaraní. The Hague, Paris,
        Mouton & Co., 1967   PM7173.G7

2047   GUDSCHINSKY, Sarah Caroline
        Proto-Popotecan. Baltimore, Waverly Pr., 1958 (i.e. 1959)
                (IUPA)   GN4.I5.mem.15

2048   HALL, Robert Anderson
        Pidgin and creole languages. Cornell Univ. Pr., 1966
                          PM7802.H3

2049   HANZELI, Victor Egon
        Missionary linguistics in New France. The Hague, Mouton,
        1969   PM603.H3

20491   HARDMAN, Martha James
        Jaqaru: outline of phonological and morphological
        structure. The Hague, Mouton, 1966   PM5788.H3

2050   HARRINGTON, John Peabody
        Vocabulary of the Kiowa language. Washington, U. S.
        Govt. Print Off., 1928 (BAEB)   E51.U55.no.84

20501   HEATH, Shirley Brice
        Telling tongues; language policy in Mexico, colony to
        nation. Teachers College Pr., 1972   PM3009.H4

2051   HESS, H. Harwood
        The syntactic structure of Mezquital Otomi. The Hague,
        Paris, Mouton, 1968   PM4149.Z9M44

2052   HOFF, B. J.
        The Carib language. The Hague, Martinus Nijhoff, 1968
                          PM5757.H6

2053   HOIJER, Harry
        An analytical dictionary of the Tonkawa language.
        Berkeley, Univ. of California Pr., 1949
                (CUPL)   P25.C25.v.5.no.1

2054   HOLMER, Nils G.
        John Campanius' Lutheran catechism in the Delaware
        language. Upsala, A.-b Lundequistska Bokhandeln, 1946
                       PM1034.L83H6

2055   JACOBS, Melville ed.
        Clackamas Chinook texts. Bloomington, Ind., 1958-59
                     PM844.J2

2056   JACOBS, Melville
        Northwest Sahaptin texts. AMS, 1969 (1934-37)
                          (CUCA)   E51.C7.v.19

2057   JONES, Robert B.
        Karen linguistic studies. Berkeley, Univ. of California Pr.,
        1961   (CUPL)   P.25.C25.v.25

20571   JOSSELIN de JONG, Jan Benjamin de
        Original Odzibwe text. Johnson Rep., 1968 PM854.J6.1968

2058   JOVER PERALTA, Anselmo
        Diccionario guaraní-español y español-guaraní. Buenos Aires,
        Editorial Tupã, 1951   PM7176.J6.1951

20581   KASCHUBE, Dorothea V.
        Structural elements of the language of the Crow Indians of
        Montana. Boulder, Univ. of Colorado Pr., 1967
                          (CUSA)   GN4.C64.no.14

2059   KEY, Mary (Ritchie)
        Comparative Tacanan phonology. The Hague, Paris, Mouton, 1968
                                          PM7088.K4

2060   KNOROZOV, IU V.
        Selected chapters from the writing of the Maya Indians.
        Cambridge, Mass. Peabody Museum of American Archaeology
        and Ethnology, 1967   PM3968.K55

2061   KROEBER, Alfred Louis
        The languages of the coast of California north of San Francisco.
        Berkeley, Univ. of California Pr., 1911
                          (UCPAE)   E51.C15.v.9.no.3

2062   KROEBER, Alfred Louis
        The languages of the coast of California south of San Francisco.
        Berkeley, Univ. of California Pr., 1904
                          (UCPAE)   E51.C15.v.2.no.2

2063   KROEBER, Alfred Louis
        Phonetic constituents of the native languages of California.
        Berkeley, Univ. of California Pr., 1911
                          (UCPAE)   E51.C15.v.10.no.1

2064   KROEBER, Alfred Louis
        Serian, Tequistlatecan, and Hokan. Berkeley, Univ. of California
        Pr., 1915   (UCPAE)   E51.C15.v.11.no.4

2065   KURODA, Sige Yuki
        Yawelmani phonology. Cambridge, Mass., M.I.T. Pr., 1967
                                          PM2681.K8

2066   LA FLESCHE, Francis
       A dictionary of the Osage language. Washington, U. S.
       Govt. Print. Off., 1932 (BAEB)   E51.U55.no.109

2067   LASTRA, Yolanda
       Cochabamba Quechua syntax. The Hague, Paris, Mouton,
       1968   PM6309.L3

2068   LAURENT, Joseph
       New familiar Abenakis and English dialogues. Quebec,
       Printed by L. Brousseau, 1884   PM551.L3

2069   LEVIN, Norman Balfour
       The Assiniboine language. Bloomington, Indiana Univ.,
       1964   PM638.L48

2070   LOWIE, Robert Harry ed. and tr.
       Crow texts. Berkeley, Univ. of California Pr., 1960
                             PM1001.L65

2071   LOWIE, Robert Harry
       Crow word lists. Berkeley, Univ. of California Pr.,
       1960   ref.PM1001.L67

2072   MAILLARD, Antoine Simon
       Grammar of the Mikmaque language of Nova Scotia. AMS,
       1970 (1864)   PM1792.M3.1970

20721   MALLERY, Garrick
       Sign language among North American Indians, compared
       with that among other peoples and deafmutes. The Hague,
       Mouton, 1972   E98.S5.M26.1972

2073   MASON, John Alden
       The Mutsun dialect of Costanoan, based on the vocabulary
       of De la Cuesta. Berkeley, Univ. of California Pr., 1916
                   (UCPAE)   E51.C15.v.11.no.7

2074   MATHIOT, Madeleine
       An approach to the cognitive study of language. Bloomington,
       Indiana Univ., 1968   PM4176.M328

2075   MATTESON, Esther
       The Piro (Arawakan) language. Berkeley, Univ. of California
       Pr., 1965   (CUPL)   P25.C25.v.42

2076   MAYERS, Marvin Keene ed.
       Languages of Guatemala. The Hague, Mouton, 1966
                             PM3361.M3.1966

2077   MENGARINI, Gregory
        A selish or Flat-Head grammar. AMS, 1970(1861) PM2262.M5.1970

2078   MILLER, Wick R.
        Uto-Aztecan cognate sets. Berkeley, Univ. of California Pr.,
        1967   (CUPL)   P25.C25.v.48

2079   MOLINA, Alonso de
        Arte de la lengua mexicana y castellana. Madrid, Ediciones
        Cultura Hispánica, 1945   PM4063.M7.1945

2080   MOLINA, Alonso de
        Vocabulario en lengua castellana y mexicana y mexicana y
        castellana. México, Editorial Porrúa, 1970 ref.PM4066.M7.1970

2081   NEWMAN, Stanley Stewart
        Yokuts language of California. Johnson Rep., 1963 (1944)
                                         PM2681.N4.1963

2082   NEWMAN, Stanley Stewart
        Zuni dictionary. Bloomington, Ind., 1958 PM2711.N4

2083   NOBLE, Gladwyn Kingsley
        Proto-Arawakan and its descendants. Bloomington, Indiana Univ.,
        1965   PM5476.N6

2084   OSGOOD, Cornelius ed.
        Linguistic structures of native America. Johnson Rep.,
        1965 (1946)   PM201.07.1965

2085   OSWALT, Robert L.
        Kashaya texts. Berkeley, Univ. of California Pr., 1964
                         (CUPL)   P25.C25.v.36

2086   PANDOSY, Marie Charles
        Grammar and dictionary of the Yakama language. AMS, 1970
        (1862)   PM2611.P3.1970

2087   PAREDES CANDÍA, Antonio
        Vocablos aymaras en el habla popular paceña. La Paz,
        Ediciones "Isla," 1963   PM5576.P3

2088   PARKER, Gary John
        Ayacucho Quechua grammar and dictionary. The Hague, Mouton,
        1969   ref.PM6303.P38

2089   Phonemic systems of Colombian languages. Norman, Summer
        Institute of Linguistics of the Univ. of Oklahoma, 1967
                                         PM5191.P5

2090   Pidginization and creolization of languages.
          Cambridge, Eng., University Pr., 1971   PM7802.P5

2091   PIKE, Kenneth Lee
          Tone languages. Ann Arbor, Univ. of Michigan Pr., 1948
                                               P25.M47.v.4

2092   PORTNOY, Antonio
          Estado actual del estudio de las lenguas indígenas que
          se hablaron en el territorio hoy argentino. Buenos Aires,
          "Coni", 1936   PM5101.P6

2093   RADIN, Paul
          The genetic relationship of the North American Indian
          languages. Berkeley, Univ. of California Pr., 1919
                          (UCPAE)   E51.C15.v.14.no.5

2094   RAND, Silas Tertius
          Dictionary of the language of the Micmac Indians.
          Johnson Rep., 1972 (1888)   PM1793.R3.1972

20941 RAU, Jack
          The codex as a book form; three Maya codices: Dresden,
          Tro-Cortesianus, Peresianus. Pre-Columbian Pr., 1970
                                               F1435.R29

2095   REICHARD, Gladys Amanda
          Navaho grammar. J. J. Augustin, 1951   PM2007.R425

2096   RIGGS, Stephen Return
          A Dakota-English dictionary. Minneapolis, Ross &
          Haines, 1968   E71.C76.1968

2097   RITUAL OF THE BACABS.
          Ritual of the Bacabs. Norman, Univ. of Oklahoma Pr.,
          1965   F1435.R54

2098   SANDOVAL, Rafael Tiburcio
          Arte de la lengua mexicana. México, Instituto de
          Investigaciones Históricas, 1965   PM4063.S3.1965

2099   SAXTON, Dean
          Dictionary: Papago & Pima to English, O'odham-Mil-gahn;
          English to Papago & Pima, Mil-gahn-O'odham. Tucson,
          Univ. of Arizona Pr., 1969   ref.PM4176.S2

20991 SCHULLER, Rodolfo R.
          ...Discovery of a fragment of the printed copy of the
          work on the Milleayae language by Luis de Valdivia.
          Cambridge, Mass., The Museum, 1913 (PMP) E51.H337.v.3.no.5

20992　SEILER, Hansjakob
　　　　Chauilla texts with an introduction. Bloomington, Indiana
　　　　University; distributed by Humanities Pr., 1970
　　　　　　　　　　　　　　　　　　PM731.Z95.E5.1970

2100　SETON, Ernest Thompson
　　　　Sign talk. Garden City, N. Y., Doubleday, Page & Co.,
　　　　1918　　　　　　　　　　　　　P135.S4

21001　SHEA, John Dawson Gilmary
　　　　_A French-Onondaga dictionary, from a manuscript of the
　　　　seventeenth century_. AMS, 1970　　　PM2076.S5.1970

2101　SITJAR, Buenaventura
　　　　Vocabulary of the language of San Antonio Mission, California.
　　　　AMS, 1970 (1861)　　　　　　　PM2251.S5.1970

2102　SMITH, Buckingham ed.
　　　　Grammar of the Pima or Nevome. AMS, 1970 (1862) PM2172.S6.1970

2103　SOLÁ, Donald F.
　　　　Gramática del quechua de Huánuco. Lima, Universidad Nacional
　　　　Mayor de San Marcos, 1967　　　PM6303.S618

2104　_Studies in southwestern ethnolinguistics_. The Hague, Paris,
　　　　Mouton & Co., 1967　　　　　　PM461.S7

21041　SUMMER INSTITUTE OF LINGUISTICS
　　　　Aztec studies. Norman, Oklahoma, Summer Institute of
　　　　Linguistics, 1969　　　　　　PM4063.S9.v.2

2105　SUMMER INSTITUTE OF LINGUISTICS.
　　　　Studies in the Athapaskan languages. Berkeley, Univ. of
　　　　California Pr., 1963　(CUPL)　　P25.C25.v.29

21051　SWADESH, Morris
　　　　Diccionario de elementos del maya yucateco colonial.
　　　　Mexico, UNAM, Coordinacion de Humanidades, 1970
　　　　　　　　　　　　　　　　　　PM3966.S9.1970

2106　SWADESH, Morris
　　　　Los mil elementos del mexicano clásico. México, Universidad
　　　　Nacional Autónoma de México, Instituto de Investigaciones
　　　　Históricas, 1966　　　　　　　PM4061.S95

2107　SWANTON, John Reed
　　　　_Linguistic material from the tribes of southern Texas and
　　　　northeastern Mexico_. Washington, U. S. Govt. Print. Off.,
　　　　1940　　　　　　　(BAEB)　　　E51.U55.no.127

2108   SWANTON, John Reed
        A structural and lexical comparison of the Tunica,
        Chitimacha, and Atakapa languages. Washington, U. S.
        Govt. Print. Off., 1919 (BAEB)   E51.U55.no.68

2109   SYMPOSIUM ON AMERICAN INDIAN LINGUISTICS, UNIVERSITY OF
        CALIFORNIA, 1951.
        Papers from the Symposium on American Indian Linguistics.
        Berkeley, Univ. of California Pr., 1954
                        (CUPL)   P25.C25.v.10

2110   THOMAS, Cyrus
        Indian languages of Mexico and Central America and their
        geographical distribution. Washington, U. S. Govt. Print.
        Off., 1911   E51.U55.no.44

2111   THOMPSON, John Eric Sidney
        A catalog of Maya hieroglyphs. Norman, Univ. of Oklahoma Pr.,
        1962   PM3962.T45

2112   THOMPSON, John Eric Sidney
        Maya hieroglyphic writing. Norman, Univ. of Oklahoma Pr.,
        1962 (1960)   PM3962.T48.1962

21121   THOMPSON, John Eric Sidney
        Maya hieroglyphs without tears. United Kingdom,
        British Museum, 1972   F1435.3.P6.T48

2113   TOVAR, Antonio
        Catálogo de las lenguas de América del Sur. Buenos Aires,
        Editorial Sudamericana, 1961   PM5008.T6

2114   TRUMBULL, James Hammond
        Natick dictionary. Washington, U. S. Govt. Print. Off.,
        1903   (BAEB)   E51.U55.no.25

2115   TURNER, Paul
        Dictionary: Chontal to Spanish-English, Spanish to Chontal.
        Tucson, Univ. of Arizona Pr., 1971   PM3651.Z5T8

2116   VAN WYNEN, Donald
        Tacana y Castellano. Cochabamba, Bolivia, 1962 PM7088.Z5V2

21161   VERWYST, Chrysostom
        Chippewa exercises; being a practical introduction into
        the study of the Chippewa language. Minneapolis, Minn.,
        Ross and Haines, 1971   PM852.V5.1971

2117   VOEGELIN, Charles Frederick
        Topological and comparative grammar of Uto-Aztecan.
        Baltimore, Waverly Pr., 1962- (IUPA)   GN4.I5.mem.17

2118   WALAM OLUM
        Walam olum. Indianapolis, Indiana Historical Society, 1954
                                        PM1034.W3.1954

2119   WALL, Leon
        Navajo-English dictionary. Phoenix?, Ariz., U. S. Dept. of
        the Interior, Bureau of Indian Affairs, Branch of Education,
        1958   ref.PM2008.W3

2120   WARES, Alan Campbell
        A comparative study of Yuman consonantism. The Hague,
        Paris, Mouton, 1968   PM2701.W3

2121   WATERHOUSE, Viola Grace
        The grammatical structure of Oaxaca Chontal. Bloomington,
        1962   PM3651.W3.1962

21211   WEBB, Nancy McIvor
        A statement of some phonological correspondences among
        the Pomo languages. Baltimore, Waverly Pr., 1971
                  (IUPA)   GN4.I5.mem.26

2122   WILLIAMS, Roger
        A key into the language of America. Providence, reprinted
        for the Rhode Island and Providence Plantations Tercentenary
        Committee, Inc., 1936   E99.N16W7

2123   WILLIAMSON, John Poage
        An English-Dakota dictionary. Minneapolis, Ross & Haines,
        1970 (1902)   PM1023.W62.1970

2124   ZEISBERGER, David
        Zeisberger's Indian dictionary. Cambridge, Mass.,
        J. Wilson and Son, 1887   ref.PM605.Z5

2125   ALEXANDER, Hartley Burr
       Manito masks. Dutton, 1925   PN3205.A6

2126   ALEXANDER, Hartley Burr
       North American mythology. Pub. for Archaeological Institute
       of America by Marshall Jones, 1937 (1916) BL25.M8.v.10

2127   APPLEGATE, Frank Guy
       Indian stories from the Pueblos. Philadelphia & London,
       J. B. Lippincott Co., 1929   E99.P9A64

2128   ARIAS LARRETA, Abraham
       Pre-Columbian literatures, Aztec, Incan, Maya-Quiché.
       Los Angeles, The New World Library, 1964 PM4068.9.A7

2129   ARMER, Laura (Adams)
       Southwest. London, New York, Longmans, Green and Co., 1935
                                  PS3501.R5285S6

2130   ARMSTRONG, Virginia Irving comp.
       I have spoken. Chicago, Sage Books, 1971 E98.O7A7.1971

2131   ARNOLD, Elliott
       Blood brother. Duell, Sloan and Pearce, 1947 PS3501.R5933B56

2132   ASTROV, Margot Luise Therese (Kröger) ed.
       American Indian prose and poetry. Capricorn Books, 1962 (1946)
                                    PM102.A8.1962

2133   ASTURIAS, Miguel Angel ed.
       Poesís precolombina. Buenos Aires, Fabril, 1968 (1960)
                                 PM4068.9.A8.1968

2134   AUSTIN, Mary (Hunter)
       One-smoke stories. Boston and New York, Houghton Mifflin Co.,
       1934   PS3501.U8057

2135   AVELEYTA ARROYO DE ANDA, Teresa
       Pueblo Limpio. México, Costa-Amic, 1963 (1962) PQ7298.1.V4P8

21351   BAGLEY, Clarence Booth
       Indian myths of the Northwest. Seattle, Washington,
       Lowman and Hanford Co., 1930   E98.F6.B14

2136   BANDELIER, Adolph Francis Alphonse
       The delight makers. Dodd, Mead and Co., 1918 PS1063.B8D4.1918

2137 BIERHORST, John comp.
         In the trail of the wind. Farrar, Straus and Giroux,
         1971   PM197.E3B5.1971

2138 BISSELL, Benjamin Hezekiah
         The American Indian in English literature of the
         eighteenth century. Hamden, Conn., Archon Books, 1968
         (1925)   PR449.I5B5.1968

21381 BLAFFER, Sarah C.
         The Black-man of Zinacantan, a Central American legend;
         including an analysis of tales recorded and translated.
         Austin, Univ. of Texas Pr., 1972   F1221.T9.B55

2139 BRANDON, William comp.
         The magic world. Morrow, 1971   PM197.E3B7

2140 BRINTON, Daniel Garrison
         Aboriginal American authors and their productions.
         Chicago, Checagou Reprints, 1970 (1883) PM108.B8.1970

2141 BRINTON, Daniel Garrison
         American hero-myths. Philadelphia, Watts, 1882 E59.R38B8

2142 BRINTON, Daniel Garrison
         Ancient Nahuatl poetry. AMS, 1969 (1890) PM4068.5.B755.1969

2143 BRINTON, Daniel Garrison comp.
         The Güegüence. AMS, 1969 (1883)   PM4070.Z77.1969

2144 BRINTON, Daniel Garrison
         The myths of the New World. Haskell House, 1968 (1896)
                                           E59.R38B85.1968

2145 BRINTON, Daniel Garrison ed.
         Rig Veda americanus. Philadelphia, D. G. Brinton, 1890
                                           PM4068.B74

2146 BROWNE, Lewis Allen
         Indian fairy tales. Boston, John W. Luce & Co., 1912
                                           E98.F6B88

2147 BURLAND, Cottie Arthur
         North American Indian mythology. Tudor, 1965 E98.R3B96

2148 CALLAHAN, Robert Elmer
         Heart of an Indian. F. H. Hitchcock, 1927 PS3505.A4346H4.1927

2149 CARPENTER, Edmund Snow ed.
         Anerca. Toronto, J. M. Dent: distributed by New Directions,
         1959   PM64.Z95E8

214

21491   CASH, Joseph H. and Herbert T. Hoover eds.
         To be an Indian; an oral history. Holt, Rinehart, and
         Winston, 1971   E77.T58

2150   CHINARD, Gilbert
         L'Amérique et le rêve exotique dans la littérature française
         au XVII et XVIII siècle. Paris. E. Droz, 1934
                                        PQ145.7.A5C5.1934

2151   CLARK, Ella Elizabeth
         Indian legends from the northern Rockies. Norman, Univ.
         of Oklahoma Pr., 1966   E78.N77C5

2152   CLARK, Ella Elizabeth
         Indian legends of the Pacific Northwest. Berkeley, Univ.
         of California Pr., 1953   E98.F6C57

2153   CLARK, LaVerne Harrell
         They sang for horses: the impact of the horse on Navajo
         and Apache folklore. Tucson, Univ. of Arizona Pr., 1966
                                        fE78.S7C55

2154   COFFIN, Tristam P.
         Indian tales of North America. Austin, Tex.,
         American Folklore Society, 1971 (1961) E98.F6C68

2155   COLE, Cornelius
         California three hundred and fifty years ago. San Francisco,
         S. Carson & Co.; New York, C. T. Dillingham, 1888
                                        PS3505.0266C3

2156   COMETTA MANZONI, Aída
         El indio en la novela de América. Buenos Aires, Editorial
         Futuro, 1960   PQ7082.N7C6

21561   CRONYN, George William ed.
         American Indian poetry; an anthology of songs and chants.
         Ballentine Books, 1972   E98.P74.C9.1972

2157   CURTIN, Jeremiah
         Creation myths of primitive America. B. Blom, 1969
                                        E98.R3C92.1969

2158   DAY, Arthur Grove
         The sky clears. Macmillan, 1951   E98.P74D39

2159   DE HUFF, Elizabeth Willis
         Taytay's tales. Harcourt, Brace and Co., 1922 E98.F6D3

2160   EMERSON, Ellen Russell
         Indian myths. Minneapolis, Ross & Haines, 1965 E98.R3E5.1965

2161   FAIRCHILD, Hoxie Neale
        The noble savage. Russell & Russell, 1961 (1955) PR146.F3.1961

2162   FAST, Howard Melvin
        The last frontier. Garden City, N. Y., Sun Dial Pr., 1944
        (1941)   PS3511.A784L3.1944

2163   FLETCHER, Alice Cunningham
        Indian story and song, from North America. Johnson Repr.,
        1970 (1900)   E98.F6F5.1970

2164   FORBES, Jack D. comp.
        Nevada Indians speak. Reno. Univ. of Nevada Pr., 1967
                                   E78.N4F6

2165   FREUCHEN, Peter
        Eskimo. H. Liveright, 1931   PT8175.F65S713

2166   FRY, Alan
        How a people die. Garden City, N. Y., Doubleday, 1970
                                 PR6056.R85H6

2167   FUNDABURK, Emma Lila ed.
        Southeastern Indians: life portraits. Luverne, Ala.,
        1958   ref.E78.S65F8

2168   GARIBAY KINTANA, Angel María ed.
        Epica náhuatl. México, Universidad Nacional Autónoma de
        México, 1964   PM4068.G28.1964

2169   GARIBAY KINTANA, Angel Maria
        Historia de la literature náhuatl. México, Editorial
        Porrúa, 1953-1954   PM4068.G29

2170   GARIBAY KINTANA, Angel Maria ed. and tr.
        Poesía náhuatl. México, Universidad Nacional Autónoma
        de México, Instituto de Historia, Seminario de Cultura
        Náhuatl, 1964-   PM4068.2.G3

2171   GAYTON, Anna Hadwick
        Yokuts and western Mono myths. Berkeley and Los Angeles,
        Univ. of California Pr., 1940 (AR)   E51.A58.v.5.no.1

2172   GILLMOR, Frances
        Flute of the Smoking Mirror. Tucson, Univ. of Arizona Pr.,
        1968 (1949)   F1219.N48G55.1968

2173   GILMORE, Melvin Randolph
        Prairie smoke. AMS, 1966   E98.F6G45.1966

2174   GORDON, Hanford Lennox
        Legends of the Northwest. St. Paul, Minn., St. Paul Book
        and Stationary Co., 1881   F597.G66

2175   GRIDLEY, Marion Eleanor
        Indian legends of American scenes. Chicago, New York,
        M. A. Donohue & Co., 1939   E98.F6G7

21751   HAMILTON, Charles ed.
        Cry of the thunderbird: the American Indian's own story.
        Norman, Univ. of Oklahoma Pr., 1972   E77.H2.1972

21752   HOUSTON, James comp.
        Songs of the dream people; chants and images from the
        Indians and Eskimos of North America. Canada, Longmans, 1972
                                  PM198.E3.H64.1972b

2176   HUNTER, Milton Reed
        Utah Indian stories. Springville, Utah, Printed by Art
        City Pub. Co., 1946   E78.U55H8

2177   INSLEY, Bernice
        Indian folklore tales. Exposition Pr., 1952 E98.F6I5

2178   JACOBS, Melville
        The content and style of an oral literature. Chicago,
        Univ. of Chicago Pr., 1959   E99.C818J32

2179   JAMES, Harry Clebourne
        Red man, white man. San Antonio, Naylor Co., 1958
                               PS3519.A485R4.1958

2180   JANVIER, Thomas Allibone
        The Aztec treasure-house. Harper, 1918 PS2129.J5A9

2181   JONES, James Athearn
        Traditions of the North American Indians. Upper Saddle River,
        N. J., Literature House, 1970   E98.F6J6.1970

2182   JONES, Louis Thomas
        Aboriginal American oratory. Los Angeles, Southwest
        Museum, 1965   E98.O7J6

2183   JUDSON, Katharine Berry
        Myths and legends of California and the old Southwest.
        Chicago, A. C. McClurg & Co., 1916 (1912) E98.F6J9.1916

2184   KEISER, Albert
        The Indian in American literature. Oxford Univ. Pr.,
        1933   PS173.I6K4

2185   KING, Charles
        Warrior gap. London, New York, Hobart, 1901 PS2172.W3.1901

2186   KOPIT, Arthur L.
        Indians. Hill & Wang, 1969   PS3521.0573I5

2187   KROEBER, Alfred Louis
        Indian myths of south central California. Berkeley,
        The University Pr., 1907 (UCPAE)   E51.C15.v.4.no.4

2188   KROEBER, Theodora
        The inland whale. Berkeley, Univ. of California Pr.,
        1964   E98.F6K82.1964

2189   LADD, Horatio Oliver
        Chunda. Eaton & Mains, 1906   PS3523.A26C5

2190   LA FARGE, Oliver
        All the young men. Boston and New York, Houghton Mifflin Co.,
        1935   PS3523.A2663A4

2191   LA FARGE, Oliver
        The enemy gods. Boston, Houghton Mifflin Co., 1937
                               PS3523.A2663E5.1937

2192   LA FARGE, Oliver
        Laughing Boy. Boston, Houghton Mifflin Co., 1957 (1929)
                               PS3523.A2663L3.1957

2193   LARNED, William Trowbridge
        American Indian fairy tales. P. F. Volland Co., 1921
                        E98.F6L3

2194   LATTA, Frank Forrest
        California Indian folklore. Shafter, Calif., 1936
                        E98.F6L34

2195   LELAND, Charles Godfrey
        The Algonquin legends of New England. Detroit, Singing
        Tree Pr., 1968 (1884)   E98.F6L5.1968

2196   LEÓN PORTILLA, Miguel
        Pre-Colombian literatures of Mexico. Norman, Univ. of
        Oklahoma Pr., 1969   PM4068.L413

2197   LEÓN-PORTILLA, Miguel
        Trece poetas del mundo azteca. México, Universidad
        Nacional Autónoma de México, Instituto de Investigaciones
        Históricas, 1967   PM4068.5.L4

2198   LESUEUR, James W.
        Indian legends. Independence, Mo., Zion's Printing and
        Publishing Co., 1928   E59.R38L6

2199   LÉVI-STRAUSS, Claude
        L'Origine des manières de table. Paris, Plon, 1968? E98.F6L58

2200   LEWIS, Richard comp.
        I breathe a new song. Simon and Schuster, 1971
                                        PM64.Z95E5.1971

2201   LINDERMAN, Frank Bird
        Indian Old-man stories. C. Scribner's Sons, 1920 E98.F6L69

2202   LONGFELLOW, Henry Wadsworth
        The song of Hiawatha. Mount Vernon, N. Y., The Peter Pauper
        Pr., 1942   PS2267.A1.1942

2203   LÓPEZ AUSTIN, Alfredo comp.
        Augurios y abusiones. México, Instituto de Investigaciones
        Históricas, 1969   PM4068.5.L6

2204   LOWIE, Robert Harry
        Studies in plains Indian folklore. Berkeley and Los Angeles,
        Univ. of California Pr., 1942 (UCPAE) E51.C15.v.40.no.1

2205   LUDEWIG, Hermann Ernst
        The literature of American aboriginal languages.
        London, Trübner and Co., 1858   ref.Z7116.L94

2206   LUMMIS, Charles Fletcher
        The man who married the moon. Century Co., 1894 E99.P9L95

2207   LUMMIS, Charles Fletcher
        Pueblo Indian folk-stories. Century Co., 1910 E99.P9L96

2208   LYBACK, Johanna R. M.
        Indian legends. Chicago, Lyons and Carnahan, 1925 E98.F6L9

2209   MACKENZIE, Donald Alexander
        Myths of pre-Columbian America. London, Gresham Pub. Co., Ltd.,
        1924   E59.R38M2

2210   MALKUS, Alida Sims
        The dragon fly of Zuñi. Harcourt, Brace and Co., 1928
                                        PS3525.A447D7

2211   MARRIOTT, Alice Lee
        American Indian mythology. Crowell, 1968 E98.F6M24

2212   MELÉNDEZ, Concha
        La novela indianista en Hispano-américa (1832-1889).
        Rio Piedras, Universidad de Puerto Rico, 1961 PQ7082.N7M4.1961

22121   MOMADAY, Natachee Scott comp.
        American Indian authors. Boston, Houghton, Mifflin Co.,
        1972   PS508.I5.M6

2213   MOON, Sheila
        A magic dwells. Middletown, Conn., Wesleyan Univ. Pr.,
        1970   BL325.C7M66

2214   NASSOUR, Sarah A.
        Skin of gods. Los Angeles, New York, Suttonhouse, 1938
                                                PS3527.A68S52

2215   NEIHARDT, John Gneisenau
        The song of the Indian wars. Macmillan, 1928 PS3527.E35S63.19:

2216   NELSON, John Louw
        Rhythm for rain. Boston, Houghton Mifflin Co., 1937
                                                PS3527.E44R45.1937

2217   NICHOLSON, Irene
        Firefly in the night. London, Faber and Faber, 1959
                                                PM4068.N5

2218   NICHOLSON, Irene
        Mexican and Central American mythology. London, Hamlyn,
        1967   F1219.3.R38N5

2219   OPLER, Morris Edward
        Dirty Boy: a Jicarilla tale of raid and war. Menasha,
        Wis., American Anthropological Assoc., 1938
                        (AAAM)   GN2.A22.no.52

2220   PATENCIO, Francisco
        Stories and legends of the Palm Springs Indians.
        Los Angeles, Times Mirror Pr., 1943   E98.F6P3

2221   PIERRE, George
        Autumn's bounty. San Antonio, Naylor, 1972 PS3566.I42A68

2222   POSTON, Charles Dibrell
        Apache-land. San Francisco, A. L. Bancroft & Co., Printers,
        1878   PS2649.P65A7

2223   POUSMA, Richard Hettema
        He-who-always-wins. Grand Rapids, Mich., W. B. Eerdmans Pub.
        Co., 1934   PS3531.O88H4

2224   PRICE, Lawrence Marsden
        Inkle and Yarico album. Berkeley, Univ. of California Pr.,
        1937   PN57.I6P7

2225   RADIN, Paul
        The road of life and death. Pantheon Books, Inc., 1945
                                                E98.D8R3

2226   RASMUSSEN, Knud Johan Victor comp. and tr.
        Beyond the high hills. Cleveland, World Pub. Co., 1961
                                                PM64.Z95E5.1961

2227   RAVICZ, Marilyn Ekdahl
        Early Colonial religious drama in Mexico. Washington,
        Catholic Univ. of America Pr., 1970   PM4068.7.R3

2228   ROBERTS, Mrs. Elizabeth (Judson)
        Indian stories of the Southwest. San Francisco, Harr Wagner
        Pub. Co., 1917   E98.F6R6

2229   ROTHENBERG, Jerome comp.
        Shaking the pumpkin. Garden City, N. Y., Doubleday, 1972
                                                PM197.E3R6

2230   SCHOOLCRAFT, Henry Rowe
        Indian legends from Algic researches. East Lansing, Michigan
        State Univ. Pr., 1956 (i.e. 1962)   E98.F6S32

22301   SHAW, Mary
        According to our ancestors; folk texts from Gwatemala and
        Honduras. Oklahoma, Oklahoma Univ. Summer Institute of
        Linguistics, 1971   F1465.3.F6.S48

2231   SIMMS, William Gilmore
        The Yemassee. Twayne Publishers, 1964   PS2848.Y5.1964

2232   SMITH, Bertha H.
        Yosemite legends. San Francisco, P. Elder and Co., 1904
                                                E98.F6S57

2233   SMITH, Dama Margaret
        Hopi girl. Stanford Univ., Stanford Univ. Pr.; London,
        H. Milford, Oxford Univ. Pr., 1931   PS3537.M3425H6

2234   SPALDING, Phebe Estelle
        The Tahquitch maiden. San Francisco, P. Elder & Co.,
        1911   PS3537.P167T3

2235   SPENCE, Lewis
        The myths of Mexico & Peru. Dingwall-Rock, 19--
                                                F1219.3.R38S754

22351   SPENCE, Lewis
        The myths of the North American Indians. D. D. Nickerson
        and Co., 1932   E98.R3.S72.1932b

2236   SWANTON, John Reed
        Myths and tales of the southeastern Indians. Washington,
        U. S. Govt. Print. Off., 1929 (BAEB)   E51.U55.nc.88

2237   THOMPSON, Stith ed.
        Tales of the North American Indians. Bloomington, Indiana
        Univ. Pr., 1966   E98.F6T32.1966

2238   ULLOM, Judith C.
        Folklore of the North American Indians. Washington, U. S.
        Govt. Print. Off., 1969   Z1209.U4

2239   UNDERHILL, Ruth Murray
        Hawk over whirlpools. J. J. Augustin, 1940 PS3541.N5H3

2240   VANDERWERTH, W. C. comp.
        Indian oratory. Norman, Univ. of Oklahoma Pr., 1971
                       E98.O7V33

2241   WARBURTON, Austen D.
        Indian lore of the north California coast. Santa Clara,
        Calif., Pacific Pueblo Pr. 1966   E78.C15W35

2242   WEATHERS, Winston
        Indian and white. Lincoln, Univ. of Nebraska Pr., 1970
                     E98.F6W42

2243   WILSON, Herbert Earl
        The lore and the lure of the Yosemite. Los Angeles,
        Wolfer Printing Co., 1932   E98.F6W77.1932

22431   WITT, Shirley Hill comp.
        The way; an anthology of American Indian literature.
        Knopf, 1972   PM197.E1.W5.1972

2244   WOOD, Charles Erskine Scott
        A book of tales. The Vanguard Pr., 1929 E98.F6W82.1929

2245   YÁÑEZ, Agustín ed.
        Mitos indígenas. México, Universidad Nacional Autónoma
        de México, 1964   F1219.Y3.1964

2246   YOUNG, Egerton Ryerson
        Stories from Indian wigwams and northern camp-fires.
        Eaton & Mains, 1892   E78.C2Y8

2247   ZITKALA-SA
        Old Indian legends. Boston and London, Ginn & Co., 1901
                     E98.F6Z5

223

2248 ADAIR, John
 The people's health. Appleton-Century-Crofts, 1970 RA801.A3

2249 AGUIRRE BELTRÁN, Gonzalo
 Medicina y magia. México, Instituto Nacional Indigenista,
 1963   R466.A5

2250 CLEMENTS, Forrest Edward
 Primitive concepts of disease. Berkeley, Univ. of California
 Pr., 1932   (UCPAE)   E51.C15.v.32.no.2

2251 COOK, Sherburne Friend
 The epidemic of 1830-1833 in California and Oregon. Berkeley,
 Univ. of California Pr., 1955 (UCPAE) E51.C15.v.43.no.3

2252 COOK, Sherburne Friend
 The extent and significance of disease among the Indians of
 Baja California, 1697-1773. Berkeley, Univ. of California
 Pr., 1937   (IAM)   F1401.I22.no.12

2253 CORLETT, William Thomas
 The medicine-man of the American Indian and his cultural
 background. Springfield, Ill., Baltimore, Md., C. C. Thomas,
 1935   E98.M4C67

2254 COURY, Charles
 La médecine de l'Amérique précolombienne. Paris, R. Dacosta,
 1969   E59.M4C6

2255 CRUZ, Martín de la
 The de la Cruz-Badiano Aztec herbal of 1552. Baltimore,
 The Maya Society, 1939   RS169.C7.1939

2256 DEVEREUX, George
 Reality and dream. New York Univ. Pr., 1969 RC465.D48.1969a

2257 HRDLIČKA, Aleš
 Tuberculosis among certain Indian tribes of the United States.
 Washington, Govt. Print. Off., 1909 (BAEB) E51.U55.no.42

2258 JAMES, George Wharton
 The Indian's secret of health; or, What the white race may
 learn from the Indian. Pasadena, Calif., The Radiant Life
 Pr., 1917   E77.J262

2259 KANE, Robert Lewis
 Federal health care (with reservations!). Springer Pub. Co.,
 1972   RA448.5.I5K3

2260   LEIGH, Rufus Wood
        <u>Dental pathology of aboriginal California</u>. Berkeley,
        Univ. of California Pr., 1928 (UCPAE) E51.C15.v.23.no.10

22601 LIGHTHALL, J. I.
        <u>Indian folk medicine guide</u>. Popular Library, 197-? E98.M4.L5

2261   MARTÍNEZ CORTÉS, Fernando
        <u>Las ideas en la medicina náhuatl</u>. México, La Prensa Médica
        Mexicana, 1965   F1219.3.M5M3

2262   POPE, Saxton Temple
        <u>The medical history of Ishi</u>. Berkeley, Univ. of California Pr.,
        1920   (UCPAE)   E51.C15.v.13.no.5

2263   ROUHIER, Alexandre
        <u>La plante qui fait les yeux émerveillés</u>. Paris, G. Doin, 1927
                                    RS165.P44R6

2264   SCULLY, Virginia
        <u>A treasury of American Indian herbs: their lore and their
        use for food, drugs, and medicine</u>. Crown, 1970 E98.B7S3.1970

2265   SEGGIARO, Luís A.
        <u>Medicina indígena de América</u>. Buenos Aires, Editorial
        Universitaria de Buenos Aires, 1969   F2230.1.M4S4

2266   STEWART, Joseph Letie
        <u>The problem of stuttering in certain North American Indian
        societies</u>. Washington, American Speech and Hearing Assoc.,
        1960   RC424.S73

2267   STONE, Eric
        <u>Medicine among the American Indians</u>. Haffner Pub. Co.,
        1962   E98.M4S8.1962

2268   U. S. DIVISION OF INDIAN HEALTH.
        <u>Health auxiliary training: instructor's guide</u>. Washington,
        U. S. Govt. Print. Off., 1966   RA801.U54

2269   U. S. DIVISION OF PUBLIC HEALTH METHODS.
        <u>Health services for American Indians</u>. Washington, U. S.
        Govt. Print. Off., 1957?   RA801.U55

2270   VOGEL, Virgil J.
        <u>American Indian medicine</u>. Norman, Univ. of Oklahoma Pr.,
        1970   E98.M4V6

2271   WEINER, Michael A.
        <u>Earth medicine-earth foods</u>. Macmillan, 1972 E98.M4W4

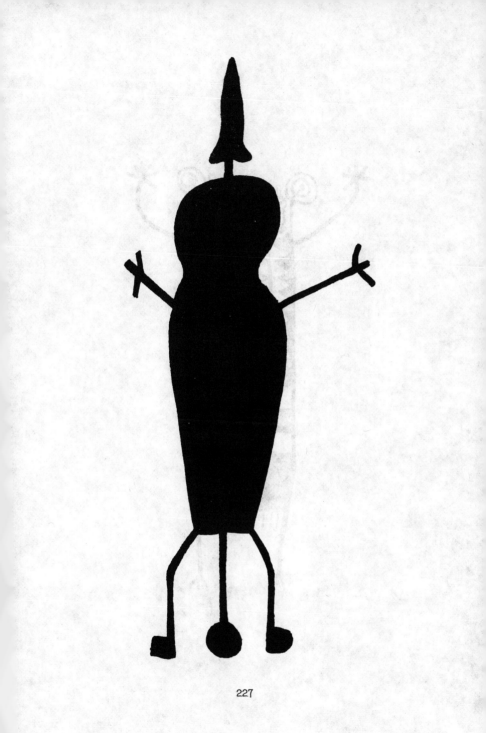

227

2272　BARRETT, Samuel Alfred
　　　The dream dance of the Chippewa and Menominee Indians of
　　　northern Wisconsin. Wilwaukee, Wis., Pub. by order of the
　　　Trustees, 1911　　　　　　　E98.D2B2

2273　BURTON, Frederick Russell
　　　American primitive music. Port Washington, N.Y., Kennikat Pr.,
　　　1969 (1909)　　　　　　　ML3557.B9.1969

2274　COLLAER, Paul
　　　Amerika: Eskimo und indianische Bevölkerung. Leipzig,
　　　VEB Deutscher Verlag Für Musik, 1967　fML89.M9.Bd.1:2

2275　CRONYN, George William
　　　The path on the rainbow, an anthology of songs and chants
　　　from the Indians of North America. Liveright Pub. Co.,
　　　1934　　　　　　　E98.P74C9

2276　DENSMORE, Frances
　　　The American Indians and their music. The Womans Pr.,
　　　1926　　　　　　　ML3557.D362

2277　DENSMORE, Frances
　　　Mandan and Hidatsa music. Washington, U. S. Govt. Print.
　　　Off., 1923　　　(BAEB)　　　E51.U55.no.80

2278　DENSMORE, Frances
　　　Music of Acoma, Isleta, Cochiti, and Zuñi Pueblos.
　　　Washington, U. S. Govt. Print. Off., 1957
　　　　　　　　　(BAEB)　　　E51.U55.no.165

2279　DENSMORE, Frances
　　　Music of the Maidu Indians of California. Los Angeles,
　　　Southwest Museum, 1958　　ML3557.D359

2280　DENSMORE, Frances
　　　Nootka and Quileute music. Washington, U. S. Govt. Print.
　　　Off., 1939　　　(BAEB)　　　E51.U55.no.124

2281　DENSMORE, Frances
　　　Yuman and Yaqui music. Washington, U. S. Govt. Print. Off.,
　　　1932　　　(BAEB)　　　E51.U55.no.110

2282　EVANS, Bessie
　　　American Indian dance steps. A. S. Barnes and Co., Inc.,
　　　1931　　　　　　　E98.D2E9

2283   FERGUSSON, Erna
        Dancing gods. Albuquerque, Univ. of New Mexico Pr.,
        1957   E98.D2F47.1957

22831   FLETCHER, Alice Cunningham
        Indian games and dances with native songs; arranged from
        American Indian ceremonials and sports. AMS, 1970
                                                E98.G2.F6.1970

2284   KENDRICK, Edith (Johnston)
        Regional dances of Mexico. Dallas, B. Upshaw, 1956 (1935)
                                                GV1627.K45

22841   KURATH, Gertrude Prokosch
        Music and dance of the Tewa Pueblos. Santa Fe, Museum
        of New Mexico Pr., 1970 (Museum of New Mexico research
        records, no. 8)   E99.T35.K85

2285   LEÓN PORTILLA, Miguel
        Los antiguos mexicanos a través de sus crónicas y cantares.
        México, Fondo de Cultura Económica, 1961 F1219.L555

2286   LOWIE, Robert Harry
        Dance associations of the Eastern Dakota. American Museum
        of Natural History, 1913 (AMNHP)   GN2.A27.v.11.pt.2

2287   LOWIE, Robert Harry
        Sun dance of the Shoshoni, Ute, and Hidatsa. American
        Museum of Natural History, 1919 (AMNHP) GN2.A27.v.16.pt.5

2288   McALLESTER, David Park
        Peyote music. 1949   ML3557.M3

2289   MARTÍ, Samuel
        Alt-Amerika. Leipzig, Deutscher Verlag Für Musik, 1970
                                                ML89.M9.Bd.2:7

2290   MARTÍ, Samuel
        Canto, danza y música precortesianos. México, Fondo de
        Cultura Económica, 1961   F1219.M38

2291   MARTÍ, Samuel
        Dances of Anáhuac. Chicago, Aldine Pub. Co., 1964
                                                F1219.3.D2M35

2292   MASON, Bernard Sterling
        Dances and stories of the American Indian. The Ronald Pr.
        Co., 1944   E98.D2M3

2293   PAIGE, Harry W.
        Songs of the Teton Sioux. Los Angeles, Westernlore Pr.,
        1970   ML3557.P3

2294   ROBERTS, Helen Heffron
        Musical areas in aboriginal North America. New Haven,
        Pub. for the Section of Anthropology, Dept. of the Social
        Sciences, Yale Univ., by the Yale Univ. Pr.; London,
        H. Milford, Oxford Univ. Pr., 1936 (YUPA) GN2.Y3.no.12

2295   SETON, Mrs. Julia (Moss)
        The rhythm of the redman. The Ronald Press Co., 1930
                                        E98.D2S4.1930

2296   SPIER, Leslie
        _The sun dance of the Plains Indians: its development and
        diffusion_. American Museum of Natural History, 1921
                        (AMNHP)   GN2.A27.v.16.pt.7

2297   SQUIRES, John L.
        American Indian dances. Ronald Press Co., 1963 E98.D2S77

2298   STEVENSON, Robert Murrell
        Music in Aztec and Inca territory. Berkeley, Univ. of
        California Pr., 1968   ML3549.S84

2299   UNDERHILL, Ruth Murray
        Singing for power. Berkeley, Univ. of California Pr., 1938
                                        ML3557.U53S4

2300   ABERLE, David Friend
        Navaho and Ute peyotism. Boulder, Univ. of Colorado Pr.,
        1957   (CUSA)   GN4.C64.no.6

2301   ALEXANDER, Hartley Burr
        The world's rim. Lincoln, Univ. of Nebraska Pr., 1967
                                                    E98.R3A4.1967

2302   AMERICAN BAPTIST CONVENTION. BOARD OF EDUCATION.
        The moccasin trail. Philadelphia, Boston, etc., The Judson Pr.,
        1932   E98.M6A45

2303   ARMITAGE, Merle
        Pagans, conquistadores, heroes, and martyrs. Fresno, Calif.,
        Academy Guild Pr., 1964 (1960)   BV2800.A8.1964

23031   BAAL, Jan van
        _Symbols for communication; an introduction to the anthropological
        study of religion._ Assen, Van Gorcum, 1971 GN470.B17

23032   BARNETT, Homer Garner
        Indian Shakers, a messianic cult of the Pacific Northwest.
        Illinois, So. Illinois Univ. Pr., 1972 E78.N77.B3

2304   BEATTY, Charles
        Journals of Charles Beatty. University Park, Pennsylvania
        State Univ. Pr., 1962 (i.e. 1963)   BX9225.B458A3.1963

2305   BEAVER, Robert Pierce
        Church, state, and the American Indians. St. Louis,
        Concordia Pub. House, 1966   BR516.B37

2306   BEAVER, Robert Pierce ed.
        Pioneers in mission. Grand Rapids, W. B. Eerdmans Pub. Co.,
        1966   BV2410.B4

2307   BENEDICT, Ruth Fulton
        The concept of the guardian spirit in North America. Menasha,
        Wis., American Anthropological Assoc., 1923
                            (AAAM)   GN2.A22.no.29

2308   BERKHOFER, Robert F.
        Salvation and the savage. Lexington, Univ. of Kentucky Pr.,
        1965   E98.M6B37

2309   BISCHOFF, William Norbert
        The Jesuits in old Oregon. Caldwell, Id., The Caxton
        Printers, Ltd., 1945   BV2801.B5

2310   BORGES, Pedro
        Métodos misionales en la cristianización de América, siglo
        XVI. Madrid, Consejo Superior de Investigaciones Cientificas,
        Departamento de Misionología Española, 1960 BV2757.B6

2311   BRAINERD, David
        The life and diary of David Brainerd. Chicago, Moody Pr.,
        1955 (1949)   E98.M6B786

2312   BURLAND, Cottie Arthur
        The gods of Mexico. Putnam, 1967   F1219.3.R38B8.1967a

2313   CARRO, Venancio Diego
        La teología y los teólogos-juristas españoles ante la
        conquista de América. Madrid, Salamanca, 1951
                         BX1790.C25.1951

2314   CHINCHILLA AGUILAR, Ernesto
        La danza del sacrificio. Guatemala, Centro Editorial
        "José de Pineda Ibarra," Ministerio de Educación Pública,
        1963   F1465.C5

2315   COLLIER, John
        Patterns and ceremonials of the Indians of the Southwest.
        Dutton, 1949   fE78.S7C6

23151   DAVIS, Edward H.
        ...The Diegueno ceremony of the death images. Museum
        of the American Indian, Heye Foundation, 1919
                  (HFM)   E51.N42.v.5.no.2

2316   DE KORNE, John Cornelius ed.
        Navaho and Zuni for Christ. Grand Rapids, Mich., Christian
        Reformed Board of Missions, 1947   F801.D4

2317   DE SCHWEINITZ, Edmund Alexander
        The life and times of David Zeisberger. Johnson Reprint,
        1971 (1871)   E98.M6Z4.1971

2318   DOMINICANS
        Doctrina cristiana en lengua española y mexicana.
        Madrid, Ediciones Cultura Hispánica, 1944 BX1968.D65

23181   DU BOIS, Cora Alice
        ...The 1870 ghost dance. Berkeley and Los Angeles,
        Univ. of California Pr., 1973 (AR)   E51.A58.v.3.no.1

2319   DUNNE, Peter Masten
        Early Jesuit missions in Tarahumara. Berkeley, Univ.
        of California Pr., 1948   BX3712.A1D795

2320   DUNNE, Peter Masten
         Pioneer black robes on the west coast. Berkeley and
         Los Angeles, Univ. of California Pr., 1940 BX3712.A1D8

2321   DURÁN, Diego
         Book of the gods and rites and The ancient calendar.
         Norman, Univ. of Oklahoma Pr., 1971   F1219.D9513

2322   EASTMAN, Charles Alexander
         The soul of the Indian. Houghton Mifflin Co., 1911
                                                E98.R3E15

2323   ENGELHARDT, Zephyrin, father
         The missions and missionaries of California.
         Santa Barbara, Calif., Mission Santa Barbara, 1929?
                                          F864.E572.Spec.Coll.

2324   Facing the future in Indian missions; part I. A social outlook
         on Indian missions, by Lewis Meriam. part II. The church
         and the Indian, by George W. Hinman. Council of Women for
         Home Missions, and Missionary Education Movement, 1932
                                          E98.M6F2

2325   GARRAGHAN, Gilbert Joseph
         The Jesuits of the middle United States. America Pr.,
         1938   BS3708.G3

2326   GIFFORD, Edward Winslow comp.
         California Indian nights entertainments. Glendale, Calif.,
         The Arthur H. Clark Co., 1930   E98.R3G45

2327   A hand-book of the church's mission to the Indians.
         Hartford, Conn., Church Missions Pub. Co., 1914 E98.M6H23

2328   HECKEWELDER, John Gottlieb Ernestus
         A narrative of the mission of the United Brethren among
         the Delaware and Mohegan Indians. Arno, 1971 (1820)
                                          E99.M9H43

2329   HOME MISSIONS COUNCIL. COMMITTEE ON INDIAN MISSIONS.
         Signs of the times in American Indian affairs; report.
         Homes Missions Council, 1918   E98.M6H6.1918

2330   HOWITT, William
         Colonization and Christianity. Negro Universities Pr.,
         1969 (1838)   JV305.H7.1969

2331   HURDY, John Major
         American Indian religions. Los Angeles, Sherbourne Pr.,
         1970   E98.R3H86

235

2332 JAMES, George Wharton
      In and out of the old missions of California. Boston,
      Little, Brown, 1905   F870.M6J3

2333 KELLAWAY, William
      The New England Company, 1649-1776. Barnes & Noble,
      1962 (1961)   E98.M6K28.1962   E98.M6K28.1962

2334 KELSEY, Rayner Wichersham
      Friends and the Indians, 1655-1917. Philadelphia, The
      Associated Executive Committee of Friends on Indian
      Affairs, 1917   E98.M6K29

2335 KLINGBERG, Frank Joseph
      Anglican humanitarianism in colonial New York.
      Philadelphia, The Church Historical Society, 1940
                                              BV2500.A6K55

2336 KROEBER, Alfred Louis
      The religion of the Indians of California. Berkeley,
      Univ. of California Pr., 1907 (UCPAE) E51.C15.v.4.no.6

2337 LA BARRE, Weston
      The peyote cult. Hamden, Conn., Reprinted by
      Shoe String Pr., 1959 (1938)   E98.R3L3.1959

2338 LADD, John
      The structure of a moral code. Cambridge, Mass.,
      Harvard Univ. Pr., 1957   E98.E84L33

2339 LEÓN PORTILLA, Miguel
      La filosofía nahuatl, estudiada en sus fuentes. Mexico,
      Universidad Nacional Autonoma de Mexico, 1966
                                        F1219.3.P5L4.1966

2340 LINTON, Ralph
      Purification of the sacred bundles. Chicago, Field Museum
      of Natural History, 1923 (CMA)   GN2.F5.no.7

2341 LOEB, Edwin Meyer
      The eastern Kuksu cult. Berkeley, Univ. of California
      Pr., 1933   (UCPAE)   E51.C15.v.33.no.2

2342 LOEB, Edwin Meyer
      The western Kuksu cult. Berkeley, Univ. of California Pr.,
      1932   (UCPAE)   E51.C15.v.33.no.1

2343 LÓPEZ AUSTIN, Alfredo comp.
      Juegos rituales aztecas. México, Universidad Nacional
      Autónoma de México, 1967   F1219.3.R38L6

2344   McGROARTY, John Steven
        Mission memories. Los Angeles, Neuner Corp. 1929 F870.M6M1

23441   MARETT, Robert Ranulph
        Faith, hope and charity in primitive religion. Blom, 1972
                                    GN470.M23.1972

2345   MARRIOTT, Alice Lee
        Peyote. Crowell, 1971   E98.R3M3.1971

23451   MATA TORRES, Ramon
        Peregrinacion del Peyote. Mexico, Guadelajara, Ed. de la
        casa de las Artesanias del Cobiern   F1219.3.R38.M3

2346   MAZZUCHELLI, Samuel Charles
        Memoirs. Chicago, Press of W. F. Hall Printing Co., 1915
                                        BX1406.M35

2347   MENDIETA, Gerónimo de
        Historia eclesiástica indiana. México, D. F., Editorial
        Salvador Chávez Hayhoe, 1945   F1219.M53.1945

2348   MOFFETT, Thomas Clinton
        The American Indian on the new trail. Missionary Education
        Movement of the United States and Canada, 1914 E98.M6M7

2349   MORIARTY, James Robert
        Chinigchinix: an indigenous California Indian religion.
        Los Angeles, Southwest Museum, 1969   E98.R3M7

2350   NICOLAR, Joseph
        The life and traditions of the Red man. Bangor, Me.,
        C. H. Glass & Co., Printers, 1893   E98.R3N6

23501   NORMAN, John
        Ghost dance. Ballantine Books, 1970   E99.D1.N6

2351   NUTTALL, Zelia
        A penitential rite of the ancient Mexicans. Cambridge,
        Mass., The Museum, 1904 (PMP)   E51.H337.v.1.no.7

2352   PALLADINO, Lawrence Benedict
        Indian and white in the Northwest. Lancaster, Pa.,
        Wickersham Pub. Co., 1922   BX1415.M9P3.1922

2353   PARSONS, Elsie Worthington (Clews)
        Hopi and Zuñi ceremonialism. Menasha, Wis., American
        Anthropological Assoc., 1933 (AAAM)   GN2.A22.no.39

2354 PÉREZ DE RIBAS, Andrés
My life among the savage nations of New Spain. Los Angeles,
Ward Ritchie Pr., 1966   BX3712.A1P533

2355 PHELAN, John Loddy
The millennial kingdom of the Franciscans in the New World.
Berkeley, Univ. of California Pr., 1970 F1219.3.M595.1970

2356 Pre-Columbian American religions, by Walter Krickeberg
[and others]. Holt, Rinehart and Winston, 1969 (1968)
                                        E59.R38R413.1969

2357 REICHARD, Gladys Amanda
Prayer: the compulsive word. J. J. Augustin, 1944
                    (MAES)   E51.A556.v.7

2358 RICARD, Robert
La "conquête spirituelle" du Mexique. Paris, Institut
d'ethnologie, 1933   BX1428.R5

2359 RICARD, Robert
La conquista espiritual de México. Mexico, Editorial Jus,
1947   BX1428.R55

2360 RICARD, Robert
The spiritual conquest of Mexico. Berkeley, Univ. of
California Pr., 1966   BX1428.R53

2361 RÍOS, Eduardo Enrique
Life of Fray Antonio Margil, O.F.M. Washington,
Academy of American Franciscan History, 1959 BX4705.M3252.R53

2362 SALPOINTE, Jean Baptiste
Soldiers of the cross. Banning, Calif., St. Boniface's
Industrial School, 1898   BX1412.S3

2363 SCHMIDT, Wilhelm
High gods in North America. Oxford, The Clarendon Pr.,
1933   E98.R3S3

2364 SÉJOURNÉ, Laurette
Burning water. Vanguard Pr., 1956?   F1219.3.R38S4

2365 SETON, Ernest Thompson comp.
The gospel of the red man. Garden City, N. Y., Doubleday,
Doran, 1936   E98.R3S4

2366 SHEA, John Dawson Gilmary
History of the Catholic missions among the Indian tribes
of the United States. 1529-1854. E. Dunigan & Brother, 1855
                                        E98.M6S53

238

2367   SHIPLEY, Nan
        The James Evans story. Toronto, Ryerson Pr., 1966
                                        BV2813.E8S5

2368   SHORRIS, Earl
        The death of the Great Spirit. Simon and Schuster, 1971
                                        E98.S67S5

23681   Systems of North American witchcraft and sorcery.
        Keith H. Basso and others., Idaho, Univ. of Idaho, 1970
                                        E98.M2.S95

2369   Tracts relating to the aborigines. No. 1-12. 1838-46.
        London, E. Marsh   BV2535.A4A5.Spec.Coll.

2370   TSA TO KE, Monroe
        The peyote ritual. San Francisco, Grabhorn Pr., 1957
                                        fE98.R3T8.Spec.Coll.

2371   UNDERHILL, Ruth Murray
        Ceremonial patterns in the greater Southwest. J. J. Augustin,
        1948   (MAES)   E51.A556.v.13

2372   UNDERHILL, Ruth Murray
        Red man's religion. Chicago, Univ. of Chicago Pr., 1965
                                        E98.R3U57

2373   WATERS, Frank
        Masked gods. Chicago, Swallow Pr., Inc., 1950
                                        E98.R3W4.1950b

23731   WATERS, Frank
        Mysticism and witchcraft. Ft. Collins, Colorado, Colorado
        State Univ., 1966   E99.H7.W35

2374   WHERRY, Joseph H.
        Indian masks and myths of the West. Funk & Wagnalls, 1969
                                        E98.M3W45

2375   WILLOYA, William
        Warriors of the Rainbow. Healdsburg, Calif., Naturegraph,
        1962   BF1809.W5

2376   WINSLOW, Ola Elizabeth
        John Eliot, apostle to the Indians. Boston, Houghton Mifflin,
        1968   E78.M4E595

2377   WISSLER, Clark
        General discussion of shamanistic and dancing societies.
        American Museum of Natural History, 1916
                            (AMNHP)   GN2.A27.v.11.pt.12

2378   YOUNG, Karl E.
        <u>Ordeal in Mexico</u>. Salt Lake City, Deseret Book Co., 1968
                                F1392.M6Y6

2379 ADNEY, Edwin Tappan
   The bark canoes and skin boats of North America. Washington,
   Smithsonian Institution, 1964   E98.B6A3

2380 ANELL, Bengt
   Running down and driving of game in North America.
   Uppsala, Inst. for allm. och jamforande etnografi, 1969
            fE98.H8A5

2381 AUSTIN, Mary (Hunter)
   The arrow maker. Duffield and Co., 1911 PS3501.U8A7.1911

2382 BARRETT, Samuel Alfred
   The material culture of the Klamath lake and Modoc Indians
   of northeastern California and southern Oregon. Berkeley,
   Univ. of California Pr., 1910 (UCPAE) E51.C15.v.5.no.4

2383 CARTER, George Francis
   Plant geography and culture history in the American Southwest.
   Johnson Reprint, 1967 (1945)   E98.A3C3.1967

2384 CASTETTER, Edward Franklin
   Pima and Papago Indian agriculture. Albuquerque, N.M.,
   The Univ. of New Mexico Pr., 1942 E99.P6C3

2385 COPE, Leona
   Calendars of the Indians north of Mexico. Berkeley,
   Univ. of California Pr., 1919 (UCPAE) E51.C15.v.16.no.4

23851 CRABTREE, Don E.
   An introduction to flintworking. Pocatello, Idaho,
   Idaho State Univ., 1972 (ISUOP) E78.I18.I4.no.28

2386 FOSTER, George McClelland
   Contemporary pottery techniques in southern and central
   Mexico. New Orleans, Middle American Research Institute,
   Tulane Univ., 1955 (TMAI) F1421.T95.no.22

2387 GAYTON, Anna Hadwick
   Yokuts and western Mono pottery-making. Berkeley, Univ. of
   California Pr., 1929 (UCPAE) E51.C15.v.24.no.3

2388 GIFFORD, Edward Winslow
   Pottery-making in the Southwest. Berkeley, Univ. of
   California Pr., 1928 (UCPAE) E51.C15.v.23.no.8

2389 HAINES, Francis
   The buffalo. Crowell, 1970   SK297.H33.1970

23891   HAMILTON, T. M.
        <u>Native American bows</u>. York, Pa., G. Shumway, 1972 E59.A68.H3

2390   HATT, Gudmund
        <u>Moccasins and their relation to the Arctic footwear</u>.
        Lancaster, Pa., Pub. for the American Anthropological Assoc.,
        The New Era Printing Co., 1916 (AAAM) GN2.A22.no.15

2391   HOLDER, Preston
        <u>The hoe and the horse on the Plains</u>. Lincoln, Univ. of
        Nebraska Pr., 1970   E78.G73H6

2392   HOLMES, William Henry
        <u>The use of gold and other metals among ancient inhabitants</u>
        <u>of Chiriqui Isthmus of Darien</u>. Washington, U. S. Govt.
        Print. Off., 1887   (BAEB)   E51.U55.no.3

2393   JAMES, George Wharton
        <u>Indian basketry</u>. Pasadena, Calif., Privately printed by
        the author, 1903   TS910.J27.1903

2394   KELLY, Isabel Truesdell
        <u>The Tajin Totonac</u>. Washington, U. S. Govt. Print. Off.,
        1952-   (SIP)   E51.S4.no.13

2395   KENT, Kate Peck
        <u>The cultivation and weaving of cotton in the prehistoric</u>
        <u>Southwestern United States</u>. Philadelphia, American Philo-
        sophical Society, 1957   fE98.T35K4

2396   KIDDER, Alfred Vincent
        <u>Pottery of the Pajarito plateau and of some adjacent regions</u>
        <u>in New Mexico</u>. Lancaster, Pa., The New Era Printing Co.,
        1915   (AAAM)   GN2.A22.no.12

2397   KIMBALL, Yeffe
        <u>The art of American Indian cooking</u>. Garden City, N. Y.,
        Doubleday, 1965   TX715.K499

2398   KISSELL, Mary Lois
        <u>Basketry of the Papago and Pima</u>. American Museum of
        Natural History, 1916 (AMNHP)   GN2.A27.v.17.pt.4

2399   KROEBER, Alfred Louis
        <u>Arrow release distributions</u>. Berkeley, Univ. of California
        Pr., 1927   (UCPAE)   E51.C15.v.23.no.4

2400   KROEBER, Alfred Louis
        <u>Fishing among the Indians of northwestern California</u>.
        Berkeley, Univ. of California Pr., 1960
                   (AR)   E51.A58.v.21.no.1

24001   LAUBIN, Reginald
        The Indian tipi; its history, construction, and use.
        Ballantine Books, 1971   E98.D9.L3.1971

2401   LAUFER, Berthold
        The reindeer and its domestication. Lancaster, Pa., Pub.
        for the American Anthropological Assoc., 1917
                            (AAAM)   GN2.A22.no.18

2402   LENZ, Hans
        Mexican Indian paper, its history and survival. Mexico,
        Editorial Libros de Mexico, printed by R. Loera y Chavez,
        1961   fF1219.3.P3L43

2403   MARQUINA, Ignacio
        Arquitectura prehispánica. México, Instituto Nacional de
        Antropología e Historia, Secretaria de Educación Pública,
        1951   fF1219.3.A6M37

2404   MASON, John Alden
        Costa Rican stonework. American Museum of Natural History,
        1945   (AMNHP)   GN2.A27.v.39.pt.3

2405   MORGAN, Lewis Henry
        Houses and house-life of the American aborigines. Chicago,
        Univ. of Chicago Pr., 1965   E98.D9M65.1965

2406   MORRIS, Earl Halstead
        The beginnings of pottery making in the San Juan area.
        American Museum of Natural History, 1927
                            (AMNHP)   GN2.A27.v.28.pt.2

2407   MURPHEY, Edith (Van Allen)
        Indian uses of native plants. Fort Bragg, Calif., Mendocino
        County Historical Society, 1969 (1959) E98.B7M8.1969

2408   NUTTALL, Mrs. Zelia
        The atlatl or spear-thrower of the ancient Mexicans.
        Cambridge, Mass., Peabody Museum of American Archaeology
        and Ethnology, 1891   (PMP)   E51.H337.v.1.no.3

2409   O'NEALE, Lila Morris
        Yurok-Karok basket weavers. Berkeley, Univ. of California
        Pr., 1932   (UCPAE)   E51.C15.v.32.no.1

24091   PETERSON, Harold Leslie
        American Indian Tomahawks. Museum of the American Indian,
        Heye Foundation, 1971 (HFM)   E51.N42.v.19.1971

2410   POPE, Saxton Temple
        Bows and arrows. Berkeley, Univ. of California Pr., 1962 (1930)
                            (UCPAE)   E51.C15.v.13.no.9.1962

2411   The pottery of Pecos. New Haven, Pub. for Phillips Academy
        by the Yale Univ. Pr.; London, H. Milford, Oxford Univ.
        Pr., 1931-36   E98.P8P77

2412   RAINEY, Froelich Gladstone
        The whale hunters of Tigara. American Museum of Natural
        History, 1947   (AMNHP)   GN2.A27.v.41.pt.2

2413   ROE, Frank Gilbert
        The Indian and the horse. Norman, Univ. of Oklahoma Pr.,
        1968   E98.H55R6

2414   ROMERO, John Bruno
        The botanical lore of the California Indians. Vantage Pr.,
        1954   QK99.R64

2415   RUSSELL, Carl Parcher
        Guns on the early frontiers. Berkeley, Univ. of California
        Pr., 1962 (1957)   TS520.R85.1962

2416   SALAS, Alberto Mario
        Las armas de la conquista. Buenos Aires, Emecé, 1950
                                              NK6614.S3

2417   STIERLIN, Henri
        Living architecture: ancient Mexican. London, Macdonald &
        1968   F1219.3.A6S713

2418   TILLEY, Martha
        3 textile traditions: Pueblo, Navaho & Rio Grande.
        Colorado Springs, Colo., Taylor Museum of the Colorado
        Springs Fine Arts Center, 1967   E98.T35T5

2419   Varia anthropologica. Berkeley, Univ. of California Pr., 1936
                        (UCPAE)   E51.C15.v.35.no.3-5

2420   VON HAGEN, Victor Wolfgang
        The Aztec and Maya papermakers. J. J. Augustin, 1944
                                              F1219.3.P3V7.1944

2421   WEATHERWAX, Paul
        Indian corn in old America. Macmillan, 1954 SB191.M2W42

2422   WHITFORD, A. C.
        Textile fibers used in eastern aboriginal North America.
        American Museum of Natural History, 1941
                        (AMNHP)   GN2.A27.v.38.pt.1

2423   WILL, George Francis
        Corn among the Indians of the upper Missouri. St. Louis, M
        The William Harvey Miner Co., Inc., 1917   E98.A3W6

2424   WISSLER, Clark
        <u>Riding gear of the North American Indians</u>. American
        Museum of Natural History, 1915 (AMNHP) GN2.A27.v.17.pt.1

2425   WOODBURY, Richard Benjamin
        <u>Prehistoric stone implements of northeastern Arizona</u>.
        Kraus Reprint Corp., 1968 (1954) (PMP) E51.H337.v.34.1968

ABNAKI

24251   MAURAULT, Joseph Pierre Anselme
        Histoire des Abenakis depuis 1605 jusqu's nos jours.
        Johnson Rep., The Hague, Mouton, 1970 (1969) E99.A13.M4.1970

ACHOMAWI

2426   KNIFFEN, Fred Bowerman
        Achomawi geography. Berkeley, Univ. of California Pr., 1928
                             (UCPAE)   E51.C15.v.23.no.5

2427   OLMSTED, David Lockwood
        Achumawi dictionary. Berkeley, Univ. of California Pr., 1966
                              (CUPL)

ACOMA

2428   JAMES, Harold L.
        Acoma; the people of the white rock. Glorieta, N.M.,
        Rio Grande Pr., 1970   E99.A16J3

2429   MILLER, Wick R.
        Acoma grammar and texts. Berkeley, Univ. of California Pr.,
        1965   (CUPL)   P25.C25.v.40

2430   STIRLING, Matthew Williams
        Origin myth of Acoma, and other records. Washington,
        U. S. Govt. Print. Off., 1942 (BAEB) E51.U55.no.135

        ACOMA
          See also: 2278

AKWA'ALA

2431   GIFFORD, Edward Winslow
        Notes on the Akwa'ala Indians of Lower California. Berkeley,
        Univ. of California Pr., 1928 (UCPAE) E51.C15.v.23.no.7

ALEUT

2432   BERGSLAND, Knut
        Aleut dialects of Atka and Attu. Philadelphia, American
        Philosophical Society, 1959 (APST) fQ11.P6.n.s.v.49.pt.3

2433   JOCHELSON, Vladimir Il'ich
        History, ethnology and anthropology of the Aleut.
        Washington, Carnegie Institution of Washington, 1933 E99.A34J7

ALGONKIN

2434   SPECK, Frank Gouldsmith
        The functions of wampum among the eastern Algonkian.
        Lancaster, Pa., American Anthropological Assoc., 1919
                      (AAAM)   GN2.A22.no.25

ALGONQUIAN

2435   DEMING, Alden O.
        Manabozho, the Indian's story of Hiawatha. Philadelphia,
        F. A. Davis Co., 1938   E99.A35D4

2436   TEICHER, Morton I.
        Windigo psychosis. Seattle, American Ethnological Society,
        1960 (i.e. 1961)   E99.A35T4

ALGONQUIAN
        See also: 0092, 0795, 1629, 1665, 2195

ALSEA

2437   DRUCKER, Philip
        Contributions to Alsea ethnography. Berkeley, Univ. of
        California Pr., 1939   (UCPAE)   E51.C15.v.35.no.7

2438   FRACHTENBERG, Leo Joachim
        Alsea texts and myths. Washington, U. S. Govt. Print.
        Off., 1920   (BAEB)   E51.U55.no.67

2439   ADAMS, Alexander B.
     Geronimo. G. P. Putnam's Sons, 1971   E99.A6G14.1971

2440   BASSO, Keith H.
     The Cibecue Apache. Holt, Rinehart and Winston, 1970
                                 E99.A6B228

2441   BASSO, Keith H.
     Western Apache witchcraft. Tucson, Univ. of Arizona Pr.,
     1969   E99.A6B23

2442   BELLAH, Robert Neelly
     Apache kinship systems. Cambridge, Mass., Harvard Univ. Pr.,
     1952   E99.A6B4

2443   BETZINEZ, Jason
     I fought with Geronimo. Harrisburg, Pa., Stackpole Co.,
     1959   E99.A6B42

2444   BOURKE, John Gregory
     The medicine men of the Apache. Glorieta, N. M., Rio Grande
     Pr., 1970   E99.A6B8.1970

2445   CHRIS
     Apache odyssey. Holt, Rinehart and Winston, 1969 E99.A6C46

2446   CLUM, John Philip
     The truth about the Apaches. Los Angeles, Adcraft, 1931
                                 E99.A6C52

2447   CLUM, Woodworth
     Apache agent. Boston, New York, Houghton Mifflin Co., 1936
                                 E99.A6C48

2448   COCHISE, Ciyé
     The first hundred years of Niño Cochise. Abeland-Schuman, Ltd.,
     1971   E99.A6C47

2449   CREMONY, John Carey
     Life among the Apaches. Glorieta, N. M., Rio Grande Pr.,
     1969   E99.A6C7.1969

2450   DAVIS, Britton
     The truth about Geronimo. New Haven, Yale Univ. Pr.;
     London, H. Milford, Oxford Univ. Pr., 1929 E99.A6D26

2451   FISKE, Elizabeth French
     I lived among the Apaches. Pasadena, Trail's End Publishing
     Co., Inc., 1947   E99.A6A55

2452   FORREST, Earle Robert
        Lone war trail of Apache Kid. Pasadena, Calif.,
        Trail's End Publishing Co., Inc., 1947 E99.A6A55

2453   GERONIMO, Apache chief
        Geronimo: his own story. Dutton, 1970 E99.A6G3.1970

2454   GETTY, Harry T.
        The San Carlos Indian cattle industry. Tucson, Univ. of
        Arizona Pr., 1963   E99.A6G34

2455   GIFFORD, Edward Winslow
        Apache-Pueblo. Berkeley, Univ. of California Pr., 1940
                        (AR)   E51.A58.v.4.no.1

2456   GODDARD, Pliny Earle
        Myths and tales from the San Carlos Apache. American
        Museum of Natural History, 1918 (AMNHP) GN2.A27.v.24.pt.1

2457   GODDARD, Pliny Earle
        San Carlos Apache texts. American Museum of Natural
        History, 1919   (AMNHP)   GN2.A27.v.24.pt.3

2458   GODDARD, Pliny Earle
        White mountain Apache texts. American Museum of Natural
        History, 1920   (AMNHP)   GN2.A27.v.24.pt.4

2459   GOODWIN, Grenville
        The social organization of the western Apache. Tucson,
        Univ. of Arizona Pr., 1969   E99.A6G65.1969

2460   HAYES, Jess G.
        Apache vengeance. Albuquerque, Univ. of New Mexico Pr.,
        1954   E99.A6A56

2461   KAYWAYKLA, James
        In the days of Victorio. Tucson, Univ. of Arizona Pr.,
        1970   E99.W36K38.1970

2462   LOCKWOOD, Francis Cummins
        The Apache Indians. Macmillan, 1938   E99.A6L6

2463   MAZZANOVICH, Anton
        Trailing Geronimo. Hollywood, Calif., A. Mazzanovich,
        1931   E99.A6M4.1931

2464   OGLE, Ralph Hedrick
        Federal control of the Western Apaches, 1848-1886. Albuquerque,
        Univ. of New Mexico Pr., 1970   E99.A6O33.1940a

2465   OPLER, Morris Edward
        An Apache life-way. Chicago, The Univ. of Chicago Pr.,
        1941   E99.A6073

2466   PARMEE, Edward A.
        Formal education and culture change. Tucson, Univ. of
        Arizona Pr., 1968   E99.A6P36

2467   SANTEE, Ross
        Apacheland. C. Scribner's Sons, 1947   E99.A6S3

2468   SCHELLIE, Don
        Vast domain of blood. Los Angeles, Westernlore Pr.,
        1968   E99.A6S36

2469   SONNICHSEN, Charles Leland
        The Mescalero Apaches. Norman, Univ. of Oklahoma Pr., 1958
                                                E99.A6S65

24691   TERRELL, John Upton
        Apache chronicle. World Pub., 1972   E99.A6.T4.1972

2470   THRAPP, Dan L.
        The conquest of Apacheria. Norman, Univ. of Oklahoma Pr.,
        1967   E99.A6T47

2471   TUNNELL, Curtis D.
        A Lipan Apache mission. Austin, Texas Memorial Museum,
        1969   GN37.A8T4.no.14

2472   U. S. BOARD OF INDIAN COMMISSIONERS.
        Peace with the Apaches of New Mexico and Arizona. Freeport,
        N. Y., Books for Libraries, 1971 (1871) E99.A6U5.1971

24721   Western Apache raiding and warfare, from the notes of Grenville
        Goodwin. Basso, Keith H. ed. Tucson, Univ. of Arizona Pr.,
        1971   E99.A6.W3

2473   WILSON, H. Clyde
        Jicarilla Apache political and economic structures.
        Berkeley, Univ. of California Pr., 1964
                        (UCPAE)   E51.C15.v.48.no.4

        APACHE
        See also: 0506, 1510, 1523, 1809, 18311, 1832
                   1865, 1926, 2011, 2153, 2222

ARAPAHO

2474   BALCOM, Royal H.
     <u>Better living for the Indian</u>. Ethete, Wyo., St. Michael's
     Mission, 1924?   E99.A7B3

2475   DORSEY, George Amos
     <u>Traditions of the Arapaho</u>. Chicago, Field Museum of
     Natural History, 1903 (FMAS)   GN2.F4.v.5

2476   HILGER, Inez
     <u>Arapaho child life and its cultural background</u>.
     Washington, U. S. Govt. Print. Off., 1952
                  (BAEB)   E51.U55.no.148

2477   KROEBER, Alfred Louis
     <u>Arapaho dialects</u>. Berkeley, Univ. of California Pr., 1916
                (UCPAE)   E51.C15.v.12.no.3

2478   TRENHOLM, Virginia Cole
     <u>The Arapahoes, our people</u>. Norman, Univ. of Oklahoma Pr.,
     1970   E99.A7T7

     <u>ARAPAHO</u>
       See also: 0155, 0861

ARIKARA

2479   DEETZ, James
     <u>The dynamics of stylistic change in Arikara ceramics</u>.
     Urbana, Univ. of Illinois Pr., 1965   E99.A8D4

2480   FLANNERY, Regina
     <u>The Gros Ventres of Montana</u>. Washington, Catholic Univ.
     of America Pr., 1953-57   E99.A87F5

2481   KROEBER, Alfred Louis
     <u>Ethnology of the Gros Ventre</u>. American Museum of Natural
     History, 1908   (AMNHP)   GN2.A27.v.1.pt.4

2482   KROEBER, Alfred Louis
     <u>Gros Ventre myths and tales</u>. American Museum of Natural
     History, 1907   (AMNHP)   GN2.A27.v.1.pt.3

2483   <u>Societies of the Arikara Indians</u>. American Museum of
     Natural History, 1915 (AMNHP)   GN2.A27.v.11.pt.8

     <u>ARIKARA</u>
       See also: 0101, 1473

ASSINIBOIN

2484   WRITERS' PROGRAM. MONTANA.
        The Assiniboines. Norman, Univ. of Oklahoma Pr., 1961
                                              E99.A84W7.1961

ASSINIBOIN
        See also: 0101, 2069

ATHAPASCAN

2485   GODDARD, Pliny Earle
        The Bear river dialect of Athapascan. Berkeley, Univ.
        of California Pr., 1929 (UCPAE)   E51.C15.v.24.no.5

ATHAPASCAN
        See also: 0090, 0796, 1229, 2105

AZTEC

2486   BALLOU, Maturin Murray
        Aztec land. Boston and New York, Houghton, Mifflin & Co.,
        1890   F1215.B19

2487   BIART, Lucien
        The Aztecs. Chicago, A. C. McClurg and Co., 1887 F1219.B57

2488   BRAY, Warwick
        Everyday life of the Aztecs. London, Batsford, New York,
        Putnam, 1968   F1219.B845

2489   CASE, Alfonso
        The Aztecs. Norman, Univ. of Oklahoma Pr., 1958
                                              F1219.3.R38C313

2490   CORDRY, Donald Bush
        Costumes and textiles of the Aztec Indians of the Cuetzalán
        region, Puebla, Mexico. Los Angeles, Southwest Museum, 1940
                        (LASM)   F869.L8S65.no.14

2491   DURAN, Diego
        The Aztecs. Orion Pr., 1964   F1219.D9443

2492   GIBSON, Charles
        The Aztecs under Spanish rule. Stanford, Calif., Stanford
        Univ. Pr., 1964   F1219.1.M53G5
                        253

2493   LEÓN-PORTILLA, Miguel
        Aztec thought and culture. Norman, Univ. of Oklahoma Pr.,
        1963   F1219.3.P5L43

24931   MADSEN, William
        The Virgin's children; life in an Aztec village today.
        Greenwood Pr., 1969   F1219.1.S2.M3.1969

2494   MORENO, Manuel M.
        La organización política y social de los aztecas. México,
        Instituto Nacional de Antropología e Historia, 1962
                                                    F1219.M82.1962

2495   NICHOLSON, Henry B.
        Two Aztec wood idols: iconographic and chronologic
        analysis. Washington, Dumbarton Oaks, Trustees for
        Harvard University, 1968 (SCAA)   E51.S85.no.5

2496   SOUSTELLE, Jacques
        The daily life of the Aztecs. Macmillan, 1962 (1961)
                                                    F1219.S723.1962

2497   VAILLANT, George Clapp
        Aztecs of Mexico. Garden City, N. Y., Doubleday, 1962
                                                    F1219.V33.1962

2498   VON HAGEN, Victor Wolfgang
        The Aztec: man and tribe. New American Library, 1961
                                                    F1219.V72.1961

        AZTEC
        See also: 1693, 1710, 1963, 1978, 21041, 2180, 2298, 2420

                              BANNOCK

2499   MADSEN, Brigham D.
        The Bannock of Idaho. Caldwell, Id., Caxton Printers, 1958

                             BELLABELLA

2500   BOAS, Franz
        Bella Bella texts. AMS, 1969 (1928) (CUCA) E51.C7.v.5

                                254

BELLACOOLA

2501   McILWRAITH, Thomas Forsyth
      The Bella Coola Indians. Toronto, Univ. of Toronto Pr.,
      1948   · E78.B9M32

BRULÉ

2502   ANDERSON, John Alvin
      The Sioux of the Rosebud. Norman, Univ. of Oklahoma Pr.,
      1971   E99.B8A6.1971

2503   DYCK, Paul
      Brulé; the Sioux people of the Rosebud. Flagstaff, Ariz.,
      Northland Pr., 1971   E99.B8D9

CADDO

2504   PARSONS, Elsie Worthington (Clews)
      Notes on the Caddo. Menasha, Wis., The American Anthropological
      Assoc., 1941   E99.C12P3

2505   SWANTON, John Reed
      Source material on the history and ethnology of the Caddo
      Indians. Washington, U. S. Govt. Print. Off., 1942
                (BAEB)   E51.U55.no.132

CAHITA

2506   BEALS, Ralph Leon
      The contemporary culture of the Cahita Indians. Washington,
      U. S. Govt. Print. Off., 1945   (BAEB)   E51.U55.no.142

CAHUÏLLA

25061   BEAN, Lowell John
      Mukat's people; the Cahuilla Indians of southern California.
      Univ. of California Pr., 1972   E99.C155.B4

CAHUILLA
    See also: 2036, 20992

2507   BRINTON, Daniel Garrison comp.
        The annals of the Cakchiquels. AMS, 1969 F1465.A61.1969

CARIB

2508   FARABEE, William Curtis
        The central Caribs. Oosterhout, Anthropological Publications,
        1967 (1924)   F2380.1.C2F2.1967

        CARIB
        See also: 2052

CATAWBA

2509   BROWN, Douglas (Summers)
        The Catawba Indians. Columbia, Univ. of South Carolina
        Pr., 1966   E99.C24B74

2510   HUDSON, Charles M.
        The Catawba Nation. Athens, Univ. of Georgia Pr., 1970
                                          E99.C24H8

2511   SPECK, Frank Gouldsmith
        Catawba texts. AMS, 1969 (1934) (CUCA) E51.C7.v.24.1969

CAYUGA

2512   SPECK, Frank Gouldsmith
        Midwinter rites of the Cayuga Long House. Philadelphia,
        Univ. of Pennsylvania Pr., 1949   E99.C3S6

CAYUSE

2513   RUBY, Robert H.
        The Cayuse Indians. Norman, Univ. of Oklahoma Pr., 1972
                                          E99.C32R8

256

2514   BROWN, John P.
        Old frontiers. Arno, 1971 (1938)   E99.C5B84.1971

2515   CLARKE, Mary Whatley
        Chief Bowles and the Texas Cherokees. Norman, Univ. of
        Oklahoma Pr., 1971   E99.C5C66

2516   CORKRAN, David H.
        The Cherokee frontier. Norman, Univ. of Oklahoma Pr.,
        1962   E99.C5C72

2517   FILLER, Louis ed.
        The removal of the Cherokee Nation. Boston, Heath, 1962
                                      E99.C5F5

2518   GEARING, Frederick O.
        Priests and warriors. Menasha, Wis., American Anthropological
        Assoc., 1962   (AAAM)   GN2.A22.no.93

2519   GULICK, John
        Cherokees at the crossroads. Chapel Hill, Institute for
        Research in Social Science, Univ. of North Carolina, 1960
                                      E99.C5G8

2520   HOLLAND, Cullen Joe
        The Cherokee Indian newspapers, 1828-1906. Ann Arbor,
        University Microfilms, 1970   PN4893.H6.1970

2521   KILPATRICK, Jack Frederick ed. and tr.
        Friends of Thunder, folktales of the Oklahoma Cherokees.
        Dallas, Southern Methodist Univ. Pr., 1964 E99.C5K48

2522   KILPATRICK, Jack Frederick comp.
        New Echota letters. Dallas, Southern Methodist Univ. Pr.,
        1968   E99.C5K47

2523   KILPATRICK, Jack Frederick
        Run toward the nightland. Dallas, Southern Methodist
        Univ. Pr., 1967   E99.C5K484

2524   KILPATRICK, Jack Frederick ed. and tr.
        The shadow of Sequoyah. Norman, Univ. of Oklahoma Pr., 1965
                                      E99.C5K485

2525   KILPATRICK, Jack Frederick
        Walk in your soul. Dallas, Southern Methodist Univ. Pr., 1965
                                      E99.C5K49

2526   LUMPKIN, Wilson
        The removal of the Cherokee Indians from Georgia. Arno,
        1969   E99.C5L9.1969

2527   MALONE, Henry Thompson
        Cherokees of the Old South. Athens, Univ. of Georgia Pr.,
        1956   E99.C5M34

2528   MOONEY, James
        Myths of the Cherokee. St. Clair Shores, Mich.,
        Scholarly Pr., 1970 (1900)   E99.C5M763.1970

2529   MOONEY, James
        The Swimmer manuscript, Cherokee sacred formulas and
        medicinal prescriptions. Washington, U. S. Govt. Print.
        Off., 1932   (BAEB)   E51.U55.no.99

2530   PARKER, Thomas Valentine
        The Cherokee Indians with special reference to their
        relations with the United States Government. Grafton Pr.,
        1907   E99.C5P3

2531   PEITHMANN, Irvin M.
        Red men of fire. Springfield, Ill., Thomas, 1964 E99.C5P38

2532   REID, John Phillip
        A law of blood. New York Univ. Pr., 1970 E99.C5R37

2533   SPECK, Frank Gouldsmith
        Decorative art and basketry of the Cherokee. Milwaukee,
        Wis., Pub. by order of the Trustees, 1920 E98.B3S74

2534   STARKEY, Marion Lena
        The Cherokee nation. A. A. Knopf, 1946   E99.C5S76

2535   STARR, Emmet
        Starr's history of the Cherokee Indians. Fayetteville,
        Ark., Indian Heritage Assoc., 1967 E99.C5S8.1967

2536   TIMBERLAKE, Henry
        The memoirs of Lieut. Henry Timberlake. Arno, 1971
        (1927)   E99.C5T62.1971

25361   TRAVELLER BIRD
        Tell them they lie; the Sequoyah myth. Los Angeles,
        Westernlore Pub., 1971   E99.C5.T75

2537   VAN EVERY, Dale
        Disinherited: the lost birthright of the American
        Indian. Morrow, 1966   E99.C5V3

25371   WASHBURN, Cephas
           Reminiscences of the Indians. Richmond, Presbyterian
           Committee of Publication. Johnson Rep:, 1971 E99.C5.W3.1971

2538   WILKINS, Thurman
           Cherokee tragedy. Macmillan, 1970   E99.C5W57

2539   WOODWARD, Grace Steele
           The Cherokees. Norman, Univ. of Oklahoma Pr., 1965 (1963)
                                          E99.C5W72

CHEROKEE
    See also: 0080, 1322, 1466, 1927, 1956, 1976, 20062

CHEYENNE

2540   BENT, George
           Life of George Bent. Norman, Univ. of Oklahoma Pr.,
           1968   E99.C53B44

2541   BERTHRONG, Donald J.
           The Southern Cheyennes. Norman, Univ. of Oklahoma Pr.,
           1963   E99.C53B46

.2542   GRINNELL, George Bird
           By Cheyenne campfires. New Haven, Yale Univ. Pr., 1962
                                    E99.C53G76.1962

2543   GRINNELL, George Bird
           The Cheyenne Indians. New Haven, Yale Univ. Pr., 1923
                                    E99.C53G77

2544   GRINNELL, George Bird
           The fighting Cheyennes. Norman, Univ. of Oklahoma Pr.,
           1956 (1915)   E99.C53G8.1956

2545   HOEBEL, Edward Adamson
           The Cheyennes. Holt, 1960   E99.C53H6

2546   JABLOW, Joseph
           The Cheyenne in Plains Indian trade relations, 1795-1840.
           J. J. Augustin, 1951   (MAES)   E51.A556.v.19

2547   LLEWELLYN, Karl Nickerson
           The Cheyenne way. Norman, Univ. of Oklahoma Pr., 1941
                                    E99.C53L54

2548   MEREDITH, Mrs. Grace E.
        Girl captives of the Cheyennes. Los Angeles,
        Gem Publishing Co., 1927   E87.G37

2549   MOONEY, James
        The Cheyenne Indians. Lancaster, Pa., 1907
                        (AAAM)   GN2.A22.no.6

2550   PETERSEN, Karen Daniels
        Howling Wolf. Palo Alto, Calif., American West Pub. Co.,
        1968   E99.C53P45

2551   PETTER, Rodolphe Charles
        Sketch of the Cheyenne grammar. Lancaster, Pa., 1907
                        (AAAM)   GN2.A22.no.6

2552   POWELL, Peter J.
        Sweet medicine. Norman, Univ. of Oklahoma Pr., 1969
                                        E99.C53P6

2553   SANDOZ, Mari
        Cheyenne autumn. Hastings House, 1965 (1953) E99.C53S2

2554   STANDS IN TIMBER, John
        Cheyenne memories. New Haven, Yale Univ. Pr., 1967
                                        E99.C53S7

        CHEYENNE
        See also: 0155, 0820

                        CHICKASAW

2555   GIBSON, Arrell Morgan
        The Chickasaws. Norman, Univ. of Oklahoma Pr., 1971
                                        E99.C55G5

        CHICKASAW
        See also: 1322

                        CHILKAT

2556   EMMONS, George Thornton
        The whale house of the Chilkat. American Museum of Natural
        History, 1916   (AMNHP)   GN2.A27.v.19.pt.1

CHILULA

2557   GODDARD, Pliny Earle
        Chilula texts. Berkeley, Univ. of California Pr., 1914
                (UCPAE)   E51.C15.v.10.no.7

2558   GODDARD, Pliny Earle
        Notes on the Chilula Indians of northwestern California.
        Berkeley, Univ. of California Pr., 1914
                (UCPAE)   E51.C15.v.10.no.6

CHIMARICO

2559   DIXON, Roland Burrage
        The Chimariko Indians and language. Berkeley, Univ. of
        California Pr., 1910   (UCPAE)   E51.C15.v.5.no.5

CHINOOK

2560   BOAS, Franz
        Chinook texts. Washington, U. S. Govt. Print. Off.,
        1894   (BAEB)   E51.U55.no.20

2561   JACOBS, Melville
        The people are coming soon. Seattle, Univ. of Washington Pr.,
        1960   E99.C818J33

25611   RAY, Verne Frederick
        Lower Chinook Ethnographic notes. Washington, Univ. of
        Washington, 1938   E99.C57.R3

        CHINOOK
        See also: 0797, 2040, 2041, 2055

CHIPPEWA

2562   BARNOUW, Victor
        Acculturation and personality among the Wisconsin Chipewa.
        Menasha, Wis., American Anthropological Assoc., 1950
                (AAAM)   GN2.A22.no.72

2563   BIRKET-SMITH, Kaj
       Contributions to Chipewyan ethnology. Copenhagen,
       Gyldendal, 1930   (TUEX)   G670.1921.R25.v.6.no.3

2564   COLEMAN, Bernard, Sister
       Ojibwa myths and legends. Minneapolis, Ross and Haines,
       1962 (1961)   E99.C6C54

2565   COPWAY, George
       The life, letters and speeches of Kah-ge-ga-gah-bowh.
       S. W. Benedict, 1850   E99.C6C754

2566   COPWAY, George, Chippewa chief
       The life, history, and travels, of Kah-ge-ga-gah-bowh
       (George Copway). Philadelphia, J. Harmstead, 1847 E99.C6C73

2567   COPWAY, George, Chippewa chief
       The traditional history and characteristic sketches of the
       Ojibway nation. Boston, B. F. Mussey & Co., 1851 E99.C6C6

2568   DENSMORE, Frances
       Chippewa customs. Washington, U. S. Govt. Print. Off.,
       1929   (BAEB)   E51.U55.no.86

2569   DENSMORE, Frances
       Chippewa music. Washington, U. S. Govt. Print. Off.,
       1910-13.   (BAEB)   E51.U55.no.45.53

2570   GUTTMANN, Allen
       States' rights and Indian removal. Boston, D. C. Heath,
       1965   E99.C5G85

2571   HICKERSON, Harold
       The Chippewa and their neighbors. Holt, Rinehart and
       Winston, 1970   E99.C6H44

2572   HICKERSON, Harold
       The southwestern Chippewa. Menasha, Wis., American
       Anthropological Assoc., 1962 (AAAM)   GN2.A22.no.92

2573   HILGER, Inez
       Chippewa child life and its cultural background. Washington,
       U. S. Govt. Print. Off., 1951 (BAEB)   E51.U55.no.146

2574   JONES, Peter
       History of the Ojebway Indians. Freeport, N. Y., Books
       for Libraries Pr., 1970   E99.C6J7.1970

2575   LANDES, Ruth
       Ojibwa religion and the Midéwiwin. Madison, Univ. of
       Wisconsin Pr., 1968   E99.C6L28.1968

2576   LANDES, Ruth
        Ojibwa sociology. AMS, 1969 (1937) (CUCA) E51.C7.v.29

2577   LANDES, Ruth
        The Ojibwa woman. AMS, 1969 (1938) (CUCA) E51.C7.v.31.1969

2578   LYFORD, Carrie Alberta
        The crafts of the Ojibwa (Chippewa). Phoenix, Printing Dept.,
        Phoenix Indian School, 1943   E98.I5U73.v.5

2579   WARREN, William Whipple
        History of the Ojibway Nation. Minneapolis, Ross & Haines,
        1957   E99.C6W3

        CHIPPEWA
        See also: 0791, 0860, 1928, 21161, 2272

                              CHOCTAW

2580   BAIRD, W. David
        Peter Pitchlynn; chief of the Choctaws. Norman, Univ. of
        Oklahoma Pr., 1972   E99.C8P62

2581   BENSON, Henry Clark
        Life among the Choctaw Indians and sketches of the South-west.
        Johnson Reprint, 1970 (1860)   E99.C8B4.1970

2582   BUSHNELL, David Ives
        The Choctaw of bayou Lacomb, St. Tammany parish, Louisiana.
        Washington, U. S. Govt. Print. Off., 1909
                              (BAEB)   E51.U55.no.48

2583   BYINGTON, Cyrus
        A dictionary of the Choctaw language. Washington, U. S.
        Govt. Print. Off., 1915 (BAEB)   E51.U55.no.46

2584   DEBO, Angie
        The rise and fall of the Choctaw Republic. Norman, Univ.
        of Oklahoma Pr., 1967 (1961)   E99.C8D4.1961

2585   DE ROSIER, Arthur H.
        The removal of the Choctaw Indians. Knoxville, Univ. of
        Tennessee Pr., 1970   E99.C8D46

2586   An early account of the Choctaw Indians. Lancaster, Pa.,
        Pub. for the American Anthropological Assoc., 1918
                              (AAAM)   GN2.A22.no.22

2587   JAMES, John
        <u>My experience with Indians</u>. Austin, Tex., Gammel's Book
        Store, 1925   E99.C8J26

2588   SWANTON, John Reed
        <u>Source material for the social and ceremonial life of the
        Choctaw Indians</u>. Washington, U. S. Govt. Print. Off.,
        1931   E99.C8S9

        <u>CHOCTAW</u>
        See also: 1322

                              CHONTAL

2589   CARRASCO y GARRORENA, Pedro
        <u>Pagan rituals and beliefs among the Chontal Indians of
        Oaxaca, Mexico</u>. Berkeley, Univ. of California Pr., 1960
                           (AR)   E51.A58.v.20.no.3

25891   TURNER, Paul R.
        <u>The Highland Chontal</u>, Holt, Rinehart and Winston, 1971,
        c1972   F1221.C58.T8
        <u>CHONTAL</u>
        See also: 2115, 2121

                             CHUMASHAN

2590   GRANT, Campbell
        <u>The rock paintings of the Chumash</u>. Berkeley, Univ. of
        California Pr., 1965   E99.C815G7

2591   GREENWOOD, Roberta S.
        <u>A coastal Chumash village</u>. Los Angeles, Southern California
        Academy of Sciences, 1969   E99.C815G73

2592   LANDBERG, Leif C. W.
        <u>The Chumash Indians of southern California</u>. Los Angeles,
        Southwest Museum, 1965 (LASM)   F869.L8S65.no.19

                              COCHITI

2593   BENEDICT, Ruth (Fulton)
        <u>Tales of the Cochiti Indians</u>. Washington, U. S. Govt.
        Print. Off., 1931   (BAEB)   E51.U55.no.98

2594   COCHITI DAM ARCHAEOLOGICAL SALVAGE PROJECT.
        The Cochiti Dam. Santa Fe, Museum of New Mexico Pr.,
        1968-   E99.C84C6

2595   DUMAREST, Noël
        Notes on Cochiti, New Mexico. Lancaster, Pa., Pub. for the
        American Antrhopological Assoc., 1919 (AAAM) GN2.A22.no.27

2596   FOX, Robin
        The Keresan Bridge. London, Athlone Pr.; New York,
        Humanities Pr., 1967   E99.C84F6

2597   GOLDFRANK, Esther Schiff
        The social and ceremonial organization of Cochiti.
        Menasha, Wis., Pub. for the American Anthropological Assoc.,
        1919   (AAAM)   GN2.A22.no.

2598   LANGE, Charles
        Cochití: a New Mexico pueblo, past and present. Austin, Univ.
        of Texas Pr., 1960 (1959)   E99.C84L3

                            COCOPA

2599   GIFFORD, Edward Winslow
        The Cocopa. Berkeley, Univ. of California Pr., 1933
                        (UCPAE)   E51.C15.v.31.no.5

                          COMANCHES

2600   HOEBEL, Edward Adamson
        The political organization and law-ways of the Comanche
        Indians. Menasha, Wis., American Anthropological Assoc.,
        1940   E99.C85H6

2601   RICHARDSON, Rupert Norval
        The Comanche barrier to south plains settlement. Glendale,
        Calif., The Arthur H. Clark Co., 1933 E99.C85R5

2602   RISTER, Carl Coke
        Comanche bondage. Glendale, Calif., A. H. Clark Co.,
        1955   E87.B4R5

2603   SIMMONS, Marc comp.
        Border Comanches. Santa Fe, N.M., Stagecoach Pr., 1967
                                                E99.C85S5

                            265

2604   VIZCAYA CANALES, Isidoro
        La invasión de los indios bárbaros al noreste de México
        en los años de 1840-1841. Monterrey, 1968   E99.C85V58

2605   WALLACE, Ernest
        The Comanches: lords of the south plains. Norman, Univ.
        of Oklahoma Pr., 1952   E99.C85W34

                                COOS

2606   FRACHTENBERG, Leo Joachim
        Coos texts. AMS, 1969 (1913) (CUCA)   E51.C7.v.1.1969

                                CORA

2607   NÁPOLI, Ignacio María
        The Cora Indians of Baja California. Los Angeles,
        Dawson's Book Shop, 1970   F1246.N313.Spec.Coll.

                                CREE

2608   CHANCE, Norman Allee
        Conflict in culture. Ottawa, Canadian Research Centre
        for Anthropology, Saint Paul Univ., 1968   E99.C88C48

2609   MANDELBAUM, David Goodman
        The Plains Cree. American Museum of Natural History,
        1940   (AMNHP)   GN2.A27.v.37.pt.2

        CREE
        See also: 0101, 0156, 0157, 1669

                                CREEK

2610   CAUGHEY, John Walton
        McGillivray of the Creeks. Norman, Univ. of Oklahoma
        Pr., 1959   E99.C9C3

                                266

2611   CORKRAN, David H.
        The Creek frontier, 1540-1783. Norman, Univ. of Oklahoma Pr.,
        1967   E99.C9C65

2612   DEBO, Angie
        The road to disappearance. Norman, Univ. of Oklahoma Pr.,
        1941   E99.C9D4

2613   GATSCHET, Albert Sammuel
        A migration legend of the Creek Indians. v. 1-2 Kraus Reprint,
        1969   E99.C9G26.1969

2614   HAYNE, Coe Smith
        Red men on the Bighorn. Philadelphia, Judson, 1929
                                                E99.C92H4

2615   MILFORT, Louis
        Memoir. Chicago, R. R. Donnelley, 1956 E99.C9M513

2616   ORRMONT, Arthur
        Diplomat in warpaint. London, New York, Abelard-Schuman,
        1968   E99.C9O7.1968

2617'   SPECK, Frank Gouldsmith
        The Creek Indians of Taskigi town. Lancaster, Pa.,
        The New Era Printing Co., 1907 (AAAM) GN2.A22.no.8

2618   SWANTON, John Reed
        Early history of the Creek Indians and their neighbors.
        Washington, U. S. Govt. Print. Off., 1922
                        (BAEB)   E51.U55.no.73

26181   SWANTON, John Reed
        Social organization and social usages of the Indians of
        the Creek confederacy. Johnson Rep., 1970 E99.C9.S9.1970

2619   WOODWARD, Thomas Simpson
        Woodward's reminiscences of the Creek, or Muscogee Indians.
        Tuscaloosa, Ala., Alabama Book Store; Birmingham, Ala.,
        Birmingham Book Exchange, 1939   E99.C9W66

2620   WRIGHT, James Leitch
        William Augustus Bowles, Director General of the Creek
        Nation. Athens, Univ. of Georgia Pr., 1967 E99.C9W7

        CREEK
          See also: 1322, 1847, 1907

2621   CARRINGTON, Margaret Irvin (Sullivant)
        Absaraka, home of the Crows. Chicago, The Lakeside Pr.,
        R. R. Donnelley & Sons, 1950   F594.C31.1950

2622   HUGHES, Ted
        Crow: from the life and songs of the crow. Harper & Row,
        1971   PR6058.U37C67.1971

26221   LINDERMAN, Frank Bird
        Pretty-shield, medicine woman of the Crows. John Day, 1972
                                               E99.C92.L59.1972

2623   LOWIE, Robert Harry
        Crow Indian art. American Museum of Natural History, 1922
                                               E99.C92L9

2624   LOWIE, Robert Harry
        The Crow Indians. Holt, Rinehart and Winston, 1956 (1935)
                                               E99.C92L913.1956

2625   LOWIE, Robert Harry
        The Crow language, grammatical sketch and analyzed text.
        Berkeley and Los Angeles, Univ. of California Pr., 1941

2626   LOWIE, Robert Harry
        A Crow text, with grammatical notes. Berkeley, Univ. of
        California Pr., 1930   (UCPAE)   E51.C15.v.29.no.2

2627   LOWIE, Robert Harry
        The material culture of the Crow Indians. American Museum
        of Natural History, 1922 (AMNHP)   GN2.A27.v.21.pt.3

2628   LOWIE, Robert Harry
        Minor ceremonies of the Crow Indians. American Museum of
        Natural History, 1924   (AMNHP)   GN2.A27.v.21.pt.5

2629   LOWIE, Robert Harry
        Myths and traditions of the Crow Indians. American Museum
        of Natural History, 1918   E99.C92L92

2630   LOWIE, Robert Harry
        The religion of the Crow Indians. American Museum of
        Natural History, 1922   (AMNHP)   GN2.A27.v.25.pt.2

2631   LOWIE, Robert Harry
        The sun dance of the Crow Indians. American Museum of
        Natural History, 1915   (AMNHP)   GN2.A27.v.16.pt.1

2632   LOWIE, Robert Harry
        The Tobacco society of the Crow Indians. American Museum
        of Natural History, 1919   E99.C92L926

26321   PLENTY-COUPS, Crow Chief
        Plenty-coups, Chief of the Crows. John Day, 1972
                             E99.C92.P55.1972

2633   U. S. CONGRESS. SENATE. COMMITTEE ON INDIAN AFFAIRS.
        A company for breeding horses on the Crow Indian reservation,
        Montana. Washington, U. S. Govt. Print. Off., 1908
                             E99.C92U58

2634   WOODRUFF, Mrs. Janette
        Indian oasis. Caldwell, Id., Caxton Printers, Ltd., 1939
                             E99.C92W6

        CROW
           See also: 0101, 0142, 0144, 0840, 0865, 20581, 2070, 2071

                           CUNA

2635   KEELER, Clyde Edgar
        Cuna Indian art. Exposition Pr., 1969 F1565.2.C8K39

2636   NORDENSKIÖLD, Erland
        An historical and ethnological survey of the Cuna Indians.
        Göteborgs Museum, Etnografiska Avdelningen, 1938
                             F2230.N82.v.10

2637   STOUT, David Bond
        San Blas Cuna acculturation. Johnson Reprint, 1964 (1947)
                           F1565.2.C8S8.1964

                        DAKOTA

26371   ARTICHOKER, John
        The Sioux Indian goes to college. So. Dak., Institute Indian
        Studies, 1959   E99.D1.A7

2638   BAUMANN, Peter
        Reise aum Sonnentanz. Berlin, Safari-Verlag, 1970 E99.D1B26

2639   BELDEN, George P.
        Belden, the white chief; or, Twelve years among the Indians
        of the plains. Cincinnati, C. F. Vent, 1870   E77.B42

2640   CRESWELL, Robert J.
        Among the Sioux. Minneapolis, University Pr., 1906 E99.D1C7

26401   EASTMAN, Charles Alexander
         Old Indian days. Fenwyn Press Books, 1970   E99.D1.E18.1970

2641   EASTMAN, Mary (Genderson)
         Dahcotah. Minneapolis, Ross & Haines, 1962 E99.D1E19.1962

2642   FISKE, Frank Bennett
         The taming of the Sioux. Bismarck, N. D., Bismarck Tribune,
         1917   E99.D1F54

2643   HANS, Frederic Malon
         The great Sioux nation. Chicago, M. A. Donohue and Co.,
         1907   E99.D1H2

2644   HASSRICK, Royal B.
         The Sioux. Norman, Univ. of Oklahoma Pr., 1964   E99.D1H3

2645   HILL, Richmond C.
         A great white Indian chief. Ossining, N. Y., Rand,
         McNally & Co., 1912   E99.D1H6

2646   HYDE, George E.
         A Sioux chronicle. Norman, Univ. of Oklahoma Pr., 1956
                                                     E99.D1H93

2647   JACKSON, Donald Dean
         Custer's gold. New Haven, Yale Univ. Pr., 1966 E99.D1J3

2648   JOHNSON, Willis Fletcher
         Life of Sitting Bull and history of the Indian war of 1890-91.
         Philadelphia, Edgewood, 1891   E99.D1J6

2649   KELLY, Mrs. Fanny (Wiggins)
         Narrative of my captivity among the Sioux Indians.
         Hartford, Conn., Mutual Pub. Co., 1871 E87.K29.1871

2650   LYFORD, Carrie Alberta
         Quill and beadwork of the western Sioux. Lawrence, Kan.,
         Printing Dept., Haskell Institute, 1940 E99.D1L9

2651   MACGREGOR, Gordon
         Warriors without weapons. Chicago, Univ. of Chicago Pr.
         1946   E99.D1M12

2652   MALAN, Vernon D.
         The Dakota Indian community. Brookings, Rural Sociology
         Dept., Agricultural Experiment Station, South Dakota
         State College, 1962   E99.D1M138

2653   MEKEEL, Scudder
        The economy of a modern Teton Dakota community. New Haven,
        Pub. for the Section of Anthropology, Dept. of the Social
        Sciences, Yale Univ., by the Yale Univ. Pr., 1936
                        (YUPA)   GN2.Y3.no.6

2654   MILLER, David Humphreys
        Ghost dance. Duell, Sloan and Pearce, 1959   E99.D1M6

2655   The Modern Sioux. Lincoln, Univ. of Nebraska Pr., 1970
                                        E99.D1M66

2656   MOONEY, James
        The ghost-dance religion and the Sioux outbreak of 1890.
        Chicago, Univ. of Chicago Pr., 1965   E98.R3M6.1965

2657   MOONEY, James
        The Siouan tribes of the East. Washington, U. S. Govt. Print.
        Off., 1894   (BAEB)   E51.U55.no.22

2658   PIDGEON, William
        Traditions of De-coo-dah. H. Thayer, 1958   E73.P61

2659   PRAUS, Alexis A.
        The Sioux, 1798-1922. Bloomfield Hills, Cranbrook Institute
        of Science, 1962   (CIB)   Q11.C95.no.44

2660   RIGGS, Stephen Return
        Mary and I; forty years with the Sioux. Minneapolis,
        Ross and Haines, 1969   E99.D1R5.1969

2661   RIGGS, Stephen Return
        Tañ-koo wah-kañ. Boston, Congregational Sabbath-School
        and Pub. Soc., 1869   E99.D1R532

2662   ROBINSON, Doane
        A history of the Dakota or Sioux Indians. Minneapolis,
        Ross and Haines, 1967   E99.D1R6

2663   STANDING BEAR, Luther, Dakota chief
        Land of the spotted eagle. Boston, Houghton Mifflin, 1933
                                        E99.D1S71

2664   STANDING BEAR, Luther, Dakota chief
        My people, the Sioux. Boston and New York, Houghton Mifflin Co.,
        1928   E99.D1S73

2665   STIRLING, Matthew Williams
        Three pictographic autobiographies of Sitting Bull.
        Washington, The Smithsonian Institution, 1938   E99.D1S623

2666   SULLIVAN, Louis Robert
        Anthropometry of the Siouan tribes. American Museum of
        Natural History, 1919 (AMNHP)   GN2.A27.v.23.pt.3

2667   THORSON, Alice Otillia
        The tribe of Pezhekee. Minneapolis, Heywood Manufacturing
        Co., 1901   E99.01T5

2668   UTLEY, Robert Marshall
        The last days of the Sioux Nation. New Haven, Yale
        University Pr., 1963   E99.D1U9

2669   VESTAL, Stanley comp.
        New sources of Indian history, 1850-1891. Norman, Univ.
        of Okalhoma Pr., 1934   E99.D1V34

2670   VESTAL, Stanley
        Sitting Bull, champion of the Sioux. Norman, Univ. of
        Oklahoma Pr., 1957   E99.D1S58.1957

2671   WALLIS, Wilson Dallam
        The Canadian Dakota. American Museum of Natural History,
        1947   (AMNHP)   GN2.A27.v.41.pt.1

2672   WHITE BULL, Dakota chief
        The warrior who killed Custer. Lincoln, Univ. of Nebraska Pr.,
        1969 (1968)   E99.D1W66

        DAKOTA
        See also: 0092, 0101, 0791, 0799, 1470, 1478, 1497, 1550,
                   1806, 1849, 1880, 1991, 2096, 2123, 2286, 2293

                              DELAWARE

2673   ADAMS, Richard Calmit
        The ancient religion of the Delaware Indians and observations
        and reflections. Washington, D. C., Law Reporter Printing
        Co., 1904   E99.D2A16

2674   BRINTON, Daniel Garrison
        The Lenâpê and their legends. Philadelphia, D. G. Brinton,
        1885   E99.D2B8

2675   WALLACE, Anthony F. C.
        King of the Delawares: Teedyuscung, 1700-1763. Philadelphia,
        Univ. of Pennsylvania Pr., 1949   E99.D2T4

26751   WESLAGER, Clinton Alfred
         The Delaware Indians; a history. New Brunswick, N.J.,
         Rutgers,Univ. Pr., 1972   E99.D2.W39

DELAWARE
See also: 0073, 1316, 1946, 2328

DIEGUEÑO

2676   KROEBER, Alfred Louis
         Phonetic elements of the Diegueño language. Berkeley,
         Univ. of California Pr., 1914 (UCPAE) E51.C15.v.11.no.2

2677   WATERMANN, Thomas Talbot
         The religious practices of the Diegueño Indians. Berkeley,
         Univ. of California Pr., 1910 (UCPAE) E51.C15.v.8.no.6

DIEGUEÑO
See also: 23151

ESKIMO

2678   BALIKEI, Asen
         The Netsilik Eskimo. Garden City, N. Y., Natural History Pr.,
         1970   E99.E7B16

2679   BANDI, Hans Georg
         Eskimo prehistory. College, Univ. of Alaska Pr.; distributed
         by Univ. of Washington Pr., Seattle, 1969 E99.E7B173

2680   BIRKET-SMITH, Kaj
         Anthropological observations on the central Eskimos.
         Copenhagen, Gyldendalske boghandel, Nordisk forlag, 1940
                        (TUEX)   G670.1921.R25.v.3.no.2

2681   BIRKET-SMITH, Kaj
         The Caribou Eskimos. Copenhagen, Gyldendal, 1929
                        (TUEX)   G670.1921.R25.v.5

2682   BIRKET-SMITH, Kaj
         The Eskimos. London, Methuen, 1959   E99.E7B865.1959

2683   BIRKET-SMITH, Kaj
         The Eyak Indians of the Copper river delta. København,
         Levin & Munksgaard, 1938   E99.E9B5

273

2684   BIRKET-SMITH, Kaj
       Five hundred Eskimo words. Copenhagen, Gyldendal, 1928
                (TUEX)   G670.1921.R25.v.3.no.3

2685   BRIGGS, Jean L.
       Never in anger. Cambridge, Mass., Harvard Univ. Pr.,
       1970   E99.E7B75

2686   BOAS, Franz
       The central Eskimo. Lincoln, Univ. of Nebraska Pr.,
       1964   E99.E7B66.1964

26861   BRUEMMER, Fred
       Seasons of the Eskimo: a vanishing way of life. New York
       Graphic Society, 1971   E99.E7.B78

2687   BULIARD, Roger
       Inuk. Farrar, Straus and Young, 1951   E99.E7B873

26871   CANADIAN ESKIMO ARTS COUNCIL.
       Sculpture/Inuit; sculpture of the Inuit, masterworks of
       the Canadian Arctic. Canada, Canadian Eskimo Art Council,
       Canada, Univ. of Toronto Pr., 1971   E99. 7.C287

2688   CARLSON, Gerald F.
       Two on the rocks. McKay, 1966   E99.E7C29

2689   CARPENTER, Edmund Snow
       Eskimo. Toronto, Univ. of Toronto Pr., 1959 fE99.E7C33

2690   CHANCE, Norman Allee
       The Eskimo of North Alaska. Holt, Rinehart and Winston,
       1966   E99.E7C5

2691   Chefs-d'oeuvre des arts indiens et esquimaux du Canada.
       Paris, Société des amis du Musée de l'homme, 1969
                                   E99.E7C53

2692   COCCOLA, Raymond de
       Ayorama. Oxford Univ. Pr., 1956   E99.E7C62

2693   COPELAND, Donalda McKillop
       Remember, nurse. Toronto, Ryerson, 1960 E99.E7C6

2694   DELALANDE, Lucien
       Sous le soleil de minuit. Montréal, Rayonnement, 1958
                                   E99.E7D4

2695   FEJES, Claire
       People of the Noatak. Knopf, 1966   E99.E7F4

2696   FORTUINE, Robert
        The health of the Eskimos.   Hanover, N. H., Dartmouth
        College Libraries, 1968   ref.E99.E7F6

2697   FREUCHEN, Peter
        Book of the Eskimos.   Cleveland, World Pub. Co., 1961
                                            E99.E7F7

2698   GIDDINGS, James Louis
        Ancient men of the Arctic.   Knopf, 1967 E99.E7G358

2699   GRABURN, Nelson H. H.
        Eskimos without igloos.   Boston, Little, Brown, 1969
                                            E99.E7G67

2700   GUBSER, Nicholas J.
        The Nunamiut Eskimos.   New Haven, Yale Univ. Pr., 1965
                                            E99.E7G83

2701   HARPER, Francis
        Caribou Eskimos of the upper Kazan River, Keewatin.
        Lawrence, Univ. of Kansas, 1964   E99.E7H3

2702   HAWKES, Ernest William
        The Laborador Eskimo.   Ottawa, Government Printing Bureau,
        1916   E99.E7H398

2703   HIMMELHEBER, Hans
        Eskimokünstler.   Eisenach, E. Röth, 1953   E99.E7H5.1953

2704   HIPPLER, Arthur E.
        Barrow and Kotzebue.   Minneapolis, Training Center for
        Community Programs in coordination with Office of Community
        Programs, Center for Urban and Regional Affairs, Univ. of
        Minnesota, 1969   E99.E7H53

27041   HONIGMANN, John Joseph
        Arctic Townsmen: ethnic backgrounds and modernization.
        Canada, Saint Paul Univ., 1970   E99.E7.H768

2705   HOUSTON, James A.
        Eskimo prints.   Barre, Mass., Barre Pub., 1967 E99.E7H85

2706   HRDLICKA, Ales
        Contributions to the anthropology of central and Smith
        sound Eskimo.   American Museum of Natural History, 1910
                        (AMNHP)   GN2.A27.v.5.pt.2

2707   HUGHES, Charles Campbell
        An Eskimo village in the modern world.   Ithaca, N.Y.,
        Cornell Univ. Pr., 1960   E99.E7H95

                            275

2708   IGLAUER, Edith
        The new people. Garden City, N. Y., Doubleday, 1966 E99.E7I35

2709   JENNESS, Diamond
        Dawn in Arctic Alaska. Minneapolis, Univ. of Minnesota Pr.,
        1957   E99.E7J451

2710   JENNESS, Diamond
        Eskimo administration. Montreal, Arctic Institute of
        North America, 1962-68   E99.E7J52

2711   JENNESS, Diamond
        The life of the Copper Eskimos. Johnson Reprint, 1970 (1923)
                                               E99.E7J53.1970

2712   JENNESS, Diamond
        The people of the twilight. Chicago, Univ. of Chicago Pr.,
        1959   E99.E7J54.1959

2713   LANTIS, Margaret
        Alaskan Eskimo ceremonialism. J. J. Augustin, 1947
                        (MAES)   E51.A556.v.11

2714   LANTIS, Margaret ed.
        Eskimo childhood and interpersonal relationships. Seattle,
        Univ. of Washington Pr., 1960   E99.E7L283

2715   LARSEN, Helge Eyvin
        Ipiutak and the Arctic whale hunting culture. American
        Museum of Natural History, 1948 (AMNHP) GN2.A27.v.42

2716   LEDYARD, Gleason H.
        And to the Eskimos. Chicago, Moody Pr., 1958 E99.E7L4

2717   MOWAT, Farley
        The desperate people. Boston, Little, Brown, 1959 E99.E7M85

2718   MOWAT, Farley
        People of the Deer. Boston, Little, Brown, 1952 E99.E7M86

27181   NELSON, Edward William
        The Eskimo about Bering Strait. Johnson Rep., 1971
                                               E99.E7.N4.1971

2719   NELSON, Richard K.
        Hunters of the northern ice. Chicago, Univ. of Chicago Pr.,
        1969   E99.E7N43

2720   OSCHINSKY, Lawrence
        The most ancient Eskimos. Ottawa, Canadian Research
        Centre for Anthropology, Univ. of Ottawa, 1964 E99.E7O78

2721   OSWALT, Wendell H.
       Alaskan Eskimos. San Francisco, Chandler Pub. Co.;
       Chicago, 1967, distributors: Science Research Assoc.
                                           E99.E7085

2722   OTTAWA. NATIONAL GALLERY OF CANADA.
       Cape Dorset. Ottawa, 1967.   E99.E7085

27221 PHEBUS, George
       Alaskan Eskimo life in the 1890's as sketched by native
       artists. Smithsonian Institution Pr., Braziller, 1972
                                           E99.E7.P46

2723   PITSEOLAK
       Pictures out of my life. Montreal, Design Collaborative
       Books in association with Oxford Univ. Pr., Toronto, 1971
                                           E99.E7P53

2724   PONCINS, Gontran de Montaigne, vicomte de
       Kabloona. Raynal & Hitchcock, Inc., 1941 E99.E7P6.1941a

2725   PRYDE, Duncan
       Nunage. Walker & Co., 1972 (1971)   E99.E7P77.1972b

2726   RASMUSSEN, Knud Johan Victor
       Alaskan Eskimo words. Copenhagen, Gyldendal, 1941
                         (TUEX)   G670.1921.R25.v.3.no.4

2727   RASMUSSEN, Knud Johan Victor
       The Alaskan Eskimos as described in the posthumous notes
       of Knud Rasmussen. Copenhagen, Gyldendal, 1952
                         (TUEX)   G670.1921.R25.v.10.no.3

2728   RASMUSSEN, Knud Johan Victor
       Intellectual culture of the Copper Eskimos. Copenhagen,
       Gyldendal, 1932   (TUEX)   G670.1921.R25.v.9

2729   RASMUSSEN, Knud Johan Victor
       Intellectual culture of the Hudson Bay Eskimos. Copenhagen,
       Gyldendal, 1930   (TUEX)   G670.1921.R25.v.7

2730   RASMUSSEN, Knud Johan Victor
       The Mackenzie Eskimos after Knud Rasmussen's posthumous
       notes. Copenhagen, Gyldendal, 1942
                         (TUEX)   G670.1921.R25.v.10.no.2

2731   RASMUSSEN, Knud Johan Victor
       The Netsilik Eskimos. Copenhagen, Gyldendal, 1931
                         (TUEX)   G670.1921.R25.v.8.no.1,2

2732   RASMUSSEN, Knud Johan Victor
          The people of the Polar north. London, K. Paul Trench,
          Trübner & Co., Ltd., 1908   E99.E7R2

2733   RAY, Dorothy Jean
          Artists of the tundra and the sea. Seattle, Univ. of
          Washington Pr., 1961   E99.E7R25

2734   RAY, Dorothy Jean
          Eskimo masks: art and ceremony. Seattle, Univ. of
          Washington Pr., 1967   E99.E7R28

2735   RAY, Dorothy Jean
          Graphic arts of the Alaskan Eskimo. Washington, U. S.
          Indian Arts and Crafts Board; for sale by the Supt. of
          Docs., U. S. Govt. Print. Off., 1969 (NAA) E98.A7N36.no.2

2736   SCHAEFER-SIMMERN, Henry
          Eskimo-Plastik aus Kanada. Kassel, F. Lometsch, 1958
                                             E99.E7S3

2737   SENUNGETUK, Joseph E.
          Give or take a century. San Francisco, Indian Historian
          Pr., 1971   E99.E7S43

2738   SHAPIRO, Harry Lionel
          The Alaskan Eskimo. American Museum of Natural History,
          1931   (AMNHP)   GN2.A27.v.31.pt.6

2739   SPENCER, Robert F.
          The North Alaskan Eskimo; a study in ecology and society.
          Washington, U. S. Govt. Print. Off., 1959
                          (BAEB)   E51.U55.no.171

2740   STEENSBY, Hans Peder
          An anthropogeographical study of the origin of the Eskimo
          culture. København, B. Lunos Bogtrykkeri, 1916 E99.E7S7

2741   SUTTON, George Miksch
          Eskimo year. Macmillan, 1936   F1106.S85

2742   SWINTON, George
          Eskimo sculpture. Toronto, McClelland and Stewart, 1965
                                             E99.E7S94

2743   VALENTINE, Victor F. comp.
          Eskimo of the Canadian Arctic. Toronto, McClelland and
          Stewart, 1968   E99.E7V17

27431 VALLEE, Francis Gerald
          Kabloona and Eskimo in the Central Keewatin. Canada, Canadian
          Res. Ctr. for Anthropology, Saint Paul Univ., 1967 E99.E7.V18

2744   VanSTONE, James W.
        Eskimos of the Nushagak River. Seattle, Univ. of Washington
        Pr., 1967   E99.E7V225

2745   VanSTONE, James W.
        Point Hope, an Eskimo village in transition. Seattle, Univ.
        of Washington Pr., 1962   E99.E7V23

2746   WASHBURNE, Heluiz (Chandler)
        Land of the good shadows. John Day Co., 1940 E99.E7B657

2747   WEYER, Edward Moffat
        The Eskimos: their environment and folkways. Hamden, Conn.,
        Archon Books, 1962 (1932)   E99.E7W48.1962

2748   WINNIPEG ART GALLERY.
        Eskimo sculpture. Winnipeg, Winnipeg Art Gallery, 1967
                       E99.E7W75

        ESKIMO
        See also: 0255, 0380, 0469, 06541, 0986, 0997, 1578, 1583,
                  1607, 1950, 1990, 20061, 2165, 21752, 2274

FOX

2749   GEARING, Frederick O.
        The face of the Fox. Chicago, Aldine Pub. Co., 1970
                       E99.F7G4

2750   JONES, William
        Ethnography of the Fox Indians. Washington, U. S. Govt. Print.
        Off., 1939   (BAEB)   E51.U55.no.125

2751   MICHELSON, Truman
        Contributions to Fox ethnology. Washington, U. S. Govt.
        Print. Off., 1927-30 (BAEB)   E51.U55.no.85,95

2752   MICHELSON, Truman
        Fox miscellany. Washington, U. S. Govt. Print. Off.,
        1937   (BAEB)   E51.U55.no.114

2753   MICHELSON, Truman
        Notes on the buffalo-head dance of the Thunder gens
        of the Fox Indians. Washington, U. S. Govt. Print. Off.,
        1928   (BAEB)   E51.U55.no.87

2754   MICHELSON, Truman
        Notes on the Fox Wâpanówiweni. Washington, U. S. Govt. Print.
        Off., 1932   (BAEB)   E51.U55.no.105

2755   MICHELSON, Truman
        Observations on the thunder dance of the Bear gens of the
        Fox Indians. Washington, U. S. Govt. Print. Off., 1929
                        (BAEB)   E51.U55.no.89

2756   STEWARD, John Fletcher
        Lost Maramech and earliest Chicago. Chicago, etc.,
        F. H. Revell Co., 1903   E99.F7S8

        FOX
        See also: 0123

                            GABRIELENO

2757   JOHNSTON, Bernice Eastman
        California's Gabrielino Indians. Los Angeles, Southwest
        Museum, 1962   E99.G15J6

2758   REID, Hugo
        The Indians of Los Angeles County. Los Angeles, Priv.
        Print., 1926; Photocopy, made by Los Angeles Public Library,
        1964   E99.G15R32.1964

                            GOSIUTE

2759   CHAMBERLIN, Ralph Vary
        The ethno-botany of the Gosiute Indians of Utah. Lancaster, Pa.
        The New Era Printing Co., 1911   (AAAM) GN2.A22.no.11

                            GUAYMI

2760   ALPHONSE, Ephraim S.
        Guaymí grammar and dictionary, with some ethnological notes.
        Washington, U. S. Govt. Print. Off., 1956
                        (BAEB)   E51.U55.no.162

HAIDA

2761   BARBEAU, Charles Marius
        Haida myths illustrated in argillite carvings. Ottawa,
        Dept. of Resources and Development, National Parks Branch,
        National Museum of Canada, 1953   E99.H2B3

2762   MURDOCK, George Peter
        Rank and potlatch among the Haida. New Haven, Pub. for the
        Section of Anthropology, Dept. of the Social Sciences, Yale
        Univ., by the Yale Univ. Pr.; London, H. Milford, Oxford
        Univ. Pr., 1936   (YUPA)   GN2.Y3.no.13

2763   SWANTON, John Reed comp.
        Haida texts and myths, Skidegate dialect. Washington, U. S.
        Govt. Print. Off., 1905 (BAEB)   E51.U55.no.29

HAISLA

2764   OLSON, Ronald LeRoy
        The social organization of the Haisla of British Columbia.
        Berkeley, Univ. of California Pr., 1940
                 (AR)   E51.A58.v.2.no.5

HAVASUPAI

2765   CUSHING, Frank Hamilton
        The Nation of the Willows. Flagstaff, Ariz., Northland Pr.,
        1965   E99.H3C8

2766   SMITHSON, Carma Lee
        Havasupai religion. Johnson Reprint, 1971 (1963)
             (UUAP)   E51.U8.no.68.1971

2767   SPIER, Leslie
        Havasupai ethnography. American Museum of Natural History,
        1928   E99.H3S65

HIDATSA

2768   BOWERS, Alfred W.
        Hidatsa social and ceremonial organization. Washington, U. S.
        Govt. Print Off., 1965 (BAEB)   E51.U55.no.194

2769   MATTHEWS, Washington
        Ethnography and philology of the Hidatsa Indians. Johnson
        Reprint, 1971 (1877)   E99.H6M4.1970

2770   PEPPER, George Hubbard
        An Hidatsa shrine and the beliefs respecting it. Lancaster,
        Pa., New Era Printing Co., 1908 (AAAM) GN2.A22.no.10

27701   SMITH, G. Hubert
        Like-a-fishhook village and Fort Berthold, Garrison Reservoir,
        North Dakota. Washington, D. C., U. S. Govt. Print. Off.,
        1972   E99.H6.S64

2771   WILSON, Gilbert Livingstone
        Hidatsa eagle trapping. American Museum of Natural History,
        1928   (AMNHP)   GN2.A27.v.30.pt.4

2772   WILSON, Gilbert Livingstone
        The horse and the dog in Hidatsa culture. American Museum
        of Natural History, 1924 (AMNHP)   GN2.A27.v.15.pt.2

        HIDATSA
        See also: 0142, 0144, 2277, 2287

                            HOPI

2773   BEAGLEHOLE, Ernest
        Hopi hunting and hunting ritual. New Haven, Pub. for the
        Section of Anthropology, Dept. of the Social Sciences,
        Yale Univ., by the Yale Univ. Pr., 1936
                        (YUPA)   GN2.Y3.no.4

2774   BEAGLEHOLE, Ernest
        Hopi of the second mesa. Menasha, Wis., American Anthropologica
        Assoc., 1935   (AAAM)   GN2.A22,no.44

2775   BEAGLEHOLE, Ernest
        Notes on Hopi economic life. New Haven, Pub. for the
        Section of Anthropology, Dept. of the Social Sciences, Yale
        Univ. by the Yale Univ. Pr.; London, H. Milford, Oxford
        Univ. Pr., 1937   (YUPA)   GN2.Y3.no.15

2776   BOELTER, Homer H.
        Portfolio of Hopi kachinas. Hollywood, Calif., H. H. Boelter
        Lithography, 1969   fE99.H7B6.Spec.Coll.

2777   BOURKE, John Gregory
        The snake-dance of the Moquis of Arizona. C. Scribner's
        Sons, 1884   E99.H7B7
                            282

2778   BRANDT, Richard B.
       Hopi ethics. Chicago, Univ. of Chicago Pr., 1954   E98.E84B73

2779   COLTON, Harold Sellers
       Hopi kachina dolls. Albuquerque, Univ. of New Mexico, 1959
                                                   E99.H7C6.1959

2780   COURLANDER, Harold comp.
       The fourth world of the Hopis. Crown Pub., 1971 E99.H7C64

2781   DENMAN, Leslie Van Ness
       Sh'a a-la-k'o Mana. San Francisco, Printed at the Grabhorn
       Pr. for W. and L. Denman, 1957   fE99.H7D394.Spec.Coll.

2782   DENNIS, Wayne
       The Hopi child. J. Wiley, 1965 (1940) E99.H7D4.1965

2783   DOCKSTADER, Frederick J.
       The kachina and the white man. Bloomfield Hills, Cranbrook
       Institute of Science, 1954   (CIB)   Q11.C95.no.35

2784   DOZIER, Edward P.
       The Hopi-Tewa of Arizona. Berkeley, Univ. of California Pr.,
       1954   (UCPAE)   E51.C15.v.44.no.3

2785   FORREST, Earle Robert
       The snake dance of the Hopi Indians. Los Angeles, Westernlore
       Pr., 1961   E99.H7F6

2786   HACK, John Tilton
       The changing physical environment of the Hopi Indians of
       Arizona. Cambridge, Mass., Peabody Museum, 1942
                          (PMP)   E51.H337.v.35.no.1

2787   HOUGH, Walter
       The Hopi Indians. Cedar Rapids, Ia., The Torch Pr., 1915
                                           E99.H7H68

2788   HOUGH, Walter
       The Moki snake dance. Chicago, Pub. by Passenger Dept.,
       The Santa Fe Route, 1902   E99.H7H82

2789   KROEBER, Alfred Louis ed.
       Walapai ethnography. Menasha, Wis., American Anthropological
       Assoc., 1935   E99.H75K7

2790   LOCKETT, Hattie Greene
       The unwritten literature of the Hopi. Tucson, Ariz.,
       Univ. of Arizona, 1933   E99.H7L84

2791   LOS ANGELES COUNTY, CALIF. OTIS ART INSTITUTE, LOS ANGELES.
       Kachinas. Los Angeles, 1967?   E99.H7L9

2792   LOWIE, Robert Harry
        Hopi kinship. American Museum of Natural History, 1929
                  (AMNHP)   GN2.A27.v.30.pt.7

2793   LOWIE, Robert Harry
        Notes on Hopi clans. American Museum of Natural History,
        1929   (AMNHP)   GN2.A27.v.30.pt.6

2794   LUMMIS, Charles Fletcher
        Bullying the Moqui. Prescott, Ariz., Prescott College Pr.,
        1968   E99.H7L8

2795   NEQUATEWA, Edmund
        Truth of a Hopi and other clan stories of Shung-opovi.
        Flagstaff, Northern Arizona Society of Science and Art,
        1936   (MNAB)   F806.M95.no.8

2796   O'KANE, Walter Collins
        The Hopis: portrait of a desert people. Norman, Univ.
        of Oklahoma Pr., 1953   E99.H7O54

2797   O'KANE, Walter Collins
        Sun in the sky. Norman, Univ. of Oklahoma Pr., 1950
                                 E99.H7O55
2798   SIKORSKI, Kathryn A.
        Modern Hopi pottery. Logan, Utah State Univ. Pr., 1968
                                 E99.H7S53

2799   SIMPSON, Ruth De Ette
        The Hopi Indians. Los Angeles, Southwest Museum, 1953
                                 E99.H7S55

2800   STEPHEN, Alexander M.
        Hopi journal of Alexander M. Stephen. AMS, 1969 (1936)
                              E99.H7S82.1969

2801   TALAYESVA, Don C.
        Sun chief. New Haven, Pub. for the Institute of Human
        Relations by Yale Univ. Pr.; London, H. Milford, Oxford
        Univ. Pr., 1942   E99.H7T25

2802   THOMPSON, Laura
        Culture in crisis. Harper, 1950   E99.H7T42

2803   THOMPSON, Laura
        The Hopi way. Russell & Russell, 1965 (1944)
                                 E99.H7T45.1965

28031   TITIEV, Mischa
       The Hopi Indians of old Oraibi: change and continuity.
       Ann Arbor, Univ. of Michigan Pr., 1972   E99.H7.T48.1972

2804   TITIEV, Mischa
       Old Oraibi, a study of the Hopi Indians of third mesa.
       Kraus Reprint, 1968 (1944) (PMP)   E51.H337.v.22.no.1.1968

2805   U. S. CENSUS OFFICE. 11th CENSUS, 1890.
       Moqui Pueblo Indians of Arizona and Pueblo Indians of
       New Mexico. Washington, U. S. Census Print. Off., 1893
                                         fE99.H7U5

2806   VOEGELIN, Charles Frederick
       Hopi domains. Baltimore, Waverly Pr., 1957
                   (IUPA)   GN4.I5.mem.14

2807   VOTH, Henry R.
       The traditions of the Hopi. Chicago, 1905 Field Museum of
       Natural History   (FMAS)   GN2.F4.v.8

2808   WATERS, Frank
       Book of the Hopi. Ballantine Books, 1971 (1963)   E99.H7W3

2809   WATERS, Frank
       Pumpkin seed point. Chicago, Sage Books, 1969   E99.H7W36

       HOPI
       See also: 06821, 2353

HUPA

2810   GODDARD, Pliny Earle
       The morphology of the Hupa language. Berkeley, The University
       Pr., 1905   (UCPAE)   E51.C15.v.3

2811   GODDARD, Pliny Earle
       The phonology of the Hupa language. pt. 1- Berkeley,
       The University Pr., 1907- (UCPAE)   E51.C15.v.5.no.1

2812   GODDARD, Pliny Earle
       Pitch accent in Hupa. Berkeley, Univ. of California Pr.,
       1928   (UCPAE)   E51.C15.v23.no.6

2813   GOLDSCHMIDT, Walter Rochs
       The Hupa white deerskin dance. Berkeley and Los Angeles,
       Univ. of California Pr., 1940   (UCPAE)   E51.C15.v.35.no.8

2814   CONNELLEY, William Elsey
        Indian myths. Rand, McNally & Co., 1928 E99.H9C68

2815   HUNTER, Andrew F.
        Huron village sites. Toronto, Printed by L. K. Cameron,
        Printer to the King's Most Excellent Majesty, 1907
                                                      E99.H9H9

2816   MITCHELL, Joseph
        The missionary pioneer. Joint Centenary Committee, 1918
                                                      E99.H9M6.1918

2817   TOOKER, Elisabeth
        An ethnography of the Huron Indians, 1615-1649. Washington,
        U. S. Govt. Print. Off., 1964 (BAEB)   E51.U55.no.190

2818   TRIGGER, Bruce G.
        The Huron farmers of the North. Holt, Rinehart and Winston,
        1969   E99.H9T7

        HURON
        See also: 1667

        INGALIK

2819   OSGOOD, Cornelius
        Ingalik material culture. New Haven, Pub. for the Dept.
        of Anthropology, Yale Univ., by the Yale Univ. Pr.;
        London, H. Milford, Oxford Univ. Pr., 1940
                        (YUPA)   GN2.Y3.no.22

2820   OSGOOD, Cornelius
        Ingalik mental culture. New Haven, Dept. of Anthropology,
        Yale Univ., 1959   (YUPA)   GN2.Y3.no.56

2821   OSGOOD, Cornelius
        Ingalik social culture. New Haven, Pub. for the Dept.
        of Anthropology, Yale Univ., by the Yale Univ. Pr., 1958
                        (YUPA)   GN2.Y3.no.53

        IROQUOIS

2822   CANFIELD, William Walker comp.
        The legends of the Iroquois. Port Washington, N.Y., I. J.
        Friedman, 1971 (1902)   286   E99.I7C23.1971

2823   CASWELL, Harriet S. (Clark)
        Our life among the Iroquois Indians. Boston and Chicago,
        Congregational Sundayschool and Publishing Society, 1892
                                    E99.S3C3

2824   CONFERENCE ON IROQUOIS RESEARCH, GLENS FALLS, N. Y., 1965.
        Iroquois culture, history, and prehistory. Albany,
        Univ. of the State of New York, State Education Dept.,
        New York State Museum and Science Service, 1967 E99.I7C77.1965

2825   FENTON, William Nelson
        The Iroquois eagle dance; an offshoot of the Calumet dance
        with An analysis of the Iroquois eagle dance and songs, by
        Gertrude Prokosch Kurath. Washington, U. S. Govt. Print. Off.,
        1953   (BAEB)   E51.U55.no.156

2826   FENTON, William Nelson
        The roll call of the Iroquois chiefs. Washington,
        Smithsonian Institution, 1950   E99.I7F46

2827   FENTON, William Nelson
        Symposium on local diversity in Iroquois culture. Washington,
        U. S. Govt. Print. Off., 1951 (BAEB) E51.U55.no.149

2828   GOLDSTEIN, Robert A.
        French-Iroquois diplomatic and military relations 1609-1701.
        The Hague, Mouton, 1969   E99.I7G6

2829   GRAYMONT, Barbara
        The Iroquois in the American Revolution. Syracuse, N. Y.,
        Syracuse Univ. Pr., 1972   E99.I7G67

2830   HALE, Horatio (Emmons)
        The Iroquois book of rites. Philadelphia, D. G. Brinton,
        1883   E99.I7H16

2831   HENRY, Thomas Robert
        Wilderness messiah. W. Sloane Assoc., 1955 E99.I7H45

2832   HUNT, George T.
        The wars of the Iroquois. Madison, The Univ. of Wisconsin Pr.,
        1960 (1940)   E99.I7H8.1960

2833   JOHNSON, Anna Cummings
        The Iroquois. D. Appleton and Co., 1855 E99.I7J65

2834   MORGAN, Lewis Henry
        League of the Ho-dé-no-sau-nee, or Iroquois. Rochester, Sage,
        1851   E99.I7M8.Spec.Coll.

2835   MORGAN, Lewis Henry
        League of the Iroquois. Corinth Books, 1962 E99.I7M85

2836   NOON, John A.
        Law and government of the Grand River Iroquois. Johnson
        Reprint, 1964 (1949)   E99.I7N76.1964

2837   PARKER, Arthur Caswell
        Parker on the Iroquois. Syracuse, N. Y., Syracuse Univ.
        Pr., 1968   E99.I7P25.1968

2838   REAMAN, George Elmore
        The trail of the Iroquois Indians. Barnes & Noble, 1967
                                            E99.I7R28

2839   RITZENTHALER, Robert Eugene
        Iroquois false-face masks. Milwaukee, Milwaukee Public
        Museum, 1969   E99.I7R57

2840   SCHOOLCRAFT, Henry Rowe
        Notes on the Iroquois. Albany, E. H. Pease, 1847
                                            E99.I7S4.Spec.Coll.

2841   SPECK, Frank Gouldsmith
        The Iroquois. Bloomfield Hills, Mich., 1955 [i.e. 1960]
                            (CIB)   Q11.C95.no.23.1955

2842   TOOKER, Elizabeth
        The Iroquois ceremonial of midwinter. Syracuse, N.Y.,
        Syracuse Univ. Pr., 1970   E99.I7T6

2843   U. S. CENSUS OFFICE. 11th CENSUS, 1890.
        Indians. Washington, U. S. Govt. Print. Off., 1892
                                            E99.I7U5

2844   WILSON, Edmund
        Apologies to the Iroquois. Farrar, Straus and Cudahy, 1960
                                            F99.I7W56

2845   YAWGER, Rose N.
        The Indian and the pioneer, an historical study. Syracuse,
        N. Y., C. W. Bardeen, 1893   E99.I7Y3

        IROQUOIS
        See also: 0080, 1951

JEMEZ

2846   ELLIS, Florence Hawley
        A reconstruction of the basic Jemez pattern of social
        organization with comparisons to other Tanoan social
        structures. Albuquerque, Univ. of New Mexico Pr., 1964
                        (NMPA)   GN2.N4.no.11

2847   PARSONS, Elsie Worthington (Clews)
        The pueblo of Jemez. New Haven, Pub. for the Dept. of
        Archaeology, Phillips Academy, Andover, Mass., by the
        Yale Univ. Pr., 1925   E99.J4P2

JICARILLA

2848   GODDARD, Pliny Earle
        Jicarilla Apache texts. American Museum of Natural History
        1911   (AMNHP)   GN2.A27.v.8

2849   OPLER, Morris Edward
        The character and derivation of the Jicarilla holiness
        rite. Albuquerque, Univ. of New Mexico Pr., 1943
                        (NMAS)   GN2.N39.v.4.no.3

2850   OPLER, Morris Edward
        Childhood and youth in Jicarilla Apache society. Los Angeles,
        The Southwest Museum, 1946   E99.J506

2851   OPLER, Morris Edward
        Dirty boy: a Jicarilla tale of raid and war. Menasha, Wis.,
        American Anthropological Assoc., 1938   E99.J5062

2852   VAN ROEKEL, Gertrude B.
        Jicarilla Apaches. San Antonio, Naylor Co., 1971   E99.J5V3

KAMIA

2853   Gifford, Edward Winslow
        The Kamia of Imperial Valley. Washington, U. S. Govt. Print.
        Off., 1931   (BAEB)   E51.U55.no.97

2854   UNRAU, William E.
       The Kansa Indians. Norman, Univ. of Oklahoma Pr., 1971
                           E99.K2U75

KANSA
    See also: 0158

KARANKAWA

2855   GATSCHET, Albert Samuel
       The Karankawa Indians, the coast people of Texas. Cambridge,
       Mass., Peabody Museum, 1891 (PMP)   E51.H337.v.1.no.2

2856   KILMAN, Edward W.
       Cannibal coast. San Antonio, Naylor Co., 1959 E99.K23K5

KARUK

2857   BRIGHT, William
       The Karok language. Berkeley, Univ. of California Pr.,
       1957   (CUPL)   P25.C25.v.13

2858   HARRINGTON, John Peabody
       Karuk Indian myths. Washington, U. S. Govt. Print. Off.,
       1932   (BAEB)   E51.U55.no.107

2859   HARRINGTON, John Peabody
       Tobacco among the Karuk Indians of California. Washington,
       U. S. Govt. Print. Off., 1932 (BAEB)   E51.U55.no.94

2860   SCHENCK, Sara (Moffatt)
       Karok ethnobotany. Berkeley, Univ. of California Pr.,
       1952   (AR)   E51.A58.v.13.no.6

KASKA

2861   HONIGMANN, John Joseph
       Culture and ethos of Kaska society. New Haven, Univ. Pr.,
       1949   (YUPA)   GN2.Y3.no.40

2862   HONIGMANN, John Joseph
       The Kaska Indians: an ethnographic reconstruction. New Haven,
       Reprinted by Human Relations Area Files Pr., 1964 (1954)
                 (YUPA)   GN2.Y3.no.51.1964

KATO

2863   GODDARD, Pliny Earle
       Elements of the Kato language. Berkeley, Univ. of California
       Pr., 1912   (UCPAE)   E51.C15.v.11.no.1

2864   GODDARD, Pliny Earle
       Kato texts. Berkeley, Univ. of California Pr., 1909
                   (UCPAE)   E51.C15.v.5.no.3

2865   LEESBERG, Arnold Cornelius Marius
       Comparative philology. Leyden, Late E. J. Brill, 1903
                                  fPL3005.L4

KAWIA

2866   BARROWS, David Prescott
       The ethno-botany of the Coahuilla Indians of Southern
       California. Chicago, Univ. of Chicago Pr., 1900   E99.K27B2

2867   HOOPER, Lucile
       The Cahuilla Indians. Berkeley, Univ. of California Pr.,
       1920   (UCPAE)   E51.C15.v.16.no.6

2868   JAMES, Harry Clebourne
       The Cahuilla Indians. Banning?, Calif., Malki Museum Pr.,
       1969   E99.K27J3.1969

2869   KROEBER, Alfred Louis
       Ethnography of the Cahuilla Indians. Berkeley, Univ. of
       California Pr., 1908   (UCPAE)   E51.C15.v.8.no.2

KERESAN

2870   GUNN, John Malcolm
       Schat-chen. Albuquerque, N. M., Albright and Anderson,
       1917   E99.K39G9

2871   GIBSON, Arrell Morgan
       The Kickapoos. Norman, Univ. of Oklahoma Pr., 1963   E99.K4G5

2872   HOAD, Louise (Green)
       Kickapoo Indian trails. Caldwell, Id., The Caxton Printers, Lt
       1944   E99.K4H6

2873   RITZENTHALER, Robert Eugene
       The Mexican Kickapoo Indians. Westport, Conn., Greenwood Pr.,
       1970   E99.K4R5.1970

2874   U. S. CONGRESS. SENATE. COMMITTEE ON INDIAN AFFAIRS.
       Affairs of the Mexican Kickapoo Indians. Washington,
       U. S. Govt. Print. Off., 1908   E99.K4U55

KIOWA

2875   BATTEY, Thomas C.
       The life and adventures of a Quaker among the Indians.
       Norman, Univ. of Oklahoma Pr., 1968   E99.K5B3.1968

2876   LOWIE, Robert Harry
       Societies of the Kiowa. American Museum of Natural History,
       1916   (AMNHP)   GN2.A27.v.11.pt.11

2877   MARRIOTT, Alice Lee
       Saynday's people. Lincoln, Univ. of Nebraska Pr., 1963
                                E99.K5M358

2878   MARRIOTT, Alice Lee
       The ten grandmothers. Norman, Univ. of Oklahoma Pr.,
       1963 (1945)   E99.K5M36

2879   MAYHALL, Mildred P.
       The Kiowas. Norman, Univ. of Oklahoma Pr., 1962 E99.K5M39

2880   MOMADAY, Natachee Scott
       The way to rainy mountain. Albuquerque, Univ. of New Mexico,
       1969   E99.K5M64

2881   NYE, Wilbur Sturtevant
       Bad medicine & good. Norman, Univ. of Oklahoma Pr., 1962
                                E99.K5N9

2882   SPIER, Leslie
       Notes on the Kiowa sun dance. American Museum of Natural
       History, 1921   (AMNHP)   GN2.A27.v.16.pt.6

KIOWA
    See also: 0868, 2050

KLAMATH

2883   BARKER, M. A. R.
       Klamath dictionary. Berkeley, Univ. of California Pr.,
       1963   (CUPL)   P25.C25.v.31

2884   BARKER, M. A. R.
       Klamath grammar. Berkeley, Univ. of California Pr.,
       1964   (CUPL)   P25.C25.v.32

2885   BARKER, M. A. R.
       Klamath texts. Berkeley, Univ. of California Pr., 1963
                           (CUPL)   P25.C25.v.30

2886   SPIER, Leslie
       Klamath ethnography. Berkeley, Univ. of California Pr.,
       1930   (UCPAE)   E51.C15.v.30

2887   STERN, Theodore
       The Klamath Tribe; a people and their reservation.
       Seattle, Univ. of Washington Pr., 1965
                           (MAES)   E51.A556.v.41

KUTCHIN

2888   McKENNAN, Robert Addison
       The Chandalar Kutchin. Montreal, 1965 E99.N22M3

2889   OSGOOD, Cornelius
       Contributions to the ethnography of the Kutchin. New Haven,
       Pub. for the Section of Anthropology, Dept. of the Social
       Sciences, Yale Univ., by the Yale Univ. Pr.; London,
       H. Milford, Oxford Univ. Pr., 1936 (YUPA) GN2.Y3.no.14

KUTENAI

2890   TURNEY-HIGH, Harry Holbert
       Ethnography of the Kutenai. Menasha, Wis., The American
       Anthropological Assoc., 1941   E99.K85T8

2891   BOAS, Franz
        Contributions to the ethnology of the Kwakiutl. AMS,
        1969 (1925)   (CUCA)   E51.C7.v.3.1969

2892   BOAS, Franz
        Geographical names of the Kwakiutl Indians. AMS, 1969
        (1934)   (CUCA)   E51.C7.v.20.1969

2893   BOAS, Franz
        Kwakiutl ethnography. Chicago, Univ. of Chicago Pr.,
        1966   E99.K9B49

2894   BOAS, Franz
        Kwakiutl tales. AMS, 1969 (1910)   E51.C7.v.2

2895   BOAS, Franz
        The religion of the Kwakiutl Indians. Columbia University
        Pr., 1930   (CUCA)   E51.C7.v.10

2896   BOAS, Franz
        The social organization and the secret societies of the
        Kwakiutl Indians. Washington, 1897   E99.K9B5

2897   CODERE, Helen
        Fighting with property; a study of Kwakiutl potlatching
        and warfare, 1792-1930. J. J. Augustin, pref. 1950

2898   DRUCKER, Philip
        To make my name good. Berkeley, Univ. of California Pr.,
        1967   E99.K9D7

2899   HAWTHORN, Audrey
        Art of the Kwakiutl Indians and other Northwest coast
        tribes. Vancouver, Univ. of British Columbia; Seattle,
        London, Univ. of Washington Pr., 1967   E99.K9H3

2900   ROHNER, Ronald P.
        The Kwakiutl. Holt, Rinehart and Winston, 1970
                                                 E99.K9R63

2901   ROHNER, Ronald P.
        The people of Gilford. Ottawa, Queen's Printer, 1967
                                                 E99.K9R6

2902   SEWID, James
        Guests never leave hungry. New Haven, Yale Univ. Pr.,
        1969   E99.K9S4

2903   WOLCOTT, Harry F.
        A Kwakiutl village and school. Holt, Rinehart and Winston,
        1967   E99.K9W6

        KWAKIUTL
        See also: 0847

LAGUNA

2904   PARSONS, Elsie Worthington (Clews)
        Laguna genealogies. American Museum of Natural History,
        1923   (AMNHP)   GN2.A27.v.19.pt.5

2905   PARSONS, Elsie Worthington (Clews)
        Notes on ceremonialism at Laguna. American Museum of
        Natural History, 1920   (AMNHP)   GN2.A27.v.19.pt.4

LUISEÑO

2906   BRIGHT, William
        A Luiseño dictionary. Berkeley, Univ. of California Pr.,
        1968   (CUPL)   P25.C25.v.51

2907   DU BOIS, Constance Goddard
        The religion of the Luiseño Indians of southern California.
        Berkeley, The University Pr., 1908   (UCPAE)
                                                E51.C15.v.8.no.3

2908   JAMES, George Wharton
        Picturesque Pala. Pasadena, Calif., Radiant Life Pr.,
        1916   E99.L9J3

2909   KROEBER, Alfred Louis
        The Sparkman grammar of Luiseno. Berkeley, Univ. of
        California Pr., 1960   (CUPL)   P25.C25.v.16

2910   McCOWN, B. E.
        Temeku, a page from the history of the Luiseño Indians.
        n.p., Archaeological Survey Assoc. of Southern California.
        1955   E99.L9M2

2911   PARKER, Horace
        The historic valley of Temecula. Balboa Island, Calif.,
        Paisano Pr., 1965   E99.L9P3

2912   SPARKMAN, Philip Stedman
        The culture of the Luiseño Indians. Berkeley, Univ. of
        California Pr., 1908   (UCPAE)   E51.C15.v.8.no.4

2913   WHITE, Raymond C.
        Luiseño social organization. Berkeley, Univ. of California Pr.
        1963   (UCPAE)   E51.C15.v.48.no.2

LUMMI

2914   STERN, Bernhard Joseph
        The Lummi Indians of northwest Washington. Columbia
        University Pr., 1934   (CUCA)   E51.C7.v.17

        LUMMI
            See also: 2839

MAHICAN

2915   SKINNER, Alanson Buck
        Notes on Mahikan ethnology. Milwaukee, Wis., Pub. by
        order of the Board of Trustees, 1925   E99.M12S52

MAIDU

2916   SHIPLEY, William F.
        Maidu grammar. Berkeley, Univ. of California Pr., 1964
                                (CUPL)   P25.C25.v.41

        MAIDU
            See also: 2279

MAKAH

2917   COLSON, Elizabeth
        The Makah Indians. Manchester, Eng., Manchester Univ. Pr.,
        1953   E99.M19C6.1953a

2918   WATERMAN, Thomas Talbot
        The whaling equipment of the Makah Indians. Seattle,
        Univ. of Washington Pr., 1967   E99.M19W32.1967

MANAHOAC

2919   BUSHNELL, David Ives
        The Manahoac tribes in Virginia, 1608. City of Washington,
        The Smithsonian Institution, 1935   E78.V7B83

MANDAN

2920   BOWERS, Alfred W.
        Mandan social and ceremonial organization. Chicago,
        Univ. of Chicago Pr., 1950   E99.M2B68

2921   CATLIN, George
        O-kee-pa, a religious ceremony. New Haven, Yale Univ. Pr.,
        1967   E99.M2C3.1967

2922   WILL, George Francis
        The Mandans: a study of their culture, archaeology and
        language. Kraus Reprint, 1967 (1906)
                                (PMP)   E51.H337.v.3.no.4

        MANDAN
          See also: 0142, 0144, 2277

MARICOPA

2923   EZELL, Paul Howard
        The Maricopas. Tucson, University of Arizona Pr., 1963
                                               E99.M25E9

MASCOUTENS

2924   SKINNER, Alanson Buck
        The Mascoutens or Prairie Potawatomi Indians. Westport, Conn.,
        Greenwood Pr., 1970   E99.M3S62

MASHPEE

2925   LANDES, Ruth
        The Mystic Lake Sioux. Madison, Univ. of Wisconsin Pr., 1968
                            297   E99.M435L3

2926   TROWBRIDGE, Charles Christopher
        Meearmeear traditions. Ann Arbor, Univ. of Michigan Pr.,
        1938   E99.M48T76

                                MAYA

2927   BENSON, Elizabeth P.
        The Maya world. Crowell, 1967   F1435.B47

2928   BRINTON, Daniel Garrison   ed. and tr.
        The Maya chronicles. AMS, 1969 (1882) F1435.C48.1969

2929   CANCIAN, Frank
        Economics and prestige in a Maya community. Stanford, Calif.,
        Stanford Univ. Pr., 1965   F1221.T9C3

2930   CARVER, Norman F.
        Silent cities: Mexico and the Maya. Tokyo, Shokokusha,
        1966   F1219.3.A6C3

2931   COE, Michael D.
        The Maya. Praeger, 1966   F1435.C72.1966a

2932   Estudios de cultura maya.
        v. 1- México, 1961-   F1435.A2

2933   FÖRSTEMANN, Ernst Wilhelm
        Commentary on the Maya manuscript in the Royal public
        library of Dresden. Cambridge, Mass., Peabody Museum,
        1906   (PMP)   E51.H337.v.4.no.2

2934   GALLENKAMP, Charles
        Maya; the riddle and rediscovery of a lost civilization.
        London, F. Muller, 1960   F1435.G16.1960

2935   GANN, Thomas William Francis
        The Maya Indians of southern Yucatan and northern British
        Honduras. Washington, U. S. Govt. Print. Off., 1918
                           (BAEB)   E51.U55.no.64

2936   GATES, William Edmond
        Commentary upon the Maya-Tzental Perez codex, with a concluding
        note upon the linguistic problem of the Maya glyphs. Cambridge,
        Mass., Peabody Museum, 1910 (PMP)   E51.H337.v.6.no.1

2937   GIRARD, Rafael
        Los mayas: su civilización, su historia, sus vinculaciones
        continentales. México, Libro Mex, 1966 F1435.G53

2938   LEÓN PORTILLA, Miguel
        Tiempo y realidad en el pensamiento maya. México,
        Universidad Nacional Autónoma de México, 1968 F1435.L4

2939   The Maya and their neighbors.
        D. Appleton-Century Co., 1962 (1940)   F1435.M45.1962

2940   Monographs and papers in Maya archaeology.
        Cambridge, Mass., Peabody Museum, 1970 (PMP) E51.H337.v.61

2941   MORLEY, Sylvanus Griswold
        The Ancient Maya. Stanford, Calif., Stanford Univ. Pr.,
        1956 (1955)   F1435.M75.1956

2942   ROYS, Ralph Loveland
        The political geography of the Yucatan Maya. Washington,
        Carnegie Institution of Washington, 1957 F1435.R79

2943   RUZ LHUILLIER, Alberto
        La civilización de los antiguos mayas. México, Instituto
        Nacional de Antropología e Historia, 1963 F1435.R95.1963

2944   SCHELLHAS, Paul
        Representation of deities of the Maya manuscripts. Cambridge,
        Mass., Peabody Museum, 1904 (PMP)   E51.H337.v.4.no.1

2945   SPINDEN, Herbert Joseph
        The reduction of Mayan dates. Cambridge, Mass., Peabody
        Museum, 1924   (PMP)   E51.H337.v.6.no.4

2946   STACY-JUDD, Robert Benjamin
        The ancient Mayas. Los Angeles, Murray & Gee, 1934
                                              F1376.S78

2947   THOMPSON, John Eric Sidney
        The civilization of the Mayas. Chicago, Field Museum of
        Natural History, 1958 (CMA)   GN2.F5.no.25

2948   THOMPSON, John Eric Sidney
        Ethnology of the Mayas of southern and central British
        Honduras. Chicago, Field Museum of Natural History, 1930
                        (FMAS)   GN2.F4.v.17.no.2

2949   THOMPSON, John Eric Sidney
        Maya archaeologist. Norman, Univ. of Oklahoma Pr., 1963
                                              F1435.T495.1963

2950   THOMPSON, John Eric Sidney
        Maya history and religion. Norman, Univ. of Oklahoma Pr.,
        1970   F1435.T496

2951   THOMPSON, John Eric Sidney
        The rise and fall of Maya civilization. Norman, Univ. of
        Oklahoma Pr., 1966   F1435.T497.1966

2952   THOMPSON, Raymond H.
        Modern Yucatecan Maya pottery making. Salt Lake City,
        Society for American Archaeology, 1958
                            (SAAM)   E51.S7.no.15

2953   TOZZER, Alfred Marston
        Animal figures in the Maya codices. Cambridge, Mass.,
        Peabody Museum, 1910   (PMP)   E51.H337.v.4.no.3

2954   TOZZER, Alfred Marston
        A Maya grammar. Kraus Reprint, 1967 (1921)
                            (PMP)   E51.H337.v.9.1967

2955   VOGT, Evon Zartman
        Zinacantán: a Maya community in the highlands of Chiapas.
        Cambridge, Belknap Pr. of Harvard Univ. Pr., 1969
                                          F1435.V733.1969

2956   VON HAGEN, Victor Wolfgang
        World of the Maya. New American Library, 1960 F1435.V75

2957   WHORF, Benjamin Lee
        The phonetic value of certain characters in Maya writing.
        Cambridge, Mass., Peabody Museum, 1933 (PMP) E51.H337.v.13.no.2

2958   WILLSON, Robert Wheeler
        Astronomical notes on the Maya codices. Cambridge, Mass.,
        Peabody Museum, 1924   (PMP)   E51.H337.v.6.no.3

        MAYA
            See also: 06771, 1693, 1729, 1747, 1781, 1791, 2024, 2060
                        20941, 21051, 2111, 2112, 21121, 2128, 2420

                                    MAYO

2959   CRUMRINE, Lynne Scoggins
        Ceremonial exchange as a mechanism in tribal integration
        among the Mayos of Northwest Mexico. Tucson, Univ. of
        Arizona Pr., 1969   F1221.M3C68

2960   CRUMRINE, N. Ross
        The house cross of the Mayo Indians of Sonora, Mexico.
        Tucson, Univ. of Arizona Pr., 1964   F1221.M3C7

                                    300

29601   IWANSKA, Alicja
       Purgatory and utopia; a Mazahua Indian village of Mexico.
       Cambridge, Mass., Schenkman Pub. Co., 1971   F1221.M33.I9

MENOMINEE

2961   DENSMORE, Frances
      Menominee music. Washington, U. S. Govt. Print. Off., 1932
             (BAEB)   E51.U55.no.102

2962   HOFFMAN, Walter James
      The Menomini Indians. Johnson Reprint, 1970 (1816)
                    E99.M44H6.1970

2963   KEESING, Felix Maxwell
      The Menomini Indians of Wisconsin. Johnson Reprint, 1971
      (1939)   E99.M44K4.1971

2964   SKINNER, Alanson Buck
      Associations and ceremonies of the Menomini Indians.
      American Museum of Natural History (AMNHP) GN2.A27.v.13.pt.2

2965   SKINNER, Alanson Buck
      Folklore of the Menomini Indians. American Museum of Natural
      History, 1915   (AMNHP)   GN2.A27.v.13.pt.3

2966   SKINNER, Alanson Buck
      Social life and ceremonial bundles of the Menomini Indians.
      American Museum of Natural History, 1913
             (AMNHP)   GN2.A27.v.13.pt.1

2967   SLOTKIN, James Sydney
      The Menomini powwow. Milwaukee, 1957   E99.M44S645

2968   SMITH, Huron Herbert
      Ethnobotany of the Menomini Indians. Westport, Conn.,
      Greenwood Pr., 1970   E99.M44S65.1970

2969   SPINDLER, Louise S.
      Menomini women and culture change. Menasha, Wis., American
      Anthropological Assoc., 1962 (AAAM)   GN2.A22.no.91

MENOMINEE
   See also: 2016, 2272

2970   ANSON, Bert
        The Miami Indians. Norman, Univ. of Oklahoma Pr., 1970
                              E99.M48A5

MICMAC

2971   BOCK, Philip K.
        The Micmac Indians of Restigouche. Ottawa, Dept. of the
        Secretary of State, 1966   E99.M6B6

29711   RAND, Silas Tertius
        Legends of the Micmacs. Johnson Reprint, 1971 E99.M6.R3.1971

      MICMAC
        See also: 2072, 2094

MIMBRENO

2972   NESBITT, Paul Homer
        The ancient Mimbreños. Beloit, Wis., The Logan Museum,
        Beloit College, 1931   E99.M63N45

MIWOK

2973   BARRETT, Samuel Alfred
        The geography and dialects of the Miwok Indians. On the
        evidences of the occupation of certain regions by the Miwok
        Indians, by A. L. Kroeber. Berkeley, Univ. of California Pr.,
        1908   (UCPAE)   E51.C15.v.6.no.2-3

2974   BARRETT, Samuel Alfred
        Myths of the Southern Sierra Miwok. Berkeley, Univ. of
        California Pr., 1919   (UCPAE)   E51.C15.v.16.no.1

2975   BROADBENT, Sylvia M.
        The Southern Sierra Miwok language. Berkeley, Univ. of
        California Pr., 1964   (CUPL)   P25.C25.v.38

2976   CALLAGHAN, Catherine A.
        Bodega Miwok dictionary. Berkeley, Univ. of California Pr.,
        1970   (CUPL)   P25.C25.v.60

2977   CALLAGHAN, Catherine A.
        Lake Miwok dictionary. Berkeley, Univ. of California Pr.,
        1965   (CUPL)   P25.C25.v.39

2978   FREELAND, L. S.
        Central Sierra Miwok dictionary. Berkeley, Univ. of
        California Pr., 1960   (CUPL)   P25.C25.v.23

2979   FREELAND, L. S.
        Language of the Sierra Miwok. Baltimore, Waverly Pr.,
        1951   (IUPA)   GN4.I5.mem.6

2980   GIFFORD, Edward Winslow
        Central Miwok ceremonies. Berkeley, Univ. of California
        Pr., 1955   (AR)   E51.A58.v.14.no.4

2981   GIFFORD, Edward Winslow
        Miwok cults. Berkeley, Univ. of California Pr., 1926
                                (UCPAE)   E51.C15.v.18.no.3

2982   GIFFORD, Edward Winslow
        Miwok moieties. Berkeley, Univ. of California Pr.,
        1916   (UCPAE)   E51.C15.v.12.no.4

2983   GIFFORD, Edward Winslow
        Miwok myths. Berkeley, Univ. of California Pr., 1927
                                (UCPAE)   E51.C15.v.12.no.8

                                MIXE

2984   BEALS, Ralph Leon
        Ethnology of the western Mixe. Berkeley, Univ. of California
        Pr., 1945   (UCPAE)   E51.C15.v.42.no.1

                                MIXTEC

2985   DAHLGREN DE JORDÁN, Barbro
        La mixteca. Mexico, Universidad Nacional Autónoma de
        México, 1966   F1221.M7D3.1966

2986   SPORES, Ronald
        The Mixtec kings and their people. Norman, Univ. of Oklahoma
        Pr., 1967   F1219.S768

                                303

2987   CURTIN, Jeremiah
        Myths of the Modocs. Boston, Little, Brown, and Co.,
        1912   E99.M7C9

2988   MILLER, Joaquin
        Unwritten history: life amongst the Modocs. Hartford,
        American Pub. Co., 1874   E99.M7M5.Spec.Coll.

2989   PAYNE, Doris (Palmer)
        Captain Jack, Modoc renegade. Portland, Or., Binford & Mort,
        1938   E99.M7J3

        MODOC
        See also: 1811, 1874, 1887, 2382

MOHAVE

2990   DEVEREUX, George
        Mohave ethnopsychiatry and suicide: the psychiatric
        knowledge and the psychic disturbances of an Indian tribe.
        Washington, U. S. Govt. Print. Off., 1961
                        (BAEB)   E51.U55.no.175

2991   GREY, Herman
        Tales from the Mohaves. Norman, Univ. of Oklahoma Pr., 1970
                                                E99.M77G7

2992   KROEBER, Alfred Louis
        Mohave pottery. Berkeley, Univ. of California Pr., 1955
                        (AR)   E51.A58.v.16.no.1

2993   KROEBER, Alfred Louis
        Phonetic elements of the Mohave language. Berkeley, University
        of California Pr., 1911 (UCPAE)   E51.C15.v.10.no.3

        MOHAVE
        See also: 0299

MOHAWK

2994   BOND, Richmond Pugh
        Queen Anne's American kings. Oxford, Clarendon Pr., 1952
                                                E99.M8B65

2995   CLARKE, Thomas Wood
        The bloody Mohawk. Macmillan, 1940   F127.M55C6

2996   GRASSMANN, Thomas
        The Mohawk Indians and their valley. Schenectady, N. Y.,
        Printed by Eric Hugo Photography and Print Co., 1969
                                                E99.M8G7

2997   LYDEKKER, John Wolfe
        The faithful Mohawks. Port Washington, N. Y., I. J. Friedman,
        1968   E99.M8L93.1968

2998   STONE, William Leete
        Life of Joseph Brant. Albany, N. Y., J. Munsell, 1865
                                                E99.M8B88

MONO

2999   GIFFORD, Edward Winslow
        The Northfork Mono. Berkeley, Univ. of California Pr.,
        1932   (UCPAE)   E51.C15.v.31.no.2

MONTAGNAIS

3000   HARPER, Francis
        The friendly Montagnais and their neighbors in the Ungava
        Peninsula. Lawrence, Univ. of Kansas, 1964   E99.M87H3

3001   LEACOCK, Eleanor
        The Montagnais "hunting territory" and the fur trade. Menasha,
        Wis., American Anthropological Assoc., 1954
                                (AAAM)   GN2.A22.no.78

NARRAGANSET

3002   SIMMONS, William Scranton
        Cautantowwit's house. Providence, Brown Univ. Pr., 1970
                                                E99.N16S5.1970

3003   SPECK, Frank Gouldsmith
        Naskapi, the savage hunters of the Labrador peninsula.
        Norman, Univ. of Oklahoma Pr., 1935   E99.N18S7

NAVAJO

3004   ABERLE, David Friend
        The peyote religion among the Navajo.   Chicago, Aldine Pub. Co.,
        1966   E99.N3A2

3005   ALLEN, T. D., pseud.
        Navahos have five fingers.   Norman, Univ. of Oklahoma Pr.,
        1963   E98.T35A5.1964

3006   AMSDEN, Charles Avery
        Navaho weaving; its technic and its history.   Chicago,
        Rio Grande Pr., 1964   E98.T35A5.1964

3007   BAADER, Ethel M.
        Indian playmates of Navajo land.   Friendship Pr., 1927
                                     E99.N3B15

3008   BABINGTON, Suren H.
        Navajos, gods and tom-toms.   Greenberg, 1950   E99.N3B17

3009   BAILEY, Flora L.
        Some sex beliefs and practices in a Navaho community.
        Cambridge, Mass., Peabody Museum, 1950
                        (PMP)   E51.H337.v.40.no.2

3010   BAILEY, Lynn Robison
        The long walk.   Los Angeles, Westernlore Pr., 1964   E99.N3B18

3011   CHRISTIAN, Jane MacNab
        The Navajo, a people in transition.   El Paso, Texas Western
        College Pr., 1964-65   E99.N3C5

3012   CLARK, Elizabeth P.
        Report on the Navajo, 1946.   n.p., 1946?   E99.N3C55

3013   COLORADO SPRINGS. FINE ARTS CENTER. TAYLOR MUSEUM.
        Navaho sandpainting.   Colorado Springs, 1960   E99.N3C75

3014   COOLIDGE, Dane
        The Navajo Indians.   Boston and New York, Houghton Mifflin Co.,
        1930   E99.N3C77

30141   CRAPANZANO, Vincent
        The fifth world of Forster Bennett; portrait of a Navaho.
        Viking Pr., 1972   E99.N3.B463.1972

3015   DALE, Kenneth Iven
        Navajo Indian educational administration. Grand Forks, N. D.,
        1949   E99.N3D3.1970

3016   DOWNES, Randolph Chandler
        Preliminary Navajo report - 1946. n.p., 1946 E99.N3D66

3017   DOWNS, James F.
        Animal husbandry in Navajo society and culture. Berkeley,
        Univ. of California Pr., 1964   E99.N3D68

30171   DOWNS, James F.
        The Navajo. Holt, Rinehart and Winston, 1972 E99.N3.D69

3018   DYKHUIZEN, Dorothy
        Go quickly and tell. Grand Rapids, Mich., Wm. B. Eerdmans
        Pub. Co., 1946   E99.N3D9

3019   ELMORE, Francis Hapgood
        Ethnobotany of the Navajo. Albuquerque, N. M., Univ. of
        New Mexico Pr., 1943   E99.N3E32

3020   FORREST, Earle Robert
        With a camera in old Navaholand. Norman, Univ. of Oklahoma
        Pr., 1970   E99.N3F6

3021   FRANCISCANS, Saint Michaels, Ariz.
        An ethnologic dictionary of the Navaho language. Leipzig,
        M. Breslauer, 1929   E99.N3F8.1929

3022   FRISBE, Charlotte Johnson
        Kinaaldá; a study of the Navaho girl's puberty ceremony.
        Middletown, Conn., Wesleyan Univ. Pr., 1967 E99.N3F84

3023   GILPIN, Laura
        The enduring Navaho. Austin, Univ. of Texas Pr., 1968
                                            E99.N3G5

3024   GODDARD, Pliny Earle
        Navajo texts. American Museum of Natural History, 1933
                        (AMNHP)   GN2.A27.v.34.pt.1

3025   HAILE, Berard
        Navaho sacrificial figurines. Chicago, Univ. of Chicago Pr.,
        1947   E99.N3H24

3026   HAILE, Berard
            Origin legend of the Navaho enemy way. New Haven, Pub.
            for the Dept. of Anthropology, Yale Univ., by the Yale
            Univ. Pr.; London, H. Milford, Oxford Univ. Pr., 1938
                            (YUPA)   GN2.Y3.nc.17

3027   HAILE, Berard
            Origin legend of the Navaho flintway. Chicago, Univ. of
            Chicago Pr., 1943   E99.N3H25

3028   HAILE, Berard
            Prayer stick cutting in a five night Navaho ceremonial of
            the male branch of Shootingway. Chicago, Univ. of Chicago
            Pr., 1947   E99.N3H26

3029   HANNUM, Alberta (Pierson)
            Paint the wind. Viking Pr., 1958   E99.N3H29

3030   HANNUM, Alberta (Pierson)
            Spin a silver dollar. Viking Pr., 1945 E99.N3H3

3031   HEGEMANN, Elizabeth (Compton)
            Navaho trading days. Albuquerque, Univ. of New Mexico,
            1966 (1963)   F811.H4

3032   HILL, Willard Williams
            The agricultural and hunting methods of the Navaho Indians.
            New Haven, Pub. for the Dept. of Anthropology, Yale Univ.,
            by the Yale Univ. Pr., 1938 (YUPA)   GN2.Y3.no.18

3033   HILL, Willard Williams
            Navajo pottery manufacture. Albuquerque, Univ. of New
            Mexico Pr., 1937   (NMAS)   GN2.N39.v.2.no.3

3034   HILL, Willard Williams
            Navaho warfare. New Haven, Pub. for the Section of
            Anthropology, Dept. of the Social Sciences, Yale Univ., by
            the Yale Univ. Pr.; London, H. Milford, Oxford Univ. Pr.,
            1936   (YUPA)   GN2.Y3.no.5

3035   HODGE, William H.
            The Albuquerque Navajos. Tucson, Univ. of Arizona Pr.,
            1969   E99.N3H58

3036   HOIJER, Harry
            Navajo phonology. Albuquerque, Univ. of New Mexico Pr.,
            1945   (NMPA)   GN2.N4.no.1

3037   HOLLISTER, Uriah S.
            The Navajo and his blanket. Denver, 1903 E99.N3H7

3038   JAMES, George Wharton
        Indian blankets and their makers. Glorieta, N. M.,
        Rio Grande Pr., 1970 (1914)   E99.N3J3.1970

3039   JETT, Stephen C.
        Navajo wildlands. San Francisco, Sierra Club, 1967
                                                fE99.N3J4

30391   JOHNSTON, Bernice Eastman
        Two ways in the desert; a study of modern Navajo-Anglo
        relations. Socio-Technical Pubs., 1972 E99.N3.J59

3040   JOHNSTON, Denis Foster
        An analysis of sources of information on the population of
        the Navaho. Washington, U. S. Govt. Print. Off., 1966
                            (BAEB)   E51.U55.no.197

30401   KAHLENBERG, Mary Hunt
        The Navajo blanket. Praeger, 1972   fE99.N3.K3

3041   KELLY, Lawrence C.
        The Navajo Indians and Federal Indian policy, 1900-1935.
        Tucson, Univ. of Arizona Pr., 1968   E99.N3K34

3042   KING, Jeff
        Where the two came to their father. Princeton, Princeton
        Univ. Pr., 1969   fE99.N3K45.1969.Spec.Coll.

3043   KLAH, Hasteen
        Navajo creation myth. Santa Fe, N. M., Museum of Navajo
        Ceremonial Art, 1942   E99.N3K5

3044   KLUCKHOHN, Clyde
        An introduction to Navaho chant practice. Menasha, Wis.,
        American Anthropological Assoc., 1940   E99.N3K535

3045   KLUCKHOHN, Clyde
        The Navaho. Cambridge, Harvard Univ. Pr.; London,
        C. Cumberlege, Oxford Univ. Pr., 1951 (1946) E99.N3K54

3046   KLUCKHOHN, Clyde
        Navaho material culture. Cambridge, Mass., Belknap Pr.
        of Harvard Univ. Pr., 1971   E99.N3K545

3047   KLUCKHOHN, Slyde
        Navaho witchcraft. Boston, Beacon Pr., 1962 (1944)
                                        E99.N3K55.1962

3048   LEIGHTON, Alexander Hamilton
        The Navaho door. Russell & Russell, 1967 (1944)
                                        E99.N3L55.1967

3049   LEIGHTON, Dorothea (Cross)
        Children of the people. Octagon Books, 1969 (1947)
                                        E99.N3L57.1969

3050   LINK, Margaret Schevill
        The pollen path. Stanford, Stanford Univ. Pr., 1956
                                        E99.N3L66

3051   LINK, Martin A. comp.
        Navajo: a century of progress, 1868-1968. Window Rock,
        Ariz., Pub. by the Navajo Tribe, 1968   fE99.N3L68

3052   LIPPS, Oscar Hiram
        The Navajos. Cedar Rapids, Ia., Torch Pr., 1909 E99.N3L7

3053   McALLESTER, David Park
        Enemy way music. Cambridge, Mass., The Museum, 1954
                    (PMP)   E51.H337.v.41.no.3

30531   McNITT, Frank
        Navajo Wars; military campaigns, slave raids and reprisals.
        Albuquerque, N. M., Univ. of New Mexico Pr., 1972 E99.N3.M32

3054   MATTHEWS, Washington
        Navaho myths, prayers and songs, with texts and translations.
        Berkeley, Univ. of California Pr., 1907
                    (UCPAE)   E51.C15.v.5.no.2

3055   MILLS, George Thompson
        Navaho art and culture. Colorado Springs, Taylor Museum
        of the Colorado Springs Fine Arts Center, 1959 E99.N3M58

3056   MORGAN, William
        Human-wolves among the Navaho. New Haven, Pub. for the
        Section of Anthropology, Dept. of the Social Sciences, Yale
        Univ., by the Yale Univ. Pr.; London, H. Milford, Oxford Univ.
        Pr., 1936   (YUPA)   GN2.Y3.no.11

30561   NAVAJO COMMUNITY COLLEGE
        Navajo studies at Navajo Community College. Many Farms, Ariz.,
        Navajo Community College Pr., 1971   E99.N3.N3

3057   The Navajo yearbook. no. 1-8. 1952-61. Window Rock, Ariz.,
        Navajo Agency   E99.N3N36

3058   NEWCOMB, Franc (Johnson)
        Hosteen Klah, Navaho medicine man and sand painter. Norman,
        Univ. of Oklahoma Pr., 1964   E99.N3N37

3059   NEWCOMB, Franc (Johnson)
       Navaho folk tales. Santa Fé, N. M., Museum of Navaho Ceremonial
       Art, 1967   E99.N3N375

3060   NEWCOMB, Franc (Johnson)
       Navaho neighbors. Norman, Univ. of Oklahoma Pr., 1966
                                              E99.N3N375

3061   NEWCOMB, Franc (Johnson)
       Navajo omens and taboos. Santa Fe, N. M., The Rydal Pr.,
       1940   E99.N3N38

3062   NEWCOMB, Franc (Johnson)
       A study of Navajo symbolism. Kraus, 1968 (1956)
                           (PMP)   E51.H337.v.32.no.3.1968

3063   O'BRYAN, Aileen
       The Dîné: origin myths of the Navaho Indians. Washington,
       U. S. Govt. Print. Off., 1956 (BAEB)   E51.U55.no.163

3064   OLD MEXICAN, Navaho Indian
       A Navaho autobiography. 1947   E99.N304

3065   PHELPS-STOKES FUND.
       The Navajo Indian problem. 1939   E99.N3P53

3066   RAPOPORT, Robert Norman
       Changing Navaho religious values. Cambridge, Mass.,
       Peabody Museum, 1954   (PMP)   E51.H337.v.41.no.2

3067   REICHARD, Gladys Amanda
       Dezba, woman of the desert. J. J. Augustin, 1939 E99.N3R34

3068   REICHARD, Gladys Amanda
       Navaho religion. Pantheon Books, 1950 E99.N3R38

3069   REICHARD, Sladys Amanda
       Navajo shepherd and weaver. J. J. Augustin, 1936 E99.N3R39

3070   REICHARD, Gladys Amanda
       Social life of the Navajo Indians. Columbia Univ. Pr.,
       1928   E99.N3R398

3071   REICHARD, Gladys Amanda
       Spider woman. Macmillan, 1934   E99.N3R4

3072   RICE, Josiah M.
       A cannoneer in Navajo country. Denver, Pub. for the Denver
       Public Library by the Old West Pub. Co., 1970 E99.N3R5.1970

3073   SANCHEZ, George Isidore
       "The people"; a study of the Navajos. Washington, U. S.
       Indian Service, 1948   E99.N3S2

3074   SAPIR, Edward
       The phonology and morphology of the Navaho language.
       Berkeley, Univ. of California Pr., 1967
                 (CUPL)   P25.C25.v.50

3075   SASAKI, Tom Taketo
       Fruitland, New Mexico: a Navaho community in transition.
       Ithaca, N. Y., Cornell Univ. Pr., 1960 E99.N3S3

3076   SHEPARDSON, Mary
       The Navajo Mountain community. Berkeley, Univ. of California
       Pr., 1970   E99.N3S46

3077   SHEPARDSON, Mary
       Navajo ways in government. Menasha, Wis., American
       Anthropological Assoc., 1963 (AAAM) GN2.A22.no.96

3078   SIMPSON, James Hervey
       Navaho expedition. Norman, Univ. of Oklahoma Pr., 1964
                       F801.S58.1964

3079   SPENCER, Katherine
       Reflections of social life in the Navaho origin myth.
       Albuquerque, Univ. of New Mexico Pr., 1947
                 (NMPA)   GN2.N4.no.3

3080   TERRELL, John Upton
       The Navajos. Harper, 1970   E99.N3T4.1970

3081   TSCHOPIK, Harry
       Navaho pottery making. Kraus, 1968 (1941)
                 (PMP)   E51.H337.v.17.no.1.1968

3082   UNDERHILL, Ruth Murray
       Here come the Navaho! n.p., 195-   E99.N3U3

3083   UNDERHILL, Ruth Murray
       The Navajos. Norman, Univ. of Oklahoma Pr., 1958 (1956)
                       E99.N3U32

3084   U. S. NATIONAL PARK SERVICE.
       Navaho life of yesterday and today. Berkeley, Calif.,
       1938   E99.N3U6

3085   VERPLANCK, James DeLancey
       A country of shepherds. Boston, Ruth Hill, 1934 E99.N3V6

3086   VOGT, Evon Zartman
        Navaho veterans. Cambridge, Mass., The Museum, 1951
                        (PMP)   E51.H337.v.41.no.1

3087   WALKER, John George
        The Navajo reconnaissance. Los Angeles, Westernlore Pr.,
        1964   F811.W3

3088   WATKINS, Frances Emma
        The Navaho. Los Angeles, The Southwest Museum, 1945
                                         E99.N3W3.1945

3089   WHITMAN, William
        Navaho tales. Boston and New York, Houghton Mifflin Co.,
        1925   E99.N3W6

3090   WOODWARD, Arthur
        A brief history of Navajo silversmithing. Flagstaff,
        Northern Arizona Society of Science and Art, 1938
                        (MNAB)   F806.M95.no.14

30901   WOODWARD, Arthur
        Navajo silver; a brief history of Navajo silversmithing.
        Flagstaff, Ariz., Northland Pr., 1971   E99.N3.W75.1971

30902   WORTH, Sol
        Through Navajo eyes; an exploration in film communication
        and anthropology. Bloomington, Indiana Univ. Pr., 1972
                                         E99.N3.W77

3091   WYMAN, Leland Clifton ed.
        Beautyway: a Navaho ceremonial. Pantheon Books, 1957
                                         E99.N3W93

3092   WYMAN, Leland Clifton
        Blessingway. Tucson, Univ. of Arizona Pr., 1970   E99.N3W935

3093   WYMAN, Leland Clifton
        Navaho classification of their song ceremonials. Menasha,
        Wis., American Anthropological Assoc., 1938
                        (AAAM)   GN2.A22.no.50

3094   WYMAN, Leland Clifton
        Navaho Indian ethnoentomology. Albuquerque, Univ. of
        New Mexico Pr., 1964   (NMPA)   GN2.N4.no.12

3095   WYMAN, Leland Clifton
        Navajo Indian medical ethnobotany. Albuquerque, Univ. of
        New Mexico Pr., 1941   (NMAS)   GN2.N39.v.3.no.5

3096   WYMAN, Leland Clifton
        The windways of the Navaho. Colorado Springs, Taylor
        Museum of the Colorado Springs Fine Arts Center, 1962
                                                    E99.N3W95

3097   YOUNG, Robert W. ed.
        Navajo historical selections. n.p., 1954 E99.N3Y6

3098   YOUNG, Robert W.
        The trouble at Round Rock. Phoenix, Ariz., Printing Dept.,
        Phoenix Indian School, 1952   E99.N3Y62

NAVAJO
See also: 0172, 0627, 07201, 07681, 0785, 0839, 0845, 09821,
           1517, 1527, 1530, 1548, 1841, 1854, 1936, 2000,
           2045, 2095, 2119, 2153, 2316, 2418

NEHALEM

3099   CHURCHILL, Claire (Warner)
        Slave wives of Nehalem. Portland, Or., Metropolitan Pr.,
        1933   E99.N45C4

3100   PEARSON, Clara
        Nehalem Tillamook tales. Eugene, Univ. of Oregon Books,
        1959   E99.N45P4

NEZ PERCÉ

3101   AOKI, Haruo
        Nez Perce grammar. Berkeley, Univ. of California Pr.,
        1970   (CUPL)   P25.C25.v.62

3102   JOSEPHY, Alvin M.
        The Nez Perce Indians and the opening of the Northwest.
        New Haven, Yale Univ. Pr., 1965   E99.N5J6

3103   McBETH, Kate C.
        The Nez Perces since Lewis and Clark. F. H. Revell Co.,
        1908   E99.N5M2

3104   McWHORTER, Lucullus Virgil
        Hear me, my chiefs! Caldwell, Id., Caxton Printers, 1952
                                                E99.N5M32

3105   PHINNEY, Archie
        Nez Percé texts. AMS, 1969 (1934) (CUCA) E51.C7.v.25.1969

3106   SPALDING, Henry Harmon
        The diaries and letters of Henry H. Spalding and Asa Bowen
        Smith relating to the Nez Percé Mission, 1838-1842. Glendale,
        Calif., A. H. Clark Co., 1958   E99.N5S67

3107   SPINDEN, Herbert Joseph
        The Nez Percé Indians. Lancaster, Pa., The New Era
        Printing Co., 1908   (AAAM)   GN2.A22.no.9

3108   WALKER, Deward E.
        Conflict and schism in Nez Percé acculturation. Pullman,
        Washington State Univ. Pr., 1968   E99.N5W3

        NEZ PERCÉ
           See also: 08321, 1821, 1827

                              NOMLAKI

3109   GOLDSMIDT, Walter Rochs
        Nomlaki ethnography. Berkeley, Univ. of California Pr., 1951
                           (UCPAE)   E51.C15.v.42.no.4

                              NOOTKA

3110   DRUCKER, Philip
        The northern and central Nootkan tribes. Washington,
        U. S. Govt. Print. Off., 1951 (BAEB) E51.U55.no.144

3111   MOZIÑO SUÁREZ de FIGUEROA, José Mariano
        Noticias de Nutka; an account of Nootka Sound in 1792.
        Seattle, Univ. of Wahsington Pr., 1970 (MAES) E51.A556.v.50

        NOOTKA
           See also: 2280

                              OGLALA

3112   BAD HEART BULL, Amos
        A pictographic history of the Oglala Sioux. Lincoln, Univ.
        of Nebraska Pr., 1967   fE99.O3B3

3113   BLACK ELK, Oglala Indian
        The sacred pipe. Norman, Univ. of Oklahoma Pr., 1953   E99.O3B5

3114   OLSON, James C.
        Red Cloud and the Sioux problem. Lincoln, Univ. of Nebraska Pr.
        1965   E99.O3O4

31141   SPINDLER, Will Henry
        Tragedy strikes at Wounded Knee, and other essays on Indian
        life in South Dakota and Nebraska. Vermillion, S. D.,
        Univ. of South Dakota, 1972   E99.O3.S63

3115   WALKER, J. R.
        The sun dance and other ceremonies of the Oglala division of
        the Teton Dakota. American Museum of Natural History, 1917
                        (AMNHP)   GN2.A27.v.16.pt.2

3116   WISSLER, Clark
        Societies and ceremonial associations in the Oglala division
        of the Teton-Dakota. American Museum of Natural History, 1912
                        (AMNHP)   GN2.A27.v.11.pt.1

                            OLMEC

3117   BERNAL, Ignacio
        The Olmec world. Berkeley, Univ. of California Pr., 1969
                                            F1219.B51713

3118   DRUCKER, Philip
        La Venta, Tabasco: a study of Olmec ceramics and art.
        Washington, U. S. Govt. Print. Off., 1952
                        (BAEB)   E51.U55.no.153

3119   HOUSTON, TEX. MUSEUM OF FINE ARTS.
        The Olmec tradition. Houston, 1963   F1219.H79

        OLMEC
        See also: 06761, 0760, 0784

                            OMAHA

3120   DORSEY, James Owen
        Omaha sociology. Johnson Reprint, 1970 (1884) E99.O4D8.1970

3121   FLETCHER, Alice Cunningham
        Historical sketch of the Omaha tribe of Indians in Nebraska.
        Washington, D. C., Judd & Detweiler, Printers, 1885 E99.O4F63
                            316

3122   FLETCHER, Alice Cunningham
        The Omaha tribe. Johnson Reprint, 1970 (1911) E99.04F65.1970

3123   FORTUNE, Reo Franklin
        Omaha secret societies. Columbia University Pr., 1932
                            (CUCA)   E51.C7.v.14

        OMAHA
           See also: 2030

                            ONEIDA

3124   LOUNSBURY, Floyd G.
        Oneida verb morphology. New Haven, Pub. for the Dept. of
        Anthropology, Yale Univ., by the Yale Univ. Pr., 1953
                            (YUPA)   GN2.Y3.no.48

                            ONONDAGA

3125   CHAFE, Wallace L.
        A semantically based sketch of Onondaga. Baltimore,
        Pub. at the Waverly Pr. by Indiana Univ., 1970
                            (IUPA)   GN4.I5.mem.25

3126   TUCK, James A.
        Onondaga Iroquois prehistory. Syracuse, N. Y., Syracuse
        Univ. Pr., 1971   E99.O58T8

        ONONDAGA
           See also: 21001

                            OSAGE

3127   LA FLESCHE, Francis
        The Osage tribe: rite of the chiefs. Johnson Reprint, 1970
        (1921)   E99.08L2.1970

3128   LA FLESCHE, Francis
        War ceremony and peace ceremony of the Osage Indians.
        Washington, U. S. Govt. Print. Off., 1939
                            (BAEB)   E51.U55.no.101

3129   MATHEWS, John Joseph
        The Osages, children of the Middle Waters. Norman, Univ.
        of Oklahoma Pr., 1961   E99.08M29

3130   MATHEWS, John Joseph
        Wah'kon-tah. Norman, Univ. of Oklahoma Pr., 1932 E99.O8M3

3131   TIXIER, Victor
        Tixier's travels on the Osage prairies. Norman, Univ. of
        Oklahoma Pr., 1940   E99.O8T7

        OSAGE
        See also: 2066

                                OTO

3132   WHITMAN, William
        The Oto. AMS, 1969 (1937) (CUCA)   E51.C7.v.28.1969

        OTO
        See also: 0093

                               PAIUTE

3133   BAILEY, Paul Dayton
        Ghost dance Messiah. Los Angeles, Westernlore Pr., 1970
                                              ˙ E99.P2W58.1970

31331   EGAN, Ferol
        Sand in a whirlwind: the Paiute Indian War of 1860.
        Doubleday, 1972   E99.P2.E45

3134   HOPKINS, Sarah Winnemucca
        Reproduction of Life among the Paiutes: their wrongs and
        claims. Bishop, Calif., Printed and distributed by Chalfant
        Pr., 1969   E99.P2H7.1969

3135   JOSEPH, Alice
        The desert people. Chicago, Univ. of Chicago Pr., 1949
                                                  E99.P25J6

.3136   KELLY, Isabel Truesdell
        Ethnography of the Surprise Valley Paiute. Berkeley,
        Univ. of California Pr., 1932 (UCPAE) E51.C15.v.31.no.3

3137   STEWARD, Julian Haynes
        Ethnography of the Owens Valley Paiute. Berkeley, Univ.
        of California Pr., 1933 (UCPAE)   E51.C15.v.33.no.3

                                318

3138   STEWARD, Julian Haynes
        Myths of the Owens Valley Paiute. Berkeley, Univ. of
        California Pr., 1936   (UCPAE)   E51.C15.v.34.no.5

3139   STEWARD, Julian Haynes
        Two Paiute autobiographies. Berkeley, Univ. of California
        Pr., 1934   (UCPAE)   E51.C15.v.33.no.5

3140   STEWART, Omer Call
        Northern Paiute. Berkeley and Los Angeles, Univ. of
        California Pr., 1941   (AR)   E51.A58.v.4.no.3

3141   STEWART, Omer Call
        The northern Paiute bands. Berkeley, Univ. of California
        Pr., 1939   (AR)   E51.A58.v.2.no.3

3142   UNDERHILL, Ruth Murray
        The northern Paiute Indians of California and Nevada.
        Washington, Education Div., U. S. Office of Indian Affairs,
        1941   E99.P2U35

3143   WATERMAN, Thomas Talbot
        The phonetic elements of the northern Paiute language.
        Berkeley, Univ. of California Pr., 1911
                              (UCPAE)   E51.C15.v.10.no.2

3144   WHEAT, Margaret M.
        Survival arts of the primitive Paiutes. Reno, Univ. of Nevada
        Pr., 1967   E99.P2W46

3145   WHITING, Beatrice Blyth
        Paiute sorcery. Johnson Reprint, 1964 (1950) E99.P2W48.1964

        PAIUTE
        See also: 0060, 0857

                          PAMUNKEY

3146   POLLARD, John Garland
        The Pamunkey Indians of Virginia. Washington, U. S. Govt.
        Print. Off., 1894   (BAEB)   E51.U55.no.17

3147   CHONA, Papago woman
        The autobiography of a Papago woman. Menasha, Wis.,
        American Anthropological Assoc., 1936   E99.P25C5

3148   DENSMORE, Frances
        Papago music. Washington, U. S. Govt. Print. Off., 1929
                        (BAEB)   E51.U55.no.90

3149   DOLORES, Juan
        Papago verb stems. Berkeley, Univ. of California Pr.,
        1913   (UCPAE)   E51.C15.v.10.no.5

3150   FONTANA, Bernard L.
        Papago Indian pottery. Seattle, Univ. of Washington Pr.,
        1962 (i.e. 1963)   E98.P8F54.1963

3151   GABEL, Norman E.
        A comparative racial study of the Papago. Albuquerque,
        Univ. of New Mexico Pr., 1949 (NMPA)   GN2.N4.no.4

3152   UNDERHILL, Ruth Murray
        A Papago calendar record. Albuquerque, Univ. of New
        Mexico Pr., 1938   (NMAS)   GN2.N39.v.2.no.5

3153   UNDERHILL, Ruth Murray
        Papago Indian religion. AMS, 1969 (1946)
                        (CUCA)   E51.C7.v.33.1969

3154   UNDERHILL, Ruth Murray
        The Papago Indians of Arizona and their relatives the Pima.
        Washington, Education Div., U. S. Office of Indian Affairs,
        1940   E99.P25U519

3155   UNDERHILL, Ruth Murray
        Social organization of the Papago Indians. AMS, 1969
        (1939)   (CUCA)   E51.C7.v.30.1969

3156   WADDELL, Jack O.
        Papago Indians at work. Tucson, Univ. of Arizona Pr.,
        1969   E99.P25W3

3157   WRIGHT, Harold Bell
        Long ago told (Huh-kew ah-kah) legends of the Papago
        Indians. D. Appleton & Co., 1929   E99.P25W94

PAPAGO
    See also: 0506, 2099, 2384, 2398

3158   KROEBER, Alfred Louis
        The Patwin and their neighbors. Berkeley, Univ. of California
        Pr., 1932   (UCPAE)   E51.C15.v.29.no.4
3159   McKERN, Will Carleton
        Functional families of the Patwin. Berkeley, Univ. of
        California Pr., 1922   (UCPAE)   E51.C15.v.13.no.7

PAWNEE

3160   DENSMORE, Frances
        Pawnee music. Washington, U. S. Govt. Print. Off., 1929
                            (BAEB)   E51.U55.no.93

3161   DORSEY, George Amos
        The Pawnee; mythology. Washington, D. C., The Carnegie
        Institution of Washington, 1906   E99.P3D6

3162   GRINNELL, George Bird
        Pawnee hero stories and folk-tales. C. Scribner's Sons,
        1893   E99.P3G8

3163   HYDE, George E.
        Pawnee Indians. Denver, Univ. of Denver Pr., 1951 E99.P3H93

3164   IRVING, John Treat
        Indian sketches. Putnam, 1888.   E99.P3I735

3165   LESSER, Alexander
        The Pawnee ghost dance hand game. AMS, 1969 (1933)
                            (CUCA)   E51.C7.v.16.1969

3166   MURIE, James R.
        Pawnee Indian societies. American Museum of Natural History,
        1914   (AMNHP)   GN2.A27.v.11.pt.7

3167   WEDEL, Waldo Rudolph
        An introduction to Pawnee archeology. Washington, U. S. Govt.
        Print. Off., 1936   (BAEB)   E51.U55.no.112

3168   WELTFISH, Gene
        The lost universe. Basic Books, 1965   E99.P3W45

        PAWNEE
        See also: 1846

31681   ANASTAS, Peter
        Glooskap's children; encounters with the Penobscot Indians
        of Maine. Boston, Beacon Pr., 1973   E99.P5.A5

3169   SPECK, Frank Gouldsmith
        Penobscot man. Philadelphia, Univ. of Pennsylvania Pr.;
        London, H. Milford, Oxford Univ. Pr., 1940   E99.P5S7

3170   SPECK, Frank Gouldsmith
        Penobscot shamanism. Lancaster, Pa., American Anthropological
        Assoc., 1919   (AAAM)   GN2.A22.no.28

3171   SPECK, Frank Gouldsmith
        Symbolism in Penobscot art. American Museum of Natural
        History, 1927   (AMNHP)   GN2.A27.v.29.pt.2

PIEGAN

3172   LANCASTER, Richard
        Piegan. Garden City, N. Y., Doubleday, 1966   E99.P58L3

PIMA

3173   AGINSKY, Bernard Willard
        Deep valley. Stein and Day, 1967   E99.P65A33

3174   Di PESO, Charles Corradino
        The Upper Pima of San Cayetano del Tumacacori. Dragoon,
        Ariz., Amerind Foundation, 1956   E78.A7D56

3175   EZELL, Paul Howard
        The Hispanic acculturation of the Gila River Pimas.
        Menasha, Wis., American Anthropological Assoc., 1961
                     (AAAM)   GN2.A22.no.90

3176   SHAW, Anna (Moore)
        Pima Indian legends. Tempe, Indian Education Center,
        College of Education, Arizona State Univ., 1963 E99.P6S5

    PIMA
        See also: 0506, 2099, 2102, 2384, 2398

31761 ALLEN, Elsie
    Pomo basketmaking; a supreme art for the weaver.
    Healdsburg, Calif., Naturegraph, 1972   E98.B3.A4

3177 BARRETT, Samuel Alfred
    Ceremonies of the Pomo Indians. Berkeley, Univ. of
    California Pr., 1917   (UCPAE)   E51.C15.v.12.no.10

3178 BARRETT, Samuel Alfred
    Pomo bear doctors. Berkeley, Univ. of California Pr.,
    1917   (UCPAE)   E51.C15.v.12.no.11

3179 BARRETT, Samuel Alfred
    Pomo Indian basketry. Berkeley, Univ. of California Pr.,
    1908   (UCPAE)   E51.C15.v.7.no.3

3180 BARRETT, Samuel Alfred   ed.
    Pomo myths. Milwaukee, Wis., Pub. by order of the Board
    of Trustees, 1933   E99.P65B25

3181 BROWN, Vinson
    The Pomo Indians of California and their neighbors.
    Healdsburg, Calif., Naturegraph, 1969   E75.A53.v.1

3182 GIFFORD, Edward Winslow
    Clear Lake Pomo society. Berkeley, Univ. of California
    Pr., 1926   (UCPAE)   E51.C15.v.18.no.2

3183 GIFFORD, Edward Winslow
    Ethnographic notes on the Southwestern Pomo. Berkeley,
    Univ. of California Pr., 1967   (AR)   E51.A58.v.25

3184 GIFFORD, Edward Winslow
    Pomo. Berkeley, Univ. of California Pr., 1937
                      (UCPAE)   E51.C15.v.37.no.4

3185 KNIFFEN, Fred Bowerman
    Pomo geography. Berkeley, Univ. of California Pr., 1939
                      (UCPAE)   E51.C15.v.36.no.6

3186 LOEB, Edwin Meyer
    Pomo folkways. Berkeley, Univ. of California Pr., 1926
                      (UCPAE)   E51.C15.v.19.no.2

3187 STEWART, Omer Call
    Notes on Pomo ethnogeography. Univ. of California Pr.,
    1943   (UCPAE)   E51.C15.v.40.no. 2

POMO
    See also: 1216, 21211

3188   HOWARD, James Henri
        The Ponca tribe. Washington, U. S. Govt. Print. Off.,
        1965   (BAEB)   E51.U55.no.195

        PONCA
        See also: 0158, 2030

POPOLOCA

3189   FOSTER, George McClelland
        Sierra Popoluca folklore and beliefs. Berkeley and Los
        Angeles, Univ. of California Pr., 1945
                            (UCPAE)   E51.C15.v.42.no.2

POTAWATOMI

3190   LANDES, Ruth
        The Prairie Potawatomi. Madison, Univ. of Wisconsin
        Pr., 1970   E99.P8L3

PUEBLO

3191   ABERLE, Sophie Bledsoe de
        The Pueblo Indians of New Mexico. Menasha, Wis., American
        Anthropological Assoc., 1948 (AAAM)   GN2.A22.no.70

3192   BROWN, Donald Nelson
        Masks, mantas, and moccasins. Colorado Springs, Fine
        Arts Center, Taylor Museum, 1962   E99.P9B7

3193   BUNKER, Robert Manson
        Other men's skies. Bloomington, Indiana Univ. Pr., 1956
                                         E99.P9B87

3194   BUNZEL, Ruth Leah
        The Pueblo potter. AMS, 1969 (1929)
                            (CUCA)   E51.C7.v.8.1969

3195   BURGESS, Marianna
        Stiya, a Carlisle Indian girl at home. Cambridge, Mass.,
        Printed at the Riverside Pr., 1891   E99.P9B9

3196   CARLSON, Roy L.
        White Mountain redware. Tucson, Univ. of Arizona Pr.,
        1970   E99.P9C28.1970

3197   CASTAÑO de SOSA, Gaspar
        A colony on the move. Santa Fe, N. M., School of American
        Research, 1965   E99.P9C313

3198   CHAPMAN, Kenneth Milton
        The pottery of Santo Domingo pueblo. Washington, D. C.,
        Press of W. F. Roberts Co., Inc., 1936 (i.e. 1938) fE98.P8C47

3199   COOLIDGE, Mary Elizabeth Burroughs (Roberts) Smith
        The rain-makers. Boston and New York, Houghton Mifflin Co.,
        1929   E99.P9C75

3200   CRANE, Leo
        Desert drums. Boston, Little, Brown, and Co., 1928 E99.P9C8

3201   CROW-WING, Hopi Indian
        A Pueblo Indian journal, 1920-21. Menasha, Wis., American
        Anthropological Assoc., 1925 (AAAM) GN2.A22.no.32

3202   CURRENT, William
        Pueblo architecture of the Southwest. Austin, Pub. for
        the Amon Carter Museum of Western Art, Fort Worth, by the
        Univ. of Texas Pr., 1971   E99.P9C82

3203   DENSMORE, Frances
        Music of Santo Domingo pueblo, New Mexico. Los Angeles,
        Southwest Museum, 1938 (LASM)   F869.L8S65.no.12

3204   DOZIER, Edward P.
        The Pueblo Indians of North America. Holt, Rinehart and
        Winston, 1970   E99.P9D6

3205   EGGAN, Frederick Russell
        Social organization of the western pueblos. Chicago,
        Univ. of Chicago Pr., 1950   E99.P9E27.1950

3206   EICKEMEYER, Carl
        Among the Pueblo Indians. Merriam Co., 1895 E99.P9E3

3207   FRENCH, David H.
        Factionalism in Isleta Pueblo. J. J. Augustin, 1948
                        (MAES)   E51.A556.v.14

3208   GILPIN, Laura
        The pueblos, a camera chronicle. Hastings House, 1941
                                                E78.S7G38

3209   HAEBERLIN, Herman Karl
        The idea of fertilization in the culture of the Pueblo
        Indians. Lancaster, Pa., Pub. for the American Anthropological
        Assoc., The New Era Printing Co., 1916 (AAAM) GN2.A22.no.13

3210   HEWETT, Edgar Lee
        The Pueblo Indian world. Albuquerque, The Univ. of New Mexico
        and the School of American Research, 1945   E99.P9H48

3211   HOLMES, William Henry
        Pottery of the ancient Pueblos. Washington, Smithsonian
        Institution, Bureau of Ethnology, 1886 E98.P8H7

3212   HOOTON, Earnest Albert
        The Indians of Pecos pueblo. New Haven, Pub. for the Dept.
        of Archaeology, Phillips Academy, Andover, Mass., by the
        Yale Univ. Pr., 1930   E98.A55H78

3123   HOUGH, Walter
        Culture of the ancient Pueblos of the upper Gila river region,
        New Mexico and Arizona. Washington, U. S. Govt. Print. Off.,
        1914   E78.N65H82

3214   KRAUSE, Fritz
        Die Pueblo-Indianer. Halle a.d.S., Druck von E. Karras,
        1907   fE99.P9K92

3215   LUMMIS, Charles Fletcher
        An appeal to the women of the United States. San Francisco,
        Indian Defense Assoc. of Central and Northern California,
        1924?   E99.P9L97

3216   MERA, Harry Percival
        The "rain bird"; a study in Pueblo design. Washington, D.C.,
        Press of W. F. Roberts Co., 1937 (i.e. 1938) fE98.A7M47

3217   MERA, Harry Percival
        Style trends of Pueblo pottery in the Rio Grande and
        Little Colorado cultural areas from the sixteenth to the
        nineteenth century. Baltimore, Waverly Pr., Inc., 1939
                                            fE98.P8M47

32171   New Perspectives on the Pueblos.
        Alfonso Oritz, ed., Albuquerque, Univ. of New Mexico Pr.,
        1972   E99.P9.N48

3218   PARSONS, Elsie Worthington
        Pueblo Indian religion. Chicago, The Univ. of Chicago Pr.,
        1939   E99.P9P37

3219 RENEHAN, Alois B.
      The Pueblo Indians and their land grants. Albuquerque,
      N. M., T. Hughes, Printer, 1923   E99.P9R3

3220 ROEDIGER, Virginia More
      Ceremonial costumes of the Pueblo Indians. Berkeley and
      Los Angeles, Univ. of California Pr., 1941 E99.P9R6

3221 SAUNDERS, Charles Francis
      The Indians of the terraced houses. G. P. Putnam's Sons,
      1912   E99.P9S25

3222 SETON, Mrs. Julia (Moss)
      The pulse of the pueblo. Santa Fe, N. M., Seton Village Pr.,
      1939   E98.S7S4

3223 SILVERBERG, Robert
      The Pueblo Revolt. Weybright and Talley, 1970 E99.P9S56.1970

3224 TYLER, Hamilton A.
      Pueblo gods and myths. Norman, Univ. of Oklahoma Pr., 1964
                                              E99.P9T9

3225 UNDERHILL, Ruth Murray
      First penthouse dwellers of America. J. J. Augustin, n.d.
                                              E99.P9U58

3226 UNDERHILL, Ruth Murray
      Work a day life of the Pueblos. Phoenix, 1946 E99.P9U33

3227 U. S. CONGRESS. SENATE. COMMITTEE ON PUBLIC LANDS AND SURVEYS.
      Pueblo Indian lands. Washington, U. S. Govt. Print. Off.,
      1923   E99.P9U54

3228 WATSON, Don
      Indians of the Mesa Verde. Mesa Verde National Park, Colo.,
      Mesa Verde Museum Assoc., 1955   E78.C6W35

3229 WHITE, Leslie A.
      The pueblo of San Felipe. Menasha, Wis., American
      Anthropological Assoc., 1942 (AAAM)   GN2.A22.no.60

3230 WHITE, Leslie A.
      The pueblo of Santa Ana, New Mexico. Menasha, Wis., American
      Anthropological Assoc., 1942 (AAAM)   GN2.A22.no.60

3231 WHITE, Leslie A.
      The pueblo of Santo Domingo, New Mexico. Menasha, Wis.,
      American Anthropological Assoc., 1935 (AAAM) GN2.A22.no.43

      PUEBLO
      See also: 0172, 0627, 0987, 1534, 1540, 1572, 1932, 2127,
                 2135, 2207, 2278, 2418

3232   SMITH, Marian Wesley
        The Puyallup-Nisqually. Columbia Univ. Pr., 1940
                (CUCA)   E51.C7.v.32

PUYALLUP
    See also: 1317

QUICHE´

32321   CARMACK, Robert M.
        Quichean civilization; the ethnohistoric, ethnographic,
        and archaeological sources. Calif., Univ. of California
        Pr., 1973   F1465.2.Q5.C27

3233   EDMONSON, Munro S.
        Quiche-English dictionary. New Orleans, Middle American
        Research Institute, Tulane Univ., 1965
                (TMAI)   F1421.T95.no.30

3234   POPOL VUH
        Antiguas historias de los ndios uichés de Guatemala.
        México, Editorial Porrúa, 1966   F1465.P815

QUILEUTE

3235   ANDRADE, Manuel Jose
        Quileute texts. AMS Pr., 1969 (1931)
                (CUCA)   E51.C7.v.12.1969

QUILEUTE
    See also: 1981, 2280

QUINAIELT

3236   OLSON, Ronald LeRoy
        The Quinault Indians. Seattle, Univ. of Washington Pr.,
        1967   E99.Q6062

SALINAN

3237   MASON, John Alden
        The ethnology of the Salinan Indians. Berkeley, Univ. of
        California Pr., 1912   (UCPAE)   E51.C15.v.10.no.4

3238   MASON, John Alden
        The language of the Salinan Indians. Berkeley, Univ. of
        California Pr., 1918   (UCPAE)   E51.C15.v.14.no.1

SALISH

3239   BALLARD, Arthur C.
        Some tales of the southern Puget Sound Salish. Seattle,
        Univ. of Washington Pr., 1927   E99.S2B23

3240   BARNETT, Homer Garner
        The Coast Salish of British Columbia. Eugene, Univ. of
        Oregon, 1955   E99.S2B3

3241   BARNETT, Homer Garner
        Gulf of Georgia Salish. Berkeley, Univ. of California Pr.,
        1939   (AR)   E51.A58.v.1.no.5

3242   EWERS, John Canfield
        Gustavus Sohon's portraits of Flathead and Pend d'Oreille
        Indians, 1854. Washington, Smithsonian Institution,
        1948   E99.S2E95

3243   JOHNSON, Olga Weydemeyer
        Flathead and Kootenay. Glendale, Calif., A. H. Clark Co.,
        1969   E99.S2J6

3244   LEWIS, Claudia Louise
        Indian families of the northwest coast. Chicago, Univ. of
        Chicago Pr., 1970   E99.S2L4

3245   MERRIAM, Alan P.
        Ethnomusicology of the Flathead Indians. Chicago, Aldine Pub.
        Co., 1967   ML3557.M49

3246   RONAN, Peter
        History of the Flathead Indians. Minneapolis, Ross &
        Haines, 1965   E99.S2R7.1965

3247   TURNEY-HIGH, Harry Holbert
        The Flathead Indians of Montana. Menasha, Wis., American
        Anthropological Assoc., 1937   E99.S2T8

3248   U. S. BOARD OF INDIAN COMMISSIONERS.
        Report upon the conditions on the Flathead Indian Reservation,
        by William H. Ketcham. Washington, D. C., 1915 E78.M9U43

3249   CHAPMAN, Kenneth Milton
      The pottery of San Ildefonso Pueblo. Albuquerque, Pub.
      for the School of American Research by Univ. of New
      Mexico Pr., 1970   fE99.S213C37

3250   MARRIOTT, Alice Lee
      María, the potter of San Ildefonso. Norman, Univ. of
      Oklahoma Pr., 1967 (1948)   E98.P8M28

3251   WHITMAN, William
      The Pueblo Indians of San Ildefonso. AMS, 1969 (1947)
                  (CUCA)   E51.C7.v.34.1969

SANTEE

3252   MEYER, Roy Willard
      History of the Santee Sioux. Lincoln, Univ. of Nebraska
      Pr., 1968 (1967)   99.S22M4

SARSI

3253   GODDARD, Pliny Earle
      Dancing societies of the Sarsi Indians. American
      Museum of Natural History, 1914 (AMNHP) GN2.A27.v.11.pt.5

3254   GODDARD, Pliny Earle
      Notes on the sun dance of the Sarsi. American Museum
      on Natural History, 1919 (AMNHP)   GN2.A27.v.16.pt.4

3255   GODDARD, Pliny Earle
      Sarsi texts. Berkeley, Univ. of California Pr., 1915
               (UCPAE)   E51.C15.v.11.no.3

SAUK

3256   SKINNER, Alanson Buck
      Observations on the ethnology of the Sauk Indians.
      Westport, Conn., Greenwood Pr., 1970   E99.S23S6.1970

SEMINOLE

3257   DENSMORE, Frances
       Seminole music. Washington, U. S. Govt. Print. Off.,
       1956   (BAEB)   E51.U55.

3258   McREYNOLDS, Edwin C.
       The Seminoles. Norman, Univ. of Oklahoma Pr., 1957
                                              E99.S28M286

32581 SPOEHR, Alexander
       Kinship system of the Seminole. Chicago, Field Museum of
       Natural History, 1942 (FMAS)   GN2.F4.v.33.no.2

3259   WILLSON, Minnie
       The Seminoles of Florida. Kingsport, Tenn., Printed and
       Bound by Kingsport Pr., 1928   E99.S28W78

SENECA

3260   CHAFE, Wallace L.
       Seneca thanksgiving rituals. Washington, U. S. Govt. Print.
       Off., 1961   (BAEB)   E51.U55.no.183

3261   FENTON, William Nelson
       An outline of Seneca ceremonies at Coldspring longhouse.
       New Haven, Pub. for the Section of Anthropology, Dept.
       of the Social Sciences, Yale Univ., by the Yale Univ.
       Pr.; London, H. Milford, Oxford Univ. Pr., 1936
                          (YUPA)   GN2.Y3.no.9

32611 HUBBARD, John Niles
       An account of Sa-go-ye-wat-ha; or, Red Jacket and his
       people, 1750-1830. B. Franklin, 1971   E99.S3.R3.1971

3262   PARKER, Arthur Caswell
       The history of the Seneca Indians. Port Washington, N.Y.,
       I. J. Friedman, 1967   E99.S3.P2.1967

3263   STONE, William Leete
       The life and times of Red-Jacket, or Sa-go-ye-wat-ha.
       St. Clair Shores, Mich., Scholarly Pr., 1970 E99.S3R4.1970

3264   WALLACE, Anthony F. C.
       The death and rebirth of the Seneca. Knopf, 1970 (1969)
                                              E99.S3W3.1970

3265   COOLIDGE, Dane
        The last of the Seris. Dutton, 1939   F1221.S43C7

3266   DeGRAZIA, Ted Ettore
        The Seri Indians. Flagstaff, Ariz., Northland Pr., 1970
                                            F1221.S43D4

3267   GRIFFEN, William B.
        Notes on Seri Indian culture, Sonora, Mexico. Gainesville,
        Univ. of Florida Pr., 1959   F1221.S43G7

3268   KROEBER, Alfred Louis
        The Seri. Los Angeles, Southwest Museum, 1931
                        (LASM)   F869.L8S65.no.6

32681   MALKIN, Borys
        Seri Ethnozoology. Pocatello, Idaho, Idaho State Univ.,
        1962   (ISUOP)   E78.I18.I4.no.7

SHAWNEE

3269   DRAKE, Benjamin
        Life of Tecumseh and of his brother the prophet. Kraus
        Reprint, 1969 (1858)   E99.S35T12.1969

3270   EGGLESTON, Edward
        Tecumseh and the Shawnee prophet. Dodd, Mead & Co., 1878
                                            E99.S35T137

3271   RAYMOND, Ethel T.
        Tecumseh. Toronto, Glasgow, Brook, 1922 E99.S35T2

3272   TUCKER, Glenn
        Tecumseh. Indianapolis, Bobbs-Merrill, 1956 E99.S35T35

3273   VOEGELIN, Charles Frederick
        The Shawnee female deity. New Haven, Pub. for the Section
        of Anthropology, Dept. of the Social Sciences, Yale Univ.,
        by the Yale Univ. Pr.; London, H. Milford, Oxford Univ. Pr.,
        1936   (YUPA)   GN2.Y3.no.10

SHAWNEE
        See also: 19431

SHOSHONEAN

3274 DORN, Edward
The Shoshoneans. Morrow, 1966 (i.e. 1967, 1966) E99.S39D6

3275 KROEBER, Alfred Louis
Notes on Shoshonean dialects of Southern California.
Berkeley, Univ. of California Pr., 1909
(UCPAE)   E51.C15.v.8.no.5

3276 KROEBER, Alfred Louis
Shoshonean dialects of California. Berkeley, Univ. of
California Pr., 1907   (UCPAE)   E51.C15.v.4.no.3

3277 LOWIE, Robert Harry
Notes on Shoshonean ethnography. American Museum of
Natural History, 1924 (AMNHP)   GN2.A27.v.20.pt.3

3278 SHINN, George Hazen
Shoshonean days. Glendale, Calif., Priv. Print. for the
Author by the Arthur H. Clark Co., 1941 E99.S39S5.Spec.Coll.

SHOSHONI

3279 CROWDER, David Lester
Tendoy, chief of the Lemhis. Caldwell, Id., Caxton Printers,
1969   E99.S4C7.1969

3280 LOWIE, Robert Harry
Dances and societies of the Plains Shoshone. American
Museum of Natural History, 1915 (AMNHP) GN2.A27.v.11.pt.10

3281 STEWARD, Julian Haynes
Nevada Shoshone. Berkeley and Los Angeles, Univ. of California
Pr., 1941   (AR)   E51.A58.v.4.no.2

3282 STEWARD, Julian Haynes
Northern and Gosiute Shoshoni. Berkeley, Univ. of California
Pr., 1943   (AR)   E51.A58.v.8.no.3

3283 TRENHOLM, Virginia Cole
The Shoshonis, sentinels of the Rockies. Norman, Univ. of
Oklahoma Pr., 1964   E99.S4T7

3284 WILSON, Elijah Nicholas
The white Indian boy. Yonkers-on-Hudson, N. Y., World Book
Co., 1919   E99.S4W72

SHOSHONI
See also: 2287

3285   EWERS, John Canfield
       The Blackfeet. Norman, Univ. of Oklahoma Pr., 1958
                              E99.S54E78

3286   EWERS, John Canfield
       The horse in Blackfoot Indian culture, with comparative
       material from other western tribes. Washington, U. S.
       Govt. Print. Off., 1955   (BAEB)   E51.U55.no.159

3287   GOLDFRANK, Esther Schiff
       Changing configurations in the social organization of a
       Blackfoot tribe during the reserve period. (The Blood of
       Alberta, Canada). J. J. Augustin, 1945
                     (MAES)   E51.A556.v.8

3288   GRINNELL, George Bird
       Blackfeet Indian stories. C. Scribner's Sons, 1913 E99.S54G8

3289   GRINNELL, George Bird
       Blackfoot lodge tales. C. Scribner's Sons, 1920
                           E99.S54G83.1920

3290   HANKS, Lucien Mason
       Observations on northern Blackfoot kinship. J. J. Augustin,
       1945   (MAES)   E51.A556.v.9

32901   HANKS, Lucien Mason
       Tribe under trust; a study of the Blackfoot reserve of
       Alberta. Canada, Univ. of Toronto Pr., 1972 E99.S54.H28.1972

3291   HARROD, Howard L.
       Mission among the Blackfeet. Norman, Univ. of Oklahoma Pr.,
       1971   E99.S54H3

3292   LEWIS, Oscar
       The effects of white contact upon Blackfoot culture, with
       special reference to the role of the fur trade. J. J. Augustin
       1942   (MAES)   E51.A556.v.6

3293   McCLINTOCK, Walter
       Old Indian trails. Boston and New York, Houghton Mifflin Co.,
       1923   E99.S54M18

3294   McCLINTOCK, Walter
       The Old North trail. London, Macmillan and Co., Ltd.,
       1910   E99.S54M2

3295   McCLINTOCK, Walter
       The tragedy of the Blackfoot. Los Angeles, Southwest
       Museum, 1930   (LASM)   F869.L8S65.no.3

3296   SCHULTZ, James Willard
           Blackfeet and buffalo. Norman, Univ. of Oklahoma Pr.,
           1962   E99.S54S27
3297   SCHULTZ, James Willard
           My life as an Indian. Boston, Houghton, Mifflin, 1914?
                                                   E99.S54S3.1914

3298   WISSLER, Clark
           Societies and dance associations of the Blackfoot Indians.
           American Museum of Natural History, 1913
                      (AMNHP)   GN2.A27.v.11.pt.4

3299   WISSLER, Clark
           The sun dance of the Blackfoot Indians. American Museum of
           Natural History, 1918   (AMNHP)   GN2.A27.v.16.pt.3

                          SINKIUSE

3300   RUBY, Robert H.
           Half-Sun on the Columbia. Norman, Univ. of Oklahoma Pr.,
           1965   E99.S55R8

                          SINKYONE

3301   NOMLAND, Gladys Ayer
           Sinkyone notes. Berkeley, Univ. of California Pr., 1935
                      (UCPAE)   E51.C15.v.36.no.2

                          SIOUX

        See Dakota

                          SOBAIPURI

3302   DI PESO, Charles Corradino
           _The Sobaipuri Indians of the Upper San Pedro River Valley,
           southeastern Arizona_. Dragoon, Amerind Foundation, 1953
                                                   E99.S67D5

                            335

SPOKAN

3303   RUBY, Robert H.
        The Spokane Indians. Norman, Univ. of Oklahoma Pr., 1970
                                   E99.S68R8

STOCKBRIDGE

33031   HOPKINS, Samuel
        Historical memoirs relating to the Housatonic Indians.
        Johnson Reprint, 1972   E99.S8.H7.1972

TALAMANCA

3304   STONE, Doris (Zemurray)
        The Talamancan tribes of Costa Rica. Cambridge, Mass.,
        Peabody Museum, 1962   (PMP)   /51.H337.v.43.no.2

TANAI

3305   VAUDRIN, Bill
        Tanaina tales from Alaska. Norman, Univ. of Oklahoma Pr.,
        1969   E99.T185V3

TAOS

3306   GRANT, Blanch Chloe
        Taos Indians. Taos, N. M., 1925   E99.T2G8

TARAHUMARE

3307   BENNETT, Wendell Clark
        The Tarahumara. Chicago, The Univ. of Chicago Pr.,
        1935; Photocopy, Ann Arbor, Mich., University Microfilms, 1966
                               F1221.T25B4.1966

3308   PENNINGTON, Campbell W.
        The Tarahumar of Mexico. Salt Lake City, Univ. of Utah Pr.,
        1963   F1221.T25P4

TARASCO

3309   BEALS, Ralph Leon
        Cherán: a Sierra Tarascan village. Washington, U. S. Govt.
        Print. Off., 1946   (SIP)   E51.S4.no.2

3310   BEALS, Ralph Leon
        Houses and house use of the Sierra Tarascans. Washington,
        U. S. Govt. Print. Off., 1944 (SIP)   E51.S4.no.2

3311   BOYD, Maurice
        Tarascan myths & legends. Fort Worth, Texas Christian Univ.
        Pr., 1969   F1221.T3B63

3312   FOSTER, Mary LeCron
        The Tarascan language. Berkeley, Univ. of California Pr.,
        1969   (CUPL)   P25.C25.v.56

3313   FRIEDRICH, Paul
        On the meaning of the Tarascan suffixes of space. Baltimore,
        Waverly Pr., 1969   (IUPA)   GN4.I5.mem.23-24

TEPEHUANE

3314   PENNINGTON, Campbell W.
        The Tepehuan of Chihuahua. Salt Lake City, Univ. of Utah Pr.,
        1969   F1221.T4P4

TETON

33141   FIRE, John
        Lame Deer, seeker of visions. Simon and Schuster, 1972
                              E99.T34.F57

3315   DOZIER, Edward P.
      Hano, a Tewa Indian community in Arizona. Holt, Rinehart
      and Winston, 1966   E99.T35D73

3316   HENDERSON, Junius
      Ethnozoology of the Tewa Indians. Washington, U. S. Govt.
      Print. Off., 1914   (BAEB)   E51.U55.no.56

3317   ORTIZ, Alfonso
      The Tewa world. Chicago, Univ. of Chicago Pr., 1969
                           E99.T3507.1969

3318   PARSONS, Elsie Worthington (Clews)
      The social organization of the Tewa of New Mexico.
      Menasha, Wis., American Anthropological Assoc., 1929
                (AAAM)   GN2.A22.no.36

3319   ROBBINS, Wilfred William
      Ethnobotany of the Tewa Indians. Washington, U. S. Govt.
      Print. Off., 1916   (BAEB)   E51.U55.no.55

      TEWA
      See also 22841

TLINGIT

3320   DE LAGUNA, Frederica
      The story of a Tlingit community: a problem in the
      relationship between archeological, ethnological, and historical
      methods. Washington, U. S. Govt. Print. Off., 1960
                (BAEB)   E51.U55.no.172

3321   JONES, Livingston French
      A study of the Thlingets of Alaska. Johnson Reprint, 1970
      (1914)   E99.T6J7.1970

3322   KRAUSE, Aurel
      The Tlingit Indians. Seattle, Pub. for the American
      Ethnological Society by the University of Washington Pr.,
      1956   E99.T6M5

3323   MILLER, Polly
      Lost heritage of Alaska. Cleveland, World Pub. Co., 1967
                           E99.T6M5

3324   OLSON, Ronald LeRoy
        <u>Social structure and social life of the Tlingit in Alaska.</u>
        Berkeley, Univ. of California Pr., 1967 (AR) E51.A58.v.26

3325   SALISBURY, Oliver Maxson
        <u>Quoth the raven.</u> Seattle, Superior Pub. Co., 1962 E99.T6S3

3326   SWANTON, John Reed
        <u>Social condition, beliefs and linguistic relationship of the</u>
        <u>Tlingit Indians.</u> Johnson Reprint, 1970 (1908) E99.T6S95.1970

TIGUA

3327   DUTTON, Bertha Pauline
        <u>Sun Father's way.</u> Albuquerque, Univ. of New Mexico Pr.,
        1963   E99.T52D8

TSATTINE

3328   GODDARD, Pliny Earle
        <u>The Beaver Indians.</u> American Museum of Natural History,
        1916   (AMNHP)   GN2.A27.v.10.pt.4

3329   GODDARD, Pliny Earle
        <u>Beaver texts, Beaver dialect.</u> American Museum of Natural
        History, 1917   (AMNHP)   GN2.A27.v.10.pt.5-6

TSIMSHIAN

3330   BOAS, Franz
        <u>Tsimshian mythology.</u> Johnson Reprint, 1970 (1916)
                            E99.T8B59.1970

3331   BOAS, Franz
        <u>Tsimshian texts</u>. Washington, U. S. Govt. Print. Off.,
        1902   (BAEB)   E51.U55.no.27

3332   GARFIELD, Viola Edmundson
        <u>The Tsimshian: their arts and music</u>. J. J. Augustin, 1951
                            E99.T8G3

3333   VOEGELIN, Charles Frederick
      Tübatulabal grammar. Berkeley, Univ. of California Pr.,
      1935   (UCPAE)   E51.C15.v.34.no.2

3334   VOEGELIN, Charles Frederick
      Tübatulabal texts. Berkeley, Univ. of California Pr.,
      1935   (UCPAE)   E51.C15.v.34.no.3

3335   VOEGELIN, Erminie (Wheeler)
      Tübatulabal ethnography. Berkeley, Univ. of California Pr.,
      1938   (AR)   E51.A58.v.2.no.1

    TUBATULABAL
      See also: 0022

TUCUNA

33351   NIMUENDAJU, Curt
      The Tukuna. Berkeley, Univ. of California Pr., 1952
                 (UCPAE)   E51.C15.v.45

TUISENO

33352   SCHOLDER, Fritz
      Scholder/Indians. Flagstaff, Arizona, Northland Pr., 1972
                              fE99.L9.S3

TUNICA

3336   HAAS, Mary Rosamond
      Tunica dictionary. Berkeley, Univ. of California Pr., 1953
             (CUPL)   P25.C25.v.6.no.2

3337   HAAS, Mary Rosamond ed.
      Tunica texts. Berkeley, Univ. of California Pr., 1950
             (CUPL)   P25.C25.v.6.no.1

3338   WALLACE, Anthony F. C.
        The model personality structure of the Tuscarora Indians as
        revealed by the Rorschach test. Washington, U. S. Govt.
        Print. Off., 1952   (BAEB)   E51.U55.no.150

TUTELO

3339   SPECK, Frank Gouldsmith
        The Tutelo spirit adoption ceremony. Harrisburg, Commonwealth
        of Pennsylvania, Dept. of Public Instruction, Pennsylvania
        Historical Commission, 1942   E99.T96S6

TWANA

3340   ELMENDORF, William Welcome
        The structure of Twana culture. Pullman, Washington Univ.,
        1960   E99.T98E4

UTE

3341   DENSMORE, Frances
        Northern Ute music. Washington, U. S. Govt. Print. Off.,
        1922   (BAEB)   E51.U55.no.75

33411   JORGENSEN, Joseph G.
        The Sun dance religion; power for the powerless. Chicago,
        Univ. of Chicago Pr., 1972   E99.U8.J67

3342   STEWART, Omer Call
        Ethnohistorical bibliography of the Ute Indians of Colorado.
        Boulder, Univ. of Colorado Pr., 1971 (CUSA) GN4.C64.no.18

3343   U. S. NATIONAL PARK SERVICE.
        Ethnology of Rocky mountain national park. Berkeley, Calif.,
        1935   E99.U8U57

UTE
    See also: 0161, 2287

WAILAKI

3344 GODDARD, Pliny Earle
Habitat of the Pitch Indians, a Wailaki division. Berkeley,
Univ. of California Pr., 1924 (UCPAE) E51.C15.v.17.no.4

WAMPANOAG

3345 WEEKS, Alvin Gardner
Massasoit of the Wampanoags. Fall River, Mass., Priv. Print.,
Plimpton Pr., 1919   E99.W2M45

WAPPO

3346 DRIVER, Harold Edson
Wappo ethnography. Berkeley, Univ. of California Pr.,
1936   (UCPAE)   E51.C15.v.36.no.3

3347 RADIN, Paul
A grammar of the Wappo language. Berkeley, Univ. of
California Pr., 1929 (UCPAE)   E51.C15.v.27

3348 RADIN, Paul
Wappo texts, 1st series. Berkeley, Univ. of California Pr.,
1924   (UCPAE)   E51.C15.v.19.no.1

3349 SAWYER, Jesse O.
English-Wappo vocabulary. Berkeley, Univ. of California Pr.,
1965   (CUPL)   P25.C25.v.43

WASHO

3350 BARRETT, Samuel Alfred
The Washo Indians. Milwaukee, Wis., Pub. by Order of the
Trustees, 1917   E99.W38B2

3351 DANGBERG, Grace Melissa   comp.
Washo tales. Carson City, Nev., 1968   E99.W38D3

3352 DANGBERG, Grace Melissa
Washo texts. Berkeley, Univ. of California Pr., 1927
(UCPAE)   E51.C15.v.22.no.3

3353   DOWNS, James F.
        The two worlds of the Washo. Holt, Rinehart and Winston,
        1966   E99.W38D6

3354   KROEBER, Alfred Louis
        The Washo language of east central California and Nevada.
        Berkeley, Univ. of California Pr., 1907
                            (UCPAE)   E51.C15.v.4.no.5

3355   LOWIE, Robert Harry
        Ethnographic notes on the Washo. Berkeley, Univ. of
        California Pr., 1939   (UCPAE)   E51.C15.v.36.no.5

        WASHO
        See also: 0060, 1577

                            WINNEBAGO

3356   BLOWSNAKE, Sam
        The autobiography of a Winnebago Indian. Berkeley, Univ.
        of California Pr., 1920   (UCPAE)   E51.C15.v.16.no.7

3357   RADIN, Paul
        The culture of the Winnebago. Baltimore, Waverly Pr.,
        1949   (IUPA)   GN4.I5.mem.2

3358   RADIN, Paul
        The evolution of an American Indian prose epic. Baltimore,
        Waverly Pr., 1954-56.   E99.W7R115

3359   RADIN, Paul
        The social organization of the Winnebago Indians.
        Ottawa, Government Printing Bureau, 1915   E99.W7R12

3360   RADIN, Paul
        The trickster. Greenwood Pr., 1969 (1956) E99.W7R142.1969

3361   RADIN, Paul
        Winnebago culture as described by themselves. Baltimore,
        Waverly Pr., 1950   (IUPA)   GN4.I5.mem.3

3362   RADIN, Paul
        Winnebago hero cycles: a study in aboriginal literature.
        Baltimore, Waverly Pr., 1948 (IUPA)   GN4.I5.mem.1

3363   RADIN, Paul
        The Winnebago tribe. Johnson Reprint, 1970 (1923) E99.W7R15.1970b

                            343

WINTUN

3364   BARRETT, Samuel Alfred
        The Wintun Hesi ceremony. Berkeley, Univ. of California Pr.,
        1919   (UCPAE)   E51.C15.v.14.no.4

3365   DU BOIS, Cora Alice
        Wintu ethnography. Berkeley, Univ. of California Pr., 1935
                      (UCPAE)   E51.C15.v.36.no.1

3366   DU BOIS, Cora Alice
        Wintu myths. Berkeley, Univ. of California Pr., 1931
                      (UCPAE)   E51.C15.v.28.no.5

WIYAT

3367   LOUD, Llewellyn Lemont
        Ethnogeography and archaeology of the Wiyot territory.
        Berkeley, Univ. of California Pr., 1918 E99.W8L8

3368   REICHARD, Gladys Amanda
        Wiyot grammar and texts. Berkeley, Univ. of California Pr.,
        1925   (UCPAE)   E51.C15.v.22.no.1

3369   TEETER, Karl V.
        The Wiyot language. Berkeley, Univ. of California Pr.,
        1964   (CUPL)   P25.C25.v.37

YANA

3370   GIFFORD, Edward Winslow
        Yana. Berkeley, Univ. of California Pr., 1936
                      (UCPAE)   E51.C15.v.37.no.2

3371   POPE, Saxton Temple
        Yahi archery. Berkeley, Univ. of California Pr., 1918
                      (UCPAE)   E51.C15.v.13.no.3

3372   SAPIR, Edward
        The fundamental elements of Northern Yana. Berkeley,
        Univ. of California Pr., 1922 (UCPAE) E51.C15.v.13.no.6

3373   SAPIR, Edward
        The position of Yana in the Hokan stock. Berkeley,
        Univ. of California Pr., 1917 (UCPAE) E51.C15.v.13.no.1

3374   SAPIR, Edward
        Yana dictionary. Berkeley, Univ. of California Pr., 1960
                              (CUPL)   P25.C25.v.22

3375   SAPIR, Edward
        Yana terms of relationship. Berkeley, Univ. of California
        Pr., 1918   (UCPAE)   E51.C15.v.13.no.4

3376   WATERMAN, Thomas Talbot
        The Yana Indians. Berkeley, Univ. of California Pr.,
        1918   (UCPAE)   E51.C15.v.13.no.2

                              YAQUI

33761   CASTANEDA, Carlos
        Journey to Ixtlan; the lessons of Don Juan. Simon and Schuster,
        1972   E99.Y3.C28

3377   CASTANEDA, Carlos
        A separate reality. Simon and Schuster, 1971   E99.Y3C29

3378   CASTANEDA, Carlos
        The teachings of Don Juan. Ballantine Books, 1969 (1968)
                                          E99.Y3C3.1969

3379   DeGRAZIA, Ted Ettore
        De Grazia paints the Yaqui Easter. Tucson, Univ. of
        Arizona Pr., 1968   fND237.D3337A44

3380   FABILA, Alfonso
        Las tribus yaquis de Sonora. México, Departamento de Asuntos
        Indígenas, 1940   E99.Y3F2

33801   GIDDINGS, Ruth Warner
        Yaqui myths and legends. Tucson, 1959 (Anthropological
        papers of the University of Arizona, no. 2)   E99.Y3.G5

3381   MOISÉS, Rosalio
        The tall candle. Lincoln, Univ. of Nebraska Pr., 1971
                                          E99.Y3M6

3382   SPICER, Edward Holland
        Potam, a Yaqui village in Sonora. Menasha, Wis., 1954
                              (AAAM)   GN2.A22.no.77

        YAQUI
           See also: 1523, 2281

                              345

3383   GIFFORD, Edward Winslow
       The southeastern Yavapai. Berkeley, Univ. of California Pr.,
       1932   (UCPAE)   E51.C15.v.29.no.3

YOKUTS

3384   GAYTON, Anna Hadwick
       Yokuts and western Mono ethnography. Berkeley, Univ. of
       California Pr., 1948   (AR)   E51.A58.v.10.no.1-2

3385   KROEBER, Alfred Louis
       Yokuts dialect survey. Berkeley, Univ. of California Pr.,
       1963   (AR)   E51.A58.v.11.no.3

3386   KROEBER, Alfred Louis
       The Yokuts language of south central California.
       Berkeley, Univ. of California Pr., 1907
                              (UCPAE)   E51.C15.v.2.no.5

3387   LATTA, Frank Forrest
       Handbook of Yokuts Indians. Bakersfield, Calif., Kern
       County Museum, 1949   E99.Y75L38

       YOKUTS
       See also: 2171, 2387

YUKIAN

3388   KELLY, Isabel Truesdell
       Yuki basketry. Berkeley, Univ. of California Pr., 1930
                              (UCPAE)   E51.C15.v.24.no.9

YUMA

3389   FORBES, Jack D.
       Warriors of the Colorado. Norman, Univ. of Oklahoma Pr.,
       1965   E99.Y94F59

3390   FORDE, Cyril Daryll
       Ethnography of the Yuma Indians. Berkeley, Univ. of California
       Pr., 1931   (UCPAE)   E51.C15.v.28.no.4

YUMAN

3391   CASTETTER, Edward Franklin
        Yuman Indian agriculture. Albuquerque, Univ. of New Mexico Pr.,
        1951   E99.Y95C3

3392   DRUCKER, Philip
        Yuman-Piman. Berkeley and Los Angeles, Univ. of California Pr.,
        1941   (AR)   E51.A58.v.6.no.3

3393   KROEBER, Alfred Louis
        Yuman tribes of the lower Colorado. Berkeley, Univ. of
        California Pr., 1920   (UCPAE)   E51.C15.v.16.no.8

        YUMAN
            See also: 2120, 2281

YUROK

3394   ERIKSON, Erik Homburger
        Observations on the Yurok: childhood and world image.
        Berkeley and Los Angeles, Univ. of California Pr., 1943
                            (UCPAE)   E51.C15.v.35.no.10

3395   KROEBER, Alfred Louis
        Yurok and neighboring kin term systems. Berkeley, Univ. of
        California Pr., 1934   (UCPAE)   E51.C15.v.35.no.2

3396   ROBINS, Robert Henry
        The Yurok language: grammar, texts, lexicon. Berkeley,
        Univ. of California Pr., 1958 (CUPL)   P25.C25.v.15

3397   SPOTT, Robert
        Yurok narratives. Berkeley and Los Angeles, Univ. of
        California Pr., 1942   (UCPAE)   E51.C15.v.35.no.9

3398   WATERMAN, Thomas Talbot
        Yurok geography. Berkeley, Univ. of California Pr.,
        1920   (UCPAE)   E51.C15.v.16.no.5

3399   WATERMAN, Thomas Talbot
        Yurok marriages. Berkeley, Univ. of California Pr., 1934
                            (UCPAE)   E51.C15.v.35.no.1

347

3400   NADER, Laura
       Talea and Juquila; a comparison of Zapotec social organization.
       Berkeley, Univ. of California Pr., 1964
                        (UCPAE)   E51.C15.v.48.no.3

ZOQUE

3401   CORDRY, Donald Bush
       Costumes and weaving of the Zoque Indians of Chiapas,
       Mexico. Los Angeles, Southwest Museum, 1941
                        (LASM)   F869.L8S65.no.15

ZUNI

3402   BENEDICT, Ruth (Fulton)
       Zuni mythology. AMS, 1969   E99.Z9B4.1969

3403   CUSHING, Frank Hamilton
       Zuni breadstuff. Museum of the American Indian, Heye
       Foundation, 1920   (HFM)

3404   CUSHING, Frank Hamilton
       Zuñi folk tales. G. P. Putnam's Sons, 1901 E99.Z9C92

3405   DENMAN, Leslie Van Ness
       Pai ya tu ma, god of all dance and his customs of the flute,
       Zuni pueblo, 1932. San Francisco?, 1955 E99.Z9D4.Spec.Coll.

3406   DRUCKER, Philip
       The Tolowa and their southwest Oregon kin. Berkeley,
       Univ. of California Pr., 1937 (UCPAE)   E51.C15.v.36.no.4

3407   GOULD, Richard A.
       Archaeology of the Point St. George site and Tolowa
       prehistory. Berkeley, Univ. of California Pr., 1966
                        E99.T7G6

3408   KROEBER, Alfred Louis
       Zuñi kin and clan. American Museum of Natural History, 1917
                        (AMNHP)   GN2.A27.v.18.pt.1

3409   KROEBER, Alfred Louis
       Zuñi potsherds. American Museum of Natural History, 1916
                        (AMNHP)   GN2.A27.v.18.pt.1

3410   LEIGHTON, Dorothea (Cross)
        People of the middle place. New Haven, Conn., Human Relations
        Area Files Pr., 1966   E99.Z9L4

3411   NEWMAN, Stanley Stewart
        Zuni grammar. Albuquerque, Univ. of New Mexico Pr., 1965
                        (NMPA)   GN2.N4.no.14

3412   PARSONS, Elsie Worthington (Clews)
        Notes on Zuñi. Lancaster, Pa., Pub. for the American
        Anthropological Assoc., 1917 (AAAM)   GN2.A22.no.19,20

3413   PARSONS, Elsie Worthington (Clews)
        The scalp ceremonial of Zuñi. Menasha, Wis., American
        Anthropological Assoc., 1924 (AAAM)   GN2.A22.no.31

3414   PARSONS, Elsie Worthington (Clews)
        Winter and summer dance series in Zuñi in 1918. Berkeley,
        Univ. of California Pr., 1922 (UCPAE)   E51.C15.v.17.no.3

3415   ROBERTS, Frank Harold Hanna
        The village of the great kivas on the Zuñi reservation,
        New Mexico. Washington, U. S. Govt. Print. Off., 1932
                                                E99.Z9R75

3416   ROBERTS, John Murray
        Zuni daily life. n.p., Human Relations Area Files Pr.,
        1965   E99.Z9R76

3417   SELTZER, Carl Coleman
        Racial prehistory in the Southwest and the Hawikuh Zunis.
        Kraus, 1968 (1944)   (PMP)   E51.H337.v.23.no.1968

3418   STEVENSON, Matilda Coxe (Evans)
        The Zuñi Indians. Johnson Rep., 1970 (1905)
                                        E99.Z9S86.1970

34181   The Zunis; self-portrayals, by the Zuni people. N. M.,
        Univ. of New Mexico Pr., 1972   E99.Z9.Z86

        ZUNI
        See also: 0494, 2082, 2210, 2316, 2353

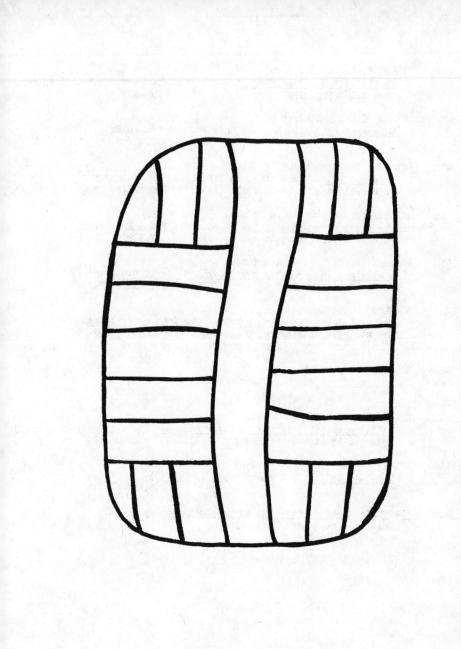

INDEX TO SERIES

AAAM	AMERICAN ANTHROPOLOGICAL ASSOCIATION. Memoirs of the American Anthropological Assoc.	GN2.A22
AMNHP	AMERICAN MUSEUM OF NATURAL HISTORY, NEW YORK. Anthropological papers	GN2.A27
APST	AMERICAN PHILOSOPHICAL SOCIETY, PHILADELPHIA. Transactions of the American Philosophical Society	fQ11.P6
AR	Anthropological records	E51.A58
ASR	WM. L. BRYANT FOUNDATION. AMERICAN STUDIES. Report	E77.8.W5
BAEB	U. S. BUREAU OF AMERICAN ETHNOLOGY. Anthropological papers	E51.U55
CIB	CRANBROOK INSTITUTE OF SCIENCE, BLOOMFIELD HILLS, MICHIGAN. Bulletin	Q11.C95
CMA	CHICAGO. NATURAL HISTORY MUSEUM. Popular series: anthropology	GN2.F5
CUCA	COLUMBIA UNIVERSITY. Columbia Univ. contributions to anthropology	E51.C7
CUPL	CALIFORNIA. UNIVERSITY. Univ. of California publications in linguistics	P25.C25
CUSA	COLORADO. UNIVERSITY. Univ. of Colorado studies	GN4.C64
CWRA	CASE WESTERN RESERVE UNIVERSITY. Studies in Anthropology	GN2.C34
DO	WASHINGTON. DUMBARTON OAKS, TRUSTEES FOR HARVARD UNIVERSITY.	E51.S85
ESAR	EASTERN STATES ARCHEOLOGICAL FEDERATION. Research publication	E51.E212
FMAS	Fieldiana: anthropology	GN2.F4
HFM	NEW YORK. MUSEUM OF THE AMERICAN INDIAN, HEYE FOUNDATION. Indian notes and monographs	E51.N45

IAM	Ibero–Americana	F1401.I22
INAH	MEXICO. INSTITUTO NACIONAL DE ANTROPOLOGIA E HISTORIA. Serie investigaciones	F1219.M627
ISUOP	IDAHO STATE UNIVERSITY. POCATELLO, IDAHO. MUSEUM Occasional Papers.	E78.I18.I4
IUPA	INDIANA. UNIVERSITY. Indiana Univ. publications in anthropology and linguistics	GN4.I5
LASM	LOS ANGELES. SOUTHWEST MUSEUM. Papers	F869.L8S65
MAES	AMERICAN ETHNOLOGICAL SOCIETY, NEW YORK. Monographs of the American ethnological society	E51.A556
MNAB	FLAGSTAFF, ARIZ. MUSEUM OF NORTHERN ARIZONA. Bulletin	F806.M95
MNMP	SANTA FE, N. M. MUSEUM OF NEW MEXICO. Papers in anthropology	E78.N65S3
NAA	Native American arts	E98.A7N36
NMAS	NEW MEXICO. UNIVERSITY. Bulletin	GN2.N39
NMPA	NEW MEXICO. UNIVERSITY. Publications in anthropology	GN2.N4
NWAF	New World Archaeologocial Foundation	E51.U75
NPSAS	U. S. NATIONAL PARK SERVICE. Archeological research series	E51.U75
PAIA	ARCHAEOLOGICAL INSTITUTE OF AMERICA. Papers of the Archaeological Inst. of America	E51.A64
PAIP	PAN AMERICAN INSTITUTE OF GEOGRAPHY AND HISTORY. Publicación	F1401.P153
PMM	HARVARD UNIVERSITY. PEABODY MUSEUM OF ARCHAEOLOGY AND ETHNOLOGY. Memoirs	fE51.H336
PMP	HARVARD UNIVERSITY. PEABODY MUSEUM OF ARCHAEOLOGY AND ETHNOLOGY. Papers	E51.H337

PPSP	AMERICAN PHILOSOPHICAL SOCIETY, PHILADELPHIA. Proceedings	Q11.P5
SAAM	SOCIETY FOR AMERICAN ARCHAEOLOGY. Memoirs	E51.S7
SASP	SOUTHERN ANTHROPOLOGICAL SOCIETY. Proceedings	GN2.S9243
SCA	SMITHSONIAN CONTRIBUTIONS TO ANTHROPOLOGY.	fGN1.S54
SCAA	Studies in pre-Columbian art and archaeology.	E51.S85
SIP	SMITHSONIAN INSTITUTION. INSTITUTE OF SOCIAL ANTHROPOLOGY. Publication	E51.S4
SIWBS	SMITHSONIAN INSTITUTION. War background studies	GN4.S6
TMAI	TULANE UNIVERSITY OF LOUISIANA. MIDDLE AMERICAN RESEARCH INSTITUTE. Publication	F1421.T95
TUEX	THULE EXPEDITION, 5th, 1921-1924. Report	G670.1921.R25.
UCAC	CALIFORNIA. UNIVERSITY. ARCHAEOLOGICAL RESEARCH FACILITY. Contributions.	E51.C2
UCPAE	CALIFORNIA. UNIVERSITY. Univ. of California publications in American archaeology and ethnology	E51.C15
UMAP	MICHIGAN. UNIVERSITY. MUSEUM OF ANTHROPOLOGY. Anthropological papers	GN2.M5
UUAP	UTAH. UNIVERSITY. DEPT. OF ANTHROPOLOGY. Anthropological papers	E51.U8
UVIA	JALAPA, MEXICO (CITY). UNIVERSIDAD VERACRUZANA. INSTITUTO DE ANTROPOLOGIA. Cuadernos	F1219.1.V47J3
YUPA	YALE UNIVERSITY. DEPT. OF ANTHROPOLOGY. Yale Univ. publications in anthropology	GN2.Y3

AUTHOR AND TITLE INDEX

358

361

362

366

373

374

375

381

401

434

455

459

461

462

463

465

McALLESTER, David Park. 2288
                                                          3053

McBETH, Kate C. 3103

McBRYDE, Felix Webster 0195

McCALLUM, James Dow 0986

McCLINTOCK, Walter 3293
                                                          3294
                                                          3295

McCLUNG, John Alexander 1421

McCOWN, Theodore Doney 0561
                                                          2910

McCRACKEN, Harold 0709

McCREIGHT, Major Israel 1122

MACEWAN, John Walter Grant 0841

MACFARLAN, Allan A. 1123
                                                          1474

McFEAT, Tom 0145

McGILLYCUDDY, Julia E. (Blanchard) 1288

McGillycuddy, agent 1288

McGillivray of the Creeks 2610

McGIMSEY, Charles Robert 02461

MACGOWEN, Kenneth 0247

MACGREGOR, Frances M. (Cooke) 1124

MACGREGOR, Gordon 2651

McGREGOR, John Charles 0444
                                                          0445

McGROARTY, John Steven 2344

McILWRAITH, Thomas Forsyth 2501

McINTOSH, John 1125

McINTIRE, William G. 0248

McKENNAN, Robert Addison 2888

McKENNEY, Thomas Loraine 1126
                                                          1127

MACKENZIE, Sir Alexander 1657
                                                          1658
                                                          1659

MACKENZIE, Donald Alexander 2209

476

482

483

504

511